Human Rights in the Age of Platfo

Information Policy Series

Edited by Sandra Braman

A complete list of the books in the Information Policy series appears at the back of this book.

Human Rights in the Age of Platforms

Edited by Rikke Frank Jørgensen

Foreword by David Kaye

The MIT Press
Cambridge, Massachusetts
London, England

The Open Access edition of this book was published with generous support from Knowledge Unlatched and the Danish Council for Independent Research.

K||| Knowledge Unlatched

This book was set in Stone Serif and Stone Sans by Jen Jackowitz. Printed and bound in the United States of America.

Library of Congress Cataloging-in-Publication Data

Names: Jørgensen, Rikke Frank, editor.
Title: Human rights in the age of platforms / edited by Rikke Frank Jørgensen.
Description: Cambridge, MA : The MIT Press, [2019] | Series: Information
    policy | Includes bibliographical references and index.
Identifiers: LCCN 2018049349 | ISBN 9780262039055 (hardcover : alk. paper)
Subjects: LCSH: Human rights. | Information society. | Information
    technology--Moral and ethical aspects.
Classification: LCC JC571 .H7695266 2019 | DDC 323--dc23 LC record available at
    https://lccn.loc.gov/2018049349

10 9 8 7 6 5 4 3 2 1

Contents

Series Editor's Introduction

Sandra Braman

One can sign away one's constitutional rights by contract, though historically that has been allowed only when there were plenty of other options. One could choose, for example, to sign a contract forbidding engaging in public political speech, even on one's personal time, in order to work for a telephone company concerned about being welcome in every home in the community—in the past, though, under conditions in which if that were not acceptable there were plenty of other jobs available on a par in terms of skills required, pay, a visible career path, and so on. You had a choice.

In contrast, already by the turn of the century, comparative analysis of the terms of service and acceptable use agreements, the contracts we sign with Internet service providers (ISPs) and platforms by clicking through on them, found the terms of these contracts across providers were converging. And they were doing so in ways destructive of the human rights that are core to most constitutions and constitution-like foundations of national law in protections for civil liberties (see "Advantage ISP"). US constitutional law, for example, forbids the use of language in laws or regulations that is vague (reasonable adults may not agree on its meaning) or overbroad (covering far more activity and types of communication than is the intended target of a particular law or regulation). Both types of language are not only rife in, but characteristic of, terms of service agreements. This convergence of the provisions of terms of service means that, on the Internet, there has been nowhere else, effectively, to go, if offered a contract you considered abusive of human rights. The subject addressed by this book, on threats to human rights from private sector entities in the online environment, could not be more important.

Theories of free speech typically focus on one problem: how to maximize the possibilities for rich and diverse public discourse about shared matters of public concern under conditions in which there may be threats to those rights from governments. As Edwin C. Baker and others have pointed out, though, with the commercial broadcasting that has dominated the globe ever since the liberalization waves of the late twentieth century, a second problem has to be solved at the same time: in economists' terms, a second market had to be served—advertisers. Thinking about free speech in a two-sided market rather than an environment conceived to serve only one "market," comprised of the needs of citizens and citizenship, makes analyses more complex. And, importantly, it inverts the relationship of the problem to policy making. Historically, thinking and practice with respect to protecting free speech have been focused on preventing the government from inappropriately affecting the speech environment in what we might think of as a single market problem. When the problem involves a two-sided market, though, the question becomes how the government can best intervene, using laws and policy, to support the public speech environment and help it thrive.

What we have now, as is pointed out in *Human Rights in the Age of Platforms*, is a third class of problem—those created by multisided market markets. With this, the challenge for policy makers of all types (whether public sector or private, organizational or individual) is that the problem becomes yet more complex again by another order of magnitude. There is a second challenge to human rights in cyberspace when framed in economic terms, as well. The information economy in which we now live is, so to speak, an expanding universe. The economic domain is itself growing by commodifying types of information and informational interactions that had not previously been treated as something that can be bought and sold. This way of conceptualizing the information economy was introduced by political economists in the 1970s as the second of the four ways of conceptualizing "the information economy" that have appeared since the 1960s, all simultaneously in use today theoretically, rhetorically, and operationally. (The first to appear was an approach that understood the information economy as one in which everything operates as it always had, but industries in the information sector had become proportionately more important than those in other economic sectors. Later, approaches appeared that focused on transformations in the nature of economic processes themselves—emphasizing cooperation and coordination for long-term economic success in addition to competition—[often referred to as *the network economy*] and, in the twenty-first century, appreciation of the ways in which representation has replaced empirical data as the foundation of economic decision-making [an approach in which the information economy is called a *representational economy*].)

By the 1990s, there were consulting firms and business schools with advice about just how to take advantage of informational opportunities to make profit from this expansion of the economic universe. The intellectual capital movement of that era developed alternative accounting schemes for these new forms of value, and the industrial classification codes so fundamental to the accounting systems of importance for regulation as well as financial purposes were revised in that era as well for the same reasons; in the US this meant replacing the Standard Industrial Classification (SIC) codes with the North American Industry Classification System (NAICS), while internationally these were transformations that took place within the International Standard Industrial Classification (ISIC) code system. This same insight into what makes the information economy different from the industrial economy was also a driving force behind the formation of the World Trade Organization (WTO) and the development of associated treaties, such as the General Agreement on Trade in Services (GATS), which for the first time incorporated trade in services into international trade agreements. (The prize for the best definition of "services" for this purpose still goes to *The Economist*, which defined it in 1984 as "anything that can be bought and sold that cannot be dropped on your foot.")

What all of this means for human rights is that the proportion of our lifeworlds, of what we all do on a daily basis with our friends, colleagues, neighbors, allies, and fellow citizens, for which human rights abuses presents threats, is growing. The emphasis here is not on the egregious examples of extraordinary situations, but on the "normal," whether that is the normal as we are coming to accept it or the normal as we would prefer it to be. We live, that is, in an expanding universe of possible human rights issues that might arise in association with our ordinary use of digital technologies or because these technologies are embedded in our habitual or expected contexts.

Spending several days at a meeting of the Internet Engineering Task Force in November 2017 was humbling in this regard. A growing number of those involved in this group, which is responsible for the always ongoing effort of Internet design, are working on the problem of inserting explicit attention to human rights issues formally into the processes through which a proposed protocol for the Internet becomes the official protocol. Spending several days in sessions under the guidance of members of this group who were sophisticated both regarding the technologies involved and the processes of the organization made clear that the problem of privacy was a whack-a-mole problem, appearing in a high percentage of conversations, each devoted to a specific technical issue, each within its own working group and topical problem track. With every new technological development, new privacy problems appear. From the human rights side, the problem may be a lack of comprehension of the technical possibilities and constraints of the systems to which critiques and demands for protection are being addressed.

Human Rights in the Age of Platforms can serve as a primer for all of us. In the gifted intellectual and editorial hands of Rikke Frank Jørgensen, these authors make visible the human rights problems specific to those environments controlled by the private sector (essentially all of them) rather than in the geopolitical and legal terms that have dominated the human rights discourses of the past. The book provides, in essence, an environmental approach in that the cases addressed range across the various facets of our lives. They bring to bear theories and insights from multiple disciplines and, for many, life experience working on human rights issues on the ground.

It is not an encouraging time to be thinking about human rights, whether in the offline or online environment. But it *is* encouraging to have such thoughtful scholars, thinkers, and practitioners to help us understand the fundamental human rights issues of our era as we seek to develop the means to address them offered by this foundational work.

Foreword

David Kaye
UN Special Rapporteur on Freedom of Expression

On the shelf beside my desk rest a number of recent and already dog-eared books about the digital age: *Consent of the Networked* by Rebecca MacKinnon, *The Attention Merchants* by Tim Wu, *China's Contested Internet* by Guobin Yang, *Twitter and Tear Gas* by Zeynep Tufekci, *The Net Delusion* by Evgeny Morozov, *Weapons of Math Destruction* by Cathy O'Neill, and *Dragnet Nation* by Julia Angwin. Stacked nearby are countless nongovernmental organization reports and academic studies about the ways in which the Internet is affecting the enjoyment of human rights, with titles like *Tainted Leaks* (Citizen Lab), *Online and on All Fronts* (Human Rights Watch), *Let the Mob Do the Job* (Association for Progressive Communications), *Troops, Trolls and Troublemakers* (Oxford Internet Institute), and *¿Quién defiende tus datos?* (Derechos Digitales).

What connects these disparate publications? Apart from all having a focus on the individual's experience in the digital age, not a single one tells a hopeful story about personal autonomy, freedom of expression, security, or privacy online. Not one of these publications highlights the ways in which the Internet has opened broad avenues of communication among cultures, permitted the sharing of information and ideas across borders, and offered vast expanses of knowledge that can be traversed from link to link and thread to thread online. Some of them focus on the repression of governments that criminalize expression online or conduct surveillance of their citizens and others. Some drill down into the ways in which private companies govern quasi-public space, share information with governments seeking access to their networks, or simply give the false impression of privacy or security in the shadow of what Peter Swire has called "The Golden Age of Surveillance."

Are there stories about private actors expanding or simply protecting human rights? Of course, they do exist. Indeed, the story that dominated about twenty years of public discourse, from about 1990 to 2010, was the story of private innovation breaking through old barriers of distance to develop technologies that have created and then forever altered the "information society." Those stories are still told, ones about atheists in religious societies using the Internet for connection, sexual minorities going online to gain knowledge about health and well-being, and critics and dissenters using the tools of social media to share information and organize for protest.

The truth is, the books on my shelf and the publications in my in-box reflect changes in the way most stakeholders now think about the Internet. According to an increasingly dominant narrative, the Internet is a place of darkness, danger, propaganda, misogyny, harassment, and incitement, which private actors are doing little to ameliorate. (Where do you read these complaints? On the Internet!) Worldwide, people are worried, legislators are energized, and the gears of regulation have been engaged. An era of Internet laissez-faire is over or at least coming to a close. To be sure, repressive governments have been imposing costs on private actors in digital space for many years, especially those actors—such as telecommunications and Internet service providers—subject to licensing rules as a condition of participation in a local market. Many perform a kind of regulation by denying entry into markets; blocking, filtering, or throttling digital traffic; providing beneficial network access to friends and limiting that access to critics; and performing other tricks of the digital censor.

But the regulatory buzz is not limited to the repressive. Some rules—such as those pertaining to intellectual property, like the Digital Millennium Copyright Act in the United States—have been in place for decades, giving some private actors the power to shape in often very problematic ways the nature of expression and creation online. Recent years have shown deepening interest in regulation, as governments are eager to gain some measure of control over Internet space in an era of digital distress. European institutions are in the lead, developing regulatory models that may be replicated worldwide. The European Court of Justice has taken on personal reputational control with the right to be forgotten (or the right to erasure), outsourcing its implementation to Google. The European Court of Human Rights has danced around the possibility of intermediary liability for third-party expression. The United States and Europe have been in deep negotiations over the future of privacy ever since the collapse of the Safe Harbour standards in the treatment of personal data of Europeans. The European Union has imposed a code of conduct for social media companies and search engines to follow in the context of extremist and terrorist content, and it seems poised at the time of this writing to enter into the fraught space of disinformation and propaganda, so-called "fake" or "junk" news.

Amid the calls for regulation in democratic societies and the acts of government repression elsewhere, there is one undeniable fact about the digital age: at the center is the private company. Whether it's the telco providing digital access, or the social media company providing space for conversation, or one of any number of other actors in sibling industries, private companies in the digital age exercise enormous control. They connect users and providers of information and ideas. They sell user data and user attention. They moderate (or regulate) user speech. They cooperate with or resist government demands. In short, they often are either the governors of space visited by billions or the mediators between the individual and the government. This is a massive role and, depending on how you see it, a vital responsibility. Just whose responsibility is subject to debate.

This volume, a collection of studies by some of the leading thinkers at the nexus of private action and public regulation in the digital age, introduces the most difficult legal and policy questions of the digital age. It presents theoretical insights about the transformations brought about by private actors. It offers specific examples of private power that implicates the rights of individual users. It provides legal frameworks for all stakeholders to think through the problems of human rights protection in an environment so dominated by private companies. All of this the volume does without either the hysteria of the moment's particular crises or, at the other end of the spectrum, a jargony disconnection from the experience of real human beings.

The real challenge for the next generation of legislators and regulators, particularly those of good faith operating in democratic societies, is to shape new laws that meet two conditions: First, at a minimum, they must promote and protect everyone's rights, such as the right to seek, receive, and impart information and ideas of all kinds, regardless of frontiers and through any media as provided by Article 19 of the International Covenant on Civil and Political Rights. They must be compliant with international human rights norms, protecting users who enjoy rights. Second, law must protect users—and society as a whole—from the harms caused by the special features of the digital age. That is easier said than done, perhaps, but the preservation of the original vision of the Internet should be at the top of all stakeholders' agendas moving forward. This volume guides us toward that goal.

Acknowledgments

I would like to thank the people who made this book possible: first and foremost, the contributors to the book, who gathered at the Danish Institute for Human Rights in January 2017 to share their initial drafts and worked together to shape the overall direction of the book. A note of thanks goes to colleagues at the Danish Human Rights Institute, Marc Bagge Pedersen, Karen Lønne Christensen, and Emilia Piechowska, who have provided crucial practical and editorial assistance; and Anja Møller Pedersen for her contribution to the authors' workshop.

I am also indebted to the MIT Press for their kind and professional assistance all the way from idea to final book, to the anonymous reviewers, and to series editor Sandra Braman for her support and substantive input ever since the idea of the book first materialized in 2016.

I am grateful for the generous support from Knowledge Unlatched and the Danish Council for Independent Research, which enabled the open access edition of this book. It is my hope that it will benefit scholars and human rights practitioners around the globe.

Introduction

Rikke Frank Jørgensen

This book is concerned with the human rights implications of the "social web."[1] Companies such as Google, Facebook, Apple, Microsoft, Twitter, LinkedIn, and Yahoo! play an increasingly important role as managers of services and platforms that effectively shape the norms and boundaries for how users may form and express opinions, encounter information, debate, disagree, mobilize, and retain a sense of privacy. The technical affordances, user contracts, and governing practices of these services and platforms have significant consequences for the level of human rights protection, both in terms of the opportunities they offer and the potential harm they can cause.

Whereas part of public life and discourse was also embedded in commercial structures in the pre-Internet era, the current situation is different in scope and character. The commercial press that is often referred to as the backbone of the Fourth Estate was supplemented by a broad range of civic activities and deliberations (Elkin-Koren and Weinstock Netanel 2002, vii). Moreover, in contrast to today's technology giants, the commercial press was guided by media law and relatively clear expectations as to the role of the press in society, meaning an explicit and regulated (although imperfect on many counts) role in relation to public deliberation and participation.

In contrast to this, the platforms and services that make up the social web are based on the double logic of public participation and commercial interest (Gillespie 2010). Arguably, over the past twenty years, these companies have facilitated a revolution in access to information and communication and have had a transformative impact on individuals' ability to express, assemble, mobilize, inform, learn, educate, and so on around the globe. At the same time, the ability of states to compel action by the companies has put the human rights implications of their practices increasingly high on the international agenda (Sullivan 2016, 7). Most recently, concern has been raised as to the democratic implications of having a group of relatively few and powerful companies moderate and govern what is effectively the "the greatest expansion of access to information in history" (Kaye 2016). Despite the civic-minded narratives used to describe their services (Jørgensen 2017b; Moore 2016), the companies ultimately answer to shareholders rather than the public interest, and especially Google's and Facebook's business practices have increasingly been under scrutiny in the public debate.

The revenue model of the widely used platforms imply that the expressions, discussions, queries, searches, and controversies that make up people's social life in the online domain form part of a personal information economy (Elmer 2004). Advertising is no longer simply the dominant way to pay for information and culture (Lewis 2016), as has long been the case within "old media," but has taken on a new dimension in that an unprecedented amount of social interaction is used to control markets. Whereas data was previously "considered a byproduct" of interactions with media, major Internet companies have become "data firms," deriving their wealth from the abilities to harvest, analyze, and use personal data rather than from "user activity proper" (van Dijck and Poell 2013, 9). The data mining of personal information is paradoxical, as there is no demand or preference for it among consumers, yet it is accepted as a kind of cultural tax that allows users to avoid paying directly for the services provided (Lewis 2016, 95). Scholars have cautioned that these current practices represent a largely uncontested "new expression of power" (Zuboff 2015) that has severe impacts on human agency and on democracy more broadly, as elaborated by Zuboff in this volume. As these new practices permeate our economies, social interactions, and intimate selves, there is an urgent need for an understanding of their relationship with human rights.

Human rights are a set of legally codified norms that apply to all human beings, irrespective of national borders. International human rights law lays down obligations of governments to act in certain ways or to refrain from certain acts, in order to promote and protect human rights of individuals or groups.[2] As such, it governs the relationship between the individual and the state, but it does not directly govern the activities of the private sector, although the state has an obligation to protect individuals against human rights harms in the realm of private parties.

In recent years there have been a variety of initiatives that provide guidance to companies to ensure compliance with human rights, most notably the Guiding Principles on Business and Human Rights, adopted by the UN Human Rights Council in 2011 (UNGPs; United Nations Human Rights Council 2011). According to these Guiding Principles, any business entity has a responsibility to respect human rights, and as part of this, to carry out human rights due diligence, which requires companies to identify, assess, address, and report on their human rights impacts. Moreover, the Guiding Principles state that businesses should be prepared to communicate how they address their human rights impacts externally, particularly when concerns are raised by or on behalf of affected stakeholders.

The commonly stated claim that human rights apply online as they do offline fails to recognize that in a domain dominated by privately owned platforms and services, individuals' ability to enjoy their human rights is closely related to whether states have decided to encode them into national regulation applicable to companies and/or the willingness of companies to undertake human rights due diligence. In Europe, for example, the former is the case with online privacy rights, which enjoy protection under the new EU General Data Protection Regulation (GDPR) irrespective of whether the data processing is carried out by a public institution or a private company.[3]

In order to address the interdisciplinary nature, scope, and complexity of these questions, the book is organized into three parts. The first is a theoretical and conceptual part that highlights areas in which datafication[4] and the social web have implications for the protection of human rights. The second is a more practice-oriented part that explores examples of platform governance and rulemaking, and the third is a legal part that discusses human rights under pressure, focusing in particular on the right to freedom of expression and privacy, but also addressing human rights and standards related to equality and nondiscrimination, participation, transparency, access to remedies, and the rule of law. The ultimate goal of the book is to contribute to a more robust system of human rights protection in a domain largely facilitated by corporate actors. While the cases and examples used are for the most part focused on a European and US context, the challenges this book addresses are global by nature as is most clearly illustrated in the chapters by Callamard and York and Zuckerman.

Before introducing the chapters in more detail, I will outline some of debates and literature that have served as inspiration for this book, most notably discourses on the "platform society" and its democratic implications. As part of this, I will briefly introduce the broad field of "human rights and technology," as well as the human rights and business framework, in order to situate the specific conceptualization of this book and the human rights questions it is concerned with.

The Platform Society

In recent years, the notion of "platform" has become the prevailing way to describe the services and revenue model that make up the social web (Helmond 2015, 5). The defining characteristic of these platforms is not that they create objects of consumption but rather that they create the world within which such objects can exist (Lazzarato 2004, 188). In short, the platforms give us our horizons, or our sense of the possible (Langlois et al. 2009, 430). Via integrating buttons (like, tweet, etc.), the platforms expand beyond single services to the extent that the platform logic is visible and present across the entire web. The code and policies of the platform impose specific boundaries on social acts, and as such, the platform allows a certain predefined kind of social engagement (see the chapter by Flyverbom and Whelan in this volume). For example, you can like and have friends, but not a list of enemies. Further, the platforms' economic interest in gathering user data implies that one cannot study a single layer but must acknowledge the intimate relationship between the technical affordances and the underlying economic interests.

Arguably, the corporate logic, algorithms, and informational architectures of major platforms now play a central role in providing the very material means of existence of online publics. These combined elements regulate the "coming into being" of a public by imposing specific possibilities and limitations on user activity (Langlois et al. 2009, 417). Effectively, these platforms construct the conditions for public participation on the web. This key role prompts us to seek an understanding of their combined articulation of code and economic interests and how this logic defines the conditions and premises for online participation—in short, the paradox that exists between tools used to facilitate and free communication and the opacity and complexity of an architecture governed by the economies of data mining (ibid., 420). The economies of data mining redefine relations of power, not merely by selling user attention but by tapping into "the everyday life" of users and refashioning it from within, guided by commercial norms such as the presumed value to advertisers (Langlois and Elmer 2013, 4). This power perspective has also been highlighted in recent software studies, albeit from a different perspective, focusing on the interests that algorithms afford and serve in their specific manifestation (Bucher 2012), and thus how these algorithms rule (Gillespie 2014, 168). Yet scholarship has only recently begun to struggle with the broader societal implications of having technology companies define the boundaries and conditions for online social life and a networked public sphere. In addition, there is an increasing awareness of the difficulty for researchers in studying the technical, economic, and political priorities that guide major platforms due to their largely inaccessible, "complex and black-boxed architecture" (Langlois et al. 2009, 416). While major platforms effectively influence whether the notion of a public sphere for democratic dialogue can be sustained into the future (Mansell 2015), we have limited knowledge of how they operate and limited means of holding them accountable to fundamental rights and freedoms.

From a regulatory perspective, the companies that control the major platforms for information search, social networking, and public discourse of all kinds "squeeze themselves between traditional news companies and their two customer segments, the audience and the advertisers" (Latzer et al. 2014, 18). They benefit from substantial economies of scale and a scope of operation that enables them to exploit enormous information assets (Mansell 2015, 20), while their global character detaches them from the close structural coupling between the systems of law and politics that is the paradigm of the nation-state (Graber 2016, 22). While the companies often frame themselves as neutral "conduits" for traffic and hosts for content creators, they have the power to influence which ideas are easily located and how boundaries for public discourse are set, as elaborated by York and Zuckerman in this volume. The capacity of these companies to screen out desirable content without the user's knowledge is as significant as their capacity to screen out undesirable content. "Citizens cannot choose to view what they are not aware of or to protest about the absence of content which they cannot discover" (Mansell 2015, 24). In short, the regulatory challenge does not concern only cases in which the companies exercise direct editorial control over content. At a more fundamental level, it is about whether their practices shape the user's online experience in ways that are inconsistent with human rights standards relating to rights of expression, public participation, nondiscrimination, media plurality, privacy, and so forth. When their gatekeeping efforts diminish the quality or variety of content accessed by citizens, result in discriminatory treatment, or lead to unwanted surveillance, there is a prime facie case for policy oversight (ibid., 3). We shall return to this point below when addressing the human rights responsibilities of these companies.

Private Control, Public Values

Since Habermas' seminal work on transformations of the public sphere, various aspects of commercialization have been raised and widely elaborated in relation to the increasing power of private media corporations over public discourse, not least concerning their economic and institutional configurations (Verstraeten 2007, 78). Since public spaces relate to general principles of democracy as locations where "dissent and affirmation become visible" (Staeheli and Mitchell 2007, 1), their configurations and modalities of ownership, regulation, and governance greatly impact individuals' means of participating in online public life. Oldenburg's (1997) original work on *The Great Good Place* (or the "third place"), for example, considers the role of physical space in democratic culture and the conflict between these spaces and the commercial imperative that informs the contemporary design of cities and communities. By contrast, the commercial aspects of the online public sphere are a less researched topic although this has begun to change as scholarship increasingly examines how the political economy of online platforms affects social practices and public discourse, and what kind of public sphere may develop as a result (Gillespie 2010, 2018; Goldberg 2011; Mansell 2015).

Arguably, the major platforms of the social web have developed an incredibly successful revenue model based on collection of users' personal data, preferences, and behavior. The platforms facilitate communications within society, while also harnessing communication in an effort to monetize it (Langlois and Elmer 2013, 2). "Corporate social media platforms constantly enact these double articulations: while on the surface they seem to promote unfettered communication, they work in their back-end of data processing and analysis to transform and translate acts of communication into valuable data" (ibid., 6). Since harnessing of personal information is at the core of this revenue model, it calls for reconsideration of both "personal" and "information" in order to adequately protect users' online privacy as discussed extensively by Mai in this volume.

On a legal level, the harnessing of personal information implies "the organized activity of exchange, supported by the legal infrastructure of private-property-plus-free-contract" (Radin 2002, 4). The value of personal information has been debated in a series of Facebook-commissioned reports on how to "sustainably maximize the contribution that personal data makes to the economy, to society, and to individuals" (Ctrl-Shift 2015, 3). It is also the topic of annual PIE (Personal Information Economy) conferences, held by Ctrl-Shift.[5] The first report explains how mass customization is enabled by information about specific things and people. "Today's practices, whether they drive the production of a coupon or a digital advertisement, employ data analysts and complex computational power to analyze data from a multitude of devices and target ads with optimal efficiency, relevance and personalization" (ibid., 9). As noted in the report, the personal information economy has given rise to a number of concerns, such as the lack of a reasonable mechanism of consent, a sense of "creepiness," fears of manipulation of algorithms, and unaccountable concentrations of data power (ibid., 15). At its core, the revenue model profiles users in order to segment customers for the purpose of targeted advertising as addressed in the chapters by Zuboff and Bermejo in this volume. A user's search activities, for example, may result in referrals to content "properties" through a variety of intermediary sharing arrangements that support targeted marketing and cross-selling (Mansell 2015, 20). The "economic turn" in Internet-related literature is also exemplified in the work of Christian Fuchs and others (Fuchs 2015; Fuchs and Sandoval 2014) who interrogate the economic logics of the social web and argue that user activity such as the production and sharing of content is exploited labor because it contributes to the production of surplus value by data-mining companies.

In the legal literature, it has been emphasized that the mantra of personalization "blurs the distinction between citizens and consumers and swaps free opinion formation for free choice of commodities" (Graber 2016, 7). Since freedom in a democratic society presupposes the "ability to have preferences formed after exposure to a sufficient amount of information" (Sunstein 2007, 45), personalization risks replacing a diverse, independent, and unpredictable public discourse with the satisfaction of private preferences,

based on previous choices (a similar concern is found in Zuckerman 2013).
In addition, there are increasing concerns about the shift in decision-
making power from humans to algorithms (Pasquale 2015) and the democratic implications of this shift as addressed by Bechmann in this volume.
In contrast to written law, which is interpreted by authorized humans in
order to take effect on a person, code is largely self-executing and implies
minimal scope for interpretation (Graber 2016, 18). While this topic is
receiving increasing attention (Council of Europe Committee of Experts on
Internet Intermediaries 2017), there is still limited scholarship addressing
the human rights and rule-of-law implications of having algorithms regulate social behavior in ways that are largely invisible and inaccessible to the
individual affected.

In sum, while recognizing the more optimistic accounts of the networked public sphere and its potential for public participation (Benkler
2006; Benkler et al. 2015; Castells 2009), this book is inspired by literature
that is concerned with the democratic implications of having an online
domain governed by a relatively small group of powerful technology companies and informed by the personal information economy.

Human Rights and Technology Literature

Scholarship related to human rights and technology is scattered around
different disciplines ranging from international law and Internet governance to media and communication studies. The interlinkage between
technology and human rights started to surface on the international policy
agenda during the first World Summit on the Information Society (WSIS)
in 2003 and 2005 (Best, Wilson, and Maclay 2004; Jørgensen 2006). The
WSIS brought together policy makers, activists, and scholars from a range
of disciplines concerned with the normative foundations of the "information society." The interrelation between technology and human rights was
still very new at this point, and far from obvious for anyone besides a small
group of committed activists and scholars. However, in the fifteen years
since WSIS a large number of books, surveys, and norm-setting documents
have been produced, as we shall see below.

The human rights and technology literature includes a growing body
of standard-setting literature that supports ongoing efforts to establish
norms for human rights protection in the online domain. The Council of

Europe's Committee of Ministers, for example, has since 2003 issued more than 50 recommendations and declarations that apply a human rights lens to a specific area of concern in the online domain, such as search engines, social media platforms, blocking and filtering, net neutrality, Internet intermediaries, big data, Internet user rights, transborder flow of information, and so forth.[6] The Council of Europe efforts in this field are elaborated in McGonagle's chapter in this volume. Also, the Organization for Security and Co-operation in Europe (OSCE) has produced a number of guidebooks, although more narrowly related to online freedom of expression, such as *Media Freedom on the Internet: An OSCE Guidebook* (Akdeniz 2016), and the UN Human Rights Council has since 2012 adopted a number of resolutions that reaffirm the protection of human rights online.[7] Further, the UN Special Rapporteur on Freedom of Expression has produced a number of important reports that have been widely used as benchmarks for understanding and applying freedom-of-expression standards in the online domain, most recently reports on freedom of expression, states, and the private sector in the digital age (Kaye 2016), and the regulation of user-generated online content (Kaye 2018).[8] In 2015, the first UN Special Rapporteur on Privacy was appointed and contributed with work that maps out the normative baseline for protecting privacy in an online context (Cannataci 2016). Scholars and activists have also contributed to norm setting by serving to "translate" human right to an online context. One example is the Internet Rights and Principles Coalition that since 2008 has been active in promoting rights-based principles for Internet governance at the global Internet Governance Forum (IGF) as well as regional IGFs and related events. The coalition has produced a number of resources, including the Charter of Human Rights and Internet Principles for the Internet, translated into twenty-five languages. Scholarly contributions include "Towards Digital Constitutionalism? Mapping Attempts to Craft an Internet Bill of Rights" (Redeker, Gill, and Gasser 2018).

Another subdivision of literature is the vast number of empirically grounded studies that illustrate how technology practice and policy may pose threats to the protection of human rights. Much of the literature on rights and freedoms in the digital era has been concerned with technology-enabled means of state violations—for example, online censorship, repression, control, and surveillance. The United Nations Educational, Scientific, and Cultural Organization (UNESCO), for instance, has been very active and contributed with dozens of reports and mappings related to the information society, such as the *Global Survey on Internet Privacy and Freedom of Expression* (Mendel et al. 2012), and the report on *Fostering Freedom Online: The Roles, Challenges and Obstacles of Internet Intermediaries* (MacKinnon et al. 2014).[9] Also, *Consent of the Networked: The Worldwide Struggle for Internet Freedom* uses a wide array of empirical examples to illustrate the current battle for freedom of expression around the globe (MacKinnon 2012). Other widely used examples include the edited volumes *Access Controlled* (Deibert et al. 2010), *Access Denied* (Deibert et al. 2008), and *Access Contested* (Deibert et al. 2011) by the OpenNet Initiative, as well as the annual *Global Information Society Watch* produced by the Association of Progressive Communication (APC) since 2007.[10] APC, especially, has broadened the discourse on human rights in the information society to include social, economic, and cultural rights, whereas the majority of works are oriented toward the right to freedom of expression and privacy. Especially from legal scholarship, numerous contributions have been made related to privacy and freedom of expression online (Agre 1994; Balkin 2014, 2018; Benedek and Kettemann 2014; Cohen 2013; Lessig 1999; Nissenbaum 2010; Solove 2008).

A subset of concerns raised in many of these works relates to the role of Internet intermediaries[11] as actors that exercise considerable control over content and services in the online domain and therefore are encouraged or enlisted to self- or coregulate. The human rights and rule-of-law implications of such practices have been raised for the past fifteen years in relation to Internet intermediaries (Angelopoulos et al. 2016; Brown 2010; Frydman and Rorive 2003; Jørgensen and Pedersen 2017; Korff 2014; Nas 2004; Tambini, Leonardi, and Marsden 2008), and the debate continues, while increasingly focusing on regulation of platforms (Belli and Zingales 2017; Laidlaw 2015; Wagner 2013). More recently, scholarship has started to interrogate the technical Internet infrastructure and standard setting from the perspective of human rights (Cath 2017; DeNardis 2014; Milan and ten Oever 2017; Rachovitsa 2017).

Taking a slightly different approach to the topic, a number of books have focused on technology as a tool for promoting human rights and social justice (Comninos 2011; Earl and Kimport 2011; Lannon and Halpin 2013; Tufekci 2017), including the Internet freedom agenda (Carr 2013; Morozov 2011; Powers and Jablonski 2015) and more recent work on data justice (Dencik, Hintz, and Cable 2016; Pasquale 2015). Ziccardi (2013), for example, in *Resistance, Liberation Technology and Human Rights in the Digital Age*, considers the role of technology in social movements and online resistance, whereas the edited volume *New Technologies and Human Rights: Challenges to Regulation* (Cunha et al. 2013) focuses on technology and human rights from the perspective of power and inequality between the Global South and the Global North (Cunha et al. 2013). More recently, the relationship between new technologies and human rights practice is explored in the edited volume *New Technologies for Human Rights Law and Practice* by Land and Aronson (2018).

Also, scholars in fields such as media and communication studies, and information ethics, increasingly incorporate considerations of human rights norms into their work—for instance, privacy norms—although these works mostly refer to human rights in a rather general sense. Not surprisingly, media and communication scholars rarely place their analysis of, for example, transformations in the online public sphere (Balnaves and Willson 2011; Papacharissi 2010), the platform society (Gillespie 2010, 2018; van Dijck 2013), or data capitalism (Fuchs 2015; West 2017; Zuboff 2015) within the framework of the human rights system of international legal standards, institutions, and actors as a lens on these topics. However, one attempt is *Framing the Net—The Internet and Human Rights* (Jørgensen 2013), which examines how different theoretical conceptions of the online domain (as Public Sphere, Infrastructure, New Media, and Culture) carry specific human rights implications. The current volume is particularly interested in such interdisciplinary conversations, and its contributors were deliberately chosen to represent both more theoretical discourses and cutting-edge legal scholarship related to protecting human rights within the platforms and services that make up the social web.

The Human Rights Responsibility of Private Actors

In recent years, several developments have placed the role of technology companies increasingly high on the human rights agenda. First, a number of high-profile cases such as individual and class action litigation by Austrian activist Max Schrems against Facebook, the debate around fake news in relation to the US presidential election in 2016, and the Cambridge Analytica scandal have led to an increasing recognition of the powers held by a small group of technology companies and raised concern as to the way their business practices may interfere with human rights and democratic processes. As part of this debate, some commentators have suggested that the size and market share of these companies make them de facto monopolies,[12] too powerful to serve the public interest, and called for regulation akin to that of public utilities[13] (Moore 2016; Srniceks 2017; Taplin 2017a, 2017b). In response to this, economics have argued that Google and the other technology giants do not constitute monopolies since they are far from supplying the entire market. Moreover, if companies develop into natural monopolies,[14] this only causes (economic) concern if they are not efficient in the service they supply.[15] Irrespective of whether these companies—in a technical sense—constitute monopolies, the debate points to the current difficulty in finding appropriate policy responses to the powers of the technology giants.

Second, there has been a general shift in the human rights and business discourse exemplified by the adoption of the UNGPs. The endorsement of the UNGPs by the United Nations Human Rights Council in 2011 established that businesses have a "responsibility" to respect human rights. The Guiding Principles focus on the human rights impact of any business conduct and elaborate the distinction that exists between the state duty to protect human rights and the corporate responsibility to respect human rights. In relation to the corporate responsibility, the framework iterates that companies have a responsibility to assess the way their practices, services, and products affect human rights and to mitigate negative impact. A key element of the human rights responsibility is the ability to know and show that the company is preventing and addressing any adverse human rights impacts that may be associated with its activities. As part of the ability to show, the companies are expected to communicate and provide a measure of transparency and accountability to individuals or groups who may be impacted and to other relevant stakeholders (United Nations Human Rights Council 2011, 25).

The UNGPs constitute a soft-law framework that addresses three different elements of the state–business nexus: first, the state duty to protect against human rights abuses, including by business enterprises; second, the corporate responsibility to respect human rights, including through human rights due diligence; and third, access for victims of business-related human rights abuses to effective remedies (United Nations Human Rights Council 2011). In terms of ensuring human rights due diligence, the UNGPs invoke human rights impact assessments (HRIAs) and set expectations of both state and business entities with regard to HRIAs. In meeting their duty to protect, states should, for instance, "(a) enforce laws that are aimed at, or have the effect of, requiring business enterprises to respect human rights, and periodically to assess the adequacy of such laws and address any gaps; (b) ensure that other laws and policies governing the creation and ongoing operation of business enterprises, such as corporate law, do not constrain but enable business respect for human rights; (c) provide effective guidance to business enterprises on how to respect human rights throughout their operations" (ibid.). The guidelines iterate that the failure to enforce existing laws that directly or indirectly regulate business respect for human rights is often a significant legal gap in state practice—for instance, in relation to labor, nondiscrimination, or privacy laws. Further, it is important for states to review whether these laws provide the necessary coverage in light of evolving circumstances. The UNGPs framework has been widely praised by both states and companies but also criticized for its slow uptake, ineffectiveness, and lack of binding obligations on companies (Aaronson and Higham 2013; Bilchitz 2013).

In practice, identifying the human rights impact of the technology sector is complicated by a number of factors, such as the diversity of the sector. In relation to the focus of this book, that is, the social web, the companies' role in facilitating rights of expression, information, and participation means that business activities intersect with human rights in ways that are different from the classical human rights and business scheme. Often, in the business and human rights landscape, there is a relatively clear and identifiable human rights violation and a relatively clear and identifiable violator. Some of the human rights violations in the technology sector look like these kinds of violations, for example, a company's poor treatment of workers. There is, however, an additional layer of human rights harms in the technology sector compared to this classical scheme as addressed extensively by Land in this volume. Besides having obligations toward their employees and the community in which they operate, the companies may affect billions of users' human rights as part of the services and platforms they provide. This particular feature of their services poses significant challenges when determining their human rights responsibilities. Thus, while the companies may be contributing to a range of human rights violations, including labor and community harms, their impact on users' ability to communicate, participate in public life, and retain a sense of privacy is unique to these companies. Effectively, their role as intermediaries and gatekeepers in the online ecosystem implies that the manner in which they collect, process, prioritize, curate, share, and remove content shapes the boundaries for public and private life on the Internet. As Kaye notes, it remains an open question how human rights concerns raised by corporate policy, design, and engineering choices should be reconciled with the freedom of private entities to design and customize their platforms as they choose (Kaye 2016, 55).

Also, it is important to recognize the distinction between human rights law that is focused on the relationship between the individual and the state, and the private law that governs the economic relations among individuals and business entities. While in general the separation of the spheres of law has been respected, the division is being demolished, not least in Europe (Collins 2011, 1). This is due to at least two developments in legal thought. First, fundamental rights and principles are increasingly regarded as constitutional values of an entire legal order that should infuse both public and private law since the legal order should be aligned with these fundamental principles (Barak 2001, 21–22). Second, private law is perceived increasingly as another arm of the regulatory state, designed to secure social goals, and like other exercises of power by agencies of the state, subject to the constraints of human rights law (Collins 2011, 2). "It becomes appropriate, for instance, to ask whether a particular result in contract law adequately protects the autonomy and dignity of an individual, or whether tort law provides sufficient protection for an individual's right to privacy" (Collins 2011, 3). Irrespective of these developments, the responsibilities for a business entity under human rights law is arguably a more blurred, soft, and unfamiliar terrain compared to private contract law, not least in the United States.

Another of the developments that have placed the role of technology companies increasingly high on the human rights agenda is the fact that the debate on Internet intermediaries and policy responses such as co- and self-regulation, while certainly not new, has taken on a new dimension with the concentration of services within technology giants. In practice, the line between co- and self-regulation is often blurred, but in general self-regulation refers to practices whereby a company defines, implements, and enforces norms without public intervention, whereas coregulation refers to the voluntary delegation of all or some part of implementation and enforcement of norms from public authorities to a company (Frydman, Hennebel, and Lewkowicz 2008, 133–134). The EU, for instance, has for the past two decades enlisted Internet companies in frameworks of self- and coregulation to assist the EU member states in preventing illegal content in the online domain (Frydman and Rorive 2003; Korff 2014; Schulz and Held 2001; Tambini, Leonardi, and Marsden 2008). While such EU policies clearly have an impact on individuals' human rights, they have largely been formulated and implemented without an explicit recognition of the human rights issues they raise (Angelopoulos et al. 2016; Jørgensen et al. 2016). "A growing amount of self-regulation, particularly in the European Union, is implemented as an alternative to traditional regulatory action. Some governments actively encourage or even place pressure on private business to self-regulate as an alternative to formal legislation or regulation which is inherently less flexible and usually more blunt than private arrangements" (MacKinnon et al. 2014, 56). Most recently, the EU has promoted self-regulation as a tool to counter hate speech on major Internet platforms, thereby affecting the ways in which users encounter content on sensitive topics, as addressed by Jørgensen and McGonagle in this volume.

Since 2016, both the UN Special Rapporteur on Freedom of Expression, and his counterpart, the UN Special Rapporteur on Privacy, have pointed to the human rights implications of technology companies as an increasingly important area of concern. "Vast social media forums for public expression are owned by private companies. Major platforms aggregating and indexing global knowledge, and designing the algorithms that influence what information is seen online, result from private endeavor" (Kaye 2016). "This increasingly detailed data-map of consumer behavior has resulted in personal data becoming a commodity where access to such data or exploitation of such data in a variety of ways is now one of the world's largest industries generating revenues calculated in hundreds of billions most usually in the form of targeted advertising" (Cannataci 2016). What remains a major challenge is to determine the human rights responsibilities of these companies, and the extent to which their business practices interfere with human rights law. As illustrated in the previous section, the literature on technology and human rights has exploded over the past twenty years; however, the human rights implications of the social web are still underresearched, including whether specific business practices invoke a positive state obligation to regulate the companies. For example, will new regulatory responses such as the GDPR provide (European) users with effective protection of their online privacy rights? (See Van Hoboken's analysis in this volume.) When does content moderation amount to a freedom-of-expression issue, and if/when it does, does this invoke a positive obligation on the state to regulate? (See the chapter by Land, in particular.) Further, and irrespective of state regulation, what is the scope of the business responsibility to respect human rights law? (See Callamard's analysis in this volume.) While there is an increasing attention to these issues, the assessment and mitigation of the companies' human rights impact have largely been left to the companies to address through corporate social responsibility frameworks and industry initiatives such as the Global Network Initiative (Maclay 2014).[16] Up until now, there has been limited research that critically assesses the frameworks governing the activities of these companies and questions whether they are sufficient to provide the standards and compliance mechanisms needed to protect and respect human rights online (Laidlaw 2015). In sum, the companies that govern the social web effectively operate in a gray zone between human rights law and corporate social responsibility, with no authoritative answer as to what their human rights responsibility entails.

In the section that follows, I will briefly explain how the book has been organized to address these urgent questions and challenges.

Contents of the Book

The first part of the book, "Datafication," highlights some of the societal shifts that are at play, focusing on the economic model of data extraction as a means to control human behavior, the corporate shaping of "informed realities," datafication and its democratic deficits, and the (inadequate) understanding of what constitutes personal information in an algorithmic age. Drawing upon a long tale of scholarly work, the contributions highlight theoretical and conceptual challenges that have implications for how we frame, engage, and resolve questions concerning the protection of human rights online.

Zuboff's chapter, "'We Make Them Dance': Surveillance Capitalism, the Rise of Instrumentarian Power, and the Threat to Human Rights," discusses the giants of the social web as a new kind of power with a radical impact on the possibility for self-determination and autonomous action. Zuboff argues that these companies represent a market project that fuses with technology to achieve its own unique brand of social domination. From the vantage point of radical indifference, the companies rely on instruments to monitor, analyze, shape, and predict our actions, in pursuit of the competitive advantage that follows. Based on a brief overview of the framework of surveillance capitalism, Zuboff unmasks the instrumentarian power that arises from the application of surveillance capitalism's economic imperatives and contrasts this new power with the totalitarian construct with which it is typically confused. The development of these conditions demands new forms of collective action, resistance, and struggle, as contests over political rights are renewed, human rights are abrogated, and even the "right to have rights" is under siege.

Flyverbom and Whelan's chapter on "Digital Transformations, Informed Realities, and Human Conduct" explores the influence of datafied forms of knowledge on human choice and agency. The chapter proposes the notion of "informed realities" to discuss how people's ways of experiencing are governed by the different types of information they access and rely on. Notably, platforms inform people's daily lives by constructing and controlling the informed realities that they live in and live with in digital spaces. The authors warn that the growing ubiquity of these platforms and services increasingly shapes the way we view the world, while constraining and directing our decision-making in invisible ways. In conclusion, the authors suggest a number of steps to keep this development in check

Bechmann next explores "Data as Humans: Representation, Accountability, and Equality in Big Data." The chapter raises questions of representation concerning the way data are treated as humans in the datafied society, and the democratic deficits this may lead to. Bechmann argues that systematic discrimination and inequality may occur through machine learning if we fail to take the preliminary measure of inscribing human rights norms in the machine learning algorithms executed by, for instance, social media. While problems of representation are not new, discrimination may now happen in a more systematic way, fostered by data mining and the closed cycles of machine learning algorithms that need to be properly governed.

Supplementing Bechmann's concern, albeit from a different perspective, Mai's chapter on "Situating Personal Information: Privacy in the Algorithmic Age" critically examines how we conceptualize personal information and thus informational privacy in a time of big data. The chapter argues that the predominant conceptualization of informational privacy as the ability to control the flow of personal information is inadequate in an age of big data, algorithms, and an economy based on data profiles. Instead, informational privacy must be concerned with the situations and practices in which the construction, analysis, and interpretation of information take place. Mai suggests that privacy cannot be limited solely to an individual, liberal right but should be expanded to an expectation of moral norms and behavior in society.

The second part of the book, "Platforms," brings us closer to actual platform practices. It considers the evolving history of business practices for capturing, measuring, and managing attention; explores content moderation in relation to public discourse; and illustrates the corporate storytelling around human rights. In short, it examines examples of how platforms and services operate, how they relate to human rights, and what the wider societal implications of their practices may be.

Bermejo's chapter on "Online Advertising as a Shaper of Public Communication" traces the history of online advertising and illustrates how the intimate link between communication and data mining in today's online public sphere is rooted in the development of the advertising model over the past two decades. Bermejo uses the process of capturing, measuring, and managing attention—the core of the advertising industry's work in the mass media era—as a blueprint for understanding the way online advertising is conducted on the social web, and to examine the wider social and democratic implications of this model.

Moving closer toward the governance practices of platforms, York and Zuckerman's chapter on "Moderating the Public Sphere" traces the history and character of content moderation as a widely used method of (private) control over public discourse. The concepts of hard and soft control are used as a lens to characterize platform authority over what can be published online versus platform authority over what users are likely to see—or not see if the content is deprioritized in the algorithms that govern a user's feed. The practices of major platforms are examined within the larger context of threats to freedom of expression, including threats from state actors and threats from individual users acting alone or in concert. The authors argue that as instances of flawed content moderation reach the public, there is the opportunity for a strong citizen movement—one that monitors the abuse of power by platforms, demands transparency, and fights for freedom of expression.

Jørgensen's chapter on "Rights Talk: In the Kingdom of Online Giants" continues the examination of platform practices, this time from the perspective of staff at Google and Facebook. Based on empirical studies, the author presents three examples of human rights storytelling within the two companies. The first narrative paints the companies as safeguards against government overreach. The second narrative concerns their role as coregulators via codes of conduct, while the third narrative presents privacy as user control over personal information. While the companies take great pride in protecting their users' right to freedom of expression and privacy from government overreach, their own business practices are not framed as a human rights issue nor subjected to the same type of scrutiny as government practices.

The third part of the book, "Regulation," considers human rights challenges raised by these developments and examples. Given the theme of the book, the relationship between human rights law and private actors is of particular significance in this part, not least the reach of international human rights law vis-à-vis soft law such as the UNGPs. The contributions explore the human rights responsibility of non-state actors, the Council of Europe approach to Internet intermediaries, and the disconnect between platform practices and users' right to privacy and, finally, suggest a human-rights-based approach to regulating Internet intermediaries.

Callamard confronts one of the overarching questions of the book, namely, "The Human Rights Obligations of Non-state Actors." Based on a wide array of examples from around the globe, the chapter discusses challenges to human rights protection—and freedom of expression in particular—in an environment shaped by global communications systems and powerful non-state actors. The chapter traces the obligations of non-state actors to international treaty provisions; explores their treatment as international human rights law duty bearers; and discusses their role in influencing, if not shaping, normative development. In conclusion, Callamard explores "meaningful self-regulation" and the development of an international legal framework as two options for stronger human rights protection in the online domain.

In "The Council of Europe and Internet Intermediaries: A Case Study of Tentative Posturing," McGonagle explores the efforts of the European

Court of Human Rights to keep apace of technological developments and to retain and revamp its general freedom-of-expression and rule-of-law principles in an online environment dominated by Internet intermediaries. As part of this, the chapter considers the legal complications involved in bringing Internet intermediaries into the fold of a traditional, international, and treaty-centric system, including the role of self-regulatory measures. The author concludes with a reflection on the rights, duties, and responsibilities of Internet intermediaries that flow from the existing system, using the case of "hate speech" to illustrate how frictional the relationship between intermediaries' rights, duties, and responsibilities—and those of their users—can be in practice.

The right to privacy faces particular pressure in an age of datafication, as outlined in the first part of the book. Van Hoboken's chapter on "The Privacy Disconnect" responds to these challenges and explores the legal questions involved in the contemporary protection of online privacy. The chapter discusses and reviews some of the major obstacles to regulation of the personal data economy, including consolidation in the Internet service industry; the erosion of restrictions on the collection of personal information; the tension between the different regulatory approaches in the United States and Europe; and the fact that privacy regulation is primarily concerned with the handling of personal data rather than a broader concern for fair data-driven treatment, data privacy, and autonomy. Van Hoboken argues that current privacy laws and policies fall short in providing for the legitimacy of current-day pervasive data-processing practices and proposes that privacy law and policy discussions become more firmly connected to the underlying power dynamics they aim to resolve.

The book concludes with Land's chapter on "Regulating Private Harms Online: Content Regulation under Human Rights Law." Land draws upon and supplements the previous analysis (not least by Callamard) by developing a human rights–based approach to regulating the impact of Internet intermediaries, focusing on content regulation in particular. As part of this approach, Land addresses three challenges: first, the inadequate understanding of what constitutes state action in the online domain; second, the tendency to neglect the duties that international human rights law imposes directly on private actors; and third, the lack of attention toward the positive duty of the state to regulate intermediaries in order to protect rights online. Land proposes a set of recommendations that can be adopted by human rights institutions such as the UN Office of the High Commissioner for Human Rights and the UN treaty bodies, in order to strengthen human rights protection in online spaces.

Notes

1. "Social web" refers to online platforms and services designed and developed to support and foster social interaction.

2. There is large body of literature related to the field of human rights. For scholarly introductions, see, for instance, Alston and Goodman (2013) and Freeman (2014).

3. Data processing performed by national police forces and courts (for certain functions) is not subject to the GDPR but regulated in a separate EU Directive on policing and criminal justice.

4. "Datafication" refers to the practice of turning numerous aspects of life into data and transforming it in order to create value. The term was introduced by Cukier and Mayer-Schoenberger in 2013 (Cukier and Mayer-Schoenberger 2013).

5. See https://www.ctrl-shift.co.uk/personal-information-economy-2016.

6. For a full list, see https://www.coe.int/en/web/freedom-expression/committee-of -ministers-adopted-texts/-/asset_publisher/C10Tb8ZfKDoJ/content.

7. A/HRC/RES/34/7 (March 23, 2017), A/HRC/RES/32/13 (July 18, 2016), A/HRC/ RES/28/16 (April 1, 2015), A/HRC/RES/26/13 (July 14, 2014), A/HRC/RES/23/2 (June 24, 2013), A/HRC/RES/20/8 (July 16, 2012), A/HRC/RES/12/16 (October 12, 2009), A/HRC/DEC/25/117 (April 15, 2014), A/HRC/DEC/18/119 (October 17, 2011).

8. For a full list, see http://www.ohchr.org/EN/Issues/FreedomOpinion/Pages/Annual .aspx.

9. For a full list of publications under UNESCO's series of Internet Freedom, see https://en.unesco.org/unesco-series-on-internet-freedom.

10. For a full list, see https://www.apc.org/en/apc-wide-activities/global-information -society-watch.

11. "Internet intermediaries" refers to "third-party platforms that mediate between digital content and the humans who contribute and access this content" (DeNardis 2014, 154).

12. "Monopoly" refers to "an organization or group that has complete control of something, especially an area of business, so that others have no share"; see https:// dictionary.cambridge.org/dictionary/english/monopoly.

13. A "public utility" refers to "a business organization (such as an electric company) performing a public service and subject to special governmental regulation"; see https://www.merriam-webster.com/dictionary/public%20utility.

14. A "natural monopoly" refers to "a situation in which one company is able to supply the whole market for a product or service more cheaply than two or more companies could"; see https://dictionary.cambridge.org/dictionary/english/natural-monopoly.

15. See, for instance, the response to Jonathan Taplin from Tim Worstall, April 23, 2017: https://www.forbes.com/sites/timworstall/2017/04/23/google-isnt-a-monopoly-so-dont-break-it-up-or-regulate-it-like-one/#68a5c3746ad0.

16. See, for instance, the Global Network Initiative report on the 2015/16 Assessments of Facebook, Google, LinkedIn, Microsoft, and Yahoo!: http://globalnetworkinitiative.org/sites/default/files/PAR-2015-16-Executive-Summary.pdf.

References

Aaronson, Susan Ariel, and Ian Higham. 2013. "Re-Righting Business: John Ruggie and the Struggle to Develop International Human Rights Standards for Transnational Firms." *Human Rights Quarterly: A Comparative and International Journal of the Social Sciences, Philosophy, and Law* 35 (2): 333–364.

Agre, Philip E. 1994. "Surveillance and Capture: Two Models of Privacy." *The Information Society* 10 (2): 101–127.

Akdeniz, Yaman. 2016. *Media Freedom on the Internet: An OSCE Guidebook*. Vienna: Office of the OSCE Representative on Freedom of the Media.

Alston, Philip, and Ryan Goodman. 2013. *International Human Rights: The Successor to International Human Rights in Context: Law, Politics and Morals: Text and Materials*. Oxford: Oxford University Press.

Angelopoulos, Christina, Annabel Brody, Wouter Hins, P. Bernt Hugenholtz, Patrick Leerssen, Thomas Margoni, Tarlach McGonagle, et al. 2016. *Study of Fundamental Rights Limitations for Online Enforcement through Self-regulation*. Amsterdam: Institute for Information Law (IViR).

Balkin, Jack M. 2014. "Old-School/New-School Speech Regulation." *Harvard Law Review* 127 (8): 2296–2342.

———. 2018. "Free Speech in the Algorithmic Society: Big Data, Private Governance, and New School Speech Regulation." *UC Davis Law Review* 51: 1149–1210.

Balnaves, Mark, and Michele A. Willson. 2011. *A New Theory of Information and the Internet: Public Sphere Meets Protocol*. New York: Peter Lang.

Barak, Aharon. 2001. "Constitutional Human Rights and Private Law." In *Human Rights in Private Law*, edited by Daniel Friedmann and Daphne Barak-Erez, 13–42. Oxford: Hart.

Belli, Luca, and Nicolo Zingales, eds. 2017. *Platform Regulations—How Platforms Are Regulated and How They Regulate Us*. Rio de Janeiro: FGV Direito Rio.

Benedek, Wolfgang, and Matthias Kettemann. 2014. *Freedom of Expression and the Internet*. Strasbourg: Council of Europe.

Benkler, Yochai. 2006. *The Wealth of Networks—How Social Production Transforms Markets and Freedom*. New Haven, CT: Yale University Press.

Benkler, Yochai, Hal Roberts, Robert Faris, Alicia Solow-Niederman, and Bruce Etling. 2015. "Social Mobilization and the Networked Public Sphere: Mapping the SOPA-PIPA Debate." *Political Communication* 32 (4): 594–624.

Best, Michael L., Ernest J. Wilson, and Colin M. Maclay. 2004. "The World Summit in Reflection: A Deliberative Dialogue on the WSIS." *Information Technologies and International Development* 1 (3–4): 1–2.

Bilchitz, David. 2013. "A Chasm between 'Is' and 'Ought'? A Critique of the Normative Foundations of the SRSG's Framework and the Guiding Principles." In *Human Rights Obligations of Business: Beyond the Corporate Responsibility to Respect?*, edited by Surya Deva and David Bilchitz, 107–137. Cambridge, MA: Cambridge University Press.

Brown, Ian. 2010. "Internet Self-regulation and Fundamental Rights." *Index on Censorship* 1: 98–106.

Bucher, Taina. 2012. "Want to Be on the Top? Algorithmic Power and the Threat of Invisibility on Facebook." *New Media & Society* 14 (7): 1164–1180.

Cannataci, Joseph A. March 8, 2016. "Report of the Special Rapporteur on Privacy, Joseph A. Cannataci." Geneva: Human Rights Council.

Carr, Madeline. 2013. "Internet Freedom, Human Rights and Power." *Australian Journal of International Affairs* 67 (5): 621–637.

Castells, Manuel. 2009. *Communication Power*. Oxford: Oxford University Press.

Cath, Corinne, and Luciano Floridi. 2017. "The Design of the Internet's Architecture by the Internet Engineering Task Force (IETF) and Human Rights." https://papers.ssrn.com/sol3/papers.cfm?abstract_id=2912308.

Cohen, Julie E. 2013. "What Privacy Is For." *Harvard Law Review* 126 (7): 1904–1933.

Collins, Hugh. April 2011. "The Impact of Human Rights Law on Contract Law in Europe." Legal Studies Research Paper Series. Cambridge: University of Cambridge.

Comninos, Alex. June 2011. "APC Issue Paper: Freedom of Peaceful Assembly and Freedom of Association and the Internet." Published by Association for Progressive Communications.

Council of Europe Committee of Experts on Internet Intermediaries. 2017. "Study on the Human Rights Dimensions of Automated Data Processing Techniques (in Particular Algorithms) and Possible Regulatory Implications." October 6. Strasbourg: Council of Europe.

Ctrl-Shift. 2015. "The Data Driven Economy: Toward Sustainable Growth." London: Facebook and Ctrl-Shift.

Cukier, Kenneth Neil, and Viktor Mayer-Schoenberger. 2013. "The Rise of Big Data: How It's Changing the Way We Think about the World." *Foreign Affairs*. May/June. https://www.foreignaffairs.com/articles/2013-04-03/rise-big-data.

Cunha, Mario Viola de Azevedo, Norberto Nuno Gomes de Andrade, Lucas Lixinski, and Lúcio Tomé Feteira, eds., 2013. *New Technologies and Human Rights: Challenges to Regulation*. Farnham, UK: Ashgate.

Deibert, Ronald J., John Palfrey, Rafal Rohozinski, and Jonathan Zittrain, eds. 2008. *Access Denied: The Practice and Policy of Global Internet Filtering*. Cambridge, MA: MIT Press.

Deibert, Ronald, John Palfrey, Rafal Rohozinski, and Jonathan Zittrain. 2011. *Access Contested: Security, Identity, and Resistance in Asian Cyberspace*. Cambridge, MA: MIT Press.

Deibert, Ronald, John Palfrey, Rafal Rohozinski, Jonathan Zittrain, and Initiative OpenNet. 2010. *Access Controlled: The Shaping of Power, Rights, and Rule in Cyberspace*. Cambridge, MA: MIT Press.

DeNardis, Laura. 2014. *The Global War for Internet Governance*. New Haven, CT: Yale University Press.

Dencik, Lina, Arne Hintz, and Jonathan Cable. 2016. "Towards Data Justice? The Ambiguity of Anti-surveillance Resistance in Political Activism." *Big Data & Society* 3 (2): 1–12.

Earl, Jennifer, and Katrina Kimport. 2011. *Digitally Enabled Social Change: Activism in the Internet Age*. Cambridge, MA: MIT Press.

Elkin-Koren, Niva, and Neil Weinstock Netanel. 2002. "Introduction: The Commodification of Information." In *The Commodification of Information*, edited by Niva Elkin-Koren and Neil Weinstock Netanel. The Hague: Kluwer Law International, vii–xi.

Elmer, Greg. 2004. *Profiling Machines: Mapping the Personal Information Economy*. Cambridge, MA: MIT Press.

Freeman, Michael. 2014. *Human Rights*. Cambridge: Polity Press.

Frydman, Benoit, Ludovic Hennebel, and Gregory Lewkowicz. 2008. "Public Strategies for Internet Co-regulation in the United States, Europe and China." In *Governance, Regulations and Powers on the Internet*, edited by Eric Brousseau, Meryem Marzouki, and Cecile Méadel, 133–150. Cambridge, MA: Cambridge University Press.

Frydman, Benoit, and Isabelle Rorive. 2003. "Constitutional Framework and Speech Freedom in Relation to Self-Regulation of Communications." Paper presented at the Self-Regulation in the Media and Communications Sectors Seminar, organized by the Comparative Law & Policy Program, Oxford University, Oxford, February.

Fuchs, Christian. 2015. *Culture and Economy in the Age of Social Media*. New York: Routledge.

Fuchs, Christian, and Marisol Sandoval. 2014. *Critique, Social Media and the Information Society*. New York: Routledge.

Gillespie, Tarleton. 2010. "The Politics of Platforms." *New Media & Society* 12 (3): 347–364.

———. 2014. "The Relevance of Algorithms." In *Media Technologies: Essays on Communication, Materiality, and Society*, edited by Tarleton Gillespie, Pablo J. Boczkowski, and Kirsten A. Foot, 167–193. Cambridge, MA: MIT Press.

———. 2018. *Custodians of the Internet: Platforms, Content Moderation, and the Hidden Decisions That Shape Social Media*. New Haven, CT: Yale University Press.

Goldberg, Greg. 2011. "Rethinking the Public/Virtual Sphere: The Problem with Participation." *New Media & Society* 13 (5): 739–754.

Graber, Christoph B. 2016. "The Future of Online Content Personalisation: Technology, Law and Digital Freedoms." i-call Working Paper No. 2016/1. Zurich: University of Zurich.

Helmond, Anne. 2015. "The Platformization of the Web: Making Web Data Platform Ready." *Social Media + Society* 1 (2): 1–11.

Jørgensen, Rikke Frank, ed. 2006. *Human Rights in the Global Information Society*. Cambridge, MA: MIT Press.

Jørgensen, Rikke Frank. 2013. *Framing the Net—The Internet and Human Rights*. Cheltenham, UK: Edward Elgar.

———. 2017a. "Framing Human Rights: Exploring Storytelling within Internet Companies." *Information, Communication & Society* 21 (3): 340–355.

———. 2017b. "What Platforms Mean When They Talk about Human Rights." *Policy & Internet* 9 (3): 280–296.

Jørgensen, Rikke Frank, and Anja Møller Pedersen. 2017. "Online Service Providers as Human Rights Arbiters." In *The Responsibilities of Online Service Providers*, edited by Mariarosaria Taddeo and Luciano Floridi, 179–199. Oxford: Oxford University Press.

Jørgensen, Rikke Frank, Anja Møller Pedersen, Wolfgang Benedek, and Reinmar Nindler. 2016. "Case Study on ICT and Human Rights, FRAME: Work Package No. 2—Deliverable No. 2.3." Brussels: European Commission.

Kaye, David. May 11, 2016. "Report of the Special Rapporteur on the Promotion and Protection of the Right to Freedom of Opinion and Expression." A/HRC/32/38. Geneva: Human Rights Council.

———. April 6, 2018. "Report of the Special Rapporteur on the Promotion and Protection of the Right to Freedom of Opinion and Expression." A/HRC/38/35. Geneva: Human Rights Council.

Korff, Douwe. 2014. "The Rule of Law on the Internet and in the Wider Digital World." Issue Paper for the Council of Europe. Strasbourg: Commissioner for Human Rights.

Laidlaw, Emily. 2015. *Regulating Speech in Cyberspace*: Cambridge: Cambridge University Press.

Land, Molly, and Jay D. Aronson. 2018. *New Technologies for Human Rights Law and Practice*. Cambrige, UK: Cambridge University Press.

Langlois, Ganaele, and Greg Elmer. 2013. "The Research Politics of Social Media Platforms." *Culture Machine* 14: 1–17.

Langlois, Ganaele, Greg Elmer, Fenwick McKelvey, and Zachary Devereaux. 2009. "Networked Publics: The Double Articulation of Code and Politics on Facebook." *Canadian Journal of Communication* 34 (3): 415–434.

Lannon, John, and Edward F. Halpin. 2013. *Human Rights and Information Communication Technologies: Trends and Consequences of Use*. Hershey, PA: Information Science Reference.

Latzer, Michael, Katharina Hollnbuchner, Natascha Just, and Florian Saurwein. 2014. "The Economics of Algorithmic Selection on the Internet." Working Paper, IPMZ. Zurich: University of Zurich.

Lazzarato, Maurizio. 2004. "From Capital-Labour to Capital-Life." *Ephemere* 4 (3): 187–208.

Lessig, Lawrence. 1999. *Code and Other Laws of Cyberspace*. New York: Basic Books.

Lewis, Justin. 2016. "The Commercial Constraints on Speech Limit Democratic Debate." In *Blurring the Lines: Market-Driven and Democracy-Driven Freedom of*

Expression, edited by Maria Edström, Andrew T. Kenyon, and Eva-Maria Svensson, 91–100. Gothenburg, Sweden: Nordicom.

MacKinnon, Rebecca. 2012. *Consent of the Networked: The Worldwide Struggle for Internet Freedom*. New York: Basic Books.

MacKinnon, Rebecca, Ellonai Hickock, Allon Bar, and Hae-in Lim. 2014. *Fostering Freedom Online: The Roles, Challenges and Obstacles of Internet Intermediaries*. Paris: United Nations Educational, Scientific, and Cultural Organization.

Maclay, Colin M. 2014. "An Improbable Coalition: How Businesses, Nongovernmental Organizations, Investors and Academics Formed the Global Network Initiative to Promote Privacy and Free Expression Online." PhD diss., The Law and Public Policy Program, Northeastern University, Boston.

Mansell, Robin. 2015. "Platforms of Power." *Intermedia* 43 (1): 20–24.

Mendel, Toby, Andrew Puddephatt, Ben Wagner, Dixie Hawtin, and Natalia Torres. 2012. *Global Survey on Internet Privacy and Freedom of Expression*. Paris: United Nations Educational, Scientific, and Cultural Organization.

Milan, Stefania, and Niels ten Oever. 2017. "Coding and Encoding Rights in Internet Infrastructure." *Internet Policy Review* 6 (1).

Moore, Martin. April 2016. *Tech Giants and Civic Power*. London: King's College London.

Morozov, Evgeny. 2011. *The Net Delusion: The Dark Side of Internet Freedom*. New York: PublicAffairs.

Nas, Sjoera. 2004. "The Future of Freedom of Expression Online: Why ISP Self-regulation Is a Bad Idea." In *Spreading the Word on the Internet*, edited by Organization for Security and Co-operation in Europe (OSCE), 165–172. Vienna: OSCE.

Nissenbaum, Helen. 2010. *Privacy in Context: Technology, Policy and the Integrity of Social Life*. Palo Alto: Stanford University Press.

Oldenburg, Ray. 1997. *The Great Good Place: Cafés, Coffee Shops, Community Centers, Beauty Parlors, General Stores, Bars, Hangouts, and How They Get You through the Day*. New York: Marlowe.

Papacharissi, Zizi. 2010. *A Private Sphere: Democracy in a Digital Age*. Cambridge: Polity Press.

Pasquale, Frank. 2015. *The Black Box Society: The Secret Algorithms That Control Money and Information*. Cambridge, MA: Harvard University Press.

Powers, Shawn M., and Michael Jablonski. 2015. *The Real Cyber War: The Political Economy of Internet Freedom*. Urbana: University of Illinois Press.

Rachovitsa, Adamantia. 2017. "Rethinking Privacy Online and Human Rights: The Internet's Standardisation Bodies as the Guardians of Privacy Online in the Face of Mass Surveillance." University of Groningen Faculty of Law Research Paper 01-2017. https://ssrn.com/abstract=2911978.

Radin, Margaret Jane. 2002. "Incomplete Commodification in the Computerized World." In *The Commodification of Information*, edited by Niva Elkin-Koren and Neil Weinstock Netanel, 3–22. The Hague: Klüver Law International.

Redeker, Dennis, Lex Gill, and Urs Gasser. February 16, 2018. "Towards Digital Constitutionalism? Mapping Attempts to Craft an Internet Bill of Rights." *International Communication Gazette* 80 (4): 302–319.

Schulz, Wolfgang, and Thorsten Held. 2001. "Regulated Self-regulation as a Form of Modern Government." In Study Commissioned by the German Federal Commissioner for Cultural and Media Affairs, Interim Report, Hamburg, Germany.

Solove, Daniel J. 2008. *Understanding Privacy*. Cambridge, MA: Harvard University Press.

Srniceks, Nick. 2017. "We Need to Nationalise Google, Facebook and Amazon. Here's Why," *The Guardian*, August 30. https://www.theguardian.com/commentisfree/2017/aug/30/nationalise-google-facebook-amazon-data-monopoly-platform-public-interest.

Staeheli, Lynn A., and Donald Mitchell. 2007. *The People's Property? Power, Politics, and the Public*. New York: Routledge.

Sullivan, David. June 2016. "APC Issue Papers—Business and Digital Rights: Taking Stock of the UN Guiding Principles for Business and Human Rights." Published by Association for Progressive Communications.

Sunstein, Cass R. 2007. *Republic.com*. Princeton, NJ: Princeton University Press.

Tambini, Damian, Danilo Leonardi, and Christopher T. Marsden. 2008. *Codifying Cyberspace: Communications Self-regulation in the Age of Internet Convergence*. London: Routledge.

Taplin, Jonathan. 2017a. *Move Fast and Break Things: How Facebook, Google, and Amazon Cornered Culture and Undermined Democracy*. New York: Hachette Book Group.

———. 2017b. "Is It Time to Break Up Google?" *New York Times*, April 22. https://www.nytimes.com/2017/04/22/opinion/sunday/is-it-time-to-break-up-google.html.

Tufekci, Zeynep. 2017. *Twitter and Tear Gas: The Power and Fragility of Networked Protest*. New Haven, CT: Yale University Press.

United Nations Human Rights Council. March 21, 2011. "Report of the Special Representative John Ruggie. Guiding Principles on Business and Human Rights: Implementing the United Nations 'Protect, Respect and Remedy' Framework." New York: United Nations.

Van Dijck, José. 2013. *The Culture of Connectivity: A Critical History of Social Media.* Oxford; NY: Oxford University Press.

Van Dijck, José, and Thomas Poell. 2013. Understanding Social Media Logic. *Media and Communication* 1 (1): 2–14.

Verstraeten, Hans. 2007. "Media, Democracy and the Public Sphere: Towards a Reconceptualisation of the Public Sphere." *South African Journal for Communication Theory and Research* 26 (1): 73–83.

Wagner, Ben. 2013. "Governing Internet Expression—The International and Transnational Politics of Freedom of Expression." PhD diss., Department of Political and Social Sciences, European University Institute.

West, Sara Myers. 2017. "Data Capitalism: Redefining the Logics of Surveillance and Privacy." *Business & Society* 1–22.

Worstall, Tim. 2017. "Google Isn't A Monopoly—So Don't Break It Up Or Regulate It Like One," *Forbes*, April 23. https://www.forbes.com/sites/timworstall/2017/04/23/google-isnt-a-monopoly-so-dont-break-it-up-or-regulate-it-like-one/#68a5c3746ad0.

Ziccardi, Giovanni. 2013. *Resistance, Liberation Technology and Human Rights in the Digital Age.* Dordrecht: Springer.

Zuboff, Shoshana. 2015. "Big Other: Surveillance Capitalism and the Prospects of an Information Civilization." *Journal of Information Technology* 30 (1): 75–89.

Zuckerman, Ethan. 2013. *Rewire: Digital Cosmopolitans in the Age of Connection.* New York: W. W. Norton.

I   Datafication

The first part of the book highlights areas in which datafication has implications for the protection of human rights. The contributions raise critical
questions concerning the rise of a new species of economic power (Zuboff),
the way digital platforms inform and constrain individuals' choice and
freedom (Flyverbom and Whelan), the discriminatory effect that may flow
from big data and machine learning (Bechmann), and the need to revisit
the idea that we can protect online privacy by controlling personal information (Mai).

1 "We Make Them Dance": Surveillance Capitalism, the Rise of Instrumentarian Power, and the Threat to Human Rights

Shoshana Zuboff

What Just Happened?

A 2002 review of "wireless telemedicine" stressed the value of home health monitoring for the elderly and the expansion of health services in remote areas. A diagram of the proposed digital architecture for such services featured only three parties: a closed loop that exclusively linked a person at home, her hospital's servers, and her physician (Pattichis et al. 2002, 143–153). Digitalized information about one's body was imagined as deeply "mine": an inalienable extension of self with which one could choose to enrich already close relationships, such as those between a patient and a trusted doctor or elderly parents and their adult children. In just a few years, however, those 2002 schematics faded like an old daguerreotype.

Many studies of health monitoring continue to emphasize its utility for the elderly and other forms of remote care, but the conversation has decisively moved on from its earlier state of grace. Researchers anticipate the fusion of "smart cities" and what's now called "m-health" to produce "smart health," defined as "the provision of health services by using the context-aware network and sensing infrastructure of smart cities" (Solanas et al. 2014, 74–81). Toward that end, there are now reliable sensors for rendering an increasing range of physiological processes as behavioral data, including body temperature, heart rate, brain activity, muscle motion, blood pressure, sweat rate, energy expenditure, and body and limb motion (Intille et al. 2012, 24–31; Mukhopadhyay 2015, 1321–1330). There are sensors that can render audio, visual, and physiological data during postsurgical patient recovery and rehabilitation (Castillejo et al. 2013, 38–49). A flexible, sensored textile patch has been developed that can render breathing, hand movements, swallowing, and walking as behavioral data (Cheng et al. 2013, 3935–3947). In other applications, "wearable micromachined sensors" provide "accurate biomechanical analysis" as you walk or run, and a "body area network" records and analyzes walking and running "under extreme conditions" (De Rossi and Veltink 2010, 37–43).

These rich data can no longer be imagined as cloistered within the intimate closed loops of family and physician or even an application and its dieters or runners. By 2016, there were more than 100,000 mobile health apps available on the Google Android and Apple iOS platforms, double the number in 2014 (Addonizio 2016). A legal review of mobile health apps concludes that most of them "take the consumers' private information and data without the consumers' permission and . . . do not generally disclose to the user that this information will be sent to advertising companies" (Dehling et al. 2015, 1–26). These conclusions are borne out by a long queue of studies.

One in-depth investigation focused on the collection, processing, and usage activities associated with nine prominent fitness trackers (Hilts et al. 2016). All but two apps transmitted every logged fitness event to the company's servers, which enabled backup and sharing with one's friends but also "data analytics" and distribution to third parties. Among many disturbing findings was the fact that some of the trackers transmitted device identification numbers; others passively and continuously transmitted the user's precise longitude and latitude coordinates. These identifiers "could link fitness and biographical data to a single mobile phone hardware, or single specific fitness wearable. . . ." None of this sensitive information was necessary for the tracker to operate effectively, and most of the privacy policies were opaque at best and allowed data to be "sold or exchanged with third parties." The researchers concluded, "We discovered severe security vulnerabilities, incredibly sensitive geolocation transmissions that serve no apparent benefit to the end user, and . . . policies leaving the door open for the sale of users' fitness data to third parties without express consent of the users."

A comprehensive study of Android-based diabetes apps published in the *Journal of American Medicine* notes that while the US Food and Drug Administration approved the prescription of a range of apps that transmit sensitive health data, the behind-the-scenes practices of these apps are *"understudied"* (italics mine; Blenner et al. 2016, 1051–1052). Researchers examined

211 diabetes apps and randomly sampled 65 of them for close analysis of data-transmission practices. In some of these apps, merely downloading the software automatically "authorized collection and modification of sensitive information." They identified many backstage operations, including apps that modify or delete your information (64 percent), read your phone status and identity (31 percent), gather location data (27 percent), view your Wi-Fi connections (12 percent), and activate your camera in order to access your photos and videos (11 percent). Between 4 and 6 percent of the apps went even further: reading your contact lists, calling phone numbers found in your device, modifying your contacts, reading your call log, and activating your microphone to record your speech.

The research team concluded that privacy policies do not matter. Of the 211 apps in the group, 81 percent did not have privacy policies, but for those that did, "not all of the provisions actually protected privacy." Of those apps *without* privacy policies, 76 percent shared sensitive information with third parties, and of those *with* privacy policies, 79 percent shared your data while only about half admitted doing so in their published disclosures. Indeed, these discoveries suggest that the very notion of a "privacy policy' has become a dangerous euphemism, when such statements are better understood as "surveillance policies."

The coda here is simple: *Once I was mine. Now I am theirs.* In 2002, intimate health and body information was assumed to be the possession of the experiencing *subject*. Now, the same information is assumed to be the possession of the owners of the means by which it is produced. The experiencing subject is transformed into a data *object*. This transformation reflects what might be thought of as a journey through the ontologies, economics, and politics of possession, alerting us to the qualities of existence and power that attend self-possession in contrast to dispossession. The journey from one to the other is not restricted to body information but rather illustrates a pattern that now engulfs every aspect of human experience. We must therefore ask, what is it that determines these states of possession? What happened between 2002 and 2018 to decisively transform the ontological, economic, and political structures of these information flows? This question is aimed at the early twenty-first century, but it is clarified in a useful way with a quick backward glance.

"We've stumbled along for a while, trying to run a new civilization in old ways, but we've got to start to make this world over." It was 1912 when

Thomas Edison laid out his vision for a new industrial civilization in a letter to Henry Ford. Edison worried that industrialism's potential to serve the progress of humanity would be thwarted by the stubborn power of the robber barons and the monopolist economics that ruled their kingdoms. He decried the "wastefulness" and "cruelty" of US capitalism: "Our production, our factory laws, our charities, our relations between capital and labor, our distribution—all wrong, out of gear" (Nevins 1954, 532). Both Edison and Ford understood that the modern industrial civilization for which they harbored such hope was careening toward a darkness marked by industrial enslavement and grinding poverty for the many and prosperity for the very few.

The two quintessentially American inventors agreed that the moral life of industrial civilization would be shaped by the practices of capitalism that rose to dominance in their time and the unbridled power that such practices enjoyed, largely unimpeded by law, regulation, or jurisprudence. They believed that US society, and eventually the world, would have to fashion a new, more rational capitalism in order to avert a future of misery and conflict. A new century had dawned, but the evolution of capitalism, like the churning of civilizations, did not obey the calendar or the clock. It was 1912, and still the nineteenth century's Gilded Age refused to relinquish its claim on the twentieth.

The same can be said of our time. Once more we look to the great structural transformations of the market economy and its novel realizations of capitalism to define our era, and once more we see their promise occluded by the emergence of a new quality of economic power whose effects are revealed in a new kind of enslavement. What happened in the years between 2002 and 2018 was the emergence of a new *surveillance capitalism*, whose mechanisms and operations are only imaginable within the digital milieu (Zuboff 2014, 2015, 2016). Surveillance capitalism produces a new species of economic power that I call *instrumentarianism*. Together, the new capitalism and its unique production of power are as untamed by law as were the capitalism and economic power of the Gilded Age, and they are just as dangerous. Despite the many splendors of the digital milieu, surveillance capitalism and instrumentarian power now inscribe our lives with their unique signature of havoc, challenging human rights in ways that we did not predict and could not anticipate. Many old inequalities are deepened, while wholly new axes of exclusion and domination threaten every unprotected dimension of human experience. Earlier contests over political rights are renewed, elemental human rights are abrogated, and even the "right to have rights" is under siege (Arendt 2004).

Indeed, when it comes to the digital future and its consequences for human rights, a single point demands our attention: The challenges to human rights that we encounter in the digital era cannot be circumscribed by a specific technology or company, though they may be expressed in technological assemblies, such as algorithms and platforms, or in the practices of a single corporation. Rather, the challenges we face originate in the rapid evolution of *a new economic order* in which wealth is largely derived from surveillance—specifically, *the unilateral dispossession of human experience for the sake of others' profit.* As was the case in the twentieth century, this new economic order seeks to fashion in its likeness human personality, society, civilization, and the frameworks of human rights that bind all three. The sudden development of these conditions of existence means that if we are to claim the future for humanity, then new forms of collective action, resistance, and struggle are required. This chapter aims to contribute to such an undertaking by illuminating this triad: a novel capitalism, its novel form of power, and their novel challenges to elemental human rights that bear upon the production of autonomous action.

What Is Surveillance Capitalism?[1]

Framework

This effort to understand surveillance capitalism begins with the recognition that *we hunt the puppet master, not the puppet.* A first challenge to comprehension is the confusion between surveillance capitalism and the technologies it employs. Surveillance capitalism is not technology; it is a logic that imbues technology and commands it into action. Surveillance capitalism is a market form that is unimaginable outside the digital milieu, but it is not the same as "the digital." As is evident in the evolution of telemedicine, the digital can take many forms depending upon the social and economic logics that direct it into action. It is the capitalism that assigns the price tag of subjugation and helplessness, not the technology. In my view it is vital to understand that surveillance capitalism cannot be reduced to "platforms," "algorithms," "machine intelligence," or any other technological manifestation. While it is impossible to imagine surveillance capitalism without the affordances of the digital, it is perfectly possible to imagine these technologies and capabilities without surveillance capitalism.

That technologies are always economic means, not ends in themselves, is not a new point. Max Weber called attention to this "economic orientation," observing that economic ends are always intrinsic to technology's development and deployment. "Economic action" determines objectives, whereas technology provides "appropriate *means.*" In Weber's framing, "The fact that what is called the technological development of modern times has been so largely oriented economically to profit-making is one of the fundamental facts of the history of technology" (Weber 1978, 67). In a modern capitalist society, technology is, was, and always will be an expression of the economic objectives that direct it into action. A worthwhile exercise would be to delete the word "technology" from our vocabularies in order to see how quickly capitalism's objectives are exposed.

The primacy of economics over technology is not new, but capitalism has long found it useful to conceal itself within the Trojan horse of technology in order that we might perceive its excesses as the inevitable expression of the machines it employs. Surveillance capitalists are no exception. For example, in 2009 the public first became aware that Google maintains search histories indefinitely. When questioned about these practices, the corporation's former CEO Eric Schmidt explained, ". . . the reality is that search engines including Google do retain this information for some time" (Newman 2009). In truth, search engines do not retain, but surveillance capitalism does. Schmidt's statement is a classic of misdirection that bewilders the public by conflating commercial imperatives and technological necessity. It camouflages the concrete practices of surveillance capitalism and the specific choices that impelled Google's brand of search into action. Most significantly, it makes surveillance capitalism's practices appear to be inevitable, when they are actually meticulously calculated and lavishly funded means to self-dealing commercial ends.

Just as surveillance capitalism is not the same as technology, this new logic of accumulation cannot be reduced to any single corporation or group of corporations. Surveillance capitalism first rooted and flourished at Google and Facebook, then quickly became the default mode for most Internet businesses, startups, and apps. By now surveillance capitalism can no longer be thought of as restricted to individual companies or even to the Internet sector. It has spread across a wide range of products, services, and economic sectors, including insurance, retail, health care, finance, entertainment, education, transportation, and more, birthing whole new ecosystems of suppliers, producers, customers, market-makers, and market players. Nearly every product or service that begins with the word "smart" or "personalized," every Internet-enabled device, every "digital assistant," operates as a supply-chain interface for the unobstructed flow of behavioral data.

Surveillance capitalism was invented at Google, where its logic and foundational mechanisms were discovered and elaborated between 2001 and 2004 in much the same way that General Motors invented and perfected managerial capitalism a century ago. Google was the pathfinder of surveillance capitalism in thought and practice, the deep pocket for research and development, and the catalyst in experimentation and implementation. As the pioneer of surveillance capitalism, Google launched an unprecedented market operation into the unmapped spaces of the Internet where it faced few impediments from law or competitors, like an invasive species in a landscape free of natural predators. Its leaders drove the systemic coherence of their businesses at a breakneck pace that neither public institutions nor individuals could follow. Indeed, both speed and secrecy were carefully crafted strategies of shock and awe essential to the company's larger ambitions of market dominance (Zuboff, 2019).

Surveillance capitalism originates in history, not in technological inevitability. Google's discovery and pursuit of surveillance capitalism cannot be separated from the unique historical conditions that first motivated the urgent search for a new market form and later nurtured and sheltered its new mechanisms of accumulation. Specifically, the young company faced extreme pressure from its investors in the teeth of the 2001 financial crisis in Silicon Valley. Surveillance capitalism was invented as the solution to this financial emergency. It proved itself a rapid methodology for the translation of investment into revenue and capital. Google also benefitted from historical circumstance, when a national security apparatus galvanized by the attacks of 9/11 was inclined to nurture, mimic, shelter, and appropriate surveillance capitalism's emergent capabilities for the sake of total knowledge and its promise of total certainty. These dynamics comprise a political condition that I call *surveillance exceptionalism*.

The combination of financial success and the politics of surveillance exceptionalism transformed the new logic of accumulation into the default model of information capitalism. Surveillance capitalism migrated to

Facebook with Google-turned-Facebook executive Sheryl Sandberg and later took hold at Microsoft under the leadership of CEO Satya Nadella. Evidence suggests that Amazon has veered toward surveillance capitalism. The lure of surveillance revenue remains a constant challenge to Apple, both as an external threat and as a source of internal debate and conflict. Surveillance capitalism is no longer confined to the competitive dramas of the large Internet companies as competitive intensity eventually drove expansion into the offline world. Its economic imperatives and foundational mechanisms now spread across every economic sector and category of goods and services.

"Laws of Motion"

Borrowed from Newton's laws of inertia, force, and equal and opposite reactions, "laws of motion" is a metaphor that has been used to describe the necessary and predictable features of industrial capitalism (Marx 1992, 91–92; Wood 2002, 76, 93, 125). While surveillance capitalism does not abandon established capitalist "laws" such as competitive production, profit maximization, productivity, and growth, these earlier dynamics now operate in the context of a new logic of accumulation that also introduces its own sui generis laws of motion. Surveillance capitalism is defined by new economic imperatives whose mechanisms and effects cannot be grasped with existing models and assumptions. This is not to say that the old imperatives—a compulsion toward profit maximization along with the intensification of the means of production, growth, and competition—have vanished. Rather, these must now operate through the novel aims and mechanisms of a new market form. Most people credit Google's success to its advertising model. But the discoveries that led to Google's rapid rise in revenue and market capitalization are only incidentally related to advertising. Google's success derives from its ability to predict the future—specifically the future of human behavior.

The Rendition of Experience: Human–Natural Resources

From the start, Google had collected data on users' search-related behavior as a by-product of query activity. Back then, these data logs were treated as waste, not even safely or methodically stored. Eventually, the young company came to understand that these logs could be used to teach and continuously improve its search engine. The problem was this: Serving users with effective search results "used up" all the value that users created when they inadvertently provided behavioral data. It was a complete and self-contained process in which users were ends in themselves. All the value that users created was reinvested in their experience in the form of improved search, a progression that I have called *the behavioral value reinvestment cycle*. In this interaction, there was nothing "left over," no surplus for Google to turn into capital. As long as the effectiveness of the search engine needed users' behavioral data about as much as users needed search, charging a fee for service was too risky. In 2001 Google was remarkable, but it wasn't yet capitalism—just one of many Internet start-ups that boasted "eyeballs" but no revenue.

The year 2001 brought the dot.com bust and mounting investor pressures at Google. Back then, advertisers selected the search term pages for their displays. Google decided to try and boost ad revenue by applying its already substantial analytical capabilities to the challenge of increasing an ad's relevance to users—and thus its value to advertisers. Operationally, this meant that Google would finally repurpose its growing cache of "useless" behavioral data. Now the data would be used to match ads with keywords, exploiting subtleties that only its access to behavioral data, combined with its analytical capabilities, could reveal.

It's now clear that this shift in the use of behavioral data was an historic turning point. Behavioral data that were once discarded or ignored were rediscovered as what I call *behavioral surplus*: data reserves that are more than what is required for product and service improvements. Google's dramatic success in "matching" ads to pages revealed the transformational value of this behavioral surplus as a means of generating revenue and ultimately turning investment into revenue.

Key to this formula was the fact that this new market exchange was not an exchange with users but rather with companies who understood how to make money from bets on users' future behavior. In this new context, users were no longer ends in themselves. Instead, they became a means to profits in a new *behavioral futures market* in which users are neither buyers nor sellers nor products. Users are instead the *human nature-al* source of free raw material that feeds a new kind of manufacturing process designed to fabricate *prediction products*. These products are calculations that predict what individuals and groups will do now, soon, and later. The more raw materials that are fed into this new machine intelligence–based "means of production," the more powerful are its prediction products. While these processes were initially aimed at online ad targeting, they are no more restricted to that application than mass production was restricted to the manufacture of automobiles, where it was first applied at scale.

Many of the facts I describe here are well-known, but their significance has not been fully appreciated or adequately theorized. Google and other surveillance platforms are sometimes described as "two-sided" or "multi-sided" markets (Rochet and Tirole 2006, 645–667), but the mechanisms of surveillance capitalism suggest something different. Google had discovered a way to translate its nonmarket interactions with users into surplus raw material for the fabrication of products aimed at genuine market transactions with its real customers: advertisers (Strandburg 2013). The translation of human experience outside the market to behavioral data that circulates inside the market finally enabled Google to convert investment into revenue. The corporation thus created out of thin air and at zero marginal cost an asset class of vital raw materials derived from users' nonmarket online experience. At first those raw materials were simply "found," a by-product of users' search action. Later those assets were hunted aggressively, procured, and accumulated—largely through unilateral operations designed to evade individual awareness and thus bypass individual decision rights—operations that are therefore best summarized as "surveillance."

That behavioral surplus became the defining element of Google's success was well understood by its leaders. Google's former CEO Eric Schmidt credits Hal Varian's early development of the firm's ad auctions with providing the eureka moment that clarified the true nature of Google's business—"All of a sudden, we realized we were in the auction business"—referring to the automated behavioral futures markets deployed in ad targeting (Polanyi 2001, 75–76). Larry Page is credited with a very different and far more insightful answer to the question "What is Google?" Google's first brand manager, Douglas Edwards, recounts a 2001 session with the founders that probed their answers to that precise query. It was Page who ruminated, "If we did have a category, it would be personal information. . . . The places you've seen. Communications. . . . Sensors are really cheap. . . . Storage is cheap. Cameras are cheap. People will generate enormous amounts of data. . . . Everything you've ever heard or seen or experienced will become searchable. Your whole life will be searchable" (Edwards 2011, 291).

Page's vision perfectly reflects the history of capitalism as a process of taking things that live outside the market sphere and declaring their new life as market commodities. In historian Karl Polanyi's 1944 grand narrative of the "great transformation" to a self-regulating market economy, he described the origins of this translation process in three astonishing and crucial mental inventions that he called "commodity fictions." The first was that human life could be subordinated to market dynamics and reborn as "labor" to be bought and sold. The second was that nature could be translated into the market and reborn as "land" or "real estate." The third was that exchange could be reborn as "money" (Polanyi 2001, 75–76). Nearly eighty years earlier, Karl Marx had described the taking of lands and natural resources as the original "big bang" that ignited modern capital formation, calling it "primitive accumulation" (Marx 1992).

Page grasped that human experience would be Google's virgin wood—that it could be extracted at no extra cost online and at a low marginal cost out in the real world, where "sensors are really cheap," thus producing a surplus as the basis of a wholly new class of market exchange. Surveillance capitalism originates in this act of *digital dispossession*, operationalized in the *rendition* of human experience as behavioral data. This is the lever that moved Google's world and shifted it toward profit, changing the trajectory of information capitalism as it claimed undefended human experience for a market dynamic that would encounter no impediment in the lawless spaces of the Internet.

The significance of behavioral surplus was lost in euphemism, both at Google and throughout the Internet industry, with labels like "digital exhaust," "digital breadcrumbs," and so on.[2] These euphemisms for behavioral surplus operate as ideological filters in exactly the same way that the earliest maps of the North American continent labeled whole regions with terms like "heathens," "infidels," "idolaters," "primitives," "vassals," or "rebels." On the strength of those labels, native peoples, their places and claims, were erased from the invaders' moral and legal equations, legitimating their acts of taking and breaking in the name of Church and Monarchy.

In the case of surveillance capitalism, camouflage and other methodologies of secrecy aim to prevent interruption of critical supply-chain operations that begin with the rendition of human experience and end with the delivery of behavioral data to machine intelligence–based production systems. These operations of secrecy by design turn us into exiles from our own behavior, denied access to or control over knowledge derived from our experience. Knowledge and power rest with surveillance capital, for which we are merely "human natural" resources. We are the native peoples, now, whose tacit claims to self-determination have vanished from the maps of our own lives.

To be sure, there are always sound business reasons for hiding the location of your gold mine. In Google's case, an explicit "hiding strategy" accrued to its competitive advantage, but there were other, more pressing reasons for concealment and obfuscation (Levy 2011, 69). Douglas Edwards writes compellingly about the corporation's culture of secrecy: According to his account, Larry Page and Sergey Brin were "hawks," insisting on aggressive data capture and retention. "Larry opposed any path that would reveal our technological secrets or stir the privacy pot and endanger our ability to gather data." Page wanted to avoid arousing users' curiosity by minimizing their exposure to any clues about the reach of the firm's data operations. He questioned the prudence of the electronic scroll in the reception lobby that displays a continuous stream of search queries, and he "tried to kill" the annual Google Zeitgeist conference that summarizes the year's trends in search terms (Edwards 2011, 340–345).

What might the response have been back then if the public were told that Google's magic derived from its exclusive capabilities in unilateral surveillance of online behavior and methods specifically designed to override awareness and thus individual decision rights? Secrecy was required in order to protect operations designed to be undetectable because they took things from users without asking and employed those illegitimately claimed resources to work in the service of others' purposes.

That Google was able to choose secrecy is itself testament to the success of its own claims and an illustration of the difference between "decision rights" and "privacy." Decision rights confer the power to choose whether to keep something secret or to share it. One can choose the degree of privacy or transparency for each situation. US Supreme Court Justice William O. Douglas articulated this view of privacy in 1967: "Privacy involves the choice of the individual to disclose or to reveal what he believes, what he thinks, what he possesses" (Douglas 1967; Farahany 2012). Surveillance capitalism laid claim to these decision rights.

The typical complaint is that privacy is eroded, but that is misleading. In the larger societal pattern, privacy is not eroded but redistributed, as decision rights over privacy are claimed for surveillance capital. Instead of many people having the right to decide how and what they will disclose, these rights are concentrated within the domain of surveillance capitalism. Google discovered this necessary element of the new logic of accumulation: it must declare its rights to take the information upon which its success depends. The extraordinary financial power of surveillance capitalism's hidden inventions was only revealed when Google went public in 2004. At that time it became clear that on the strength of its secrets, the firm's revenue had increased 3,590 percent in less than four years.

Today's owners of surveillance capital have thus declared a fourth fictional commodity expropriated from the experiential realities of human beings whose bodies, thoughts, and feelings are as blameless as nature's once plentiful meadows and forests before they fell to the market dynamic. In this new logic, *human experience is subjugated to surveillance capitalism's market mechanisms and rendered as "behavior."* Behavior is reduced to data, ready to take their place in a numberless queue that feeds the machines for fabrication into predictions and eventual exchange in behavioral futures markets. The experiencing individual is not essential to this market action, except as the source of raw material.

The summary of these developments is that the behavioral surplus upon which Google's fortune rests can be considered as *surveillance assets*. These assets are critical raw materials in the pursuit of *surveillance customers* for the sake of *surveillance revenues* and their translation into *surveillance capital*. The entire logic of this capital accumulation is most accurately understood as *surveillance capitalism,* which is the foundational framework of a surveillance-based economic order: a *surveillance economy.* The big pattern here is one of subordination and hierarchy, in which earlier reciprocities between the firm and its users are subordinated to the derivative project of behavioral surplus captured for others' market aims. Individual "users" are not the subjects of value realization. Nor are they, as some have insisted, "the product" in the sales process. Instead, they are the objects from which raw materials are extracted and expropriated for Google's prediction factories: they are the means to others' ends. This is how in our lifetimes we observe capitalism shifting under our gaze: once profits from products and services, then profits from financial speculation, and now profits from surveillance.

The Extraction Imperative: Economies of Scale

The accumulation of behavioral surplus is the master motion of surveillance capitalism from which key economic imperatives can be induced. The quality of prediction products depends upon volume inputs to machine processes. Volume surplus is thus a competitive requirement. This dynamic establishes the *extraction imperative*, which expresses the necessity of *economies of scale in surplus accumulation* and depends upon automated systems that relentlessly track, hunt, and induce more behavioral surplus. These systems, which began in the online environment and later spread to the "real" world, constitute an *extraction architecture* that has evolved in the direction of ubiquity, just as Larry Page anticipated in 2001 and as the evolution of digital "health" information amply demonstrates. Under the lash of the extraction imperative, the once simple closed loops have been transformed into a global, sensate, computational, connected architecture of behavioral surplus capture and analysis, fulfilling computer scientist Mark Weiser's 1999 vision of "ubiquitous computing" memorialized in two legendary sentences: "The most profound technologies are those that disappear. They weave themselves into the fabric of everyday life until they are indistinguishable from it" (Weiser 1999).

The Prediction Imperative: Economies of Scope

Surveillance profits awakened intense competition over the revenues that flow from behavioral futures markets. In this second phase of competitive intensity, the volume of surplus became a necessary but insufficient condition for success. Even the most sophisticated process of converting behavioral surplus into products that accurately forecast the future is only as good as the raw material available for processing. In the race for higher degrees of certainty, it became clear that the best predictions would have to approximate observation. The next threshold was defined by the quality, not just the quantity, of behavioral surplus. These pressures led to a search for new supplies of surplus that would more reliably foretell the future. This marks a critical turning point in the trial-and-error elaboration of surveillance capitalism and crystallizes a second economic imperative—the *prediction imperative*—as the expression of these competitive forces. The prediction imperative drives the diversification of extraction architectures to accommodate, first, economies of scope in surplus accumulation and, later, economies of action.

The shift toward economies of scope represents a new set of aims: behavioral surplus must be vast, but it must also be varied. These variations have been developed along two dimensions. The first is the *extension* of extraction operations from the virtual world into the "real" world of embodied human experience. Surveillance capitalists understood that their future wealth would depend upon new supply routes that extend to real life on the roads, among the trees, throughout the cities. Extension wants your bloodstream and your bed, your breakfast conversation, your commute, your run, your refrigerator, your parking space, your living room, your pancreas.

Economies of scope also proceed along a second *depth* dimension. The idea here is that more predictive, and therefore more lucrative, behavioral surplus can be plumbed from intimate patterns of the self. These supply operations are aimed at your personality, moods, and emotions; your lies and vulnerabilities. (For a detailed discussion, see Zuboff 2019, chapters 8 and 9.) Emergent rendition techniques are trained on successive levels of intimacy where new supplies can be automatically captured and flattened into a tidal flow of data points that proceed toward manufactured certainty.

As the prediction imperative drives deeper into the self, the value of its surplus becomes irresistible, and the competitive pressures to corner lucrative sources of supply escalate. It is no longer a matter of surveillance capital wringing surplus from what I search, buy, and browse. Surveillance capital wants more than my body's coordinates in time and space. Now it violates the inner sanctum, as machines and their algorithms decide the meaning of my sighs, blinks, and utterances; the pattern of my breathing and the movements of my eyes; my jaw muscles; the hitch in my voice; and the exclamation points in a Facebook post that I offered in innocence and hope.

There are many glosses that divert attention from the logic of these operations and their economic origins: "ambient computing," "ubiquitous computing," and the "Internet of Things" are but a few examples. The labels differ, but they share a consistent vision: the everywhere, always-on instrumentation, datafication, connection, communication, and computation of all things, animate and inanimate, and all processes—natural, human, physiological, chemical, machine, administrative, vehicular, financial . . . This new architecture provides the means through which human experience is continuously rendered—from phones, cars, streets, homes, shops, bodies, trees, buildings, airports, and cities—and translated to the digital realm where it finds a new market life.

The Prediction Imperative: Economies of Action

The capital requirements of these automated architectures are justified by the lure of surveillance revenues, continuously ratcheting up the competitive intensity of the prediction imperative. Just as scale became necessary but insufficient for higher quality predictions, the demands of the prediction imperative eventually encountered the limitations of economies of scope. While behavioral surplus must be vast and varied, surveillance capitalists gradually came to understand that the surest way to predict behavior is to intervene at its source and shape it. The processes invented to achieve this goal are what I call *economies of action.*

Economies of scale and scope are well-known industrial logics, but economies of action are distinct to surveillance capitalism and its digital milieu. In order to achieve these economies, machine processes are configured to intervene in the state of play in the real world among real people and things. These interventions are designed to augment prediction products in order that they approximate certainty by "tuning," "herding," and conditioning the behavior of individuals, groups, and populations. These economies of action apply techniques that are as varied as inserting a specific phrase into your Facebook news feed, timing the appearance of a BUY button on your phone with the rise of your endorphins at the end of a run, shutting down your car engine when an insurance payment is late, or employing population-scale behavioral microtargeting drawn from Facebook profiles. Indeed, the notorious manipulations of the data firm Cambridge Analytica, which scandalized the world in 2018, simply appropriated the means and methods that are now both standard and necessary operations in the surveillance capitalism arsenal (Zuboff 2019, 295–330).

As the prediction imperative gathers force, it gradually becomes clear that economies of scale and scope were the first phases of a more ambitious project. Economies of action mean that ubiquitous machine architectures must be able *to know* as well as *to do.* What began as an extraction architecture now doubles as an *execution architecture* through which hidden economic objectives are imposed upon the vast and varied field of behavior. As surveillance capitalism's imperatives and the material infrastructures that perform extraction and execution operations begin to function as a coherent whole, they produce a twenty-first-century *means of behavioral modification* to which the means of production is subordinated as merely one part of this larger whole.

The means of behavioral modification does not aim to compel conformity to or compliance with social norms, as has been the case with earlier applications of the behaviorist paradigm. Rather, this new complex aims to produce behavior that reliably, definitively, and certainly leads to predicted commercial results for surveillance customers. The research director of Gartner, the respected business advisory and research firm, makes the point unambiguously when he observes that mastery of the "Internet of Things" will serve as "a key enabler in the transformation of business models from 'guaranteed levels of performance' to *'guaranteed outcomes'*" (italics mine; Pettey 2016). This is an extraordinary statement, because there can be no such guarantees in the absence of the power to make it so. The wider complex of "the means of behavioral modification" is the expression of this gathering power. The prospect of businesses competing on the promise of guaranteed outcomes enabled by a global digital architecture alerts us to the force of the prediction imperative, which now demands that surveillance capitalists make the future for the sake of predicting it.

Surveillance capitalists' interests have shifted from using automated machine processes to know about your behavior to using machine processes to shape your behavior according to their interests. Given the conditions of increasing ubiquity, it has become difficult, if not impossible, to escape this web. Under this regime, ubiquitous computing is not just a knowing machine; it is an actuating machine designed to produce more certainty *about* us and *for* them. The nearly two-decade trajectory since the collection and analysis of health data was conceived as a simple closed loop has taken us from automating information flows about behavior to *automating behavior.* Just as industrial capitalism was driven to the continuous intensification of the means of production, so surveillance capitalists are now locked in a cycle of *continuous intensification of the means of behavioral modification.* While it is possible to imagine something like a ubiquitous, connected, sensate computational architecture without surveillance capitalism, the means of behavioral modification depend entirely on this pervasive networked architecture.

Economies of scale and scope ignored privacy norms and laws, relying on weak legitimation processes like "sadistic contracts" and meaningless mechanisms of notice and consent to accumulate decision rights in the surveillance capitalist domain (Bakos, et al. 2014; Becher and Zarsky 2015; Kar 2013; Kim 2013; Preston 2015; Radin 2012). But economies of action go further. These new systems and procedures take direct aim at individual autonomy, systematically replacing self-determined action with a range of hidden operations designed to shape behavior at the source. Economies of action are constructed through systematic experimentation that began with apparent banalities like the A/B testing of web-page design elements and eventually progressed to more complex undertakings. One example is the secret manipulation of social contagion demonstrated in Facebook's vast experiments in shaping social behavior, about which the corporation's researchers concluded, "Emotional states can be transferred to others via emotional contagion, leading people to experience the same emotions without their awareness. . . . Online messages influence our experience of emotions, which may affect a variety of offline behaviors" (Kramer, Guillory, and Hancock 2014). Another is the population-scale social herding experiments popularized by the Google-incubated augmented reality application of Niantic Labs' Pokémon Go, in which innocent players are herded to eat, drink, and purchase in the restaurants, bars, fast-food joints, and shops that pay to play in the company's behavioral futures markets (see the discussion in Zuboff 2019).

Ultimately behavioral modification capabilities are institutionalized in "innovative" commercial practices in which individuals fund their own domination. One finds digital tuning, herding, and conditioning embedded in such varied practices as the insurance industry's embrace of "behavioral underwriting," the gamification of retailing, the remote-control operations of automotive telematics, or the "personalized services" of so-called "digital assistants" such as Amazon's "Alexa," Google's "Google Assistant," and Microsoft's "Cortana." What they share is the explicit aim to produce planned behavioral outcomes with methods of behavioral modification that operate through unprecedented and proprietary digital architectures, while carefully circumventing the awareness of human targets.

The conflation of economic imperatives and behavior modification at scale locates the surveillance capitalist project squarely in the paradigm of radical behaviorism associated with B. F. Skinner, which draws upon formulations in early theoretical physics, especially the philosophical work of Max Planck (2007a, 2007b). Following Planck, radical behaviorism insists on the reduction of human experience to observable, measurable behavior purged of inwardness, thus establishing psychological science as the objective study of behaving objects comparable to the research paradigms of the natural sciences. Max Meyer, a student of Planck's and the early-twentieth-century experimental psychologist most admired by Skinner, called this approach "the psychology of the Other-One" (Skinner 1991, 4–6; see also Meyer 1921). Human behavior would yield to scientific inquiry only if psychologists learned to view humans as "others," a "viewpoint of observation" considered an absolute requirement for an "objective science of human behaviour" (Meyer 1912, 371). Central to this new viewpoint was Meyer's insistence that the human being should be regarded as an "organism among organisms," distinguishable from a lettuce, a moose, or an inchworm only in degree of complexity (Esper 1967, 114; Meyer 1912, 1921).

Skinner embraced Meyer's "viewpoint of observation," which led to his discovery of the principles of "operant conditioning" in which a carefully designed "schedule of reinforcements" is imposed on the animal in order to shape specific behavioral patterns by amplifying some actions at the expense of others. While Skinner focused his work on mice and pigeons, the epistemology of radical behaviorism enabled easy generalizations across species (Blanshard 1967; Meyer 1912, 1921; Skinner 1976, 1991, 2002, 2012; Wozniak 1997). Even the complexities of human reasoning, choice, problem-solving, and reflection render themselves to the viewpoint of the Other-One:

> When a man controls himself, chooses a course of action, thinks out the solution to a problem, or strives toward an increase in self-knowledge, he is behaving. He controls himself precisely as he would control the behavior of anyone else—through the manipulation of variables of which behavior is a function. His behavior in so doing is a proper object of analysis, and eventually it must be accounted for with variables lying outside the individual himself. (Skinner 2012, 228–229)

It was Skinner who first imagined a ubiquitous "technology of behavior" that would enable the application of operant conditioning across entire human populations. He argued that "the field of human behavior" would never achieve scientific status without "instruments and methods" as powerful as those available to physicists and biologists (Skinner 2002, 4–5). Such instruments would finally illuminate the laws of human action, enabling scientists to shape and predict behavior.

There would be challenges. New technologies of behavior would have to continually push the envelope of the public–private divide in order to access all the data relevant to behavioral prediction and control. Like today's surveillance capitalists, Skinner was confident that the slow drip of technological invention would eventually push privacy to the margins of human experience, where it would join "freedom," "autonomy," and other troublesome illusions. All of these would be replaced by the viewpoint of the Other-One embodied in new instruments and methods:

> The line between public and private is not fixed. The boundary shifts with every discovery of a technique for making private events public. Behavior which is of such small magnitude that it is not ordinarily observed may be amplified. Covert verbal behavior may be detected in slight movements of the speech apparatus. . . . The problem of privacy may, therefore, eventually be solved by technical advances . . . we are still faced with events which occur at the private level and which are important to the organism without instrumental amplification. How the organism reacts to these events will remain an important question, even though the events may some day be made accessible to everyone. (Skinner 2012, 282)

Skinner's technologies of behavior have finally come to life as a market project. The conflation of economic orientation, the means of behavioral modification, and the digital architectures and devices that are its medium are now a taken-for-granted feature of the surveillance capitalist milieu. This theme and the necessity of its concealment are reiterated throughout the interviews that I conducted with data scientists and software engineers between 2012 and 2015 as one element of a larger study of surveillance capitalism.[3] The means of behavioral modification are the subject of creative elaboration, experimentation, and application, but always outside the awareness of its human targets. For example, the chief data scientist for a national drugstore chain described how his company designs automated digital reinforcers to subtly tune customers' behaviors: "You can make people do things with this technology. Even if it's just 5% of people, you've made 5% of people do an action they otherwise wouldn't have done, so to some extent there is an element of the user's loss of self-control." A software engineer specializing in the Internet of Things explained his company's approach to conditioning: "The goal of everything we do is to change people's actual behavior at scale . . . we can capture their behaviors and identify good and bad. Then we develop 'treatments' or 'data pellets' that select good behaviors." Another recounted the operational mechanisms of herding: "We can engineer the context around a particular behavior and force change that way. . . . *We are learning how to write the music, and then we let the music make them dance.*"

How do they get away with it? Dozens of surveys conducted since 2008 attest to substantial majorities in the United States, the EU, and around the world that reject the premises and practices of surveillance capitalism, yet it persists, succeeds, and dominates. In other work I have detailed sixteen factors that enabled this new logic of accumulation to root and flourish (Zuboff 2019), and here I want to underscore two of these.

The first is *dependency*. Surveillance capitalism now controls many of the operations that are essential for social participation. Early on, the free services of Google, Facebook, and other applications appealed to the latent needs of second-modernity individuals seeking resources for effective life in an increasingly hostile institutional environment (Beck and Beck-Gernsheim 2002; Zuboff and Maxmin 2002). Once bitten, the apple was irresistible. A 2010 BBC poll found that 79 percent of people in twenty-six countries considered Internet access to be a fundamental human right (BBC 2010). Six years later, in 2016, the United Nations Human Rights Council would adopt specific language on the importance of Internet access. In the United States, many people call the emergency services number, 911, on those rare occasions when Facebook is down (LA Times 2014). Most people find it difficult to withdraw from these utilities, and many ponder if it is even possible (Alter 2017; Andreassen et al. 2012; Casale and Fioravanti 2015; Cheng and Li 2014; Dreifus 2017; Griffiths, Kuss, and Demetrovics 2014; Schou Andreassen, and Pallesen 2014).

As surveillance capitalism spread across the Internet, the means of social participation became coextensive with the means of behavioral modification, eroding the choice mechanisms that adhere to the private realm—exit, voice, and loyalty. There can be no exit from processes that we cannot detect and upon which we must depend for the effectiveness of daily life.

Users are not customers and thus far lack institutionalized means of collective action that would establish reliable channels for voice. Loyalty is an empty suit, as continued participation is better explained in terms of helplessness, resignation, and the foreclosure of alternatives.

Next I turn to the second key answer to the question "How do they get away with it?" That answer is *power*.

The Rise of Instrumentarian Power

The internal pressures exerted by surveillance capitalism's economic imperatives produce the compulsion to "make them dance." First, production is subordinated to extraction, and then the means of production is subordinated to the means of behavioral modification. Finally, what is produced is the guarantee of outcomes, or at least the ever-improving approximation to such guarantees. These guarantees have value, but in the novel logic of surveillance capitalism, their value is a function of markets that bear no organic reciprocities with their populations, now repurposed as the source of unlimited raw material supplies. This analysis brings us to the edge of a new terrain, but no further. I have suggested that there can be no *guarantee* of outcomes without the power to make it so. In order to proceed, it is necessary to answer the question, *what is this new power to "make them dance"?* The answer offers a glimpse into the dark heart of surveillance capitalism as a usurper of rights and a civilizational force.

The first key point is that there is no historical precedent for the quality of power that now confronts us. It is, I argue, an unprecedented species of power that emerges in the unprecedented digital milieu of surveillance capitalism and its unprecedented economic logic founded on the dispossession of human behavior as the new source of capital accumulation. Any encounter with the unprecedented is itself a genuine intellectual and existential challenge, and this fact itself merits our attention. That which is unprecedented is necessarily unrecognizable, tacitly interpreted through the lens of familiar categories. This mental operation renders invisible precisely those dimensions of experience for which there are no established mental sets. A classic example is the notion of the "horseless carriage" to which people reverted when confronted with the unprecedented facts of the automobile. Existing lenses illuminate the familiar and obscure the original by turning the unprecedented into an extension of the past. The sociology of the unprecedented multiplies this effect. Once the abnormal is normalized, habituation and psychic numbing make contest even more unlikely (Baehr 2002; Lifton 2010; Slovic et al. 2011; van Der Kolk and Saporta 1991).

In the years during and immediately following World War II, scholars confronted these barriers of cognition, imagination, and language as they tried to name and grasp another unprecedented configuration of power, what would come to be known as "totalitarianism." In the early phases of this effort, critics appropriated the horseless-carriage language of "imperialism" as the only framework at hand with which to articulate and resist the new power's murderous threats. With a few important exceptions, it was only after the Nazi defeat that the program of naming began in earnest.

That confrontation with the unprecedented is reflected in the moving accounts of the first scholars determined to lift the veil on their era's gruesome truths. The systematic accretion of violence and complicity that engulfed whole populations at extreme velocity invoked a kind of bewilderment that ended in paralysis, even for many of the greatest minds of the twentieth century. Harvard political scientist Carl Friedrich was among the first scholars of totalitarianism to address this experience of improbability writing in 1954: "Virtually no one before 1914 anticipated the course of development which has overtaken Western civilization since then . . . none of the outstanding scholars in history, law, and the social sciences discerned what was ahead . . . which culminated in totalitarianism. To this failure to foresee corresponds a difficulty in comprehending" (Friedrich 1954, 1–2).

Nearly every intellectual who turned to this project in the period immediately following the war cites the feeling of astonishment at the suddenness with which, as Friedrich put it, totalitarianism had "burst upon mankind . . . unexpected and unannounced" (Friedrich 1954, 1). Its manifestations were so novel and unanticipated, so shocking, rapid, and unparalleled, that all of it eluded language, challenging every tradition, norm, value, and legitimate form of action. Hannah Arendt described the defeat of Nazi Germany as "the first chance to try to tell and to understand what had happened . . . still in grief and sorrow and . . . a tendency to lament, but no longer in speechless outrage and impotent horror" (Arendt 2004, 387). Later, historian Robert Conquest would document the similar failure of journalists, scholars, and Western governments in reckoning the full weight of Soviet totalitarianism's monstrous achievements. The most salient reason for this failure, he observed, was that the actual facts were so "improbable" that it was difficult even for specialists to grasp their truth. "Plenty of information was available contradicting the official picture," wrote Conquest. "The Stalin epoch is replete with what appear as improbabilities to minds unfitted to deal with the phenomena" (Conquest 2008, 486).

Ultimately, a courageous body of scholarship would evolve to meet the challenge of comprehension. It yielded different models and schools of thought, each with distinct emphasis and insights, but these shared common purpose in the work of naming. "Totalitarianism has discovered a means of dominating and terrorizing human beings from within," wrote Arendt, the German-born philosopher who would spend the six years after World War II writing her extraordinary study of totalitarian power, published in 1951 as *The Origins of Totalitarianism* (Arendt 2004, 431). Arendt's was a detailed disclosure and a pioneering attempt to theorize what had just occurred. "Comprehension," she said, is the necessary response to the "truly radical nature of Evil" disclosed by totalitarianism. "It means . . . examining and bearing consciously the burden which our century has placed on us—neither denying its existence nor submitting meekly to its weight." Totalitarianism was bent on the "destruction of humanity" and "the essence of man," but, she insisted, "to turn our backs on the destructive forces of the century is of little avail" (Arendt 2004, xxvii). Essential here was the deletion of all ties and sources of meaning other than "the movement": "Total loyalty—the psychological basis for domination—can be expected only from the completely isolated human being who, without any other social ties to family, friends, comrades, or even mere acquaintances, derives his sense of having a place in the world only from his belonging to a movement, his membership in the party" (Arendt 2004, 429).

Midcentury scholars such as Friedrich, Adorno, Gurian, Brzezinski, and Aron added to these themes, recognizing totalitarianism's insistence on domination of the human soul (Adorno 1966, 1985, 1991; Aron 1968; Friedrich 1954, 1956). The Russian-born political scientist Waldemar Gurian, who escaped Nazi Germany in 1939, argued that totalitarianism functioned as a "secularized political religion" that requires "absolute obedience" and demands "active acclamation" (Gurian 1954, 119–129). Political scientists Carl Friedrich and Zbigniew Brzezinski emphasized totalitarianism's reliance on terror to drive and sustain "human remolding," "re-educative measures," and "extensive revisions" of self and psyche (Friedrich and Brzezinski 1956, 130–133). Activist and theorist Franz Neumann's courageous analysis of National Socialism from 1933 to 1944 also elevated terror to the highest-order principle of action. Neumann described the Third Reich's subordination of the means of production to the "means of violence," as the Nazis asserted authority over property and production, both through the expropriation of Jewish assets and through the party's command and control of key industries (Neumann and Hayes 2009, 470–76, 632–634).

Totalitarianism was bent on the purification of the human species through the dual mechanisms of genocide and the "engineering of the soul." In this way totalitarian regimes could achieve their fantastical aim of "the People-as-one," as Claude Lefort describes it. "Social unanimity corresponds to inner unanimity, held in place by hatred activated toward the 'enemies of the people'" (Lefort 1986, 297–298). But to command populations right down to their souls requires unimaginable effort, which was one reason why totalitarianism was unimaginable. It measures success at the cellular level, penetrating to the quick, where it subverts and commands each unspoken yearning in pursuit of the genocidal vision that historian Richard Shorten calls "the experiment in reshaping humanity" (Shorten 2012, 50). Each individual inner life must be claimed and transformed by the perpetual threat of terror: punishment without crime. This craftwork requires the detailed orchestration of isolation, anxiety, fear, persuasion, fantasy, longing, inspiration, torture, dread, and surveillance. Arendt describes the relentless process of "atomization" and fusion in which terror destroys the ordinary human bonds of law, norms, trust, and affection, "which provide the living space for the freedom of the individual" (Arendt 1994, 343).

Arendt's project of naming was embedded in a larger wave of postwar reform determined to inoculate civilization from the genocidal impulse and institutionalized in the 1948 Universal Declaration of Human Rights (UDHR), beginning with the assertion, "All human beings are born free and equal in dignity and rights." As Michael Ignatieff has argued, the UDHR founded a "judicial revolution," establishing a global juridical framework of human rights that both ignited and legitimated the justice demands of colonial subjects, civil rights groups, and other movements originating in exclusion and oppression (Ignatieff 2001; see also Franck 2000).

Now a new surveillance-based economic order casts us adrift in a different dark sea of original and thus difficult-to-discern dangers, where the abrogation of human rights does not always or easily correspond to the historical development of human rights and its established juridical frameworks. And just as the scholars of totalitarianism once looked to nineteenth-century imperialism to explain the violence of their time, it is we who now reach for the familiar vernaculars of twentieth-century power like lifesaving driftwood. Invariably we look to the specter of totalitarianism as the lens through which to interpret today's threats. The result is that Google, Facebook, and the larger field of commercial surveillance are frequently criticized as "Big Brother" or "digital totalitarianism" (Blakely 2014; Borowicz 2014; Doctorow 2017; Economist 2004; Hirsh 2015; Menell 2013; Schulz 2016; Sorell and Draper 2012). I admire those who have stood against the incursions of commercial surveillance, but I also suggest that the equation of its new power with totalitarianism and the Orwellian trope impedes our understanding as well as our ability to resist, neutralize, and ultimately vanquish its potency. Instead, we need to grasp the specific inner logic of a conspicuously twenty-first-century conjuring of power to which the past offers no adequate compass. Its aims are in many ways just as ambitious as those of totalitarianism, but they are also utterly and profoundly distinct. The work of naming a strange form of power unprecedented in the human experience must begin anew for the sake of effective resistance and the creative power to insist on a future of our own making.

As to the new species of power, I have suggested that it is best understood as *instrumentarianism*, defined as *the instrumentation and instrumentalization of behavior for the purposes of modification, prediction, monetization and control*. In this formulation, "instrumentation" refers to the ubiquitous, sensate, computational, actuating global architecture that renders, monitors, computes, and modifies human behavior. Surveillance capitalism is the puppet master that imposes its will through the vast capabilities of this connected puppet to produce instrumentarian power, replacing the engineering of souls with the engineering of behavior. There is no brother here of any kind, big or little, evil or good—no family ties, however grim. Instead, this new global apparatus is better understood as a *Big Other* that encodes the viewpoint of the Other-One as a pervasive presence, finally bringing Skinner's longed for "technology of behavior" to life. "Instrumentalization" denotes the social relations that orient the puppet masters to human experience, as surveillance capital overrides long-standing reciprocities of market democracy, wielding its machines to transform us into the means to others' market ends. Although he did not name it, Mark Weiser, the visionary of ubiquitous computing, foresaw the immensity of instrumentarian power as a totalizing societal project. He did so in a way that suggests both its utter lack of precedent and the danger of confounding it with what has gone before: "Hundreds of computers in every room, all capable of sensing people near them and linked by high-speed networks, have the potential to make totalitarianism up to now seem like sheerest anarchy" (Weiser 1999, 89). In fact, all those computers are not the means to a digital hypertotalitarianism. They are, as I think Weiser sensed, the foundation of an unprecedented power that can reshape society in unprecedented ways. If instrumentarian power can make totalitarianism look like anarchy, then what might it have in store for us?

While all power yearns toward totality, instrumentarian power's specific purposes and methods are not only distinct from totalitarianism but they are in many ways its *precise opposite*. Surveillance capitalists have no interest in murder or the reformation of our souls. Instrumentarian power, therefore, has no principle to instruct. There is no training or transformation for spiritual salvation, no ideology against which to judge our actions. It does not demand possession of each person from the inside out. It has no interest in exterminating or disfiguring our bodies and minds in the name of pure devotion. Totalitarianism was a political project that converged with economics to overwhelm society. Instrumentarianism is a market project that converges with the digital to achieve its own unique brand of social domination. Totalitarianism operated through the means of violence, but instrumentarian power operates through the means of behavioral modification. And this is where our focus must shift. What passes for social relations and economic exchange now occurs across the medium of this robotized veil of abstraction.

Instrumentarianism's specific "viewpoint of observation" was forged in the controversial intellectual domain of "radical behaviorism." Thanks to Big Other's capabilities, instrumentarian power reduces human experience to measurable, observable behavior, while remaining steadfastly indifferent to the meaning of that experience. It is profoundly, infinitely, and, following its behaviorist origins, *radically* indifferent to our meanings and motives. This epistemology of *radical indifference* produces *observation without witness*. Instead of an intimate violent political religion, Big Other's way of knowing us yields the remote but inescapable presence of impenetrably complex systems and the interests that author them, carrying individuals on a fast-moving current to the fulfillment of others' ends. Big Other has no interest in soiling itself with our excretions, but it may aggressively hunt data on the behavior of our blood and shit. It has no appetite for our grief, pain, or terror, although it welcomes the behavioral surplus that leaches from our anguish.

Trained on measurable action, Big Other cares only about observing what we do and ensuring that we do it in ways that are *accessible* to its ever-evolving operations of rendition, reinforcement, calculation, and monetization. Instrumentarianism's radical indifference is operationalized in Big Other's dehumanized methods of evaluation that produce *equivalence without equality* by reducing individuals to the lowest common denominator of sameness—an organism among organisms.

In the execution of economies of action, Big Other simulates the behaviorists' "vortex of stimuli," transforming "natural selection" into the "unnatural selection" of variation and reinforcement authored by market players and the competition for surveillance revenues. We may confuse Big Other with the behaviorist god of the vortex, but only because it effectively conceals the machinations of surveillance capitalism that are the wizard behind the digital curtain. The gentle seductive voice crafted on the yonder side of this veil—*Google, is that you?*—gently herds us along the path that coughs up the maximum of behavioral surplus and the closest approximation to certainty.

Instrumentarian Power Thrives in Lawless Space

Instrumentarianism is not murderous, but it is as startling, incomprehensible, and new to the human story as totalitarianism was to its witnesses and victims. Thanks to Big Other's capabilities to know and to do, instrumentarian power aims for a condition of *certainty without terror* in the form of "guaranteed outcomes." In pursuit of this certainty, the locus of economic power shifts from ownership of the means of production to ownership of the means of behavioral modification. Instrumentarian power produces endlessly accruing knowledge and control for surveillance capitalists and diminished self-determination for its populations who now fund their own domination as targets of extraction and modification.

The paradox is that because instrumentarianism does not claim our bodies for some grotesque regime of pain and murder, we are prone to undervalue its effects and lower our guard. Instead of death, torture, reeducation, or conversion, instrumentarianism effectively expels us from our own behavior. It severs our insides from our outsides, our subjectivity and interiority from our observable actions. Otherized behavior takes on a life of its own that delivers our actions now, soon, and later to surveillance capitalism's aims and interests.

Under the regime of instrumentarian power, the mental agency and self-possession of autonomous human action are gradually submerged beneath a new kind of automaticity: a lived routine of stimulus–response–reinforcement that operates outside of awareness and is aggregated as statistical phenomena: the comings and goings of mere organisms. Our conformity is irrelevant to instrumentarianism's success. There is no need for mass submission to social norms, no loss of self to the collective induced by terror and compulsion, no inducements of acceptance and belonging as a reward for bending to the group. All of that is superseded by a market-based digital order that thrives within things and bodies, transforming volition into reinforcement and action into conditioned response.

Using Polanyi's lens, we have seen that surveillance capitalism annexes human experience to the market dynamic so that it is reborn as behavior: the fourth "fictional commodity." However, Polanyi's first three fictional commodities—land, labor, and money—were eventually subjected to law. Although these laws have been imperfect, the institutions of labor law, environmental law, and banking law provided regulatory frameworks intended to defend society (and nature, life, and exchange) from the worst excesses of raw capitalism's destructive power. Surveillance capitalism's translation of human experience into market commodities has thus far faced no such impediments.

In earlier work I detail the historical conditions and forms of corporate action that enabled surveillance capitalism's successful pursuit and sustenance of lawless space (Zuboff 2019). While a reprise of those arguments exceeds the space of this chapter, two conditions float above them all, and they merit emphasis. The first reverts to the sociology of the unprecedented, as the original action of instrumentarian power works its will before it can be adequately understood, thus enjoying a substantial lag in social evolution and the eventual production of law. This problem is already evident in the commoditization of human experience, which does not easily correspond to established legal frameworks, such as those that concern privacy rights or anticompetitive corporate practices. For example, laws that pertain to "data ownership" or "data protection" overlook what is original in this latest "original sin," namely, the assertion that human experience is free for unilateral (and secret) rendition into behavioral data in the first place.

A second condition that has enabled the pursuit and protection of lawless operational spaces derives from surveillance capitalism's historical and material origins as both American born and "born digital." On both counts, surveillance capital has benefitted from the antiregulatory zeitgeist of US neoliberal economic policy and political ideology (Cohen 2016; Hoofnagle 2017; Short 2011). In this respect surveillance capitalists have enjoyed a political windfall, not unlike the Gilded Age titans who exploited the absence of industry regulation in their time to claim undefended territory for their own interests, declare the righteousness of their self-authorizing prerogatives, and defend their brand of raw capitalism from democracy (Nasaw 2005). Imbued with the conviction that "the state had neither right nor reason to interfere in the workings of the economy," Gilded Age millionaires joined forces to defend the "rights of capital" and limit the role of elected representatives in setting policy or developing legislation (Nasaw 2005, 124–125). There was no need for law, they argued, when one had the "law of evolution," the "laws of capital," and the "laws of industrial society." John Rockefeller insisted that his outsized oil fortune was the result of "the natural law of trade development." Jay Gould, when questioned by Congress on the need for federal regulation of railroad rates, replied that "the laws of supply and demand, production and consumption" already regulate rates (Nasaw 2005, 132).

Gilded Age business elites determined that the most effective way to protect the original sin of that economic era was, as historian David Nasaw puts it, "to circumscribe democracy." They did this by lavishly funding their own political candidates as well as through the careful honing and aggressive dissemination of an ideological attack on the very notion of democracy's right to interfere in the economic realm (Friedman 2004, 14–28; Nasaw 2005, 146, 148).

A similar determination to conduct surveillance capitalism free of democratic oversight dominates Google's short but remarkable history. Its ability to discern, construct, and stake its claim to the unregulated territories of the Internet not yet subject to law and, in the United States at least, free from constitutional constraints, was essential to its frictionless accumulation of surplus as the means to its frictionless accumulation of power and capital.

Eric Schmidt and Jared Cohen celebrate their claim to operational spaces beyond the reach of political institutions on the very first page of their book on the digital age: "The online world is not truly bound by terrestrial laws . . . it's the world's largest ungoverned space" (Schmidt and Cohen 2014).

Surveillance capitalists are impelled to pursue lawlessness by the logic of their own creation. Google and Facebook vigorously lobby to kill online privacy protection, limit regulations, weaken or block privacy-enhancing legislation, and thwart every attempt to circumscribe their practices because such laws threaten the flow of behavioral surplus (Dougherty 2016; Google Transparency Project 2016, 2017; Mullins and Nicas 2017; Shaban 2017a, 2017b; Statista 2017; Taplin 2017). Schmidt, Brin, and Page have ardently defended their right to freedom from law even as Google grew to become what is arguably the world's most powerful corporation (Khosla 2004). Their efforts have been marked by a few consistent themes: that technology companies such as Google move faster than the state's ability to understand or follow; that any attempts to intervene or constrain are therefore fated to be ill-conceived and inept; that regulation is always a negative force that impedes innovation and progress; and that lawlessness is the necessary context for innovation (Cunningham 2011; Gobry 2011; Jenkins 2010; Yarow 2013).

Many hopes today are pinned on the new body of EU regulation known as the General Data Protection Regulation (GDPR), which became enforceable in May 2018. In time the world will learn if the GDPR can move out in front of Big Other, successfully challenging the legitimacy of surveillance capitalism, its means of behavioral modification, and its production of instrumentarian power. Scholars and specialists debate the implications of the sweeping new regulations, some arguing the inevitability of decisive change, and others arguing the likelihood of continuity over dramatic reversals of practice (Keller 2017; Mayer-Schönberger and Padova 2016; Rossi 2016; Wachter 2017; Zarsky 2017). The only possible answer is that everything will depend upon how European societies interpret the new regulatory regime in legislation and in the courts. It will not be the wording of the regulations but rather popular movements on the ground that shape these interpretations. Just as a century ago workers joined in collective action to tip the scales of power, today's "users" will have to mobilize in new ways that assert society's rejection of an economic order based on the dispossession of human experience as a means to the prediction and control of human behavior for others' profit.

As a result of its successful pursuit of lawlessness and in the absence of the typical mechanisms of private governance associated with exit, voice, and loyalty, surveillance capitalism has wielded its instrumentarian power to bypass older distinctions between market and world, market and society, market and home, or market and person. Instrumentarianism opens these borderlands to profit seeking, as market operations fill the void where democratic institutions should be. It is already clear that instrumentarian power produces specific contests over the constitutionally established rights of citizens. For example, when US scholars and jurists assess the ways in which digital capabilities challenge Fourth Amendment doctrine, the focus is typically on the relationship between individuals and the state. It is of course vital that Fourth Amendment protections reflect the realities of twenty-first-century data production and dispossession (Brennan-Marquez and Henderson 2017; Gray 2017a, 2017b; Kerr 2005, 531–585; Wydra et al. 2017). The problem is that even expanded protections from state surveillance do not shield users from the assaults of instrumentarian power animated by surveillance capitalism's private economic imperatives (Daskal 2015; Kerr 2005).

Legal scholarship is just beginning to reckon with these new facts. Fourth Amendment scholar Andrew Guthrie Ferguson concludes, "If billions of sensors filled with personal data fall outside of Fourth Amendment protections, a large-scale surveillance network will exist without constitutional limits" (Ferguson 2015, 879–880). Dutch scholars make a similar case for the inadequacy of Dutch law as it trails behind Big Other, no longer able to effectively assert the sanctity of the home from the invasive action of either industry or the state. "The walls no longer shield the individual effectively from the outside in the pursuing of . . . personal life without intrusion . . ." (Van Dongen and Timan 2017).

These and other contests over the extension of juridical rights to surveillance capitalism's market domain point us toward an even deeper crisis of human rights, delivering us head-on to Hannah Arendt's meta-formulation of the "right to have rights." Arendt's assertion peels away juridical achievements—she refers to these as the "Rights of Man"—revealing the a priori grounds upon which the very possibility of juridical rights rests. It is here on the ground of what I shall refer to as "elemental human rights" that

I propose to consider the implications of surveillance capitalism and its instrumentarian power for the prospects of human freedom.[4]

Instrumentarian Power as a Coup from Above

For Arendt, the "right to have rights" stands in contrast to juridical rights as indelible, "Man, it turns out, can lose all so-called Rights of Man without losing his essential quality as man, his human dignity" (Arendt 2004, 377). This is because the "right to have rights" equates to the "right of every individual to belong to humanity," and it "should be guaranteed by humanity itself" (Arendt 2004, 379). What does this belonging signify? For Arendt it means, above all, the possibility of effective life through voice and action, possibilities that are given in the elemental condition of inclusion in the human community. To belong to humanity is to belong to a world in which one can choose one's actions and exercise one's voice in ways that effectively further the aims of one's own life and the life of one's group.

How does the elemental condition of belonging to humanity translate into a "right to have rights"? Arendt argues that this conversion from elemental condition to explicit right arises only in the confrontation with a threat to the condition of inclusion:

> We became aware of the existence of a "right to have rights" (and that means to live in a framework where one is judged by one's actions and opinions) and a right to belong to some kind of organized community, only when millions of people emerged who had lost and could not regain these rights because of the new global political situation. . . . Not the loss of specific rights, then, but the loss of a community willing and able to guarantee any rights whatsoever, has been the calamity which has befallen ever-increasing numbers of people. Only the loss of a polity itself expels him from humanity. (Arendt 2004, 376–377)

Only exclusion from humanity itself, and thus exclusion from the elemental freedoms of voice and action, can abrogate the "right to have rights." "The fundamental deprivation of human rights is manifested first and above all in the deprivation of a place in the world which makes opinions significant and actions effective" (Arendt 2004, 376).

In this Arendt foreshadows the linguistic philosopher John Searle's "pragmatic considerations of the formulation of rights" (Searle 2010, 194–195). Searle argues that elemental conditions of existence are crystallized as formal human rights only at that moment in history when they come under systematic threat. So, for example, the ability to speak is an elemental condition. The concept of "freedom of speech" as a formal juridical right emerged only when society evolved to a degree of political complexity that the freedom to speak came under threat. Searle observes that speech is not more central to human life than breathing or being able to move one's body. No one has declared a "right to breathe" or a "right to bodily movement" because these elemental conditions have not come under attack and therefore do not require formal protection. What counts as a basic right, Searle argues, is both "historically contingent" and "pragmatic" (Searle 2010, 194–195).

It is not surprising then, that Arendt wrestled with the elemental human conditions of inclusion, voice, and action at a time when totalitarianism forced many philosophers and social theorists to question the structure of human freedom (Adorno 2008; Arendt 1983; Sartre 1957, 1992). Were there elemental constituents of human freedom that remain ineradicable, even in the teeth of "no escape" from a totalizing power? For the Arendt of *Origins* "action" was an indelible manifestation of freedom. Of those deprived of human rights under totalitarianism she wrote, "They are deprived, not of the right to freedom, but of the right to action" (Arendt 2004, 376).

It was a theme that she would elaborate throughout her life: action *initiates*. It asserts beginnings that diverge from established lines of force. Action inserts itself into the already composed human world to make something new. "To act . . . means to take an initiative, to begin . . . to set something into motion" (Arendt 1998, 176–177). Arendt observes that every beginning, seen from the perspective of the framework that it interrupts, is a miracle. The capacity for performing such miracles is uniquely human. "What usually remains intact in the epochs of petrification and foreordained doom is the faculty of freedom itself, the sheer capacity to begin, which animates and inspires all human activities and is the hidden source . . . of all great and beautiful things" (Arendt 1993, 169).

Key to our discussion is Arendt's insistence that "this insertion is not forced upon us by necessity. . . . It may be stimulated by the presence of others whose company we may wish to join, but it is never conditioned by them; its impulse springs from the beginning which came into the world when we were born and to which we respond by beginning something new on our own initiative" (Arendt 1993, 177). She explores this "impulse" in her extensive examination of "will," which she characterizes as the "organ for the future" in the same way that memory is the mental organ for the past. When we recall the past, we see only objects, but the view to the future brings "projects" that are latent in our will but have not yet come to be. Will is the organ with which we summon our futures into existence as we project ourselves into the future tense, make promises, and close the gap between present and future by fulfilling those promises as we translate the latent into the real.

These initiatives could have been "left undone" but for the inward freedom to project our commitments into the future and impose our will to see them through. It is not only that we make new beginnings, but also that these beginnings would not come into existence in the absence of our willing to undertake them. In this way, the future remains contingent on our will to create it and must therefore be understood as intrinsically unpredictable. Will is the human counterpoint to the fear of uncertainty that suffocates original action: "A will that is not free is a contradiction in terms" (Arendt 1978, 13–14).

These elemental manifestations of human self-determination, Arendt argues, derive from the capacity "to dispose of the future as though it were the present." Will is the means by which we annex the future tense, transforming it into a territory for deliberation, choice, promises, and the initiation of new beginnings in the fulfillment of those promises. This is how we manage the inescapable uncertainty of existence and achieve, as individuals and as communities, some "limited independence from the incalculability of the future." Arendt thus describes promises as "islands of predictability" and "guideposts of reliability" in an "ocean of uncertainty." They are, she argues, the only alternative to a different kind of "mastery" that relies on "domination of one's self and rule over others" when the lust for certainty produces the impulse "to cover the whole ground of the future and to map out a path secured in all directions" (Arendt 1998, 243–247). In this way human action as an elemental source of freedom expresses a dynamic biography born in the inwardness of will in order to flourish in the embrace of a human community where wills are joined to produce effective life, promising and keeping promises in shared purpose.

We have seen that the "right to have rights" is crystallized only in the historical moment when inclusion in humanity comes under threat. But what of action's birthplace in the elemental functions of human will and its annexation of the future? Arendt's metaphor of will asserts the inalienable status of this elemental inward capacity. What happens when the uniquely human capacity to dispose of the future as though it were the present—the right to count the future as one's field of action—is threatened with suppression or extinction? Following Arendt's and Searle's logic, such a threat demands the translation of this elemental condition of human freedom into a right, that it might be recognized as fundamental to effective life and accorded the protection of the political community.

This elemental condition in which we annex the future to the present as the field of autonomous action is what I have called *the right to the future tense* (Zuboff 2019). It asserts the inalienable capacity to will the future into existence through the force of one's own choice and commitment, and it recognizes this capacity as a baseline condition of effective human life. In claiming the future as a potential field of self-determined action, the right to the future tense asserts the unbroken biography of will and action that founds Arendt's "right to have rights." The right to the future tense and the "right to have rights" are twinborn. Expressed in action and guaranteed by inclusion in the human group, the "right to have rights" already presupposes the future tense as the ground on which the inner organ of the will is made manifest in the shared reality of the human community. Each is essential to the meaning and manifestation of the other, joined in the biographical arc of birth and adulthood. If the right to the future tense is abrogated, the miracle of human action is subordinated to others' plans that favor others' certainty. In the absence of the right to the future tense, the "right to have rights" is shorn of its origins in will and drifts into memory, a token of earlier unpredictable times.

I suggest that we now face the moment in history when the elemental condition in which we claim the future for autonomous action is threatened by the laws of motion of a new economic order in which wealth derives from the predictability of human behavior. The competitive dynamics of this new order require economies of action that operate to configure human behavior in ways that facilitate predictability. These operations grow more muscular with the escalation of competitive intensity, driving the evolution of predictability toward certainty. They are made manifest in a ubiquitous digital architecture of behavior modification owned and operated by surveillance capital outside of meaningful legal boundaries, indecipherable, and largely hidden. Motive and means combine to produce a new instrumentarian power that supplants freedom as the crucible of human action for the sake of guaranteed outcomes and the competitive advantages that they confer in markets that trade in the future of human behavior.

Instrumentarian power employs the logic of radical behaviorism to exile persons from their own behavior, reducing action to measurable behavior and severing interior meaning from observable performance. In this process, the human person is reduced to an organism among organisms. This constitutes a bloodless methodology through which not only are persons excluded from humanity but, for the sake of others' market success, humanity itself is excluded from the calculative knowledge that shapes the future. These new information territories are private and privileged, known only to the machines, their priests, and the market participants who pay to play in these new market spaces. Although it is obviously the case that we are excluded because the knowledge thus accumulated is not for us, the demands of economies of action suggest an even deeper structural basis for exclusion: *the ability to evade individual awareness, and therefore individual will, is an essential condition for the efficient exercise of instrumentarian power and its economic objectives.* Autonomous human action is costly friction that threatens surveillance revenues. In this way a new form of domination and its maps of a certain future override the right to the future tense.

Instrumentarian power does not simply destroy elemental rights; it usurps them. Such processes of expropriation were first evident in the transfer of decision rights over personal information from individuals to surveillance capitalists. The competitive demand for economies of action and the elaboration of the means of behavioral modification extends the pattern of expropriation to the elemental right to the future tense, which is the right to count the future as one's field of action, to initiate beginnings, and thus, to borrow from Machado, to make the road as you go (Machado 2003).

For this reason surveillance capitalism and its instrumentarian power are best described as a market-driven coup from above—not a *coup d'état* in the classic sense but rather a *coup de gens*: an overthrow of the people concealed in the technological Trojan horse that is Big Other. Instead of unpredictable human actors, the organism among organisms is manipulated for the sake of others' certainty at the expense of the arc of autonomous action that begins with the inner organ of free will and is completed in the mutual elaboration of a human community that guarantees the right to manifest one's will in action. Instrumentarian power is the hammer that suppresses human freedom in favor of others' market certainty. First to be extinguished in this coup is the pure impulse to initiate action that constructs social life as a miracle of unpredictable beginnings and distinguishes human beings as those who are born to replicate the natal miracle in original action. Arendt anticipated the possibility of this threat to human freedom at the hands of a behaviorist project elevated by global capital to world-historic power. She feared that the "last stage of the laboring society" would reduce its members to "automatic functioning," forced to acquiesce "in a dazed, 'tranquilized,' functional type of behavior":

> The trouble with modern theories of behaviorism is not that they are wrong but that they could become true, that they actually are the best possible conceptualization of certain obvious trends in modern society. It is quite conceivable that the modern age—which began with such an unprecedented and promising outburst of human activity—may end in the deadliest, most sterile passivity history has ever known. (Arendt 1998, 322)

Now it is the surveillance capitalists who enjoy the right to the future tense and who claim the "right to have rights" over the fields of action and knowledge. Instrumentarian power accomplishes the dispossession of human experience as an economic imperative, decisively prosecuting the redistribution of elemental human rights from individuals to capital. Surveillance capitalism's economic imperatives cannot be satisfied without these incursions into social and political territories that extend far beyond the traditional boundaries of private capital. In this way surveillance capitalism and its instrumentarian power are revealed as a profoundly antidemocratic constellation. They do not simply evade democratic oversight, but rather they undermine the foundations of such oversight for the sake of guaranteed outcomes. Surveillance capitalists accumulate not only surveillance assets and capital but also the elemental right to action, which is to say, freedom.

Just as industrial civilization flourished at the expense of nature and now threatens to cost us the earth, surveillance capitalism and its unprecedented instrumentarian power will thrive at the expense of human nature and threaten to cost us our humanity. The industrial legacy of climate chaos fills us with dismay, remorse, and fear. As surveillance capitalism founds a new economic order, what fresh legacy of damage and regret will be mourned by future generations? By the time you read these words, the reach of this new order will have grown, as more sectors, firms, start-ups, app developers, and investors mobilize around this one plausible version of information capitalism. This mobilization and the resistance it engenders will define a key battleground at the new frontier of power where elemental human rights will be contested in the name of humanity and the future. Who will write the music? Who will dance?

Notes

1. For readers who seek more detail, surveillance capitalism, its production of instrumentarian power, and many of its rights implications are fully analyzed in *The Age of Surveillance Capitalism: The Fight for a Human Future at the New Frontier of Power* (Zuboff 2019).

2. A typical example is this statement from the *Economist*: "Google exploits information that is a by-product of user interactions, or data exhaust, which is automatically recycled to improve the service or create an entirely new product." "Clicking for Gold," *Economist*, February 25, 2010, http://www.economist.com/node/15557431.

3. Between 2012 and 2015 I interviewed fifty-two data scientists from nineteen different companies with a combined 586 years of experience in high technology corporations and start-ups, primarily in Silicon Valley. These interviews were conducted as I developed my "ground truth" understanding of surveillance capitalism and its material infrastructure.

4. I mean to introduce here a distinction between "elemental" and "fundamental" human rights. For example, "equality under the law" is a fundamental right. In contrast, "breathing" or "moving one's arms" are elemental rights. Such rights are given under the condition of being alive and are rarely formalized as fundamental or juridical rights unless they come under direct threat of prohibition.

References

Addonizio, Gabrielle. 2016. "The Privacy Risks Surrounding Consumer Health and Fitness Apps with HIPAA's Limitations and the FTC's Guidance." *Health Law Outlook* 9 (1). http://scholarship.shu.edu/health-law-outlook/vol9/iss1/1.

Adorno, Theodor. 1966. "Education after Auschwitz," in *Critical Models: Interventions and Catchwords*. New York: Columbia University Press.

———. 1985. "On the Question: 'What Is German?,'" *New German Critique* 36 (Fall): 121–131.

———. 1991. "The Schema of Mass Culture," in *Culture Industry: Selected Essays on Mass Culture*. New York: Routledge.

———. 2008. *History and Freedom*. Cambridge: Polity Press.

Alter, Adam. 2017. *Irresistible: The Rise of Addictive Technology and the Business of Keeping Us Hooked*. New York: Penguin Press.

Andreassen, Cecilie Schou, Torbjørn Torsheim, Geir Scott Brunborg, and Ståle Pallesen. 2012. "Development of a Facebook Addiction Scale." *Psychological Reports* 110 (2): 501–517. https://doi.org/10.2466/02.09.18.PR0.110.2.501-517.

Arendt, Hannah. 1968. *The Origins of Totalitarianism*. Orlando, FL: Harcourt.

———. 1978. *The Life of the Mind: Volume Two, Willing*. New York: Harcourt Brace Jovanovich.

———. 1983. *Men in Dark Times*. New York: Harcourt Brace.

———. 1993 "What Is Freedom?," in *Between Past and Future: Eight Exercises in Political Thought*. New York: Penguin.

———. 1994. *Essays in Understanding*. New York: Schocken.

———. 1998. *The Human Condition*. Chicago: University of Chicago Press.

———. 2004. *The Origins of Totalitarianism*. New York: Schocken.

———. 2006. *Between Past and Future: Eight Exercises in Political Thought*. New York: Penguin Books.

Aron, Raymond. 1968. *Democracy and Totalitarianism*. London: Weidenfeld & Nicolson.

Baehr, Peter. 2002. "Identifying the Unprecedented: Hannah Arendt, Totalitarianism, and the Critique of Sociology." *American Sociological Review* 67 (6): 804–831. https://doi.org/10.2307/3088971.

Bakos, Yannis, et al. 2014. "Does Anyone Read the Fine Print? Consumer Attention to Standard-Form Contracts." *Journal of Legal Studies* 43 (1): 1–35. https://doi.org/10.1086/674424.

BBC. 2010. "Internet Access 'a Human Right.'" *BBC News*, March 8. http://news.bbc.co.uk/2/hi/8548190.stm.

Becher, Shmuel I., and Tal Z. Zarsky. 2015. "Online Consumer Contracts: No One Reads, but Does Anyone Care? Comments on Florencia Marotta-Wurgler's Studies." *Jerusalem Review of Legal Studies* 12 (1): 105–120. https://doi.org/10.1093/jrls/jlv005.

Beck, Ulrich, and Elisabeth Beck-Gernsheim. 2002. *Individualization: Institutionalized Individualism and Its Social and Political Consequences*. London: Sage.

Blakely, Rhys. 2014. "'We Thought Google Was the Future but It's Becoming Big Brother.'" *The Times*, September 19. http://www.thetimes.co.uk/tto/technology/internet/article4271776.ece.

Blanshard, Brand. 1967. "The Problem of Consciousness: A Debate with B. F. Skinner." *Philosophy and Phenomenological Research* 27 (3): 317–337.

Blenner, Sarah R. et al. 2016. "Privacy Policies of Android Diabetes Apps and Sharing of Health Information." *JAMA* 315 (10): 1051–1052. https://doi.org/10.1001/jama .2015.19426.

Borowicz, Wojciech. 2014. "Privacy in the Internet of Things Era," *Next Web*, October 18. http://thenextweb.com/dd/2014/10/18/privacy-internet-things-era-will-nsa -know-whats-fridge.

Brennan-Marquez, Kiel, and Stephen E. Henderson. 2017. "Fourth Amendment Anxiety." SSRN Scholarly Paper ID 2955077. Rochester, NY: Social Science Research Network. https://papers.ssrn.com/abstract=2955077.

Casale, Silvia, and Giulia Fioravanti. 2015. "Satisfying Needs through Social Networking Sites: A Pathway towards Problematic Internet Use for Socially Anxious People?" *Addictive Behaviors Reports* 1 (Supplement C): 34–39. https://doi.org/ 10.1016/j.abrep.2015.03.008.

Castillejo, P., J. F. Martínez, J. Rodríguez-Molina, and A. Cuerva. 2013. "Integration of Wearable Devices in a Wireless Sensor Network for an E-health Application," *IEEE Wireless Communications* 20 (4): 38–49.

Cheng, Cecilia, and Angel Yee-lam Li. 2014. "Internet Addiction Prevalence and Quality of (Real) Life: A Meta-Analysis of 31 Nations across Seven World Regions." *Cyberpsychology, Behavior and Social Networking* 17 (12): 755–760. https://doi .org/10.1089/cyber.2014.0317.

Cheng, J., O. Amft, G. Bahle, and P. Lukowicz. 2013. "Designing Sensitive Wearable Capacitive Sensors for Activity Recognition." *IEEE Sensors Journal* 13 (10): 3935–3947.

Cohen, Julie E. 2016. "The Regulatory State in the Information Age." *Theoretical Inquiries in Law* 17 (2). http://www7.tau.ac.il/ojs/index.php/til/article/view/1425.

Conquest, Robert. 2008. *The Great Terror: A Reassessment.* Oxford: Oxford University Press.

Cunningham, Lillian. 2011. "Google's Eric Schmidt Expounds on His Senate Testimony." *Washington Post*, September 30. http://www.washingtonpost.com/national/ on-leadership/googles-eric-schmidt-expounds-on-his-senate-testimony/2011/09/30/ gIQAPyVgCL_story.html.

Daskal, Jennifer. 2015. "The Un-Territoriality of Data." *Yale Law Journal* 125 (2): 326–559. http://www.yalelawjournal.org/article/the-un-territoriality-of-data.

De Rossi, D and P. Veltink. 2010. "Wearable Technology for Biomechanics: E-Textile or Micromechanical Sensors?" *IEEE Engineering in Medicine and Biology Magazine,* May 20, 37–43.

Dehling, Tobias et al. 2015. "Exploring the Far Side of Mobile Health: Information Security and Privacy of Mobile Health Apps on IOS and Android." *JMIR MHealth and UHealth* 3 (1): 1–26, https://doi.org/10.2196/mhealth.3672.

Der Kolk, Bessel A. van, and Jose Saporta. 1991. "The Biological Response to Psychic Trauma: Mechanisms and Treatment of Intrusion and Numbing." *Anxiety Research* 4 (3). https://doi.org/10.1080/08917779108248774.

Doctorow, Cory. 2017. "Unchecked Surveillance Technology Is Leading Us Towards Totalitarianism—Opinion." *International Business Times*, May 5. http://www.ibtimes.com/unchecked-surveillance-technology-leading-us-towards-totalitarianism-opinion-2535230.

Douglas, J. 1967. "Dissenting Statement of Justice Douglas, J. Regarding Warden v. Hayden, 387 U.S. 294" (US Supreme Court, April 12, 1967). https://www.law.cornell.edu/supremecourt/text/387/294.

Dougherty, Conor. 2016. "Tech Companies Take Their Legislative Concerns to the States," *New York Times*, May 27.

Dreifus, Claudia. 2017. "Why We Can't Look Away from Our Screens." *New York Times*, March 6. https://www.nytimes.com/2017/03/06/science/technology-addiction-irresistible-by-adam-alter.html.

Economist. 2004. "Move over, Big Brother," *Economist*, December. http://www.economist.com/node/3422918.

Edwards, Douglas. 2011. *I'm Feeling Lucky*. Boston: Houghton Mifflin Harcourt.

Elizabeth B. Wydra, Brianne J. Gorod, and Brian R. Frazelle. 2017. "Timothy Ivory Carpenter v. United States of America—On Writ of Certiorari to the United States Court of Appeals for the Sixth Circuit—Brief of Scholars of the History and Original Meaning of the Fourth Amendment as Amici Curiae in Support of Petitioner." Supreme Court of the United States.

Esper, Erwin A. 1967. "Max Meyer in America." *Journal of the History of the Behavioral Sciences* 3 (2): 107–131.

Farahany, Nita A. 2012. "Searching Secrets." *University of Pennsylvania Law Review* 160 (5): 1271.

Ferguson, Andrew Guthrie. 2015. "The Internet of Things and the Fourth Amendment of Effects." Rochester, NY: California Law Review. https://papers.ssrn.com/abstract=2577944.

Franck, Thomas M. 2000. *The Empowered Self: Law and Society in an Age of Individualism*. Oxford: Oxford University Press.

Friedman, Lawrence M. 2004. *American Law in the 20th Century*. New Haven: Yale University Press.

Friedrich, Carl J. 1954. "The Problem of Totalitarianism—An Introduction," in *Totalitarianism*, ed. Carl J. Friedrich. New York: Grosset & Dunlap.

———, ed. 1954. *Totalitarianism*. New York: Grosset & Dunlap.

Friedrich, Carl J., and Zbigniew Brzezinski. 1956. *Totalitarian Dictatorship and Autocracy*. Cambridge: Harvard University Press.

Gobry, Pascal-Emmanuel. 2011. "Eric Schmidt to World Leaders at EG8: Don't Regulate Us, or Else." Business Insider. May 24, 2011. http://www.businessinsider.com/eric-schmidt-google-eg8-2011-5.

Google Transparency Project. 2016. "Google's Revolving Door Explorer (US)." April 15. http://www.googletransparencyproject.org/googles-revolving-door-explorer-us.

———. 2017. "Google's European Revolving Door." September 25. http://google transparencyproject.org/articles/googles-european-revolving-door.

Gray, David. 2017a. "The Fourth Amendment Categorical Imperative." *Michigan Law Review*. http://michiganlawreview.org/the-fourth-amendment-categorical-imperative.

———. 2017b. *The Fourth Amendment in an Age of Surveillance*. New York: Cambridge University Press.

Griffiths, Mark D., Daria J. Kuss, and Zsolt Demetrovics. 2014. "Social Networking Addiction." In *Behavioral Addictions*, edited by Kenneth Paul Rosenberg and Laura Curtiss Feder, 119–141. Elsevier. https://doi.org/10.1016/B978-0-12-407724-9.00006-9.

Gurian, Waldemar. 1964. "Totalitarianism as Political Religion." In *Totalitarianism*, edited by Carl J. Friedrich, 119–129. New York: Grosset & Dunlap.

Harvey, David. 2005. *The New Imperialism*. New York: Oxford University Press.

Hilts, Andrew, Christopher Parsons, and Jeffrey Knockel. 2016. "Every Step You Fake: A Comparative Analysis of Fitness Tracker Privacy and Security." *Open Effect*. https://openeffect.ca/fitness-trackers.

Hirsh, Michael. 2015. "We Are All Big Brother Now," *POLITICO Magazine*, July 23 https://www.politico.com/magazine/story/2015/07/big-brother-technology-trial-120477.html.

Hoofnagle, Chris Jay. 2017. "FTC Regulation of Cybersecurity and Surveillance." Public Law Research Paper ID 3010205. Berkeley, CA: UC Berkeley. https://papers.ssrn.com/abstract=3010205.

Ignatieff, Michael. 2001. *Human Rights as Politics and Idolatry*. Princeton, NJ: Princeton University Press.

Intille, Stephen S., Jonathan Lester, James F. Sallis, and Glen Duncan. 2012. "New Horizons in Sensor Development." *Medicine & Science in Sports & Exercise* 44 (January): S24–31. https://doi.org/10.1249/MSS.0b013e3182399c7d.

Jenkins, Holman W. 2010. "Google and the Search for the Future." *Wall Street Journal*, August 14. http://www.wsj.com/articles/SB10001424052748704901104575423294099527212.

Kar, Robin Bradley. 2013. "The Challenge of Boilerplate." Illinois Public Law and Legal Theory Research Paper Series. University of Illinois College of Law. http://juris.jotwell.com/the-challenge-of-boilerplate.

Keller, Daphne. 2017. "The Right Tools: Europe's Intermediary Liability Laws and the 2016 General Data Protection Regulation." SSRN Scholarly Paper ID 2914684. Rochester, NY: Social Science Research Network. https://papers.ssrn.com/abstract=2914684.

Kerr, Orin S. 2005. "Searches and Seizures in a Digital World." *Harvard Law Review* 119, 531–585.

Khosla, Vinod. 2014. "Fireside Chat with Google Co-Founders, Larry Page and Sergey Brin." Khosla Ventures, July 3. http://www.khoslaventures.com/fireside-chat-with-google-co-founders-larry-page-and-sergey-brin.

Kim, Nancy S. 2013. *Wrap Contracts: Foundations and Ramifications*. Oxford: Oxford University Press.

Kramer, Adam D. I., Jamie E. Guillory, and Jeffrey T. Hancock. 2014. "Experimental Evidence of Massive-Scale Emotional Contagion through Social Networks." *Proceedings of the National Academy of Sciences of the United States of America* 111 (24): 8788–8790. https://doi.org/10.1073/pnas.1320040111.

LA Times. 2014. "911 Calls about Facebook Outage Angers L.A. County Sheriff's Officials." *Los Angeles Times*, August 1. http://www.latimes.com/local/lanow/la-me-ln-911-calls-about-facebook-outage-angers-la-sheriffs-officials-20140801-htmlstory.html.

Lefort, Claude. 1986. *The Political Forms of Modern Society: Bureaucracy, Democracy, Totalitarianism*, ed. John B. Thompson. Cambridge: MIT Press.

Lemley, Mark A. 2006. "Terms of Use." *Minnesota Law Review* 91 (July). https://papers.ssrn.com/abstract=917926.

Levy, Steven. 2011. *In the Plex: How Google Thinks, Works, and Shapes Our Lives*. New York: Simon & Schuster.

———. 2009. "Secret of Googlenomics: Data-Fueled Recipe Brews Profitability." *Wired*, May 22. http://archive.wired.com/culture/culturereviews/magazine/17-06/nep_googlenomics.

Lifton, Robert Jay. 2010. "Beyond Psychic Numbing: A Call to Awareness." *American Journal of Orthopsychiatry* 52 (4): 619–629. https://doi.org/10.1111/j.1939-0025.1982.tb01451.x.

Machado, Antonio. 2003. *There Is No Road: Proverbs by Antonio Machado*. Buffalo, NY: White Pine Press.

Marx, Karl. 1992. *Capital: A Critique of Political Economy*, vol. 3. Translated by David Fernbach. London: Penguin.

"Max Karl Ernst Ludwig Planck." 2017. Nobel-Winners.Com, December 16. http://www.nobel-winners.com/Physics/max_karl_ernst_ludwig_planck.html.

"Max Planck Facts, Information, Pictures | Encyclopedia.Com Articles about Max Planck." n.d. http://www.encyclopedia.com/people/science-and-technology/physics-biographies/max-planck.

Mayer-Schönberger, Viktor, and Yann Padova. 2016. "Regime Change? Enabling Big Data through Europe's New Data Protection Regulation." *Columbia Science & Technology Law Review* 17: 315–335.

Menell, Peter S. 2013. "2014: Brand Totalitarianism." UC Berkeley Public Law Research Paper. Berkeley: University of California. http://papers.ssrn.com/abstract=2318492.

Meyer, Max. 1912. "The Present Status of the Problem of the Relation between Mind and Body." *Journal of Philosophy, Psychology and Scientific Methods* 9 (14): 365–371. https://doi.org/10.2307/2013335.

Meyer, Max Friedrich. 1921. *Psychology of the Other-One*. Columbia, MO: Missouri Book Publishers. http://archive.org/details/cu31924031214442.

Mukhopadhyay, S. C. 2015. "Wearable Sensors for Human Activity Monitoring: A Review." *IEEE Sensors Journal* 15 (3): 1321–1330. https://doi.org/10.1109/JSEN.2014.2370945.

Mullins, Brody, and Jack Nicas. 2017. "Paying Professors: Inside Google's Academic Influence Campaign." *Wall Street Journal*, July 14. https://www.wsj.com/articles/paying-professors-inside-googles-academic-influence-campaign-149978528.

Nasaw, David. 2005. "Gilded Age Gospels." In *Ruling America: A History of Wealth and Power in a Democracy*, edited by Steve Fraser and Gary Gerstle, 123–148. Cambridge, MA: Harvard University Press.

Neumann, Franz L., and Peter Hayes. 2009. *Behemoth: The Structure and Practice of National Socialism, 1933–1944*. Chicago: Ivan R. Dee.

Nevins, Allan. 1954. *Ford: The Times, the Man, the Company*. New York: Charles Scribner's Sons.

Newman, Jared. 2009. "Google's Schmidt Roasted for Privacy Comments." *PCWorld*, December11,2009.http://www.pcworld.com/article/184446/googles_schmidt_roasted _for_privacy_comments.html.

Pattichis, C. S. et al. 2002. "Wireless Telemedicine Systems: An Overview," *IEEE Antennas and Propagation Magazine* 44 (2): 143–153.

Pettey, Christy. 2016. "Treating Information as an Asset." *Smarter with Gartner*, February 17. www.gartner.com/smarterwithgartner/treating-information-as-an-asset.

Planck, Max. 2007a. "Phantom Problems in Science." In *Scientific Autobiography and Other Papers*, 52–79. New York: Philosophical Library.

———. 2007b. *Scientific Autobiography and Other Papers*. New York: Philosophical Library.

Polanyi, Karl. 2001. *The Great Transformation: The Political and Economic Origins of Our Time*. Boston: Beacon Press.

Preston, Cheryl B. 2015. "'Please Note: You Have Waived Everything': Can Notice Redeem Online Contracts?" *American University Law Review* 64 (3): 535–590. http:// digitalcommons.wcl.american.edu/cgi/viewcontent.cgi?article=1950&context=aulr.

"Promotion, Protection, and Enjoyment of Human Rights on the Internet, The." 2016. United Nations Human Rights Council. https://www.article19.org/data/files/ Internet_Statement_Adopted.pdf.

Preston, Cheryl B. 2015. "'Please Note: You Have Waived Everything': Can Notice Redeem Online Contracts?" *American University Law Review* 64 (3): 535–590. http:// digitalcommons.wcl.american.edu/cgi/viewcontent.cgi?article=1950&context=aulr.

Radin, Margaret Jane. 2012. *Boilerplate: The Fine Print, Vanishing Rights, and the Rule of Law*. Princeton, NJ: Princeton University Press.

Rochet, Jean-Charles, and Jean Tirole. 2006. "Two-Sided Markets: A Progress Report." *RAND Journal of Economics* 37 (3): 645–667.

Rossi, Anna. 2016. "Respected or Challenged by Technology? The General Data Protection Regulation and Commercial Profiling on the Internet." SSRN Scholarly Paper ID 2852739. Rochester, NY: Social Science Research Network. https://papers .ssrn.com/abstract=2852739.

Sandel, Michael J. 2013. *What Money Can't Buy: The Moral Limits of Markets*. New York: Farrar, Straus and Giroux.

Sartre, Jean-Paul. 1957. *Existentialism and Human Emotions*. New York: Philosophical Library.

———. 1992. *Being and Nothingness*. New York: Washington Square Press.

Schmidt, Eric, and Jared Cohen. 2014. *The New Digital Age: Transforming Nations, Businesses, and Our Lives*. New York: Vintage.

Schou Andreassen, Cecilie, and Stale Pallesen. 2014. "Social Network Site Addiction—An Overview." *Current Pharmaceutical Design* 20 (25): 4053–4061. http://www.ingentaconnect.com/content/ben/cpd/2014/00000020/00000025/art00007.

Schulz, Martin. 2016. "Transcript of Keynote Speech at Cpdp2016 on Technological, Totalitarianism, Politics and Democracy," *Scribd*. https://www.scribd.com/docu ment/305093114/Keynote-Speech-at-Cpdp2016-on-Technological-Totalitarianism -Politics-and-Democracy.

Searle, John R. 2010. *Making the Social World: The Structure of Human Civilization*. Oxford: Oxford University Press.

Shaban, Hamza. 2017a. "Google Spent the Most It Ever Has Trying to Influence Washington: $6 Million." *Washington Post*, July 21. https://www.washingtonpost .com/news/the-switch/wp/2017/07/21/google-spent-the-most-it-ever-has-trying-to -influence-washington-6-million.

———. 2017b. "Google Is the Highest-Spending Company for Federal Lobbying." *Technocracy News*, September 19. https://www.technocracy.news/index.php/2017/ 09/19/google-highest-spending-company-federal-lobbying.

Short, Jodi L. 2011. "The Paranoid Style in Regulatory Reform." *Hastings Law Journal* 63 (January): 633–694.

Shorten, Richard. 2012. *Modernism and Totalitarianism—Rethinking the Intellectual Sources of Nazism and Stalinism, 1945 to the Present*. New York, Palgrave Macmillan. http://www.palgrave.com/us/book/9780230252066.

Skinner, B. F. 1976. *About Behaviorism*. New York: Vintage Books.

———. 1991. *The Behavior of Organisms: An Experimental Analysis*. Acton, MA: Copley.

———. 2002. *Beyond Freedom & Dignity*. Kindle. Indianapolis, IN: Hackett.

———. 2012. *Science and Human Behavior*. New York: Free Press.

Slovic, Paul, David Zionts, Andrew Keane Woods, Ryan Goodman, and Derek Jinks. 2011. "Psychic Numbing and Mass Atrocity." Public Law Research Paper 11–56. New York: NYU School of Law. http://papers.ssrn.com/abstract=1809951.

Solanas, A. et al. 2014. "Smart Health: A Context-Aware Health Paradigm within Smart Cities." *IEEE Communications Magazine* 52 (8): 74–81. https://doi.org/10.1109/ MCOM.2014.6871673.

Sorell, Tom, and Heather Draper. 2012. "Telecare, Surveillance, and the Welfare State." *American Journal of Bioethics* 12 (9): 36–44. https://doi.org/10.1080/15265161 .2012.699137.

Statista. 2017. "Google Is the Biggest Lobbying Spender in Tech: Chart." *Statista*, July 24. https://www.statista.com/chart/10393/lobbying-expenditure-of-tech-companies.

Strandburg, Katherine J. 2013. "Free Fall: The Online Market's Consumer Preference Disconnect." Working Paper, New York University Law and Economics. New York: NYU.

Taplin, Jonathan. 2017. "Why Is Google Spending Record Sums on Lobbying Washington?" *Guardian*, July 30. http://www.theguardian.com/technology/2017/jul/30/ google-silicon-valley-corporate-lobbying-washington-dc-politics.

Van Der Kolk, Bessel A., and Jose Saporta. 1991. "The Biological Response to Psychic Trauma: Mechanisms and Treatment of Intrusion and Numbing." *Anxiety Research* 4 (3): 199–212. https://doi.org/10.1080/08917779108248774.

Van Dongen, Lisa, and Tjerk Timan. 2017. "Your Smart Coffee Machine Knows What You Did Last Summer: A Legal Analysis of the Limitations of Traditional Privacy of the Home under Dutch Law in the Era of Smart Technology." SSRN Scholarly Paper ID 3090340. Rochester, NY: Social Science Research Network. https://papers .ssrn.com/abstract=3090340.

Wachter, Sandra. 2017. "Normative Challenges of Identification in the Internet of Things: Privacy, Profiling, Discrimination, and the GDPR." SSRN Scholarly Paper ID 3083554. Rochester, NY: Social Science Research Network. https://papers.ssrn.com/ abstract=3083554.

Weber, Max. 1978. *Economy and Society: An Outline of Interpretive Sociology*. Berkeley: University of California Press.

Weiser, Mark. 1999. "The Computer for the 21st Century." *Scientific American*, July, 3–11.

Wells, Bruce R. 2009. "The Fog of Cloud Computing: Fourth Amendment Issues Raised by the Blurring of Online and Offline Content." *University of Pennsylvania Journal of Constitutional Law* 12: 223–240.

Wiebe, Robert H. 1967. *The Search for Order: 1877–1920*. New York: Hill and Wang.

Wood, Ellen. 2002. *The Origin of Capitalism: A Longer View*. London: Verso.

World Unplugged, The. n.d. https://theworldunplugged.wordpress.com.

Wozniak, Robert H. 1997. "Max Meyer and *The Fundamental Laws of Human Behavior*." Bryn Mawr College. http://www.brynmawr.edu/psychology/rwozniak/meyer .html.

Wydra, Elizabeth B., Brianne J. Gorod, and Brian R. Frazelle. 2017. "Timothy Ivory Carpenter v. United States of America—On Writ of Certiorari to the United States Court of Appeals for the Sixth Circuit—Brief of Scholars of the History and Original Meaning of the Fourth Amendment as Amici Curiae in Support of Petitioner." Supreme Court of the United States.

Yarow, Jay. 2013. "Google CEO Larry Page Wants a Totally Separate World Where Tech Companies Can Conduct Experiments on People." Business Insider. May 16. http://www.businessinsider.com/google-ceo-larry-page-wants-a-place-for-experi ments-2013-5.

Zarsky, Tal. 2017. "Incompatible: The GDPR in the Age of Big Data." SSRN Scholarly Paper ID 3022646. Rochester, NY: Social Science Research Network. https://papers. ssrn.com/abstract=3022646.

Zuboff, Shoshana. 2014. "A Digital Declaration." *Frankfurter Allgemeine Zeitung*, September 15. http://www.faz.net/aktuell/feuilleton/debatten/the-digital-debate/shoshan -zuboff-on-big-data-as-surveillance-capitalism-13152525.html.

———. 2015. "Big Other: Surveillance Capitalism and the Prospects of an Information Civilization." *Journal of Information Technology* 30 (1): 75–89. https://doi .org/10.1057/jit.2015.5.

———. 2016. "Google as a Fortune Teller: The Secrets of Surveillance Capitalism." *Frankfurter Allgemeine Zeitung*, March 5. http://www.faz.net/aktuell/feuilleton/ debatten/the-digital-debate/shoshana-zuboff-secrets-of-surveillance-capitalism -14103616.html.

———. 2019. *The Age of Surveillance Capitalism: The Fight for a Human Future at the New Frontier of Power.* New York: PublicAffairs.

Zuboff, Shoshana, and James Maxmin. 2002. *The Support Economy: Why Corporations Are Failing Individuals and the Next Episode of Capitalism.* New York: Viking.

2 Digital Transformations, Informed Realities, and Human Conduct

Mikkel Flyverbom and Glen Whelan

Introduction

The information that people search for, collect, and utilize on a daily basis is now largely sourced through what Jørgensen, in the Introduction to this volume, terms "the social web." As many have recognized, this results in the most popular platforms—such as Google, Facebook, Twitter, and Instagram—being able to influence and direct human activities in relatively novel ways (Flyverbom et al. 2016; Gillespie 2014; Whelan 2019a; Zuboff 2015, 2019). Despite various backlashes against these commercial platforms (such as that relating to the Facebook and Cambridge Analytica scandal of 2018), the perceived convenience and value of such services—in terms of consuming, communicating, socializing, and learning for example (cf. Hargittai and Marwick 2016; Varian 2010, 2014)—seem far from abating.

Given this context, we use the present chapter to introduce a framework that helps conceive of how these platforms construct what we term "informed realities." Like many before us, we are intrigued by the fact that, while people are free to act, they only ever act within environments that they have played, at best, a minimal role in constructing (Bourdieu 1977; Certeau 1984; Foucault 1977). More specifically, and just as popular platforms (Schmidt and Cohen 2013) and their critics (Vaidhyanathan 2011) have also recognized, we seek to highlight how choice is constrained and directed by the continuously restructured platform interfaces that help people satisfy their various desires (Flyverbom 2016; Mansell 2017). Further to the impacts it is having in terms of privacy (see chapter 10), freedom of expression (see chapters 8 and 9), and democratic accountability (see chapter 3), then, the social web impacts upon our personal freedom and individual autonomy. While perhaps harder to define, these more general ideas are nevertheless central to human rights theory and practice (Campbell 2006, 55–58; Nickel 2006, 63–64) and thus in need of discussion in the present volume.

With these considerations providing our motivation, we use the chapter's next section to conceive of informed realities as the relationship between different sorts of data, information, and knowledge. We then differentiate between three types of informed realities—that is, "expert," "popular," and "algorithmic"—that exist in digital platforms to different degrees. Finally, we conclude with some brief comments on how the risks that informed realities present for autonomy and freedom might be managed at the individual and organizational level.

Informed Realities

Google's (2019) mission is to "organize the world's information and make it universally accessible and useful." As this indicates, the information that one accesses through Google Search, Google Scholar, Google Maps, and so on, is anything but unstructured. The same is true for other platforms that we utilize. Twitter and Facebook, for example, regularly make suggestions as to which tweets and posts users might be most interested in, and online rating sites like TripAdvisor draw attention to listings that are deemed the most popular by their users.

In such ways, these different platforms can be conceived as informed realities: for they are comprised of different assemblages of data, information, and knowledge that result in users being made more or less aware of, or in their being directed toward, different news stories, websites, posts, and so on (Alaimo and Kallinikos 2017; Flyverbom and Murray 2018). So defined, questions about informed realities are far from new. Prior work on knowledge production (Berger and Luckmann 1966), communication processes (Meyrowitz 1985), and public opinion (Zaller 1992), for example, articulates how socio-material information environments create particular possibilities for acting and thinking, and how such developments contribute to social ordering. Likewise, it has long been recognized that informed realities have an impact on human freedom and autonomy. Habermas (1989, 160–178), in particular, is famous for detailing the move from a public sphere characterized by "rational-critical debate" to one dominated by "manipulative publicity."

With regard to the social web, the idea of informed realities is important because it provides a counterpoint to the oft-noted ways in which digital technologies have contributed to the democratization of cultural production (Lessig 2008), to new possibilities in terms of decentralized communication and organization (Whelan, Moon, and Grant 2013), and to increased choice and productive capacities (e.g., Benkler 2006). In doing so, and without denying that digital technologies do contribute to autonomy and freedom in these and other ways, the idea of informed realities suggests that platforms can also diminish the extent to which we freely make decisions. Just as road systems encourage people to go to certain destinations, and to get there in certain ways, informed realities encourage us, in potentially much more subtle ways, to visit a particular website or to pursue an issue in one way rather than another.

This basic idea is suggested by Zuboff (2015, 82) when she writes of there being no escape from the "Big Other" that far exceeds anything that Jeremy Bentham imagined with his panopticon, and that results in "mental agency and self-possesion" becoming submerged within "a new kind of automaticity." Likewise, Langolis et al. (2009, 420) suggest this idea with their talk of different technical systems and architectures producing "a human-understandable visual interface" that imposes "specific constraints" on us, and so too Lazzarato (2004), when he proposes that we now exist in capitalist-produced worlds that require that we adopt or become inscribed with specific forms of subjectivation.

Although these ideas are sometimes considered in opposition to those of Habermas (e.g., Langolis et al. 2009, 416), they appear to share Habermas's (1996, 92–94) concern with maintaining or protecting Kantian-influenced notions of individual autonomy. Without going into undue detail, and alongside such other matters as the capacity to make rationally sound and universalizable moral claims, Kant (1785) associated individual autonomy with establishing, and judging between, our own means and ends. As a consequence, he would have likely been concerned, as the above-mentioned authors are, that the social web is diminishing the complex decision making capacities that are often thought to comprise our "humanity and human judgement" (Rainie and Anderson 2017, 46, 51).

Such claims can appear excessive and even melodramatic. Yet, as the social web has become the backbone that supports many parts of social life, we need to consider how this shapes our decision-making. For this reason, we use the chapter's following section to detail three generic types of informed realities that populate the online domain to varying degrees. But before we can turn to this task, we need to first identify the components that comprise informed realities: that is, data, information, and knowledge. As each of these components could easily be made the subject of book-length treatment, we emphasize that the following discussions are far from exhaustive, and that our reason for providing them is the result of our heuristic concern, namely to differentiate between three types of informed realities.

Data

Data can be understood as traces of phenomena: for example, events, experiences, and experiments. In this way, data refer to discernible, experienceable differences that provide the resources from which (communicable) information is subsequently constructed (Boisot and Canals 2004; Zins 2007). While it is tempting to think that we can somehow experience data "in and of themselves," this is generally recognized as naive because of post-Kantian understandings of perception (Hacking 1979, 383), and because of data often being collected with a purpose and thus structured in certain ways while being collected and experienced (Flyverbom and Madsen 2015; Gitelman 2013).

Despite such concerns, and through more or less complex and detailed means of argumentation and deliberation that enable people to attain the "objectivation of experienceable happenings" (Habermas 1978, 369), it is commonplace for people to reach agreement on what they experience in everyday life: for example, two people will often be able to agree that they have both seen the same post on Twitter; or that a Google search query results in one link being returned at the top of the first page of results (on a given laptop, at a given time and place). In these ways, we consider data to be one element that can help qualify and distinguish between different types of informed realities.

Information

The same data can be presented to people, or communicated to users, in different forms. Such structuring is comprised of labels, classifications, tropes, and so on (Bowker and Star 1999), that strategically and purposefully mark differences in data, and that present data in certain ways. Academic writing, for example, can make use of different genres—such as the detective story—to inform readers of, and explain the importance of, the same empirical findings (Czarniawska 1999).

Of course, once data have been turned into information, this information can, in its turn, be treated as data by someone else: as when an academic uses other academic writings—which are themselves characterized by an informational structure—as the basis for a literature review. In addition to being widespread in academic circles, this tendency to treat already constructed pieces of information as data are a very prominent feature on the social web. To get a sense of just how widespread, it will suffice to once again note that Google's mission is to "organize the world's information and make it universally accessible and useful." More generally, the point is that the ways in which different platforms inform their users about, and direct their users toward, different sets of data, is the second key component used to discuss informed realities.

Knowledge

Two points are commonly emphasized in discussions of knowledge. First, it is often noted that regimes of knowledge associated with different disciplines and professions actively shape how we perceive, understand, and construct the phenomenal world. Such "knowledge" regimes, it tends to be emphasized, dictate, in a more or less automatic fashion, both the means and the ends of learning. Second, and consequently, it is often suggested that "real" or "genuine" knowledge is a critically reflective, and commonly deliberative, exercise (Dewey 1933; Habermas 1978; Kant 1784; Rabinow 2011).

Despite these points tending to be critical of (overly) instrumental understandings of knowledge, it remains commonplace to associate knowledge levels with specific know-how and with the attainment of specific qualifications. A computer science professor, for example, might be expected to teach a course on data compression, and a computer science undergraduate might be expected to prove capable of working with, and developing, data-compression algorithms. Further to this, it is commonplace to presume that those associated with prestigious institutions are more knowledgeable than those associated with an institution that is somehow deemed less prestigious. Whilst widespread, such credentialism is often critiqued for distracting people from knowledge for knowledge's sake (Dewey 1933, 216, 224), and due to the role it plays in perpetuating class distinctions (e.g., Bourdieu 1984, 1988; Davies and Rizk 2018).

Whatever their normative worth, both the instrumentalist and credentialist understandings of knowledge are important for our understanding of informed realities. Instrumentalist understandings are important because platforms wouldn't exist in the absence of those that possess the requisite skill to construct them (e.g., computer scientists). More credentialist understandings, on the other hand, are important because it is often thought that an emphasis on formal educational achievements is in the process of being disrupted by the "hackers" who have helped construct the platforms and who are often presented as caring more about results than about accreditations (Turner 2009). Likewise, such credentialism is being challenged by the more "democratic" potential of the social web, which provide the (formally uneducated) masses with increased opportunities to express their voice (e.g., Whelan, Moon, and Grant 2013). For such reasons, knowledge comprises the third component of "informed realities."

Influencing Action and Decision-Making on the Social Web

The above suggests that different and often recursive combinations of data, information, and knowledge contribute to the construction of different informed realities. These informed realities shape our experiences and actions. This, in itself, is no bold or surprising claim and is largely in line with ideas about social construction (Berger and Luckmann 1966) and socio-material affordances (Hutchby 2001). Nevertheless, we believe that such ideas are worth revisiting given that platforms direct and constrain our freedom and autonomy, and thus impact a multitude of human rights concerns such as access to information, freedom of expression, and collective mobilization (Foucault 1991; Hansen and Flyverbom 2015; Nardi and O'Day 1999; Whelan, Moon, and Grant 2013). Moreover, as the corporations that develop and control such ecosystems sometimes downplay these capacities (Zuckerberg 2016), and as they can also be very selective when it comes to their own transparency (Flyverbom 2015), it seems important that the scholarly community direct attention to the ways in which these powerful corporations shape everyday experience for many people worldwide.

Three Kinds of Informed Reality

In building on the distinction between data, information, and knowledge, we now identify three types of informed reality that populate the online domain, and that contribute to our freedom and autonomy being directed and constrained in different ways.

Expert Informed Realities

Expert informed realities often take the form of explicit evaluation and guidance and are generally associated with the opinions of specialists related to established, legitimate institutions of one sort or another. While arguably of diminished importance when compared to the role they played in the age of mass media, expert informed realities continue to be of influence. Indeed, given the emergence of blogging platforms like Blogger, Medium, and WordPress, the expert guidance that these informed realities are associated with can appear more populous, and more readily available, than ever before.

The knowledge used to construct expert informed realities is of a classically recognized sort. The experts involved will be distinguished from the rest of the population in terms of their training, their accomplishments, and often their privilege (Gabriel 1998, 3). Their training will have contributed to their capacity to make relatively fine distinctions between seemingly similar objects. And their understanding of particular phenomena, genres and styles, and/or historical periods, will often result in their view of some given development being more critical than that of the broader population.

The reputable mainstream media, such as the British newspaper *The Guardian*, provides a good example of what expert informed realities have historically looked like. And, as noted by the paper's former readers' editor Chris Elliott (2011), such newspapers have long been accused of having an "Oxbridge" bias due to 81 percent of the UK's leading journalists being educated at the world-renowned Oxford and Cambridge universities.

Just as the knowledge that is used in the creation of expert informed realities will tend to be more or less closely connected with, and even inseparable from, experts themselves (because of their education and personal experiences), so too will the data utilized. Social scientists, for example, often rely on elaborate methods for collecting and analyzing data and on secondary evidence from trusted sources. And experts in a particular profession, such as gastronomy or architecture, will often rely on data that they have gathered through their own professional activities. In short, the data drawn upon in expert informed realities tends to be limited to an expert's personal experiences and resources.

One type of information that experts produce is the narrative review or report. Such reviews will generally describe what the expert or critic thought was remarkable or prosaic, or enjoyable or annoying, about a given experience, event, product, or service. Expert information will also commonly proceed in a standard structure and will be written for a target audience with a presumed educational background.

The online publishing platform Medium provides one clear example of an expert informed reality. As noted at the top of its "Our Story" page (Medium 2019),

> Medium taps into the brains of the world's most insightful writers, thinkers and storytellers to bring you the smartest takes on topics that matter. So whatever your interest, you can always find fresh thinking and unique perspectives.

Some of the experts that Medium associates itself with include the renowned author of *The Circle* (2014), Dave Eggers, and Eve L. Ewing, whose brief biography on Medium lists her as a sociologist of race and education at the University of Chicago. In terms of writing style, the following remarks made by Miles Klee (2018) for his Medium piece on male victims in the #MeToo era is fairly representative of Medium's style, and that of expert informed realities more generally:

> my eighth grade math teacher . . . informed us that men can be victims [of sexual assault], too. . . . She . . . arrived at an anecdote that changed her whole demeanor. It was about a man whose girlfriend handcuffed him to their bed and started inserting foreign objects into his rectum—painfully and against his protests. As the woman listed the items used, including a pencil, she was taken by a giggling fit. "I'm sorry," she gasped, "It's not funny, I shouldn't laugh." But she did, and so did the class. I cannot forget the queasy jolt this laughter gave me. It was clear that although we had to be grimly mature in discussing the terrifying abuse and violence women face, a man suffering that way could be viewed as a weird exception, if not an outright absurdity. He's a punchline.

By drawing upon his own school memories, and in using a fairly classical sort of structure, Klee—whose professional description on Medium asserts his expertise by noting that he is author of IVYLAND and TRUE FALSE:—complies with the above-noted points regarding the tendency of expert informed realities to encourage (suitably knowledgeable) contributors to draw on their own personal experiences as data and to make use of narrative as a way of informing their audience. Medium implicitly encourages such an approach by proposing that good writing is about what an author knows and loves.

While the likes of Medium are making it easier for more experts to get their voice out there, they may also be contributing to what some suggest is the death of expert informed realities more generally (Mendelsohn 2012). One reason why is that expert informed realities only really make sense if there are a limited number of experts. Another reason why is that, by increasing the number of accessible "experts," expert informed realities provide users with an increased capacity to pick and choose among the experts they like.

While such choice also existed in the age of mass media, the choice or potential "openings" that one finds online (Isin and Ruppert 2015; Whelan, Moon, and Grant 2013) clearly outstrip those which could (and still can) be found in mainstream, reputable newspapers. Unlike the other informed realities discussed below, then, the world of expert informed realities looks more like a wild, unruly, and ungoverned frontier than it does an "information superhighway" (Dzieza 2014).

Popular Informed Realities

Examples of digital platforms that are characterizable as popular informed realities include Airbnb, Amazon, TripAdvisor, Twitter, and Facebook. Such popular informed realities publish people's opinions, reactions, and rankings (e.g., 4 out of 5 stars) with regard to products, services, and experiences and enable users to like or circulate posts that are made by other users. In this fashion, popular informed realities can be understood as explicitly shaped by the value judgments of their users and customers.

Thus, whereas the knowledge of expert informed realities is characterized by its relatively rarified and specialized nature, the knowledge of popular informed realities is characterized by its much more general, democratic, and informal, nature. Moreover, while the knowledge of expert informed realities is, by and large, produced by an isolated individual, the knowledge of popular informed realities is intersubjective, majoritarian, and nonhierarchical (Vaidhyanathan 2011, 60–61).

Just as the form of knowledge associated with popular informed realities is diffuse and popular, so too is the data. In contrast with expert informed realities, once again, which are characterized by their data sets being

confined to that which a limited number of people can experience, popular informed realities can build on much larger sets of data. Rather than
building on one person's reading of a particular book, one person's visit to a
given restaurant, or one person's perspective on a given politician, popular
informed realities can build on the experiences of a large number of users.
Dot Hutchison's 2016 thriller *The Butterfly Garden*, for example, had over
10,000 reviews (61 percent 5 out of 5 stars) on Amazon.com before Christ-
mas that same year.

Popular informed realities now guide decisions and inform experiences
in important ways, and they are often seen to derive legitimacy and value
from their scale and possibilities for comparisons. As individual experiences and reactions are combined and transformed into numbers (such
as a score from 1–5) by the platforms where they are compiled, they gain
value as both qualitative and quantitative forms of information that can
guide experiences and conduct (Hansen and Flyverbom 2015). Increasingly, such aggregations of popular information are combined with others, enabling the creation of sites such as Metacritic, where a wide range
of reviews are assembled and made available for scrutiny. Such packag-
ing of qualitative reactions into quantitative representations increases
the distance from their experiential origins and thus enables information
mobility and increases the possibility for "action at a distance" (Miller and
Rose 1990).

By providing more opportunities for individual expression and engagement, popular informed realities enable the (partial) circumvention of
expert informed realities. The basic sense of this was captured nicely in
Time magazine's decision, given the emergence of social web platforms, to
name YOU—rather than a president or other public figure—as person of
the year in 2006. Nevertheless, popular informed realities can also be seen
to diminish human agency and individual intent in a variety of ways.

Positive consumer reviews, for example, are widely considered as vital to
the success of online retailers, service providers, and sharing platforms. The
reason for this is that positive or negative reviews, or the correct number of
both, strongly encourage users to purchase a given product or service. As
the quality of reviews is also important, the likes of Amazon seek to bolster
trust in them by asking users to rate each other's reviews: for example, "26
of 31 people found the following review helpful" (Mudambi and Schuff
2010, 186).

By and large, the efforts that Amazon and other prominent platforms like Yelp and Facebook are making to encourage their users to utilize reviews in their decision-making seem to be working. BrightLocal's 2017 "Local Consumer Review Survey," for example, found that "97% of consumers looked online for local business in 2017, with 12% looking for a local business online every day"; that "85% of consumers trust online reviews as much as personal recommendations"; and that "49% of consumers need at least a four-star rating before they choose to use a business."

In a sense, such reviews encourage users to outsource their critical decision-making facilities to the public at large. Moreover, they can be seen as part of a general shift toward populism on the social web. In the political sphere, for example,

> Populists are [the current] stars in political cyberspace, far outshining their centrist opponents. The 2015 Facebook posts of the United Kingdom Independence Party, the leading voice of the Brexit campaign, received 4,000 likes on average, twice the number received by the Conservative Party. While Dutch voters rejected the populist, anti-immigrant candidate Geert Wilders in its recent election, Wilders' social media following greatly outpaces that of other Dutch party leaders. (Hendrickson and Galston 2017)

Rather than being considered meaningfully democratic, then, popular informed realities are often perceived as little more than superficial forums that "chip away" at individual autonomy and social democracy.

Algorithmically Informed Realities

In contrast to expert and popular informed realities, which are structured through the decisions and choices of distinct individuals and a mass of individuals, respectively, algorithmically informed realities are primarily structured through the decisions made by automated systems. Although humans currently remain a key part of the assemblage that designs, trains, and tweaks the algorithms that enable computers to make such decisions (Martin 2018), algorithmically informed realities can still be understood as the least human-centric of the informed realities here identified. They can also be understood as the most novel of the three informed realities, and are arguably the most important of the informed realities that are found within the online domain (Madsen et al. 2016).

In terms of data, algorithmically informed realities build on the traces left by people and objects as they interact through digital technologies.

Every click, search, or like on social media, every product or service purchased online, and every GPS followed movement, can be digitally recorded and surveilled (Whelan 2019b; Zuboff 2015). In turn, these digital traces, and various other digitized sources—such as books, paintings, news stories, maps, and video recordings—combine to provide what was, up until recently, an unimaginable amount of data that is only analyzable with the help of machines (Whelan 2019a).

The knowledge that drives algorithmically informed realities is ultimately associated with a long line of specialists in computer science. Google's basic search algorithm, for example, was famously created by Larry Page and Sergey Brin when they were computer science PhD students at Stanford University in the late 1990s. Increasingly, however, the knowledge that drives algorithmically informed realities is associated with machines themselves.

In the case of deep learning technologies—which comprise an input layer (e.g., a web page, a sound recording), a set of hidden layers that represent an input in an increasingly abstract fashion, and an output layer that identifies something (e.g., a sound as an ambulance siren or a web page as a porn site; Goodfellow, Bengio, and Courville 2016, 6, 13, 168)—this means that it can be difficult not just for the general public but also for experts in machine learning to know why a machine makes the decisions it does (Ananny and Crawford 2016; Burrell 2016). Indeed, Yoshua Bengio has suggested that it is "exactly because we can't mathematically pick apart a decision made by deep learning software that it works so well" (Pearson 2016). This opacity is obviously problematic in terms of democratic accountability, but it can lead to significant instrumental benefits (Danaher 2016).

Perhaps the classic example of such algorithmically informed instrumental benefits is provided by Google search, whose initial popularity was the result of it turning the "dynamic and messy . . . World Wide Web" (Vaidhyanathan 2011, 61) into an easily navigated list of results hierarchized in accord with expected utility and general popularity (Vise 2005, 37). As such search capacities have continued to develop, and to be combined with other sets of data relatable to a given user—such as the user's age, nationality, educational background, travel history, reading history, video viewing history, and so on—algorithms have come to inform user experiences in increasingly specific ways.

Spotify's Discover Weekly provides a case in point. Every Monday morning users of Spotify find a list of thirty songs on their Discover Weekly playlist. This service has proved very popular and has resulted in what can only be termed a number of gushing testimonies. Ciocca (2017) for example, writes that

> I'm a huge fan of Spotify, and particularly Discover Weekly. Why? It makes me feel *seen*. It knows my musical tastes better than any person in my entire life ever has, and I'm consistently delighted by how satisfyingly *just right* it is every week, with tracks I probably would never have found myself or known I would like.

And in an interview with Pasick (2015), the person overseeing the Discover Weekly service, Matthew Ogle, explained,

> We now have more technology than ever before to ensure that if you're the smallest, strangest musician in the world, doing something that only 20 people in the world will dig, we can now find those 20 people and connect the dots between the artist and listeners. . . . Discovery Weekly is just a really compelling new way to do that at a scale that's never been done before.

Through a combination of techniques that include collaborative filtering models which analyze and compare users' behavior; natural language processing which analyzes text; and audio models that use deep learning to analyze a song's "time signature, key, mode, tempo and loudness" (Ciocca 2017)—Spotify's Discover Weekly works its "magic." Discover Weekly thus significantly reduces the work that individuals need to undertake to discover new music. Of course, the predictive capacities of such algorithmically informed realities also mean that they are commonly understood as constituting "a good first step toward controlling our behavior" (Morozov 2011, 158). Given such conflicting positions, the ways in which algorithmically informed realities shape (cultural) tastes, popularity, quality, and so on, is deserving of more (critical) attention than it currently receives.

Conclusion

With this chapter we have proposed that expert informed realities, popular informed realities, and algorithmically informed realities constrain and direct human choice and decision-making on the social web. Although we are aware that such informed realities also enable human freedom and autonomy in different ways (e.g., through enabling voice and providing alternatives to other media sources), we have chosen here to focus on their more directive and constraining aspects.

One reason why is that, despite the controlling and manipulative capacities of the online domain being relatively well understood in the scholarly literature, the general population still seems surprised by stories and leaks about the darker sides of technology use (e.g., Edward Snowden's release of the NSA files, Christopher Wylie's blowing the whistle on Facebook and Cambridge Analytica). Moreover, and despite a growing trend toward the leaders of such platforms being portrayed as supervillains in Hollywood (Harrison 2018), they continue to portray themselves, and the platforms they control, as being driving forces of the "open and connected," "free world" (read almost any Facebook or Google press release).

Although it appears that the constraining and directive capacities of the major platforms and services are likely to grow, potentially significantly, in the foreseeable future, there are a number of steps that might keep this in check. At the social or organizational level, efforts could be made to end the dominance of "sites and services owned and operated by Facebook and Google," which "account for over 70 percent of all internet traffic" (Cuthbertson 2017).

A recent piece in the conservative US publication the *National Review*, for example, has suggested that while it may not be time to smash Google, Facebook, and Amazon "to pieces . . . perhaps we should reign in some of their most egregious practices," such as Google's "leveraging its monopoly over Web search to take other companies' business" (Verbruggen 2017). And with ultimately similar concerns in mind, Bryan Lynn and Matt Stoller (2017) of the Open Market Institute have proposed that, while it is unclear how to "ensure Google, Facebook and the other giant platform monopolists truly serve the political and commercial interests of the American people," their dominance might be slowed down by stopping them from buying other companies.

Presuming the political will exists—in North America; in Europe, whose Commissioner for Competition, Margrethe Vestager, has been described as "a scourge of big technology companies" (Birnbaum 2018); or elsewhere—then these sorts of measures would likely result in consumers being provided with an increasing number of platforms and platform owners to choose from. Nevertheless, these measures would still not address the fact that digital platforms, and those associated with popular and algorithmically informed realities in particular, tend to constrain and direct human decision-making by design. So while it would likely be better for there to be a multitude of corporate, state, or nonprofit owners of social media platforms, such platforms will, on the current evidence, continue to direct and constrain human freedom in what are likely to prove increasingly sophisticated ways. Moreover, if platforms continue to be seen as having more benefits (e.g., entertainment, socializing) than costs (e.g., privacy, manipulation), then their usage rates will grow (Varian 2014).

Whether one ultimately thinks the social web is for good or bad, it seems prudent for people to recognize, and understand, the extent to which their decision-making is constrained and directed by it. If people then proceed—perhaps following a series of meaningful, and even antagonistic, series of debates (Whelan 2013)—to continue engaging with their preferred platforms, then it would seem contrary to the freedom and autonomy at the heart of the human rights project for others to deny them such choice.

References

Alaimo, Cristina, and Jannis Kallinikos. 2017. "Computing the Everyday: Social Media as Data Platforms. *Information Society* 33 (4): 175–191.

Ananny, Mike, and Kate Crawford. 2016. "Seeing without Knowing: Limitations of the Transparency Ideal and Its Application to Algorithmic Accountability." *New Media & Society* 20 (3): 973–989.

Benkler, Yochai. 2006. *The Wealth of Networks—How Social Production Transforms Markets and Freedom*. New Haven, CT: Yale University Press.

Berger, Peter L., and Thomas Luckmann. 1966. *The Social Construction of Reality: A Treatise in the Sociology of Knowledge*. New York: Anchor Books.

Birnbaum, Michael. 2018. "Europe's Antitrust Cop, Margrethe Vestager, has Facebook and Google in Her Crosshairs." *The Washington Post*, May 12. https://www .washingtonpost.com/world/europe/europes-antitrust-cop-margrethe-vestager-has -facebook-and-google-in-her-crosshairs/2018/05/10/519eb1a0-47cd-11e8-8082 -105a446d19b8_story.html?noredirect=on&utm_term=.a8fa16418a60.

Boisot, Max, and Agustí Canals. 2004. "Data, Information and Knowledge: Have We Got It Right?" *Journal of Evolutionary Economics* 14 (1): 43–67.

Bourdieu, Pierre. 1977. *Outline of a Theory of Practice*. Cambridge: Cambridge University Press.

———. 1984. *Distinction: A Social Critique of the Judgement of Taste*. Translated by Richard Nice. Cambridge, MA: Harvard University Press.

———. 1988. *Homo Academicus*. Stanford, CA: Stanford University Press.

Bowker, Geoffrey C., and Susan Leigh Star. 1999. *Sorting Things Out: Classification and Its Consequences*. Cambridge, MA: MIT Press.

BrightLocal. 2017. "Local Consumer Review Survey." https://www.brightlocal.com/ learn/local-consumer-review-survey.

Burrell, Jenna. 2016. "How the Machine 'Thinks': Understanding Opacity in Machine Learning Algorithms." *Big Data and Society*. doi:10.1177/2053951715622512.

Campbell, Tom. 2006. *Rights: A Critical Introduction*. London: Routledge.

Certeau, Michel de. 1984. *The Practice of Everyday Life*. Berkeley: University of California Press.

Ciocca, Sophia. 2017. "How Does Spotify Know You So Well?" *Medium*, October 10. https://medium.com/s/story/spotifys-discover-weekly-how-machine-learning-finds -your-new-music-19a41ab76efe.

Cuthbertson, Anthony. 2017. "Who Controls the Internet? Facebook and Google Dominance Could Cause the 'Death of the Web.'" *Newsweek*, November 2. http:// www.newsweek.com/facebook-google-internet-traffic-net-neutrality-monopoly -699286.

Czarniawska, Barbara. 1999. "Management She Wrote: Organization Studies and Detective Stories." *Studies in Cultures, Organizations and Societies* 5 (1): 13–41.

Danaher, John. 2016. "The Threat of Algocracy: Reality, Resistance and Accommodation." *Philosophy and Technology* 29: 245–268.

Davies, Scott, and Jessica Rizk. 2018. "Three Generations of Cultural Capital Research: A Narrative Review." *Review of Educational Research* 88 (3): 331–365.

Dewey, John. 1933. *How We Think: A Restatement of the Relation of Reflective Thinking to the Educative Process*, New Edition. Boston: Houghton Mifflin.

Dzieza, Josh. 2014. "A History of Metaphors for the Internet." *The Verge*, August 20. https://www.theverge.com/2014/8/20/6046003/a-history-of-metaphors-for-the -internet.

Eggers, Dave. 2014. *The Circle*. New York: Alfred A. Knopf.

Elliott, Chris. 2011. "Open Door: Does the Guardian Employ Too Many Oxbridge Graduates?" *The Guardian*, May 20. https://www.theguardian.com/commentisfree/ 2011/may/30/open-door-guardian-oxbridge-graduates.

Flyverbom, Mikkel. 2015. "Sunlight in Cyberspace? On Transparency as a Form of Ordering." *European Journal of Social Theory* 18 (2): 168–184.

———. 2016. "Disclosing and Concealing: Internet Governance, Information Control and the Management of Visibility." *Internet Policy Review—Journal on Internet Regulation* 5 (3).

Flyverbom, Mikkel, and Anders Koed Madsen. 2015. "Sorting Data Out: Unpacking Big Data Value Chains and Algorithmic Knowledge Production." In *Die Gesellschaft der Daten: Über die Digitale Transformation der Sozialen Ordnung*, edited by Florian Süssenguth, 123–144. Bielefeld: Transcript Verlag.

Flyverbom, Mikkel, and John Murray. 2018. "Datastructuring: Organizing and Curating Digital Traces into Action." *Big Data & Society* 5 (2).

Flyverbom, Mikkel, Paul Leonardi, Cynthia Stohl, and Michael Stohl. 2016. "The Management of Visibilities in the Digital Age." *International Journal of Communication* 10: 98–109.

Foucault, Michel. 1977. *Discipline and Punish: The Birth of the Prison*. New York: Random House.

———. 1991. "Governmentality." In *The Foucault Effect: Studies in Governmentality*, edited by Graham Burchell, Colin Gordon, and Peter Miller, 87–104. Chicago: University of Chicago Press.

Gabriel, John. 1998. *Whitewash: Radicalized Politics and the Media*. London: Routledge.

Gillespie, Tarleton. 2014. "The Relevance of Algorithms." In *Media Technologies: Essays on Communication, Materiality, and Society*, edited by Tarleton Gillespie, Pablo J. Boczkowski, and Kirsten A. Foot, 167–193. Cambridge, MA: MIT Press.

Gitelman, Lisa, ed. 2013. *"Raw Data" Is an Oxymoron*. Cambridge, MA: MIT Press.

Goodfellow, Ian, Yoshua Bengio, and Aaron Courville. 2016. *Deep Learning*. Cambridge, MA: MIT Press.

Google. 2019. *About Google*. https://www.google.com/about.

Habermas, Jürgen. 1978. *Knowledge and Human Interests*. 2nd ed. Translated by J. J. Shapiro. London: Heinemann.

———. 1989 (1962). *The Structural Transformation of the Public Sphere: An Inquiry into a Category of Bourgeois Society*. Translated by Thomas Burger with Frederick Lawrence. Cambridge: Polity Press.

———. 1996. *Between Facts and Norms: Contributions to a Discourse Theory of Law and Democracy*. Translated by William Rehg. Cambridge, MA: MIT Press.

Hacking, Ian. 1979. "Imre Lakatos's Philosophy of Science." *The British Journal for the Philosophy of Science* 30 (4, December): 381–402.

Hansen, Hans Krause, and Mikkel Flyverbom. 2015. "The Politics of Transparency and the Calibration of Knowledge in the Digital Age." *Organization* 22 (6): 872–889.

Hargittai, Esther, and Alice Marwick. 2016. "'What Can I Really Do?' Explaining the Privacy Paradox with Online Apathy." *International Journal of Communication* 10: 3737–3757.

Harrison, Angus. 2018. "Kill the Tech Bro, Save the World: How CEOs Became Hollywood's New Supervillains." *The Guardian*, June 6. https://www.theguardian.com/technology/2018/jun/06/tech-bros-ceo-hollywood-supervillains.

Hendrickson, Clara, and William A. Galston. 2017. "Why Are Populists Winning Online? Social Media Reinforces Their Anti-establishment Message." *Brooking Tech Tank*, April 28. https://www.brookings.edu/blog/techtank/2017/04/28/why-are-populists-winning-online-social-media-reinforces-their-anti-establishment-message.

Hutchby, Ian. 2001. "Technologies, Texts and Affordances." *Sociology* 35: 441–456.

Hutchison, Dot. 2016. *The Butterfly Garden*. Seattle, WA: Thomas & Mercer.

Isin, Engin, and Evelyn Ruppert. 2015. *Being Digital Citizens*. London: Rowman and Littlefield.

Kant, Immanuel. 1784. "An Answer to the Question: What Is Enlightenment?" In Immanuel Kant, 2006, *Toward Perpetual Peace and Other Writings on Politics, Peace and History*, edited by Pauline Kleingeld and translated by David L. Colclasure, 17–23. New Haven, CT: Yale University Press.

———. 1785 (1987). *Groundwork of the Metaphysics of Morals*. Edited by Mary Gregor. Cambridge: Cambridge University Press.

Klee, Miles. 2018. "Brendan Fraser's #MeToo Story Is Why More Male Victims Don't Speak Out." *Medium*, June 7. https://medium.com/mel-magazine/brendan-frasers-metoo-story-is-why-more-male-victims-don-t-speak-out-26ddbe49de70.

Langolis, Ganaele, Greg Elmer, Fenwick McKelvey, and Zachary Devereaux. 2009. "Networked Publics: The Double Articulation of Code and Politics on Facebook." *Canadian Journal of Communications* 34 (3): 415–434.

Lazzarato, Maurizio. 2004. "From Capital-Labour to Capital-Life." *Ephemera* 4 (3): 187–208.

Lessig, Lawrence. 2008. *Remix: Making Art and Commerce Thrive in the Hybrid Economy*. London: Bloomsbury.

Lynn, Barry, and Matt Stoller. 2017. "How to Stop Google and Facebook from Becoming Even More Powerful." *The Guardian*, November 2. https://www.theguardian.com/commentisfree/2017/nov/02/facebook-google-monopoly-companies.

Madsen, Anders Koed, Mikkel Flyverbom, Martin Hilbert, and Evelyn Ruppert. 2016. "Big Data: Issues for an International Political Sociology of Data Practices." *International Political Sociology* 10 (3): 275–296.

Mansell, Robin. 2017. "Our Digitally Mediated Society." In *Shifting Baselines of Europe: New Perspectives beyond Neoliberalism and Nationalism*, edited by D. Büllesbach, M. Cillero, and L. Stolz, 120–130. Bielefeld: Transcript Verlag.

Martin, Kirsten. 2018. "Ethical Implications and Accountability of Algorithms." *Journal of Business Ethics*. doi:10.1007/s10551-018-3921-3.

Medium. 2019. *Welcome to Medium.* https://medium.com/about.

Mendelsohn, Daniel. 2012. "A Critic's Manifesto." *The New Yorker*, August 28. http://www.newyorker.com/books/page-turner/a-critics-manifesto.

Meyrowitz, Joshua. 1985. *No Sense of Place: The Impact of Electronic Media and Social Behavior.* Oxford: Oxford University Press.

Miller, Peter, and Nikolas Rose. 1990. "Governing Economic Life." *Economy and Society* 19: 1–31.

Morozov, Evgeny. 2011. *The Net Delusion: How Not to Liberate the World.* London: Allen Lane.

Mudambi, Susan M., and David Schuff. 2010. "What Makes a Helpful Online Review? A Study of Customer Reviews on Amazon.com." *MIS Quarterly* 34 (1): 158–200.

Nardi, Bonnie A., and Vickie O'Day. 1999. *Information Ecologies: Using Technology with Heart.* Cambridge, MA: MIT Press.

Nickel, James W. 2006. *Making Sense of Human Rights.* 2nd ed. Malden, MA: Blackwell.

Pasick, Adam. 2015. "The Magic That Makes Spotify's Discover Weekly Playlists So Damn Good." *Quartz*, December 21. https://qz.com/571007/the-magic-that-makes-spotifys-discover-weekly-playlists-so-damn-good.

Pearson, Jordan. 2016. "When AI Goes Wrong, We Won't Be Able to Ask It Why." *Vice (Motherboard)*, July 6. http://motherboard.vice.com/read/ai-deep-learning-ethics-right-to-explanation.

Rabinow, Paul. 2011. "Dewey and Foucault: What's the Problem?" *Foucault Studies* 11: 11–19.

Rainie, Lee, and Janna Anderson. 2017. *Code-Dependent: Pros and Cons of the Algorithm Age.* Pew Research Center, February 2017. http://www.pewinternet.org/2017/02/08/code-dependent-pros-and-cons-of-the-algorithm-age.

Schmidt, Eric, and Jared Cohen. 2013. *The New Digital Age: Reshaping the Future of People, Nations, and Business.* London: John Murray.

Turner, Fred. 2009. "Burning Man at Google: A Cultural Infrastructure for New Media Production." *New Media & Society* 11 (1–2): 73–94.

Vaidhyanathan, Siva. 2011. *The Googlization of Everything (and Why We Should Worry)*. Berkeley: University of California Press.

Varian, Hal R. 2010. "Computer Mediated Transactions." *American Economic Review* 100 (2): 1–10.

———. 2014. "Beyond Big Data." *Business Economics* 49 (1): 27–31.

Verbruggen, Robert. 2017. "Google, Facebook, Amazon: Our Digital Overlords." *National Review*, December 12. https://www.nationalreview.com/2017/12/google -facebook-amazon-big-tech-becoming-problem.

Vise, David A. 2005. *The Google Story*. London: Pan Books.

Whelan, Glen. 2013. "The Value of Radical Dissent within Corporate Constructed Public Spheres: Differentiating Consensual from Dissensual Corporate Social Responsibility." *Journal of Business Ethics* 115 (4): 755–769.

———. 2019a. "Born Political: A Dispositive Analysis of Google and Copyright." *Business & Society* 58 (1): 42–73.

———. 2019b. "Trust in Surveillance: A Reply to Etzioni." *Journal of Business Ethics* 156 (1): 15–19.

Whelan, Glen, Jeremy Moon, and Bettina Grant. 2013. "Corporations and Citizen-ship Arenas in the Age of Social Media." *Journal of Business Ethics* 118 (4): 777–790.

Zaller, John R. 1992. *The Nature and Origins of Mass Opinion*. Cambridge: Cambridge University Press.

Zins, Chaim. 2007. "Conceptual Approaches for Defining Data, Information and Knowledge." *Journal of the American Society for Information Science and Technology* 58 (4): 479–493.

Zuboff, Shoshana. 2015. "Big Other: Surveillance Capitalism and the Prospects of an Information Civilization." *Journal of Information Technology* 30: 75–89.

———. 2019. *The Age of Surveillance Capitalism: The Fight for a Human Future at the New Frontier of Power*. New York: PublicAffairs.

Zuckerberg, Mark. 2016. "Some Thoughts." *Facebook*. November 12. https://www .facebook.com/zuck/posts/10103253901916271.

3 Data as Humans: Representation, Accountability, and Equality in Big Data

Anja Bechmann

Introduction

This chapter examines the democratic implications of how we treat data as humans in the datafied society, and how we process such data through machine learning algorithms. Democracy as a concept has a long history in political and social sciences. The focus of the chapter will be limited to the connection between the processing of *data as humans* in learning algorithms and the democratic values of representation (including participation), accountability, and equality.[1] In line with existing studies, I illustrate how systematic discrimination and inequality may occur through machine learning if we do not take the preliminary measure of inscribing these democratic values in the machine learning algorithms executed by, for instance, social media platforms. Moreover, I argue that free and open communication is an ideal that we must strive for if we wish to avoid democratic deficits. The chapter theorizes on whom data represents, what we (as society) do with data, and how we govern these practices. I argue that while some problems of representation in the datafied society are not new, problems of discrimination may now happen in a more systematic manner without yet receiving the same regulatory impact.

In the pursuit of as many different data points as possible, technology companies develop products that intersect and datafy every aspect of human existence from self-reports (social media) to location data (self-driving cars and maps) and biometrics (health apps, exercise wearables, and biojewelry). These data traces are increasingly used to inform product and processual decisions by companies that want to "listen" to the user and optimize recommendations, products, and revenue accordingly or by politicians and governments that want to "adjust" behavior using large data streams and big data methods. One example would be the recent Cambridge Analytica controversy and the use of social media data and microtargeting campaigns during the 2016 election of Donald Trump as US president that came as a shock to many citizens, including the press. Many blamed social media, because these platforms insisted on preserving the algorithm that provides users primarily with content that confirmed their social and political adherences (Bakshy, Messing, and Adamic 2015) and at the same time allowed for third parties to implement microtargeted campaigns.

It is important for social media companies to keep users on the platform for as long as possible in order to increase advertising profits through monetizing data (see Bermejo, this volume), and one way to do this is to display content that users agree with (Bakshy, Messing, and Adamic 2015). A platform like Facebook represents a large public forum for reading, viewing, listening to, and participating in discussions; however, the company is registered as a technology company, not a media company with press responsibilities. On Facebook, we do not know the principles and values (as opposed to journalistic values as outlined in International Federation of Journalists 1986) behind the editing done by the algorithm and are unable to see each other's personalized news feeds. This is radically different from traditional editorials, where we can discuss the principles, and printed papers where we were/are able to purchase or subscribe to full papers with different viewpoints.

The chapter seeks to discuss such problems not only on the algorithmic level but also on the level of data, which plays an increasingly important role in everyday life (Schäfer and van Es 2017). The data that we leave behind when we use online platforms are central elements of the global online economy and a defining and pertinent characteristic of a citizen in the digital age, as is the processing of such data. Critical voices question whether informed consent is an option anymore, as it is impossible for companies to provide a comprehensible account of the vast places data is being used (Bechmann 2014; Nissenbaum 2011). Despite the right to access and transport one's own data (Regulation [EU] 2016/679 of the European Parliament and of the Council L 119/1), it is debatable how this right should be executed and controlled. Opting out of the datafied society is no longer an option. Even so, exclusion from data-enriched decisions may also have profound consequences for the equal representation of individuals in society (Ananny 2016). In response to these challenges, my questions are these:

How does democratic society strive to ensure that all humans are properly and equally represented—that is, that data traces actually represent the user and that all users are part of the data processing on equal terms? And how does it ensure that algorithmic decisions are transparent and reliable?

These questions cannot be answered easily, but they must be addressed; therefore, they drive the discussion in this chapter. Theoretically, the chapter draws on pragmatism (Dewey 1927) and cyberfeminist theory (Bowker and Star 1999; Haraway 1991; Star 1990) to account for the meaning of underrepresentation, unaccountability, discrimination, and inequality as constituting democratic deficits in the use of big social data and machine learning. The chapter will draw on previous empirical work carried out primarily with social media data, focusing on Facebook data as one of the most well-known sources of data enrichment and the use of big data methods such as cluster analysis, neural networks, and deep learning to account for usage patterns as a source of insight into human behavior and preferences. The purpose of the chapter is to provide critical insights into the consequences of (a lack of) data quality in machine learning processing.

Representation and Participation as Democratic Values

Let us begin by examining social media platforms and how such platforms themselves, and the datafied society at large (third parties), use social media as a data source for prediction through machine learning. In considering democracy in the datafied society, I will turn to the encounter between Lippmann and Dewey in the 1920s in which Lippmann criticizes the public as "the phantom public" (Lippmann 1927) and the ability for citizens to represent public opinion based on democratic values. In brief, Lippmann (ibid.) sees experts, facts, and science as the solution to the problem of the public and the sustainability of democratic values. Dewey (Dewey 1927; Bybee 1999) recognizes the problem but disagrees on the solution. Instead of relying on experts, facts, and science, he argues that democracy is created, situated, and negotiated through the agency of citizens and their participation in the construction of democracy, thereby empowering both individuals *and* the social group:

> [Democracy] consists in having a responsible share according to capacity in forming and directing the activities of the groups to which one belongs and in participating according to need in the values which the groups sustain. From the

standpoint of the groups, it demands liberation of the potentialities of members of a group in harmony with the interests and goods which are common. Since every individual is a member of many groups, this specification cannot be fulfilled except when different groups interact flexibly and fully in connection with other groups . . . there is a free give-and-take: fullness of integrated personality is therefore possible of achievement, since the pulls and responses of different groups reinforce one another and their values accord. (Dewey 1927, 148)

In this sense, Dewey wants to restore agency to the users or citizens as a way of negotiating values and meanings in smaller or larger groups.[2] He does not consider democracy to be something that relates solely to politics and the public sphere but rather as a basic social construct in groups. Democracy happens in both the public and private spheres and does not connect only to public opinion. He also argues for an epistemological politics of "By what right do we act?" instead of "What are the facts?" (Dewey 1927, 69). Open and free communication plays a central role in this value creation, enabling "a public to act as a public" (Dewey 1927, 55) and to judge how actions influence shared interests. Communication thereby creates the "very meaning that will be called knowledge" (ibid.).

Lippmann and Dewey's debate on democratic values and the public is relevant when it comes to user participation in social media today (posts, comments, likes, and shares) and the way algorithms control how communication is handled—whether on social media sites themselves or for data collected from them for predictions in other domains such as targeting and manipulation in political campaigns, risk assessments in financial sectors, or diagnoses and treatments in the health sector. On social media, individuals are represented through their data and connected and processed through algorithms. Users develop networks of, and memberships in, several groups and communicate on broad or narrow topics of interest, with a broader or narrower group of people, and with strong or weak ties (Bechmann, Kim, and Søgaard 2016). In many ways, social media is the ideal participation platform in Dewey's terminology, as it allows people to participate in debates across spheres. However, the transparency of who we are talking to and sharing behavioral data with and the overlap between groups have been the subject of extensive critical analysis (Bakshy, Messing, and Adamic 2015; Marwick and boyd 2014; Stutzman, Gross, and Acquisti 2012). This topic has received renewed interest in the light of recent cases and events such as Cambridge Analytica, Brexit, and the election of Trump as US president, raising the issues of informed consent (Bechmann 2014), free and open communication, and the need for different groups to meet as the basis for participatory democracy in Dewey's sense. This debate reinforces the necessity of considering how data is constructed as a representation of the individual and the way algorithms encourage exchanges across groups *with different interests.*

Equality and Accountability as Democratic Values

Dewey's focus is not primarily on whether all individuals have the same premises for participating in the creation of knowledge and democratic values and how free and open communication can be accounted for. This is a key concern of cyberfeminist theory as set out in Haraway (1991) and Star (1990). Haraway's theory of the integration of technology and humans generates an interesting perspective: data not as something "apart" or alienated from the individual but as an equal part of humans just like the body. Data cannot then be rejected as something alienating or "out there" (see also Mai's discussion on personal information in this volume). Users may experience data as something bad or something that has been violated; the sense of "embodiment" contained in this feeling is striking in earlier studies on, for instance, cyber rape (Turkle 1995). Thus, from an algorithmic or developer's point of view, data cannot be treated as something that is *nonhuman*—if we view it from the perspective of Haraway's cyborg discussion, it is indeed an integrated part of the human being. There is no mother-and-child or host-and-guest relationship, nor any extension of the body as described in McLuhan (1964). Haraway's point is that developing a perspective on data similar to that set out in McLuhan's medium theory allows for alienation and a critical discussion of technology and data as something potentially harmful that can turn against humans. On the other hand, if we do not hierarchize the relationship, then we are already technology, data is already us.

Still, just as earlier cases of census and statistical data in aggregate show (Anderson 2015; Desrosières 2002), data does not equally represent all humans. The difference between traditional survey data and social media data is that in social media settings some humans create more data points than others. Star (1990) has a strong focus on the underrepresented in specific socio-technical networks. Building on Law (1990), she also argues for technology as an arena for modulation, tacit power relations, interests, and conflicts. I will argue that questions of inclusion and exclusion (Kroll et al. 2017; Law 1990) also become relevant in the discussion on democracy, social big data, and machine learning processing. Star (Bowker and Star 1999; Star 1990) has a strong focus on the outliers—the underrepresented or "monsters" (Law 1990) that give meaning to the normal (Crawford and Calo 2016; Metcalf and Crawford 2016). To her, underrepresentation and abnormality can take many forms, from sexuality and gender to being allergic. What they all have in common is that such individuals do not decide on the shared knowledge or meaning that binds the socio-technical network together in the manner suggested by Dewey. Unable to act, they are nonetheless important as a nonagent and as a confirmation of the rules for inclusion and exclusion. In the next section I will exemplify how I see such underrepresentation encoded into the algorithmic processing of social big data and how this may subsequently lead to discrimination against protected classes (Charter of Fundamental Rights of the European Union, Article 21).

Bowker and Star (1999) suggest that by accounting for the different levels of exclusion, we are able to understand how the socio-technical is political by nature. Accountability then also becomes an interesting aspect in terms of democracy. Although Star does not explicitly discuss democracy, I will combine her proposals with those of Dewey to argue that accountability of underrepresentation and inequalities (Calo 2017; Crawford and Calo 2016; Kroll et al. 2017) in the socio-technical is part of the transparency of participation processes that Dewey considers to be the core of democracy. I will argue that the accountability of data input and machine learning processing workflows rather than a focus on the transparency of the algorithm itself (Ananny and Crawford 2018) is essential if we are to maintain an understanding of inclusion and exclusion rules *as well as* transparency in data processing. Still, this accountability does not solve the participation dilemma generated by social media platforms—thus the difficulty for citizens of both participating *and* resisting datafication. This dilemma shows that Dewey-inspired participation in a datafied society may conflict with the right to privacy (see also van Hoboken's analysis of datafication and privacy in chapter 10 of this volume).

The Politics of Algorithms

Machine learning is built into social media algorithms as the backbone of the service, and by third-party companies as a way to interpret user behavior and preferences. Algorithms are programs that control the logic and presentation of digital platforms and services, the specific recipe behind any computational decision:

> Algorithms are now a communication technology; like broadcasting and publishing technologies, they are now "the scientific instruments of a society at large," (Gitelman 2006, 5) and are caught up in and are influencing the ways in which we ratify knowledge for civic life, but in ways that are more "protocological" (Galloway 2004), i.e. organized computationally, than any medium before. (Gillespie 2014, 169)

This chapter builds on the basic argument that the algorithms we use in data-driven decision-making are not objective tools that simply compute data. They are highly error prone, interpretive, and in need of adjustments to perform optimally, and in that sense, they are political and normative in nature. This argument is present in many existing critical contributions on algorithms within communication and media studies (Ananny and Crawford 2018; Bodle 2015; Bucher 2012; Cheney-Lippold 2011; Kitchin 2014; Leese 2014; Pasquale 2015; Turow 2011).[3] These studies focus on algorithms as a cultural phenomenon with unintended consequences for society. One such consequence relates to the exploitation of user data, the commodification of personal data, and resulting challenges concerning the right to privacy (Cheney-Lippold 2011; Leese 2014; Solove 2004; Turow 2011).

Other critical accounts focus on surveillance mechanisms, where the discourse on algorithms does not relate primarily to how such computational processes violate individual privacy but rather, on the basis of Foucault (1977), considers how they function as power tools for centralized entities such as a state or a government to control, adjust, and impose certain values upon the potentially surveilled citizen (Introna and Wood 2004; Lyon 2007).

Another array of studies show how algorithms have consequences for what is presented to us as relevant information and communication. Algorithms as filters are discussed in terms of filter bubbles, echo chambers, and digital divides (Bodle 2015; Bucher 2012; Introna and Nissenbaum 2000; Mager 2012; Rogers 2009). These bodies of literature focus on the democratic values of freedom of expression and social cohesion as threatened in a personalized online space controlled by a small number of powerful gatekeepers such as Google, Facebook, Microsoft, Amazon, and Apple.

Taken together, these critical algorithmic studies offer important insights into the societal consequences of algorithms and, indirectly, into how basic human rights and democratic values can potentially be violated through algorithms in a manner that is subtle, sometimes undeliberate, yet highly effective. A fairly new interdisciplinary approach to critical algorithmic studies consists of "audit" (Sandvig et al. 2014), "decipher" (Rieder 2005), or reverse engineering studies that seek to discuss the communicative consequences of algorithmic processing through a close analysis of the actual structures and logics of specific statistical models or algorithmic constructions (Diakopoulos and Koliska 2017; Mackenzie 2015; Rieder 2017). These studies show that algorithms encode certain types of values (Mackenzie 2015) in the way they classify (Rieder 2017), cluster, or sort the data for a certain purpose without the developers knowing exactly how the statistical model or algorithm leads to a particular optimal pattern or outcome predictor. I will supplement this interesting body of literature with my own empirical work to provide examples of how underrepresentation and inequality can occur in practice.

Big Social Data as Population and Census Data

All machine learning processing is conducted with the aim of recognizing patterns in order to predict outputs, which for instance can then be used for persecution, credit scores and subsequent insurance and loan offerings, health care, and propaganda. As algorithms become widely used to structure our culture and democracy, it is crucial for society, in an interdisciplinary manner, to illustrate errors and interpretative spaces and to inscribe the "human" in standardized processes carried out to execute decisions fast and seamlessly. This is of particular importance when algorithmic decision-making moves from product and service optimization and marketing into the realm of governmental data and when such data is paired with social media data. Algorithmic decisions made here not only affect the media "bubbles" we live in, the people we engage with or exclude in consumer society (Bauman 2000)—they also affect our health care, educational opportunities, and probability of being a political target (Noyes 2015). In this section, I will focus on Facebook as an arena for the creation of big social data that is often used for data enrichment to understand and predict user behavior both on and outside Facebook.

I will then examine more closely the critical algorithmic theories on the processes at work in machine learning models and provide examples from my own experience applying such models to Facebook data in order to illustrate the interpretive spaces and politics of such algorithms. In this way, I will focus on both the data layer and the model layer in algorithmic processing (Diakopoulos and Koliska 2017).

Facebook data is an example of an overwhelming pool of data that developers could access and use for various purposes, ranging from systematic surveillance to recruiting, political campaigning, and service optimization.[4] Currently, Facebook is globally only surpassed by Reddit as the online platform people spend the most time on (alexa.com), and Facebook data contains a wealth of different data points from self-reported demographics, interests (likes and shares), and personal accounts and opinions (status updates, photos, links, and comments) to network and behavioral data (visit to external sites with Facebook plug-ins). The overwhelming amount of data both vertically and horizontally (over time) often lead to *data rush*—overly enthusiastic and bold uses of the data as an example of human behavior and opinions worldwide. Often, people are portrayed solely in terms of data for the purposes of predictions and subsequent decisions. This has fundamental consequences for the representation of individuals in decisions based on those data. For example, a study of the total amount of private status updates, shared links, and photos among 1,000 Danes over a period of eight years (Bechmann, 2019 in press) shows that the number of data traces created varies greatly when broken down into demographics, especially age. This means that when one is using such data—for example, in connection with the provision of public services —those who only read or listen are underrepresented and excluded from the data set that informs decision-making. Furthermore, although Facebook has a large penetration rate in many countries—often higher than Twitter, Snapchat, Instagram, and noninternational platforms—the data fails to represent those who are not active users of these platforms. Active users are here understood as those who leave data traces behind to be processed by algorithms (Hargittai and Walejko 2008). Thus, when using social big data as an input in machine learning processing to represent populations, the data pool may be extremely large but the sample bias is also significant. Often people "game" the Facebook advertising algorithm (Bechmann 2015; Marwick and boyd 2014) by deliberately reporting fake demographic parameters, rendering the data quality weaker and, potentially, the predictions made from such data false if the calculations are not enriched with other data.

Sample bias is nothing new and as a concept has existed throughout the history of the political and social sciences (Desrosières 2002). Critics would argue that representation is always a problem when we have to reduce populations via aggregation and work with census data (Anderson 2015), so what is new? There are at least two differences here. Social media data is produced in private domains with limited transparency obligations. When enriching public data with, for instance, social media data to create a more detailed understanding of personal behaviors and preferences, it is difficult to account for sample biases in detail and, consequently, for how the data sets used for predictions are effectively balanced. Furthermore, the data functions not only as a one-step analytical phase but also as training data for machine learning algorithms. This training data is often not provided from the same data pool. These data steps therefore obscure even further the results of the analysis and research phase before decision-making takes place. Cambridge Analytica is a good example of this, where people's data was used to train a model to find the most predictive Facebook behaviors and attributes (e.g., like profiles) for a certain psychological profiles that again allowed the company to target specific voters with carefully tailored content.

Machine Learning and Training Data

Data in machine learning processing therefore becomes an issue not only in terms of the quality of data input itself but also in terms of its suitability for training the algorithms to recognize patterns and clusters and to create classifications. The more data and the more diversified training data you have, the better your algorithm potentially is at recognizing new data. The algorithm can only interpret data and predict patterns from the data that it has already seen (training data). However, studies and incidents have shown that training data is biased historically, culturally, and contextually. Google, for instance, labeled black people as gorillas (Cohen 2019), and a study has shown how women were described with discriminatory words due to the historical role of women as, for instance, housewives (Bolukbasi et al. 2016). To generate enough training data for the algorithm to recognize patterns and connect those patterns to certain labels, researchers and developers often use data that spans a wide historical period. In such cases, training data creates a preservative construct of associated meanings and words with key concepts that may, for instance, enforce a conservative cultural understanding of the role of women. While societal values and interpretations are in general moving toward a more inclusive and diverse society and the nondiscrimination principle operates with protected classes, decisions and predictions automated through machine learning may reinforce historical biases. This, in turn, pulls societal values in the opposite direction from inclusiveness and diversity. Still, one could claim that the data is sound proof of Dewey's participatory democracy in the sense that the data is a result of what people do with data in a particular domain or context, not what they ought to be doing according to democratic values of representation, accountability, and equality.

Similar problems arise when training data is used in, for instance, picture recognition and classification algorithms through deep convolutional neural networks. Here, training data is also the most important factor in high performance. Such algorithms are usually trained on what is available, which often means large picture databases such as ImageNet with its 1,000 classes of pictures (e.g., dogs, trees, flowers) as the potential outcome of the algorithmic processing (the last layer in the network). To Internet industries such as IBM (Watson), Alphabet (Google), Amazon, Facebook, Tesla, and Microsoft, having a large and diverse pool of annotated training data becomes a lucrative business that potentially puts their algorithms and products at the forefront of the machine learning field. However, using algorithms trained on certain types of data may lead to decisions based on a false interpretation of the data source. If a picture classification algorithm is trained on a data set containing various types of annotated data (human as well as animal), the interpretation of human faces may resemble that of animal faces and thereby lead to false, and in terms of inclusion deeply problematic, classifications and decisions. In our own research lab, we tried to use vision convolutional neural networks pretrained on ImageNet to classify social media pictures (Bechmann 2017). The performance was very poor when compared to manual annotation and may indicate that contextual sensitivity in the training data is essential for the performance of the algorithms and consequently as the basis for sustainable predictions and actions. In our case sensitivity toward social media features such as the importance of text in pictures and image focus led to false classifications of the picture from a sociological perspective. Also, the interpretation of clothes generated false output categories because the training data presumably contained health care–related pictures in which staff wore uniforms that resemble white leisure wear; thus the model tried to interpret leisure clothes as business attire and provided a completely wrong prediction of the picture.

So how can we create context-sensitive annotated training data? Natural language processing researchers Derczynski, Bontcheva, and Roberts (2016) suggest that if the right type of data is available as training data, social media data is best annotated by a combination of experts/researchers and a diverse crowd of social media users. They also show how crowd training and continual performance measurements are a clear feature of social media annotations. Furthermore, they discuss how the reduction of output categories to between seven and ten is important for automatic clustering. However, despite higher performance with reduced multidimensional complexity in output categories, this reduction of complexity can be problematic for representation and democratic actions. Although a small number of computationally isolated categories do enable higher performance, the reduction in itself may give a false picture of data as humans. For instance, Facebook operates with six different categories of "like" in the data structure in order to understand the emotional reactions toward a post, despite the psychological field suggesting eight categories and twenty-four associated emotional dimensions (Plutchik 2001). The reduction of multidimensionality in data processing may simply lead to measurement errors and false conclusions, predictions, and decisions in the use of data as humans.

Mathematical Models, Abnormality and Outliers

In the model layer (Diakopoulos and Koliska 2017), working with statistical learning models in machine learning and related interpretations and decisions may also lead to underrepresentation and inequality, as with the selections previously considered in the data layer. Rieder (2017) shows how Bayes classifiers, the most widespread prediction model within big data, produce "a basis for decision-making that is not a clear-cut formula, but an adaptive statistical model containing potentially hundreds of thousands of variables" (Rieder 2017, 110). Accountability for the calculation of such variables may be very complicated. This was also true for the use of learning models (e.g., topic models and convolutional neural networks) tested at my research lab (datalab.au.dk). In our experience with topic models, it can be very time-consuming, if at all possible, to understand the statistical logic of clusters and the implications of such logic for clusters. In other words, why do these particular clusters result from the machine learning processing? The logic appears on a linguistic level (Jurafsky and Martin 2008; Manning and Schütze 1999) that does not necessarily relate to human field-specific interpretations. This discrepancy potentially distorts the actions carried out on the basis of the clusters found. The choices made in the preprocessing of data can create very different cluster predictions depending on what kind of words are included or omitted from the data set. Omitting words that have a tendency to occur in connection with certain groups of people or minorities in order to normalize data and create "meaningful" clusters reduces their representation and "voices" in the final actions, just as omitting data from abnormal users would in classical social and behavioral sciences. Another example is that the developer's choice of the optimal number of topics or distance between the different clusters significantly influences the visibility of less normal behavior or "monsters" (Law 1990) in the data. A larger distance creates less sensitivity toward diversity, whereas a smaller distance will potentially provide sensitivity to differences and diversity in the data. Setting the optimal numbers of clusters or distance requires closer examination and judgment based on data explorations, as we sought to ensure when balancing redundancy against diversity (Bechmann, Kim, and Søgaard 2016). On the other hand, microsegmentation (Bechmann, Bilgrav-Nielsen, and Jensen 2016) creates potential challenges to privacy, as abnormal or deviant usages and users *light up* in models with a large number of clusters. Such visibility can be used against users' interests in risk assessments and behavioral adjustments by authoritarian regimes and other oppressive entities.

In our work with convolutional neural networks on pictures it is equally difficult, if not more difficult, to account for meaningful subclusters created in the various layers of the network, even though researchers are able to account for the mathematical logic in different machine learning models (Davenport and Harris 2007; Freedman 2005; Zumel and Mount 2014).

Consequently, accounting for the exact reasons for certain predictions is very difficult (Bechmann 2017). For businesses with an interest in performance this is not relevant, but for a democratic society that values accountability in decision-making processes it is a major issue (Calo 2017). False positives and false negatives may be hard to account for and instead have to be adjusted for through manual/human alerts and new training and test data iterations. With the development of still more complex models with an increasing number of layers, the challenge of accountability grows. And if such machine learning models have a still more widespread and seamless use in various products, services, and decisions, the processing of manual reports of false positives and negatives may not be prioritized enough, as this requires significant resources from industry and government. Abnormal patterns or "monsters" thereby have a potential to create false positives and negatives because the training data is not sufficient to take these patterns into account in the interpretation and prediction of clusters, or the training data is not labeled sufficiently to take into account such rare or abnormal occurrences. This was also the case before machine learning, but the layers of adjusting for abnormality now become more complex. The lack of training data or labels for innovative structures, minorities, and deviant picture patterns have consequences for the ability of the datafied society to process data as humans on equal terms, especially if this is not a focal point in the design, training, and documentation of the models and their use in specific contexts.

These applied examples illustrate cases in which accountability is difficult and underrepresentation, inequality, and discrimination may easily occur. However, these are just examples of choices made when working with big social data and machine learning that have profound consequences for the democratic values of representation, accountability, and equality. Other examples include the choice of accuracy measures, confidence values, and interpretations of uncertainty information (Diakopoulos and Koliska 2017). The scientific field of machine learning thus filters out outliers but at the same time strives to achieve near-human processing (Harnad 2000; Turing 1950). Machine learning tries to avoid a simple human model but at the same time uses models that normalize data and find similar results (Ananny 2016) instead of concentrating on diversity, for instance in terms of outliers. To create a deeper understanding of the data processing that occurs and ideally enable equal treatment of all humans, documentation of the algorithmic processing is *not* a stand-alone solution (Ananny and Crawford 2018; Cohen 2019). Even if we demanded a circumvention of the intellectual property rights of companies and/or accountability for public data processing, this would be too complex to account for and also insufficient, because discrimination happens when the algorithm is applied to the data as described in this section.

Conclusion

The chapter has provided a conceptual background for data as humans on the basis of Dewey's theory of participatory democracy, and a further development of this theory using cyberfeminist theory to highlight problems with the interpretation of data as humans. It has highlighted challenges to representation, accountability and equality as democratic values and exemplified how such underrepresentation, discrimination, and unaccountability can take place in specific uses of machine learning processing on social big data. These examples have shown how the selection and processing of social big data is profoundly political in nature, thus the examples support existing critical voices in algorithmic studies.

Taking social media as its starting point, the chapter has analyzed democracy on two different levels; as media for democratic debate in Dewey's sense and as a data source for decision-making on a broader scale that defines the citizen in a datafied society (here, social media data plays a role for interpreting the citizen).

Firstly, the chapter has suggested that we should focus not on accounting for the algorithm itself as a standalone solution, but on the *social values* that have been encoded into the algorithm directly or indirectly as (political) choices made by developers. Examples might be: What are the social values of the choices made by Facebook to only show posts people agree with in order to maximize time spent on the platform, or to censor nude pictures? Western media (which social media platforms deliberately avoid registering as) are accustomed to transparency on such issues, but they are challenged by increasingly global social media that also target non-Western societies. Furthermore, such transparency is challenged by Facebook's content moderators situated in different cultures from the ones they serve and with very little editorial education compared to journalists. Can we internationally agree on shared values such as human rights and if not, would it serve democracy and the online public debate to regulate for market cultural sensitivity, that is, sensitivity toward different cultural interpretations of gender equality?

Secondly, the chapter has suggested a political and regulatory focus on documentation and accountability—not as open access to the actual (and often, in private domains, legally protected) algorithm as the only solution, but in terms of an increased focus on normalization logics and the potential negative consequences for protected classes, abnormal behavior, minorities, and underrepresented groups as a part of documenting compliance with international human rights law and the democratic values of representation, accountability and equality. We need new standards for how we create balanced big data data sets, and how we document such balance. Ultimately, if we do not find an effective modus operandi for demanding this documentation of balance and compliance, we will widen the divides already experienced in society more systematically. Again, critical voices would claim that these divides already exist, but I would argue that the systematic and integrated nature of these divides is what sets them apart as new. We no longer have a process of analysis and research followed by actions: instead, we now have a single computational process that operates in loops. If we do not account for balance and compliance with social values, citizen data mining (including in the welfare state) may develop into systematic self-reinforcing loops of discrimination due to the closed learning cycles of machine learning algorithms, informed by big social data.

Dewey's ideal of participatory democracy is not without negative consequences, especially in terms of user privacy when data points increase in tandem with participation. Apart from this big dilemma, future research needs to focus not only on how accountability is created in the different stages of machine learning processing for big (social) data, but also on how such accountability is made accessible to society at large. Finally, "Underrepresented" and outlier focus accounts (e.g., due to false negatives and positives) are a radically different way of approaching big data compared to engineering approaches tackling data-processing techniques and computational optimization. This emphasizes the need for media and communication sociologists to engage and contribute to the field of machine learning so that the analytical models we use in future research as well as in wider society can be tailored to a humanistic approach. This means accounting in detail for the human, both in terms of data and in terms of human decisions in the data processing through machine learning algorithms. By doing so, we may provide a deeper and more detailed account of how power relations are enacted through algorithms and how platforms and services are shaped by designers and users, and in turn shape society.

Notes

1. The right to equality and nondiscrimination is recognized in Article 2 of the Universal Declaration of Human Rights and is a crosscutting standard in different UN human rights instruments. Accountability is a process value related to transparency and the rule of law (see also McGonagle, chapter 9, this volume).

2. This perspective is also found in the growing body of literature on data activism (see, e.g., Gray 2018; Milan 2013).

3. For more references, see https://socialmediacollective.org/reading-lists/critical-algorithm-studies.

4. Facebook restricted the API for third party use in 2019 and has now chosen to commercialize the data and knowledge within the company's own platforms, preventing anyone from monitoring their use of this data.

References

Ananny, Mike. 2016. "Toward an Ethics of Algorithms: Convening, Observation, Probability, and Timeliness." *Science, Technology, & Human Values* 41 (1): 93–117. https://doi.org/10.1177/0162243915606523.

Ananny, Mike, and Kate Crawford. 2018. "Seeing without Knowing: Limitations of the Transparency Ideal and Its Application to Algorithmic Accountability." *New Media & Society* 20 (3): 973–989.

Anderson, Margo J. 2015. *American Census: A Social History*. 2nd ed. New Haven, CT: Yale University Press.

Bakshy, Eytan, Solomon Messing, and Lada A. Adamic. 2015. "Exposure to Ideologically Diverse News and Opinion on Facebook." *Science* 348 (6239): 1130–1132. https://doi.org/10.1126/science.aaa1160.

Bauman, Zygmunt. 2000. *Liquid Modernity*. Cambridge: Polity Press.

Bechmann, Anja. 2014. "Non-Informed Consent Cultures: Privacy Policies and App Contracts on Facebook." *Journal of Media Business Studies* 11 (1): 21–38.

———. 2015. "Managing the Interoperable Self." In *The Ubiquitous Internet: User and Industry Perspectives*, edited by Anja Bechmann and Stine Lomborg, 54-73. New York: Routledge.

————. 2017. "Keeping It Real: From Faces and Features to Social Values in Deep Learning Algorithms on Social Media Images." *Proceedings of the 50th Hawaii International Conference on System Sciences*, 1793–1801. Hilton Waikoloa Village, Hawaii. https://doi.org/10.24251/HICSS.2017.218.

————. 2019 (in press). "Inequality in Posting Behavior over Time: A Study of Danish Facebook Users." *Nordicom Review* 40 (1).

Bechmann, Anja, Kirstine Bilgrav-Nielsen, and Anne-Louise K. Jensen. 2016. "Data as a Revenue Model." *Nordicom Information* 38 (1): 76–82.

Bechmann, Anja, Jiyoung Ydun Kim, and Anders Søgaard. 2016. "What We Use Facebook Groups For: A Cross-National Comparison of Private Facebook Groups." Paper presented at the Annual Seminar for Association of Media Researchers in Denmark. Middelfart, Denmark: SMID.

Bodle, Robert. 2015. "Predictive Algorithms and Personalization Services on Social Network Sites: Implications for Users and Society." In *The Ubiquitous Internet*, edited by Anja Bechmann and Stine Lomborg, 130–145. New York: Routledge.

Bolukbasi, Tolga, Kai-Wei Chang, James Y. Zou, Venkatesh Saligrama, and Adam T. Kalai. 2016. "Man Is to Computer Programmer as Woman Is to Homemaker? Debiasing Word Embeddings." *Advances in Neural Information Processing Systems*, 4349–4357.

Bowker, Geoffrey C., and Susan Leigh Star. 1999. *Sorting Things Out: Classification and Its Consequences*. Cambridge, MA: MIT Press.

Bucher, Taina. 2012. "Want to Be on the Top? Algorithmic Power and the Threat of Invisibility on Facebook." *New Media & Society* 14 (7): 1164–1180.

Bybee, Carl. 1999. "Can Democracy Survive in the Post-Factual Age? A Return to the Lippmann-Dewey Debate about the Politics of News." *Journalism & Communication Monographs* 1 (1): 28–66.

Calo, Ryan. 2017. "Artificial Intelligence Policy: A Primer and Roadmap." *U.C. Davis Law Review* 51: 399–436.

Cheney-Lippold, John. 2011. "A New Algorithmic Identity: Soft Biopolitics and the Modulation of Control." *Theory, Culture & Society* 28 (6): 164–181.

Cohen, Julie E. 2019. "Turning Privacy Inside Out." *Theoretical Inquiries in Law* 20 (1). https://papers.ssrn.com/abstract=3162178.

Crawford, Kate, and Ryan Calo. 2016. "There Is a Blind Spot in AI Research." *Nature News* 538 (7625): 311. https://doi.org/10.1038/538311a.

Davenport, Thomas H., and Jeanne G. Harris. 2007. *Competing on Analytics: The New Science of Winning*. Boston: Harvard Business Press.

Derczynski, Leon, Kalina Bontcheva, and Ian Roberts. 2016. "Broad Twitter Corpus: A Diverse Named Entity Recognition Resource." In *Proceedings of COLING 2016*, 1169–1179. https://aclanthology.info/papers/C16-1111/c16-1111.

Desrosières, Alain. 2002. *The Politics of Large Numbers*. Cambridge, MA: Harvard University Press.

Dewey, John. 1927. *The Public and Its Problems*. New York: Holt, reprint 1946.

Diakopoulos, Nicholas, and Michael Koliska. 2017. "Algorithmic Transparency in the News Media." *Digital Journalism* 5 (7): 809–828.

Foucault, Michel. 1977. *Discipline and Punish: The Birth of the Prison*. New York: Vintage Books.

Freedman, David. 2005. *Statistical Models: Theory and Practice*. New York: Cambridge University Press.

Galloway, Alexander R. 2004. *Protocol: How Control Exists after Decentralization*. Cambridge, MA: MIT Press.

Gillespie, Tarleton. 2014. "The Relevance of Algorithms." In *Media Technologies: Essays on Communication, Materiality, and Society*, edited by Tarleton Gillespie, Pablo J. Boczkowski, and Kirsten A. Foot, 167–193. Cambridge, MA: MIT Press.

Gitelman, Lisa. 2006. *Always Already New*. Cambridge, MA: MIT Press.

Gray, Jonathan. 2018. "Three Aspects of Data Worlds." *Krisis: Journal for Contemporary Philosophy* (1): 4–17.

Haraway, Donna. 1991. *Simians, Cyborgs and Women: The Reinvention of Nature*. New York: Routledge.

Hargittai, Eszter, and Gina Walejko. 2008. "The Participation Divide: Content Creation and Sharing in the Digital Age." *Information Communication & Society* 11 (2): 239–256.

Harnad, Stevan. 2000. "Minds, Machines and Turing." *Journal of Logic, Language and Information* 9 (4): 425–445.

International Federation of Journalists. 1986. *Principles of Conduct of Journalism*. https://www.ifj.org/who/rules-and-policy/principles-on-conduct-of-journalism.html.

Introna, Lucas, and Helen Nissenbaum. 2000. "Shaping the Web: Why the Politics of Search Engines Matters." *The Information Society* 16 (3): 169–185.

Introna, Lucas, and David Wood. 2004. "Picturing Algorithmic Surveillance: The Politics of Facial Recognition Systems." *Surveillance & Society* 2 (2–3). https://ojs.library.queensu.ca/index.php/surveillance-and-society/article/view/3373.

Jurafsky, Daniel, and James H. Martin. 2008. *Speech and Language Processing*. 2nd ed. Upper Saddle River, NJ: Prentice Hall.

Kitchin, Rob. 2014. *The Data Revolution: Big Data, Open Data, Data Infrastructures and Their Consequences*. London: Sage.

Kroll, Joshua A., Joanna Huey, Solon Barocas, Edward W. Felten, Joel R. Reidenberg, David G. Robinson, and Harlan Yu. 2017. "Accountable Algorithms." *University of Pennsylvania Law Review* 165: 633–699.

Law, John. 1990. "Introduction: Monsters, Machines and Sociotechnical Relations." *The Sociological Review* 38 (S1): 1–23.

Leese, Matthias. 2014. "The New Profiling: Algorithms, Black Boxes, and the Failure of Anti-Discriminatory Safeguards in the European Union." *Security Dialogue* 45 (5): 495–511.

Lippmann, Walter. 1927. *The Phantom Public*. New Brunswick, NJ: Transaction.

Lyon, David. 2007. *Surveillance Studies: An Overview*. Cambridge: Polity Press.

Mackenzie, Adrian. 2015. "The Production of Prediction: What Does Machine Learning Want?" *European Journal of Cultural Studies* 18 (4–5): 429–445.

Mager, Astrid. 2012. "Algorithmic Ideology." *Information, Communication & Society* 15 (5): 769–787.

Manning, Christopher D., and Hinrich Schütze. 1999. *Foundations of Statistical Natural Language Processing*. Cambridge, MA: MIT Press.

Marwick, Alice E., and danah boyd. 2014. "Networked Privacy: How Teenagers Negotiate Context in Social Media." *New Media & Society* 16 (7): 1051–1067.

McLuhan, Marshall. 1964. *Understanding Media: The Extensions of Man*. New York: Signet.

Metcalf, Jacob, and Kate Crawford. 2016. "Where Are Human Subjects in Big Data Research? The Emerging Ethics Divide." *Big Data & Society* 3 (1). https://doi.org/ 10.1177/2053951716650211.

Milan, Stefania. 2013. *Social Movements and Their Technologies: Wiring Social Change*. New York: Palgrave MacMillan.

Nissenbaum, Helen. 2011. "A Contextual Approach to Privacy Online." *Daedalus* 140 (4): 32–48.

Noyes, Katherine. 2015. "Will Big Data Help End Discrimination—Or Make It Worse?" *Fortune*. http://fortune.com/2015/01/15/will-big-data-help-end-discrimination-or-make -it-worse.

Pasquale, Frank. 2015. *The Black Box Society: The Secret Algorithms That Control Money and Information*. Cambridge, MA: Harvard University Press.

Plutchik, Robert. 2001. "The Nature of Emotions: Human Emotions Have Deep Evolutionary Roots, a Fact That May Explain Their Complexity and Provide Tools for Clinical Practice." *American Scientist* 89 (4): 344–350.

Rieder, Bernhard. 2005. "Networked Control: Search Engines and the Symmetry of Confidence." *International Review of Information Ethics* 3 (1): 26–32.

———. 2017. "Scrutinizing an Algorithmic Technique: The Bayes Classifier as Interested Reading of Reality." *Information, Communication & Society* 20 (1): 100–117.

Rogers, Richard. 2009. "The Googlization Question, and the Inculpable Engine." In *Deep Search: The Politics of Search beyond Google*, edited by Konrad Becker and Felix Stalder, 173–184. New Brunswick, NJ: Transaction.

Sandvig, Christian, Kevin Hamilton, Karrie Karahalios, and Cedric Langbort. 2014. "Auditing Algorithms: Research Methods for Detecting Discrimination on Internet Platforms." Paper presented at Data and Discrimination: Converting Critical Concerns into Productive Inquiry, May 22, Seattle, WA.

Schäfer, Mirko Tobias, and Karin van Es. 2017. *The Datafied Society*. Amsterdam: Amsterdam University Press.

Solove, Daniel J. 2004. *The Digital Person: Technology and Privacy in the Information Age*. New York: NYU Press.

Star, Susan Leigh. 1990. "Power, Technology and the Phenomenology of Conventions: On Being Allergic to Onions." *The Sociological Review* 38 (S1): 26–56.

Stutzman, Fred, Ralph Gross, and Alessandro Acquisti. 2012. "Silent Listeners: The Evolution of Privacy and Disclosure on Facebook." *Journal of Privacy and Confidentiality* 4 (2): 7–41.

Turing, Alan M. 1950. "Computing Machinery and Intelligence." *Mind* 59 (236): 433–460.

Turkle, Sherry. 1995. *Life on the Screen: Identity in the Age of the Internet*. New York: Simon & Schuster.

Turow, Joseph. 2011. *The Daily You: How the New Advertising Industry Is Defining Your Identity and Your Worth*. New Haven, CT: Yale University Press.

Zumel, Nina, and John Mount. 2014. *Practical Data Science with R*. Greenwich, CT: Manning.

4 Situating Personal Information: Privacy in the Algorithmic Age

Jens-Erik Mai

Introduction

Informational privacy is often understood as the ability or right to have control over one's personal information. In fact, as discussed in the Introduction to this volume, there is a growing concern that platforms use personal information in ways that compromise their users' right to privacy. In his classic definition, Westin stated that privacy is "the claim of individuals, groups, or institutions to determine for themselves when, how, and to what extent information about them is communicated to others" (Westin 1967, 7). This basic idea of a tight link between informational privacy and personal information is echoed in today's two major approaches to informational privacy: the *access* approach in which privacy is about the ability to "limit or restrict others from information about" oneself (Tavani 2008, 141) and the *control* approach in which privacy is the ability to have "control of personal information" (Solove 2008, 24). These notions of informational privacy turn on the basic assumption that *informational privacy is about the protection of personal information*. In this chapter, I will discuss and problematize this assumption and explore the notion of personal information as it is formed in the age of algorithms, datafication, and big data.

The notion of "information" often assumes that information somehow represents, relates to, corresponds to, or points to particular people, places, or things in the world. This use of "information" follows a tradition in the philosophy of information that takes data and information to be reified entities that can be manipulated and subjected to abstract, rational analysis and that exist independent of context, situation, time, and place. In this sense, information *just is*—or as information philosopher Tom Stonier

(1990, 21) stated, "*Information exists*. It does not need to be *perceived* to exist. It does not need to be *understood* to exist. It requires no intelligence to interpret it. It does not have to have *meaning* to exist. It exists."

I will argue, however, that personal information is in fact created in contexts, in situations, in use, and via conversations and constructions about the significance of the information. As such, *information doesn't simply exist*. The understanding of information I use here is based on semiotic communication theory that places the construction of meaning as central to understanding information (cf., e.g., Fiske 2011). It follows that information is best understood as a semiotic sign in communicative practices.

In the following section, I will review how a few central privacy theories have used the notion of information. Next, I present three cases that illustrate how data and information are collected, processed, and used in the algorithmic age. In the final section, I outline a theoretical framework for understanding information as a sign, and I discuss the consequences of such an approach for informational privacy.

To Control Information

The idea that information *just is* is most clearly articulated in the tradition that considers informational privacy to be concerned with property rights over information—that information has thinglike characteristics and is owned by specific people. Moore (2010, 5) conceptualizes privacy as the "right to control access to and use of physical items, like bodies and houses, and information, like medical and financial facts" and defends a "control over access and use" (ibid., 5) definition of privacy. The claim to privacy is a claim to "control access to places and ideas" (ibid., 23) which can be "written, recorded, spoken, or fixed in some other fashion" (ibid., 23). The basic idea is that we have a property right to our personal information and the condition of privacy is one of "voluntary seclusion or walling off" (ibid., 26) and making "personal information inaccessible" (ibid., 26). This idea was most clearly articulated by Murphy (1996, 2383–2384), who asserted about personal information that "such information, like all information, is property" and therefore the basic question is simply to determine "[w]ho owns the property rights to such information" (ibid., 2384).

Solove (2008, 29) criticizes the control theory for being "too vague, too broad, or too narrow." It is too vague because it fails to define the various types of information in play in privacy situations; it is too broad because it fails to accommodate the relational nature of information and the fact that not all personal information is private; and lastly it is too narrow because it fails to account for privacy situations that are not informational in nature. Instead, Solove proposes that we "identify the various types of information and matters that are private" (ibid., 67) and determine those types of information in which intimacy or sensitivity is involved. The traditional approach has been to classify information as "public or private under the assumption that these are qualities that *inhere* in the information [emphasis added]" (ibid., 69). Solove proposes—from a grounding in "philosophy of pragmatism" (ibid., 46)—a contextual approach to privacy with a focus on specific privacy problems that there is a need to address, and he proposes that instead of defining privacy from a general perspective, the aim should be to start with practical problems that privacy theory and practice ought to solve and let those contexts define the privacy problems at hand and whether information is public or private.

Nissenbaum (2010) is likewise critical of the control approach to informational privacy. She argues that the control approach relies on the notion of a distinction between a public realm and a private realm and the ability to master the location of the information. Nissenbaum suggests that the social norms governing a given situation should provide the context to understand the privacy issues at stake. As such, Nissenbaum's focus is on the contextual, social norms that determine whether some information belongs in the public realm or in the private realm—the basic idea being that the information itself can be moved from the public realm to the private realm without having an effect on the information itself; the same information can exist in the public realm and in the private realm. Rubel and Biava (2014, 2424) are also critical of the control approach to informational privacy and suggest that informational privacy is better understood as a relation between three entities: "some person or persons, some domain of information, and some other person or persons." The point is that nothing is said beforehand about the nature of these relations, merely that those are the relations to be analyzed and understood in a given privacy situation or context. The nature of the relations then defines the particular privacy issue at stake and makes it possible to compare various privacy situations.

Common for these—and other similar—conceptualizations is that they take a pragmatic approach and aim to give voice to the contextualization of privacy issues, arguing that there are norms, specifics, or matters within a given situation that define and limit the privacy issues at play. However, they do not explicitly consider how the notion of information might be affected by their pragmatic, contextual, situational interpretation stance—they maintain the basic idea that information *just is*, that information is an entity that can be manipulated and moved between different spheres or domains.

Being Pragmatic

One route to conceptualize the role of information in informational privacy theories is to determine the "various types of information or matters that are private" (Solove 2008, 67) and which other types of information or matters are not private and to use this distinction to draw a line between privacy and non-privacy. A common approach is to draw this line based on the "intimacy or sensitivity" (ibid., 67) of the information in question; information that by nature is intimate or sensitive is personal information, while other types of information are not.

Solove (2008) suggests that a better approach is to look at the purposes for which the information is used to analyze the privacy issues involved; "information is public or private depending upon the purposes for which people want to conceal it and the uses that others might make of it" (ibid., 69). In other words, the focus ought to be on the nature of the purpose for which the information is applied. This is similar to Nissenbaum's (2010, 3) call for "contextual integrity" in which "finely calibrated systems of social norms, or rules, govern the flow of personal information."

Both Solove and Nissenbaum—as well as other privacy scholars—have been influenced by the idea that the particular situation or context is of importance to understanding the privacy issues at play. What is not discussed is the status or conceptualization of information; except for the use of notions such as sensitive, personal, intimate, or private about the information and the acknowledgement that it can take different forms (written, recorded, spoken, etc.), nothing is said about the nature of information involved in informational privacy. Solove and Nissenbaum seem to hold "the self constant" and ignore "the problem of the evolving subjectivity" (Cohen 2012, 20). That is, while they recognize the importance of the specific situation or context, their analyses are limited to understanding the privacy situation as specific and unique and to acknowledging that it is a mistake to assume that information by nature is either private or public.

In this chapter I augment these contextual approaches to privacy by arguing that information itself is a contextual, situational, and pragmatic construct. As such, the present chapter builds upon and expands the work of Nissenbaum, Solove, and others who have advocated a contextual approach to privacy. This chapter augments their work by providing a contextual understanding of personal information.

The concept of information is tricky, and it is used in several different ways with various connotations. As Agre once noted,

> Computers are frequently said to store and transmit information. The term information, though, conceals a significant ambiguity. On one hand, information can be defined (as per Shannon and Weaver) as a purely mathematical measure of information and information-carrying capacity, without regard for the content. On the other hand, information is information also about something. (Agre 1994, 107)

In this sense, the scholars discussed above can be said to use a notion of information where information has an information-carrying capacity. What is of concern for these scholars is not so much the content of the information as the information itself; in such conceptualizations, information *just is*.

However, as Agre noted, information can also be conceptualized as information about something; as Westin (1967, 7) originally noted, privacy is the claim to determine the "extent information about them is communicated to others." To reuse Warren and Brandeis's (1890, 214) famous question—"What is the thing which is protected?"—is informational privacy concerned with protecting the stuff called "information" or with protecting the state of affairs that the information is about? The answer to that question will lead to different kinds of informational privacy theories. Therefore, we need to ask "What is information?" But first, let us pause to clarify the interrelation between information and personal information.

Information and Personal Information

As a way to avoid the larger philosophical discourse about the notion of information, one could suggest that information and personal information should be regarded as separate notions that are not related (figure 4.1). In

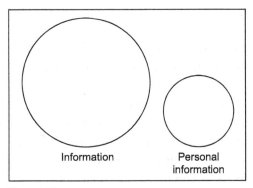

Figure 4.1

this sense, information and personal information are different in nature; they do not share characteristics or have properties in common. In such an understanding, information and personal information would be different concepts, and one would conceptualize personal information as a unique ontological unit. This understanding would allow one to define personal information as a specific set of ontological concepts that operate in specific and unique ways, independent of discussions of the notion of information as such. My sense is that this is not an attainable understanding and that personal information in many ways behaves in the same way as information per se and entails the same challenges. In this chapter, I will therefore regard information and personal information as the same conceptual unit.

We could consider personal information to share characteristics with information per se—and it could be argued that personal information is in fact just a small subset of information (figure 4.2). That is, we could single

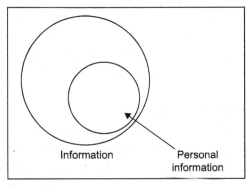

Figure 4.2

out personal information as a special kind of information—as a subset of information—defining it as "data about an individual that is identifiable to that individual—for example, my genetic code, my video preferences, my sexual preference, my credit history, my eye color, my income" (Murphy 1996, 2383) or as "any information relating to an identified or identifiable natural person" (Data Protection Working Party 2007, 4).

In this chapter, however, I will argue two things about this relation between information and personal information. First, the distinction is not as sharp as figures 4.1 and 4.2 might imply. As we will see in the next section of this chapter, the flow, use, and production of information in digital environments can blur the distinction between information about individuals (personal information) and information about all other things—in fact, if we were to maintain the distinction between information and personal information, there would probably be very little information in the digital information environment that would not be personal information (figure 4.3). As Cohen (2012) has noted, the idea of designating some information as "intimate" or "sensitive" and of specific interest in a privacy context is problematic considering today's data and information practices:

> Although privacy law purports to recognize a . . . principle, that . . . operates primarily to protect small islands of concededly "intimate" or "sensitive" information and correspondingly small enclaves of acknowledged physical seclusion. In an age of distributed information processing, moreover, even those islands are eroding. (Cohen 2012, 248)

In the algorithmic age, most information can be used in the construction of personal profiles—and thus the distinction between information and

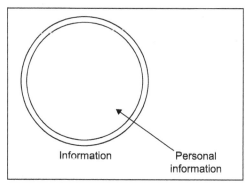

Figure 4.3

personal information becomes less clear, as lots of seemingly casual and informal information is used in the algorithmic creation of personal data profiles. There would, of course, still be some information that we would not regard as personal information, such as tree rings or fossils—until they are picked up by an individual and entered into a personal sphere at which point tree rings and fossils might in fact also become personal information, as pointed out by Van Hoboken (Joris van Hoboken, comments to author, January 12, 2017).

My second argument about the relations between information and personal information is that to understand the nature of information and appreciate the challenges of constructing a theory of informational privacy, we need to conceive of information as signs in a communicative process. What is interesting about personal information is that it is stuff that means *something about something*, and we ought to be concerned with the situations in which that meaning is produced. In other words, information is not best conceptualized as footprints of a state of affairs but as signs in a communicative process (Mai 2016b).

For a better understanding of informational privacy, we need a more granular understanding of the concept of information, as well as a more nuanced language to discuss it. With these in place, we can explore and articulate different approaches to what informational privacy is about and the avenues one might take to address current challenges. However, before digging into theories of information, let us first explore a few cases of information and data in the wild.

Three Examples of Datafication

I present three examples below in which there is an intersection between the collection, processing, and use of personal information and privacy. These examples will demonstrate how the control-oriented approach to privacy is too weak and insufficient in today's algorithmic age.

The first example is the application of algorithms in basically any and all digital platforms today, which has resulted in algorithms playing "an increasingly important role in selecting which information is considered relevant to us" (Gillespie 2014, 167). Such algorithms increasingly dominate our daily interactions with social media; they are an integral component of search engines, recommender systems, online newspapers, social networking platforms, and so forth. The use of algorithms and the degree to which they "black box" (Pasquale 2015) information processes and decisions has been widely discussed. However, as Burrell (2016, 2) argues, "what is *new* in this domain is the more pervasive technologies and techniques of data collection, the more vast archives of personal data including purchasing activities, link clicks, and geospatial movement." Although these algorithms are already nestled "into people's daily lives and mundane information practices" (Gillespie 2014, 183), there is still very little known about the "ways in which users know and perceive that algorithms are part of their 'media life'" (Bucher 2017, 31). One challenge, of course, is that people rarely understand—*because it is black boxed*—which information about them has been collected and how that information is processed and used to generate the personalized services offered by platforms. As Gillespie (2014, 173–174) has noted,

> The most knowable information (geo-location, computing platform, profile information, friends, status updates, links followed on the site, time on the site, activity on other sites that host "like" buttons or cookies) is a rendering of that user, a "digital dossier" or "algorithmic identity" that is imperfect but sufficient. What is less legible or cannot be known about users falls away or is bluntly approximated.

Sophisticated Internet users might be able to determine that personal information is being collected in their daily interaction with various digital media; many people are aware that whatever data and information they themselves provide is being collected, and that hardware information about their devices is collected as well. But, as Gillespie notes, that is rarely enough information to provide detailed personalized services—much is approximated in the construction of personal profiles. Bucher (2017, 34) gives the example of Shannon, a professional career counsellor in her forties, who has blogged about Taylor Swift and then starts receiving "Facebook ads for products that younger people might like." The reason for this might be that Facebook's algorithm has recomputed her age given the information about Taylor Swift and makes the assumption that Shannon is younger than she actually is. Shannon is rather relaxed about this and finds that it is "rather amusing" though she often finds "Facebook ads to be 'slightly offensive as they make assumptions about me, which I don't like to think are true'" (ibid., 34).

Bucher's example is a good illustration of Cohen's (2012, 26) point that "raw information . . . is not terribly useful to anyone"; the fact that Shannon has blogged about Taylor Swift says very little about Shannon without an understanding of the contextual situation in which Shannon has generated this information. The meaning of the information that is entered into the algorithms and personal data profiles, therefore, is best understood within the context of the "origins, purposes, and effects of [the] socially situated processes of sorting and categorization" (ibid., 26). The challenge, as Burrell (2016, 1) has pointed out, is that "the inputs themselves may be entirely unknown or known only partially"; once the information has been collected, it has been separated from the context in which it was produced and now interpreted and used in new contexts and therefore "is both already desiccated and persistently messy" (Gillespie 2014, 170).

The second example I will present here is the widely used but very illustrative Target case. The Target case illustrates the point that the distinction between ordinary, everyday information and sensitive information is not as clear-cut as sometimes imagined. The case was first reported in the *New York Times* by Charles Duhigg (2012), who told the story of a father who went to a Target store complaining that his daughter had received coupons for maternity clothing and baby products. Like many other chain stores, Target assigns each customer a unique "Guest ID number." This allows Target to identify and track each customer, provide customers with personalized services, and offer customers coupons that are tailored to their shopping interests. One set of customers of interest are pregnant women. Through research and data mining, Target assigns each customer a "pregnancy prediction" score, representing the likelihood that the customer is pregnant. Target is even able to calculate an expected due date. Target had found that they could assign the pregnancy score fairly precisely by analyzing the purchasing history for approximately twenty-five products, such as "quantities of unscented lotion," "supplements like calcium, magnesium and zinc," "scent-free soap," "extra-big bags of cotton balls," "hand sanitizers," and "washcloths" (Duhigg 2012). It is valuable for Target to know that a customer might be pregnant because this is a "watershed moment for couples" (Mayer-Schönberger and Cukier 2013, 57) in which they might change their shopping habits and develop new brand loyalties.

It could be argued that the daughter had control of the information regarding her purchases of the twenty-five products used to calculate her pregnancy prediction score that she provided to Target through her membership card, and that she benefitted from the transaction through coupons and discounts. The challenge is that it is not misuse of personal information that in itself creates a privacy problem; rather, the issue is that Target is able to produce sensitive personal information through predictive analysis of the young girl's purchasing history. As Inness (1992, 58) argues, "[I]t is the *intimacy* of this information that identifies a loss of privacy." The fact that Target knows a customer's purchase history for, say, washcloths might not feel like a violation of their privacy, especially if the information is traded for a discount on washcloths. However, most people would probably consider knowledge about their health—such as whether or not they are pregnant—too personal and intimate to share with Target. This example demonstrates that in the age of big data, predictive analysis, algorithms, and machine learning, the challenges to informational privacy are less about the control of personal information and more about what companies know about their customers. The focus has "shifted from concerns about revealing information about oneself to others to concerns about the new insights that others can generate based on the already available data" (Mai 2016a, 199).

The last example I will present here is Cheney-Lippold's (2011) Quancast case. Quancast builds profiles of Internet users based on their interactions with a range of sites and platforms. These profiles are constructed based on the users' seemingly meaningless data collected as they go about their daily activities; the data about these interactions flows "into rigid database fields as part of the subsumption implicit in data mining" (ibid., 169). One element in the process is the establishment of a user's gender:

> As a user travels across these networks, algorithms can topologically striate her surfing data, allocating certain web artifacts into particular, algorithmically-defined categories like gender. The fact that user X visits the web site CNN.com might suggest that X could be categorized as male. And additional data could then buttress or resignify how X is categorized. As X visits more sites like CNN. com, X's maleness is statistically reinforced, adding confidence to the measure that X may be male. As X visits more sites that are unlike CNN.com, X's maleness might be put into question or potentially resignified to another gender identity. (Cheney-Lippold 2011, 169–170)

The data collected about an individual user is analyzed and checked against other statistical analyses to ultimately establish the gender of the user. However, as new data is collected and analyzed, the gender of the user might change, and, as such, "gender becomes a vector" (ibid., 170) that is de-essentialized and constructed on a purely digital basis merely to develop marketing information about the users, which Quancast can then sell. The construction of gender within the context of Quancast becomes decontextualized from the social and cultural construction of gender; for Quancast the category of "gender" is merely a category "embedded in the logic of consumption" (ibid., 171) and is divorced from real, actual, and lived gender experiences.

Cheney-Lippold's (2011) Quancast example shows that data is collected to establish personal information about an individual, for example, "X is male" (ibid., 170). This establishment of maleness, however, has little to do with X as a human being; it is merely for marketing purposes. X's gender is established through predictive and inferential analyses of X's interactions with various sites and platforms, and X's gender is established through algorithmic analyses based on information that might not in the first place be regarded as personal information.

A common question raised for these three examples is whether they involve the notion of privacy. It is my sense that we could explore and read the cases from the perspective of privacy and discuss in which ways and to what extent the individuals' personal information was used in improper ways, and whether they had control over their personal information in the situations. I think most of us would agree that there is at least some degree of privacy involved, and that the individuals involved are at risk at least to some degree, given specific interpretations of the cases and the data practices involved. However, I would submit that we cannot meaningfully understand and analyze the privacy issues at play in these scenarios using the framework of control of personal information. In fact, I believe applying a control approach would cause us to misread the privacy concerns at stake in these examples for two reasons. The first reason is that the three cases demonstrate that the issue here has less to do with the data provided by the users/customers, and everything to do with the new insights and information the companies produce about them. The users/customers have no direct control over this new information and will, in most circumstances, not know that the information even exists. On the other hand, the fact that such information is produced and exists currently provides a flourishing personal data economy, as outlined by Zuboff in the first chapter of this volume.

The second reason for this potential misreading of the privacy concerns in the examples is that we have mistakenly based the idea of informational privacy on a specific understanding of information. When informational privacy is reduced to the challenge of controlling information, then it necessarily objectifies information, turning it into a reified entity that can be managed, that can be manipulated, and to which we can restrict access. If we regard information as a sign, as *something about something*, then informational privacy becomes concerned with the fact that something is known about someone and how we might act in such a situation. Information then becomes less central to informational privacy, because we cannot control and regulate the interpretation and production of meaning. Rather we must "control" the situations in which meaning is ascribed: the use of data.

At this point we need to return to and address the basic question for this exploration of the conceptual foundation of informational privacy, namely, *what is information?*

Information as Signs

One way to answer the question "What is information?" is to list all the things that one considers to be information: books, numbers, addresses, health records, phone bills, names, DNA codes, computer programs, weblogs, credit card statements, purchasing records, e-mails, likes on Facebook, and so on—a list of everything in the world that we consider to be informative. Such a list might end up containing almost everything in the world: cows, cups, and coffee are quite informative, but "if anything is, or might be, informative, then everything is, or might well be, information" (Buckland 1991, 356). This "extensional approach" (Furner 2016, 289) to determining the answer to the question of what is information has been labeled "information realism" (Fox 1983, 17) in the sense that it is an ontological quest for finding and listing the things in the world that are informative and therefore are information.

Another approach to understanding the nature of information is to adopt what Furner (2016, 289) calls an "intentional approach," in which the "properties that something must have" (ibid., 289) to be treated as information are identified. These might be that the information must be true to be information, that it can be used to generate knowledge, that it can be used as a vehicle for communication, that it represents some state of affairs, or some combinations of such sets of properties. One dominant approach along these lines is advocated by Floridi (2008, 2010), who has developed a philosophy of information for "fields that treat data and information as reified entities, that is, stuff that can be manipulated (consider, for example, the now common expressions 'data mining' and 'information management')" (Floridi 2010, 20). Floridi defines information as "meaningful independent of an informee" (ibid., 22) and thereby constructs a notion of information that does not rely on a knowing subject. Dretske (2008) takes a similar approach to understanding information; he suggests that information "is independent of what we think or believe. It is independent of what we know" (ibid., 31) because information is "answers to questions" (ibid., 29) and "not just any answers . . . [but] true answers" (ibid., 29). Information cannot simply be understood in terms of meaning—as in what the information is *about*—because, as he explains, "[M]eaning is fine. You can't have truth without it" but "information, unlike meaning, has to be true" (ibid., 29).

In this sense information exists before human activities, language, and thought. It is true, and it has no agency. Cohen (2012, 20) has criticized these approaches to information within the context of informational privacy for accepting "liberal individualism's commitments to immateriality and disembodiment" and, as such, creating a construct of information that "appears to be the ultimate disembodied good, yielding itself seamlessly to abstract, rational analysis" (ibid., 20). These conceptualizations of "information" follow a tradition of conceptualizing "information" as what has been called "natural information," following Grice's (1957, 1989) distinction between natural and nonnatural meaning.

Natural and Nonnatural

Grice uses "natural" and "nonnatural" meaning to distinguish between statements that entail their meaning and statements that mean through conventions. As an example, Grice (1957, 213) uses the statement "Those spots mean (meant) measles" to illustrate statements that entail meaning; if someone utters that sentence, we would rightly expect that there is an actual correlation to a state of affairs in which someone has the measles. In other words, one cannot say, "Those spots meant measles, but he hadn't got measles" (ibid., 213); if someone has these particular spots, then he or she has measles. There is no room for uncertainty and debate. Grice's notion of natural meaning is a notion of meaning where a statement entails a given state of affairs; it is true and objectively correct.

If we regard information to be natural, as in natural meaning, then information is regarded as a state of affairs. In this approach, information is viewed as that which reflects what is actual and true—and, as such, information can be manipulated and analyzed to gain knowledge about people's actual affairs, interests, and intentions. For people to enjoy freedom from surveillance and enjoy privacy, they should merely be able to control the flow of the material representations of information. If one controls when, how, and to what extent others have access to the material information, then one enjoys privacy.

Under this tradition, the fact that Shannon writes about Taylor Swift *entails* a particular age, the fact that a girl shops for particular products at Target *entails* that she is pregnant, and the fact that an Internet user visits certain web sites *entails* a particular gender.

Contrast that with the example of nonnatural meaning, which Grice (1957, 214) gives as "Those three rings on the bell (of the bus) mean that the bus is full." This utterance does not in the same way *entail* a particular state of affairs. One could very reasonably, "go on and say, 'But it isn't in fact full—the conductor made a mistake'" (ibid., 214). In this instance, someone has the intention of communicating something; there is a human agent present who can be correct or incorrect in his or her understanding of the actual state of affairs. There is no direct entailment between the statement and the fact that the bus is or is not full. The meaning of the statement is based on conventions—we have agreed that three rings mean that the bus is full. There is room for uncertainty, debate, and interpretation.

Grice's concept of nonnatural meaning is those situations in which meaning emerges out of use and in context. It is the type of meaning that is based on conventions and intentions; a statement means something because we have agreed on the correct usage of that statement. Similarly, with information, information is created and used in particular contexts and situations, and we can only understand information within those boundaries. In other words, to assign meaning and significance to Shannon writing about Taylor Swift, a girl shopping for particular products at Target, and an Internet user visiting CNN.com outside those particular contexts is, to use Gillespie's (2014, 174) words, "bluntly approximated." To suggest that these people ought to be able to protect their informational privacy by using their abilities to control their personal information would be a mistake.

Within philosophy of information, Grice's work on the distinction between natural and nonnatural meaning is used to develop the notions of natural information and nonnatural information (Søe 2016). While natural information only allows for true, objectively correct information, nonnatural information allows for mistakes, misinterpretations, and misuse—and hence opens the way for concepts such as (personal) misinformation, that is, unintended misleading information, and (personal) disinformation, that is, information which is intentionally misleading (Søe 2016). Following Grice's conceptualization of meaning, and his grounding in semiotic thinking, we could articulate the core properties of information by stating that it functions as a vehicle used in the production and exchange of meaning. That is, information is a sign (Mai 2013).

If we regard information as a sign, and personal information as nonnatural information—then we arrive at a significantly different understanding of informational privacy. Information gains meaning through interpretations with specific contexts, situations, and usages. In this conceptualization, informational privacy cannot be reduced to the flow and control of information but must be understood in the sense of what is known and knowable about the individuals in question.

However, what is known and knowable about individuals is always constructed at an interpretive distance and is always one take on the meaning of what is being said and done. So, let us now consider practices that involve the production and use of information about individuals.

Situating Informational Practices

Big data has been associated with a particular ideology or belief system about the world, that is, specific understandings of how humans operate in the world and how people make sense of the world and communicate—this ideology can be labeled "data behaviorism" (Rouvroy 2013, 143) or "dataism" (van Dijck 2014, 198). Common for much work in big data is the belief in "the objective quantification and potential tracking of all kinds of human behavior and sociality through online media technologies" (ibid., 198), and "prediction is the hallmark" (Ekbia et al. 2015, 1529) for work in big data. However, in practice, it may be difficult to attain the goal of objectivity and disinterestedness, because "big data does not arrive in the hands of analysts ready for analysis" (ibid., 1531); data has to be cleaned or conditioned to be usable, which involves deciding which attributes and variables to keep and which to ignore. In fact, in a study of working data scientists, Carter and Sholler found that,

> disinterest may not always be possible, especially for workers in business settings that involve contact with a client. Analysts might aspire to objectivity but be forced by circumstances to recognize their own positioning and the role of communication in data analysis. (Carter and Sholler 2016, 2317)

So, even if "dataism presumes *trust* in the objectivity of quantified methods" (van Dijck 2014, 204), in reality, this trust does not hold up.

The drive behind big data is a belief in the decontextualization of data—that data has meaning beyond particular situations and that more data will lead to more meaning and better understanding. The hope is that ultimately, we can do away with theories, perspectives, and interpretation. As Chris Anderson (2008) wrote, in a small piece in *Wired* where, even before big data was in vogue, he foresaw a future where it would be possible to harvest massive amounts of data, "With enough data, numbers would speak for themselves" (Anderson 2008). This is a hype, of course, but a dangerous hype that "leads to the withering away of interpretation—not through the actions of a cabal, but through a sociologic excluding from the archive all data which is not big" (Bowker 2014, 1797) and which, "thanks to relatively simple algorithms allowing, on a purely inductive statistic basis, to build models of behaviors or patterns, without having to consider either causes or intentions" (Rouvroy 2013, 143).

The challenge is that both the individuals interacting with platforms producing personal information and the analysts trying to make sense of their data are "real embodied people [who] do not experience 'information' in the abstract; [but] rather . . . through the lens of embodied perception" (Cohen 2012, 33). When people interact with digital platforms and write about Taylor Swift, shop at Target, or surf various websites, they produce data. This data can be used to infer something about them: that they are of a certain age, that they are pregnant, or that they are a certain gender. These are categories. Big data analysis, machine learning, and predictive analysis are ways to categorize—techniques to place people, objects, and phenomena into categories. Until recently, categories were thought to be unproblematic containers:

> They were assumed to be abstract containers, with things either inside or outside
> the category. Things were assumed to be in the same category if and only if they
> had certain properties in common. And the properties they had in common were
> taken as defining the category. (Lakoff 1987, 6)

However, scholarship across the social sciences and humanities as it has played out at least since the *linguistic turn* in the middle of the twentieth century (Rorty 1967) has found that categories, meaning, and understanding are embodied experiences. It is now widely accepted that categories are constructions; categories are not objectively *in* the world. They are constructed to make sense of and explain the world.

Even for simple concepts or categories—such as "dog"—there is no objective and universal meaning or sense. A dog is a *pet*; it is sometimes *owned* by people as their *property*; it is a *mammal*, a *guard*, a *dish*; it sometimes lives in *houses* and other times in *herds*; and it may even be a *show dog*. The notion of dog does not have a life or a meaning per se. There is nothing that is *the* concept dog or *the* properties that define dog:

> Our concept of the dog involves a lot more than a list of dog-like properties—it
> involves knowledge of how the dog operates in the world and how it is related
> to other things in that world. Concepts are not isolated entities. In order to grasp
> a concept, we require not only definitional, but also encyclopedic knowledge.
> (Bryant 2000, 59)

To understand the notion of dog, we need to be part of the usage and situations in which the concept is used. If we do not know the concept, we might look it up in a dictionary, but "'dictionary words' . . . must be defined in terms of other dictionary words" (Eco 1984, 50). Dictionaries and dictionary-like definitions require encyclopedic knowledge of the culture, the context, and the languages in which they are used.

There is no such thing as *raw* data, just as there is no such thing as *the* meaning of a word: "*The meaning of a word is its use in the language*" (Wittgenstein 1958, §43). Similarly, with categories, we understand the world not merely through individual concepts "but also in terms of *categories* of things," and if we change those categories, "we change our understanding of the world" (Lakoff 1987 9).

We might attribute meaning and properties to the facts that Shannon *writes about* Taylor Swift, that a young girl who *is shopping* for particular products at Target is pregnant, or that *people create* particular patterns of surf history as they visit various websites. However, that meaning and those properties will only be one of many possible interpretations, one particular take on what the data could show or tell us about the people who engaged in activities and thereby produced data. Hence, personal information is *signs* open for interpretation, analysis, and (mis)use.

Conclusion

It is commonly suggested that informational privacy seeks to protect people's personal information, the basic idea being that people's ability to enjoy privacy is tied to their ability to control the flow of their personal information. However, the notion of personal information has remained largely unmarked and undertheorized in the privacy literature, leaving behind an understanding of personal information in which information *just is*.

Privacy scholars have tended to focus on *informational control* as "the claim of individuals, groups, or institutions to determine for themselves when, how, and to what extent information about them is communicated to others" (Westin 1967, 7)—when in fact the core challenge is the processes by which personal information is created. If one focuses on the term "information," one might start to list all the things we consider personal information and then argue that people have property rights over those things, that they ought to be able to control the flow of those things, or that they should give consent for the use of such things—and then believe that once those property rights, control, or consent issues are in place, then people can enjoy privacy. However, the challenge that privacy ought to be concerned with is the situation in which meaning is created; thus we must ask, "What does it mean that others have information *about* individuals, groups, or institutions? And when does a certain use of information constitute a privacy intrusion?"

Digital platforms and services utilize big data analyses, predictive analysis, algorithms, and machine learning to produce (personal) information about individuals. The next major challenge for informational privacy theory is thus to develop a foundation that recognizes the complex and often opaque processes by which that (personal) information is produced. As Van Hoboken argues in this volume, this might lead to the position that regulation should turn away from regulating the *collection* of personal information altogether and instead regulate the *use* of (personal) information. In fact, people might only be able to enjoy informational privacy once digital platforms and services' business practices are based on ethical foundations in which their practices are truly virtuous. Privacy cannot be limited solely to an individual, liberal right but should be expanded to an expectation of how society allows individuals to be treated by companies. The next generation of informational privacy theory should establish and make explicit the internal goods, norms, and standards of the algorithmic age, which should include as necessary components "justice, courage, and honesty" (MacIntyre 1981, 191).

References

Agre, Philip E. 1994. "Surveillance and Capture: Two Models of Privacy." *The Information Society* 10 (2): 101–127.

Anderson, Chris. 2008. "The End of Theory: The Data Deluge Makes the Scientific Method Obsolete." *Wired* 16 (7).

Bowker, Geoffrey C. 2014. "The Theory/Data Thing." *International Journal of Communication* 8 (2043): 1795–1799.

Bucher, Taina. 2017. "The Algorithmic Imaginary: Exploring the Ordinary Affects of Facebook Algorithms." *Information, Communication & Society* 20 (1): 30–44.

Buckland, Michael. 1991. "Information as Thing." *Journal of the American Society for Information Science* 42 (5): 351–360.

Burrell, Jenna. 2016. "How the Machine 'Thinks': Understanding the Opacity of Machine Learning Algorithms." *Big Data & Society* January–June 2016: 1–12.

Bryant, Rebecca. 2000. *Discovery and Decision: Exploring the Metaphysics and Epistemology of Scientific Classification*. Cranbury, NJ: Associated University Presses.

Carter, Daniel, and Dan Sholler. 2016. "Data Science on the Ground: Hype, Criticism, and Everyday Work." *Journal of the Association for Information Science and Technology* 67 (10): 2309–2319.

Cheney-Lippold, John. 2011. "A New Algorithmic Identity: Soft Biopolitics and the Modulation of Control." *Theory, Culture & Society* 28(6): 164–81.

Cohen, Julia E. 2012. *Configuring the Networked Self: Law, Code, and the Play of Everyday Practices*. New Haven, CT: Yale University Press.

Data Protection Working Party. 2007. *Opinion 4/2007 on the Concept of Personal Data*. Article 29, WP 136. Brussels: European Commission.

Dretske, Fred. 2008. "Epistemology and Information." In *Handbook of the Philosophy of Science, Philosophy of Information*, vol. 8, edited by Pieter Adriaans and Johan van Benthem, 29–47. Amsterdam: Elsevier.

Duhigg, Charles. 2012. "How Companies Learn Your Secrets." *New York Times*, February 16, 2012. http://www.nytimes.com/2012/02/19/magazine/shopping-habits.html.

Eco, Umberto. 1984. *Semiotics and the Philosophy of Language*. London: Macmillan.

Ekbia, Hamid, Michael Mattioli, Inna Kouper, G. Arave, Ali Ghazinejad, Timothy Bowman, Venkata Ratandeep Suri, et al. 2015. "Big Data, Bigger Dilemmas: A Critical Review." *Journal of the Association for Information Science and Technology* 66 (8): 1523–1545.

Fiske, John. 2011. *Introduction to Communication Studies*. 3rd ed. London: Routledge.

Floridi, Luciano. 2008. "Trends in the Philosophy of Information." In *Handbook of the Philosophy of Science, Philosophy of Information*, vol. 8, edited by Pieter Adriaans and Johan van Benthem, 113–131. Amsterdam: Elsevier.

———. 2010. *Information: A Very Short Introduction*. Oxford: Oxford University Press.

Fox, Christopher J. 1983. *Information and Misinformation: An Investigation of the Notions of Information, Misinformation, Informing, and Misinforming*. Westport, CT: Greenwood Press.

Furner, Jonathan. 2016. "'Data': The Data." In *Information Cultures in the Digital Age*, edited by Matthew Kelly and Jared Bielby, 287–306. London: Springer.

Gillespie, Tarleton. 2014. "The Relevance of Algorithms." In *Media Technologies: Essays on Communication, Materiality, and Society*, edited by Tarleton Gillespie, Pablo J. Boczkowski, and Kirsten A. Foot, 167–193. Cambridge, MA: MIT Press.

Grice, H. Paul. 1957. "Meaning." In *Studies in the Way of Words*, edited by H. Paul Grice, 213–223. Cambridge, MA: Harvard University Press.

———. 1989. *Studies in the Way of Words*. Cambridge, MA: Harvard University Press.

Inness, Julie C. 1992. *Privacy, Intimacy, and Isolation*. New York: Oxford University Press.

Lakoff, George. 1987. *Women, Fire and Dangerous Things: What Categories Reveal about the Mind*. Chicago: University of Chicago Press.

MacIntyre, Alasdair. 1981. *After Virtue: A Study in Moral Theory*. Notre Dame, IN: University of Notre Dame Press.

Mai, Jens-Erik. 2013. "The Quality and Qualities of Information." *Journal of the American Society for Information Science and Technology* 64 (4): 675–688.

———. 2016a. "Big Data Privacy: The Datafication of Personal Information." *The Information Society* 32 (3): 192–199.

———. 2016b. "Personal Information as Communicative Acts." *Ethics and Information Technology* 18 (1): 51–57.

Mayer-Schönberger, Viktor, and Kenneth Cukier. 2013. *Big Data: A Revolution That Will Transform How We Live, Work, and Think*. New York: Houghton Mifflin Harcourt.

Moore, Adam D. 2010. *Privacy Rights: Moral and Legal Foundations*. University Park: Pennsylvania State University Press.

Murphy, Richard S. 1996. "Property Rights in Personal Information: An Economic Defense of Privacy." *Georgetown Law Journal* (83): 2381–2417.

Nissenbaum, Helen. 2010. *Privacy in Context: Technology, Policy, and the Integrity of Social Life*. Stanford, CA: Stanford University Press.

Pasquale, Frank. 2015. *Black Box Society: The Secret Algorithms That Control Money and Information*. Cambridge, MA: Harvard University Press.

Rorty, Richard, ed. 1967. *The Linguistic Turn: Recent Essays in Philosophical Method*. Chicago: University of Chicago Press.

Rouvroy, Antoinette. 2013. "The End(s) of Critique: Data Behaviourism versus Due Process." In *Privacy, Due Process and the Computational Turn: The Philosophy of Law Meets the Philosophy of Technology*, edited by Mireille Hildebrandt and Katja de Vries, 143–167. Oxon, UK: Routledge.

Rubel, Alan, and Ryan Biava. 2014. "A Framework for Analyzing and Comparing Privacy States." *Journal of the Association for Information Science and Technology* 65 (12): 2422–2431.

Solove, Daniel J. 2008. *Understanding Privacy*. Cambridge, MA: Harvard University Press.

Stonier, Tom. 1990. *Information and the Internal Structure of the Universe: An Exploration into Information Physics*. London: Springer.

Søe, Sille Obelitz. 2016. "The Urge to Detect, the Need to Clarify: Gricean Perspectives on Information, Misinformation and Disinformation." PhD diss., University of Copenhagen, Faculty of Humanities.

Tavani, Herman T. 2008. "Informational Privacy: Concepts, Theories, and Controversies." In *The Handbook of Information and Computer Ethics*, edited by Kenneth Einar Himma and Herman T. Tavani, 131–164. Hoboken, NJ: Wiley.

Van Dijck, José. 2014. "Datafication, Dataism and Dataveillance: Big Data between Scientific Paradigm and Ideology." *Surveillance & Society* 12 (2): 197–208.

Warren, Samuel D., and Louis D. Brandeis. 1890. "The Right to Privacy." In *Information Ethics: Privacy, Property, and Power*, edited by Adam D. Moore, 209–225. Seattle, WA: University of Washington Press.

Westin, Alan F. 1967. *Privacy and Freedom*. New York: Atheneum.

Wittgenstein, Ludwig. 1958. *Philosophical Investigations*. New York: Macmillan.

II Platforms

The second part of the book takes a closer look at digital platform practices, in particular how the online advertising model has developed into its
current form, the dynamics (and conflicts) related to content moderation,
and the sense making around human rights at Google and Facebook. The
contributions point to the intimate link between the revenue model of the
social web and practices of data capture (Bermejo); the threats that content
moderation pose to the networked public sphere and to freedom of expression (York and Zuckerman); and the way corporate narratives frame and
delimit the commitment to human rights (Jørgensen).

5   Online Advertising as a Shaper of Public Communication

Fernando Bermejo

Introduction

The privatization of the Internet in the mid-1990s opened the door to its commercialization (Greenstein 2000, 2015). A technological infrastructure that had for decades been financed and controlled by different government agencies was immediately, and almost completely, shaken by business interests (Abbate 1999). As a result, and two decades later, a handful of companies have emerged as central actors of the online public sphere. With the advent of the social web, the arena in which individuals communicate and discuss collective issues and problems is to a large extent supported by digital platforms controlled by corporations. Their practices, policies, and technologies play a fundamental role in shaping private communications and public discourse and affect the exercise and level of protection of a range of human rights, as illustrated throughout this volume.

In order to understand these "new media" companies and how they shape communication and affect human rights, it is necessary to pay attention to their business logic, to the ways in which they generate revenue and maximize profits.

This chapter attempts to do that, first, by linking the idea of revenue model to that of control over the communication process and by showing how these revenue models have evolved over the history of public communication. It presents a brief overview of the evolutionary line that goes from models in which control is purely physical to those in which it is informational and in which advertising is central.

It then proceeds to examine the transformation of the advertising model as the main source of revenue for online communication platforms. The understanding of the Internet, and especially of the World Wide Web, as a tool for publishing and consuming information allowed the advertising industry to lead the charge in the commercialization of the Internet in the 1990s (Donaton and Sloan 1995). Advertisers and media had been dealing with human attention for decades and were ready to do the same in the new digital environment: measurement tools were adapted and invented, data collection processes were implemented, new metrics and analysis techniques were applied. The goal was to reproduce the model that had served the broadcasting and advertising industries so well. However, online advertising quickly evolved around the turn of the century. Understanding this evolution and placing it in context helps us explain the influence of advertising on public communication in the second decade of the twenty-first century.

The chapter ends with an examination of some of the key influences of advertising over the shape of the online public sphere. In particular, it considers the oligopolistic tendencies favored by online advertising through its dependence on ever-increasing amounts of data, the ability of advertising to influence the content circulating in the public sphere, and the subservient situation in which users are placed by a small number of companies that have become essential to a range of human activities and require data to fuel their business.

Control and the Business of Communication

The establishment of a revenue model around communication processes responds to a variety of factors. The general characteristics of these processes and of the technologies that facilitate them constitute an essential element, since the modes and degrees of control that can be exerted bias in specific ways the viability of the different models.[1] Different modes of communication, and different technologies, make some revenue models more viable than others. By looking back at the history of forms of public communication and the different modes of control they favor, it is possible to better understand and examine the way control over public communication is currently exercised.

Early forms of public communication, which in a Western cultural context are often traced back to public spectacles in ancient Greece and Rome (McQuail 1997), were not technologically mediated. They can be described as live performances, such as a play performed in a theater, a concert, or a sports competition, which are clearly defined by time and space—they happen in a particular place at a specific moment. These space/time constraints facilitate a direct and hard form of control that seems to naturally lead to a simple revenue model based on payment. The simplest way to turn a performance into a business is to control access to the auditorium and demand some kind of compensation for the right to enter.[2] This is a physical form of control that has to do with bodily presence and that is able to sustain a revenue model in which other forms of control—softer, more complex, and having to do with information gathering—are not strictly necessary.

While such live performances continue to be an important ingredient of public communication, the use of technology became, centuries ago, an essential component of it. The first significant uses of technology as facilitator of public communication had to do with the ability to inscribe a message in a physical medium, as was the case with writing (Ong 1982). Technological mediation transformed, to a large degree, the nature of public communication and the afforded forms of control over it. Time and space lost their prominence as defining features since written texts could be read far from where and when they were written. Once the message has been inscribed, the author easily loses the ability to control it. There is, however, a way of retaining control: if reading does not require presence at a particular place in a specific moment, it requires at least access to the physical substrate on which words are written. Controlling the container allows for control over the process. This specific form of control would actually be key when the ability to copy and reproduce messages at scale thanks to the printing press transformed writing into a business (Eisenstein 1979). In fact, all cultural industries are based on this premise: the ability to mechanically copy a message—words, music, images—at scale and to control access to the physical medium in which this is copied—book, disc, videocassette—in order to demand compensation from those interested in consuming it. While the producers of messages lose control over the container once it is sold and thus cannot prevent pass-along readers/listeners/viewers, this situation allows for the creation of a viable revenue model based on payments.

The advent of the mass media would transform public communication at many levels, including the way in which a revenue model could be established. Newspapers, with different formats, periodicity, and content, had existed for centuries. And they had relied on the model of the cultural industries by demanding a fee in exchange for the medium in which messages were recorded, the paper. However, in the nineteenth century, newspapers consolidated a revenue model based on a two-sided market structure (Baldasty 1992). Part of the revenue would come from the sales of the paper, but an increasing portion of those revenues would be provided by advertisers eager to sell products and services to the growing number of readers. The reliance on advertising could only be sustained if new forms of control were implemented, controls that had to do with the collection of information and could guarantee advertisers that they were getting the product they were paying for: audiences (Smythe 1977). In consequence, the physical container, the paper, was taken as the first source of information, and the number of copies printed or delivered through the mail became a data point relevant for this new advertising market. The conflicting interest over the precise value of this data point—publishers were keen to inflate the number, while advertisers were keen to deflate it—led to the creation of independent third parties tasked to control how many copies of a publication did actually reach the readers, and thus certify circulation figures. Audit bureaus of circulation, in different forms and shape, started to appear in the first decades of the twentieth century (Beniger 1986).

Auditing circulation has obvious limitations in terms of what can be learned about the communication process and the audiences. In fact, and because of the lack of control over the container once it is sold, there is no way of knowing how many people end up consuming the message, let alone who they are. New measurement techniques for controlling the communication process were needed, and they would be fully developed upon the arrival of broadcasting as a powerful force that would upend public communication (Beville 1988; Buzzard 1990). The broadcasting technology broke any direct link between senders and receivers, between producers and consumers.[3] The signal was up in the air for anyone to capture and consume, with no record of how often this happened. In this context, it was impossible to replicate the revenue models of live performances and cultural industries. For some time, the sale of receiving sets was seen as a viable revenue model, while content production was considered as an ancillary activity. But it was soon clear that wrapping content with advertising would be a natural fit for the new mode of communication (Smulyan

1994). To make this a viable model, a whole series of breakthroughs were required, such as the development of sampling theory, the implementation of telephone surveys, and the invention of meter technology for audience measurement (Bermejo 2009; Beville 1988). Once in place, these innovations created the right environment for a thriving revenue model in which the audience would be traded as a currency produced through measurement (Ang 1991). In the broadcasting mode of control, the measurement of media consumption was structured around independent third parties (such as Nielsen or Arbitron) that used data collection techniques (such as surveys and panels) to produce syndicated studies that homogeneously covered most media outlets and offered quantifications of media exposure (mostly in terms of time) of a collectivity of individuals (usually referred to as the audience) who resided in a delimited geographical area (a market) and were classified according to a series of sociodemographic variables to yield a profile on which advertisers would rely to target their commercial messages. In this model, instead of demanding payment, the media would provide their content to the audience for free, and the content would serve as bait to capture the audience's attention, which would then be sold to advertisers for a profit (Jhally and Livant 1986; Smythe 1977). Advertisers would rely on measurement data as evidence that showed they were getting their product (the audience) and as a tool to make their investment decisions and choose which media and which audiences to target (Napoli 2003). Audiences would receive free content but in exchange, and in aggregate, would indirectly pay for it by purchasing advertised goods.

This general description accounts for the bulk of the revenue model of broadcasting throughout the second half of the twentieth century. There are, however, a couple of additional elements that have to be taken into consideration to complete the picture. The first one has to do with the possibility of controlling access to television programs. While the technology of broadcasting, consisting of sending a signal into the ether, made it impossible to control who consumed that signal, new technologies for the distribution of television signals—such as cable and satellites—achieved popularity, and techniques for encrypting and decrypting signals were developed. This allowed for the introduction of conditional access to the content being distributed and, thus, for the use of a revenue model based on payment. Though not prevalent, and almost exclusively applied to television rather than radio, this revenue model achieved great prominence in some countries (most notably, the US) and was often combined with the pure advertising model described above.

The second element that has to be considered is the idea of public service. As broadcasting became a central venue for public communication, the idea that it played a pivotal role in national communication systems led to the creation of public broadcasting services. These services became most prominent in European countries, where they were primary actors in the popularization of radio and television and acted as barriers to their commercialization and to the influence of advertising interests. Despite their relevance, public broadcasting systems were weakened in the last decades of the twentieth century under the forces of privatization (Servaes and Wang 1997).

The different forms of control of mediated communication described here, and the revenue models established around them, did not supersede one another. Rather, they accumulated over the course of the past century to produce a complex environment. In this environment, the cultural industries attempted to maintain control over their products in order to generate revenues in the form of fees, and while public service broadcasting played a significant role in some countries (especially in Western Europe), and pay television achieved a growing prominence, the majority of the mass media relied on the advertising industry as their mode of sustenance. This is the context in which the Internet arrived and that would be shaken by it.

Control and Business Models in Online Communication

The Internet was in incubation for a couple of decades within defense and academic circles, shaped by alternative technology movements, and under the umbrella of governments that provided the necessary resources for its development (Abbate 1999). Over these formative decades, there was no revenue model to speak of. In fact, any commercial activity over the Internet was explicitly prohibited (Greenstein 2000). But this situation would drastically change in the 1990s with the privatization, commercialization, and popularization of the Internet.[4] Different factors contributed to this change. The privatization of the Internet affected all different layers, from the physical backbones of the network to end users' activities (Greenstein

2000; Shah and Kesan 2007). The wave of privatization in telecommunications and broadcasting that took place in the 1980s (Feigenbaum 2009); the cultural influence of the hacker, alternative, and libertarian tech culture (Himanen 2001); and the fact that the epicenter of the Internet was located in a country with a weak culture of communication media as public service (Avery and Stavitsky 2003) all help to explain the lack of any counterbalancing forces that could have advocated for a stronger role of the state in the online environment. The popularization of the Internet was also motivated by different factors, such as the increased availability and affordability of personal computers, the growing number of Internet service providers, and most prominently the advent in the early 1990s of the World Wide Web. The creation of a popular and private network in which the ban on commercial activities imposed by the National Science Foundation's Acceptable Use Policy was lifted led to an increasingly business-driven environment, in which commercial online services (such as AOL and CompuServe) made large strides, e-commerce began to take shape, and advertising started to penetrate the online communication fabric.

Because the advent of a new technology does not occur in a vacuum, the Internet was necessarily affected by existing dynamics, stakeholders, and interests—while affecting these in turn. A first moment of friction took place when the cultural industries, in particular the music industry, realized that the ability to produce and distribute a large number of copies of a specific cultural product was no longer exclusive to them. Any Internet user with minimal investment and rudimentary digital tools was able to copy and distribute at scale the products from which the cultural industries harvested their revenues. The popularization of peer-to-peer networks, most prominently the success of Napster, made clear that the revenue model of these industries was under threat. They responded by using the law in an aggressive campaign to stop what the technology has made not only possible but easy and convenient, while in parallel attempting to protect their interests by reinforcing copyright regulation and trying to come up with a technological solution that would restrict the ability to copy and distribute their products (Gillespie 2009; Lessig 2004).

While the cultural industries tried to prevent the loss of control generated by digital technology, the mass media attempted to replicate the advertising model that had successfully supported them for decades. The ever-growing offer of content and the ease with which this could be copied or replicated, coupled with the lack of new and convenient forms of micro-payment and with the general perception that the Internet was "free," as in "free beer" (Williams 2002), contributed to pointing to advertising as the natural source of revenue of the nascent online public sphere. Starting in the mid-1990s, the advertising industry made a concerted effort to adjust to the online environment the structures and procedures that had served to sustain this model. Organizations that were involved in auditing press circulation, together with some new players, started to measure online activities through log files analysis; joint industry committees and private companies that had been measuring the mass media through the use of surveys began to use this same technique to account for online behavior; and electronic measurement panels that paralleled the ones used to measure broadcasting audiences appeared in many countries around the world. The proliferation of online advertising agencies and the standardization of online advertising formats contributed to this effort (Bermejo 2007).

These developments were based on the assumption that the web was but a new publishing platform. The large number of new users, the lack of editing capabilities in popular web browsers, the increasingly visual elements in online content, the use of dynamic IP addresses, and reduced upload speeds all pointed to a new era in which the mass communication structure, with a limited number of content providers and a large number of consumers, would prevail (Berners-Lee 1999; Napoli 1998; Roscoe 1999). Despite the obvious similarities, the replication of the advertising model did not quite succeed. Advertising would remain the main source of revenue, but it would undergo a significant transformation. Part of the reason had to do with the inability of the audience measurement operations to provide a credible and widely acceptable currency to fuel the system. The technological complexity of the new medium and the diverse use patterns led to the coexistence of competing methodologies, all of them with their problems and limitations, and of competing measuring organizations, each of them fighting for a space in the new market (Bermejo 2007; Buzzard 2012; Napoli 2010). While the audience measurement market in the mass media, save for a few exceptions, had converged in every country into a single measurement operation per medium, this was never the case in the online world (Bermejo 2007; Buzzard 2002). An additional problem was the inflation of advertising spaces, which caused a generalized reduction in the price of the audience product generated by the media.

A technical feature of the web further hindered the possibility of replicating the mass media advertising model in the online realm. For the first time, the decision on which ad to show next to a piece of content was completely individualized and ad hoc. On the Internet there's no permanent connection between content and ads, and the management of both content and advertising can be done in parallel and independently (Evans 2009). Two users can thus be consuming the same content while being exposed to completely different ads. This meant that the idea of the audience as a collective that was sold by the media began to disappear, since individual users could be targeted in different ways, and advertisers did not have to buy the whole audience as a collective but could choose certain segments or individuals. Also, the idea that the role of measurement was to produce a quantification of that collective and a profile of it began to lose sense, giving way to the field of web analytics (Kaushik 2007).

At the turn of the century, it seemed clear that the advertising model had to reinvent itself to adapt to the online environment. A first and very successful adaptation was search advertising. The idea that query terms are a valuable piece of information to target ads created a novel system in which users were shown ads based on their interests expressed in the searches they performed (Battelle 2005). This system fueled the growth of what is now known as search engine marketing, which became a substantial source of revenue and turned Google into one of the most powerful online companies. But it also presents some limitations. First, it is only applicable to a particular type of online player, search engines, and thus cannot be expanded to generate revenue for other types of online services and products. Second, search engine marketing falls on the side of demand satisfaction rather than creation. In the mass media, advertising played a dual role: it both provided information about products for people already interested in purchasing, and it generated the purchase intent through persuasion (Pope 1983). Over the course of the twentieth century the latter role became increasingly important, but search advertising did a poor job at playing that role since it was conceived as a mechanism to match products and services to manifested interests. Thus, the advertising model had to find ways of expanding throughout the Internet and of compensating for the lack of demand creation.

The idea of using language as a targeting tool was soon applied to e-mail, and thus users of free web mail accounts began to see next to their messages ads that were selected according to the words used in those messages. Also, some advertising programs scanned the content on blogs and other web pages and chose the ads to be shown accordingly (Bermejo 2011). But these applications of language-related targeting proved to be much less successful than search engine advertising, since the keywords in the content being consumed were not so indicative of users' purchase intent as the keywords used in searches.

The solution was found in the identification of interests, desires, and intents not explicitly stated but gleaned from users' behavior and from any data point left in their online activities. Rather than producing demand through persuasion, it was generated through targeting techniques that became much more precise by inferring from online traces which products and services would appeal to each individual user (Evans 2009). The way to do so was to gather information on all users' online activities and transform the Internet from a tool for information publishing to a tool for information collection. But because the web is based on a stateless protocol, and thus treats each request as independent of any other request, new techniques for linking actions and attributing them to specific users had to be developed. The first one was the cookie, created in 1994 to support e-commerce in the Netscape web browser (Montulli 2013). Cookies quickly evolved to expand their reach, both in terms of their life span and in terms of their ability to track users across the web, with the use of permanent cookies and third-party cookies. New tracking mechanisms, such as JavaScript tags, were also introduced to create user profiles for targeting purposes (Kaushik 2007).

There were additional developments in the direction of increased control over users' identities and activities. The creation of different kinds of online pointers able to track users through their online activities was a way to compensate for the statelessness and anonymity of the web, turn the open web into a marked space, and in the process make of it a viable advertising vehicle. By linking activities, an identity was created (Cheney-Lippold 2011). The opposite strategy toward the same goal was to start with the user identity by offering personalized services. The first successful wave came in the form of free web mail accounts. The next one, even more transformative, was social networking sites. By creating individual services to which users had to log in, it was possible to link all subsequent activity to specific people. Using a web mail service, or having a social network profile, greatly simplifies the tracking process, since logins serve as identity pointers.

The advent of the mobile Internet deepened this process of increased individualization. One of the traditional limitations of online tracking has to do with the possibility of having multiple users of the same machine, or a single user of multiple machines. With the spread in the use of laptops and smartphones these phenomena greatly diminished, as it could be assumed that each device corresponded to one user, facilitating the creation of profiles. In addition, the mobile Internet introduced a new axis for control: location (Gordon and de Souza 2011). Through the situation of Wi-Fi networks, the triangulation of cell phone towers positions, and the information from GPS systems, the location of most users became part of the routine menu of data points collected online. The mobile web also brought with it a new set of artifacts (applications, apps, or widgets) that created controlled environments that greatly facilitated the collection of personal information (Wang, Xu, and Grossklags 2011).

In sum, the attempts at replicating online the advertising business model that has served the mass media industry so well failed at a certain level but were immensely successful at another level. They failed in the sense that it was impossible to replicate the specific structure of the revenue model in which the mass media captured people's attention through attractive programming, the audience measurement industry measured this attention in aggregate and created the audience product, and the advertising industry allocated resources based on this measurement and bought a collective of potential customers. It was, however, successful at maintaining advertising as the main sustenance of public communication, even though the shape of the model changed significantly. The need to collect information in aggregate about media consumption and some basic sociodemographic variables gave way to a system of data collection at the individual level affecting every facet of human behavior. The pivotal role in this system is not played by companies in the content creation and distribution business, but rather by companies in the business of organizing and aggregating at scale content produced by others while collecting in the process the personal information that fuels the system, as eloquently argued by Zuboff in the first chapter.

The Impact of Advertising

While the effects of a particular revenue model in the dynamics of public communication are necessarily important, it is always difficult to isolate those effects from other contributing factors. Nonetheless, it is possible to explore some of the consequences of the advertising model prevalent on the social web and to examine them by looking at three different elements: companies, content, and users.

First, while there is a long tail of small enterprises that collect data from apps, online services, and digital gadgets, the social web is dominated by a handful of big players that benefit from economies of scale. The tendency toward markets dominated by a single platform or service has to do with the need for large provisions of capital required to sustain any large-scale online operation, but it is also related to network effect (Katona, Zubcsek, and Sarvary 2011) and learning mechanisms (Joachims and Radlinski 2007). Social networking sites, in particular, benefit from network externalities that make them more attractive as they grow their number of users, making them hard to compete with once they have achieved a certain size. Search engines, in turn, become more attractive as they learn from prior use, providing a competitive advantage to those with a large user base and a record of user activity. But the tendency toward a few dominant platforms is also related to the logic of data-driven advertising, in which the more that is known about the largest possible number of individual users, the better the interests of advertisers will be served (Krishnamurthy and Wills 2009). In this context, traditional media are clearly disadvantaged, since they are but one possible point of contact with users that visit many other destinations and use many other services, and that can be targeted anywhere across the Internet. Only companies with the scale to follow a significant portion of Internet users across a good portion of the online domain are in a situation to fully benefit from the advertising revenue model. And these companies, in return, have an unprecedented power over individual expression and public communication, as discussed by Land and by Callamard in this volume.

Second, the business logic sustaining public communication has a significant impact on the type of content that is produced and distributed. When advertising began to play an important role in funding the press through the creation of a dual market of readers and advertisers, publications began to consider content production not just in terms of what could interest readers but also what could attract advertisers, leading to the creation of new newspaper sections (Baldasty 1992). In broadcasting, the influence of advertisers led to the direct production of programming and the creation of specific genres, like the soap opera (Barnouw 2004). On the Internet, the influence of advertising on content can be perceived at two levels: what is discouraged and even prohibited and what is produced and promoted. Because an important share of the circulating online content is produced by users, online platforms supported by advertising and carrying this content have to set limits on what is acceptable and what is not as, illustrated by York and Zuckerman (see chapter 6 of this volume). Demotion in search engine results, and "community rules"[5] and blockage in social network sites, help to mark the contours of acceptable discourse and contribute to creating a friendly environment for advertising. In turn, a large amount of content is created with the only goal being to attract attention and advertising, explaining the existence of content farms and the phenomenon of clickbait. While tailoring content production to consumers' demands is a core practice of any commercial medium, the online unbundling of content and audiences introduces a level of sophistication, individualization, and adaptability that calls into question the very idea of a public sphere (Pariser 2011; Turow 2011).

Third, for users the social web involves the acceptance of the data capture that serves to fuel the advertising model. While the vast majority of the content they consume and the services they use are free in the sense that they do not require a monetary transaction, the payment here takes a different form. In order to enjoy the benefits of the services, users not only need to accept the terms of use and the boundaries for communication programmed into the platforms but they also have to allow for intensive data mining. Moreover, since the social web is increasingly described as a sort of utility, a social infrastructure that supports and facilitates personal and professional activities,[6] there is little room for choice, agency, or negotiation. Technical limitations are hardwired, terms of use are nonnegotiable, and intensive collection of personal data is part of the experience of being online.

Conclusion

This chapter has traced the evolution of revenue models and forms of control over the history of public communication, focusing on the transformation of advertising over the past two decades, and ending with an examination of how this transformation influences the current state of the online public sphere. It has shown how different modes of control facilitate different revenue models, which influence the activities of commercial enterprises and, in turn, have consequences for the exercise of human rights.

Advertising, as a revenue model, has no doubt fueled a dynamic communicative ecosystem online. Much of the content, tools, and services available to Internet users might have never existed if they had not been supported by ads. But it has also shaped the nature of public communication in specific ways. It has favored the creation of a few large and powerful platforms with a tremendous power over public discourse, it has set limits with respect to acceptable discourse while flooding the Internet with ad-friendly content, and it has created a system of data harvesting from which it is almost impossible to escape.

The growing perception of these negative consequences of the prevalent model of data harvesting and advertising targeting has not produced any viable alternative to it, at least yet. The peer production economy that emerged with the open source software movement (Moody 2001; Weber 2004) is in retreat and has only been able to produce a significant impact in online public communication with the creation of an online repository of knowledge such as Wikipedia. Besides the recent implementation of the European General Data Protection Regulation, the role of the state in the online environment seems to oscillate, depending on the countries, between minimal intervention and authoritarian control (Kalathil and Boas 2003). The increasing role of philanthropy in subsidizing online content, besides difficult to maintain over time, is dwarfed by the sheer size of the advertising-supported domain (Deighton, Kornfeld, and Gerra 2017). And pay models, demanded in some quarters as an alternative to the intrusive nature of data capture, face major barriers. If the goal is to know everything about everyone, why let the most valuable users, those with the disposable income to pay for online content and services, evade the *panoptic.com*?

Notes

1. For a detailed analysis of the idea of control, and of its relationship with communication technology, see Beniger (1986).

2. The process of exerting control over live performances can also affect many other elements, such as lighting, seating arrangements, or stage design, but the analysis of these different facets of control exceeds the scope of this chapter. For details on the evolution of control over live performances in the United States, see Butsch (2000).

3. The original meaning of the word "broadcasting," according to the *Oxford English Dictionary*, refers to the act of scattering seeds in a field.

4. These three processes are closely related but distinct. Privatization occurred when government agencies transferred control over the Internet to corporations, commercialization occurred when different companies began to make money out of Internet-related activities, and popularization occurred with the rapidly increasing number of users. For more detail on these processes, see chapter 4 in Bermejo (2007).

5. The concept of "community rules" has a flavor of enlightened despotism ("everything for the people, nothing by the people"), since they are rarely defined by the community but enforced in its name.

6. "Utility" and "infrastructure" are used here to refer to services regarded as essential or foundational for certain activities. See Sandvig (2013) for an elaboration of the idea of the Internet as infrastructure.

References

Abbate, Janet. 1999. *Inventing the Internet*. Cambridge, MA: MIT Press.

Ang, Ien. 1991. *Desperately Seeking the Audience*. London, : Routledge.

Avery, Robert K., and Alan G. Stavitsky. 2003. "U.S. Public Broadcasting and the Business of Public Service." In *Broadcasting and Convergence: New Articulations of the Public Service Remit*, edited by Gregory Ferrell Lowe and Taisto Hujanen, 137–146. Gothenburg, Sweden: Nordicom.

Baldasty, Gerald. 1992. *The Commercialization of News in the Nineteenth Century*. Madison: University of Wisconsin Press.

Barnouw, Eric. 2004. *The Sponsor: Notes on Modern Potentates*. New Brunswick, NJ: Transaction.

Battelle, John. 2005. *The Search: How Google and Its Rivals Rewrote the Rules of Business and Transformed Our Culture*. New York: Portfolio.

Beniger, James. 1986. *The Control Revolution: Technological and Economic Origins of the Information Society*. Cambridge, MA: Harvard University Press.

Bermejo, Fernando. 2007. *The Internet Audience: Constitution and Measurement*. New York: Peter Lang.

———. 2009. "Audience Manufacture in Historical Perspective: From Broadcasting to Google." *New Media & Society* 11 (1–2): 133–154.

———. 2011. "Online Advertising: Origins, Evolution, and Impact on Privacy." OSF, Mapping Digital Media No. 14. https://www.opensocietyfoundations.org/sites/default/files/mapping-digital-media-online-advertising-20111111.pdf.

Berners-Lee, Tim. 1999. *Weaving the Web: The Past, Present and Future of the World Wide Web by Its Inventor*. London: Orion Business Books.

Beville, Hugh M. 1988. *Audience Ratings: Radio, Television, and Cable*. Hillsdale, NJ: Lawrence Erlbaum.

Butsch, Richard. 2000. *The Making of American Audiences: From Stage to Television, 1750–1990*. Cambridge: Cambridge University Press.

Buzzard, Karen. 1990. *Chains of Gold: Marketing the Ratings and Rating the Markets*. Metuchen, NJ: Scarecrow Press.

———. 2002 "The Peoplemeter Wars: A Case Study of Technological Innovation and Diffusion in the Ratings Industry." *Journal of Media Economics* 15 (4): 273–291.

———. 2012. *Tracking the Audience: The Ratings Industry from Analog to Digital*. New York: Routledge.

Cheney-Lippold, John. 2011. "A New Algorithmic Identity: Soft Biopolitics and the Modulation of Control." *Theory, Culture & Society* 28(6): 164–181.

Deighton, John, Leora Kornfeld, and Marlon Gerra. 2017. *Economic Value of the Advertising-Supported Internet Ecosystem*. Interactive Advertising Bureau. https://www.iab.com/wp-content/uploads/2017/03/Economic-Value-Study-2017-FINAL2.pdf.

Donaton, Scott, and Pat Sloan. 1995. "Control New Media: Artzt Spurs Advertisers to Seek Greater Role in Programming." *Advertising Age*, March 13, p. 1.

Eisenstein, Elisabeth. 1979. *The Printing Press as an Agent of Change*. Cambridge: Cambridge University Press.

Evans, David S. 2009. "The Online Advertising Industry: Economics, Evolution, and Privacy." *Journal of Economic Perspectives* 23 (3): 37–60.

Feigenbaum, Harvey. 2009. "The Paradox of Television Privatization: When More Is Less." *Policy & Society* 27 (3): 229–237.

Gillespie, Tarleton. 2009. *Wired Shut: Copyright and the Shape of Digital Culture*. Cambridge, MA: MIT Press.

Gordon, Eric, and Adriana de Souza. 2011. *Net Locality: Why Location Matters in a Networked World*. Malden, MA: Wiley Blackwell.

Greenstein, Shane. 2000. "Commercialization of the Internet: The Interaction of Public Policy and Private Choices or Why Introducing the Market Worked so Well." *NBER Innovation Policy and the Economy* 1: 151–186.

———. 2015. *How the Internet Became Commercial: Innovation, Privatization, and the Birth of a New Network*. Princeton, NJ: Princeton University Press.

Himanen, Pekka. 2001. *The Hacker Ethic and the Spirit of the Information Age*. New York: Random House.

Jhally, Sut, and Bill Livant. 1986. "Watching as Working: The Valorization of Audience Consciousness." *Journal of Communication* 36 (3): 124–143.

Joachims, Thorsten, and Filip Radlinski. 2007. "Search Engines That Learn from Implicit Feedback." *Computer* 40 (8): 34–40.

Kalathil, Shanti, and Taylor Boas. 2003. *Open Networks, Closed Regimes: The Impact of the Internet on Authoritarian Rule*. Washington, DC: Carnegie Endowment for International Peace.

Katona, Zsolt, Peter Zubcsek, and Miklos Sarvary. 2011. "Network Effects and Personal Influences: The Diffusion of an Online Social Network." *Journal of Marketing Research* 48 (3): 425–443.

Kaushik, Avinash. 2007. *Web Analytics: An Hour a Day*. Indianapolis, IN: Wiley.

Krishnamurthy, Balachander, and Craig E. Wills. 2009. "Privacy Diffusion on the Web: A Longitudinal Perspective." Paper presented at WWW 2009, Madrid, Spain, April 2009.

Lessig, Lawrence. 2004. *Free Culture: How Big Media Uses Technology and the Law to Lock Down Culture and Control Creativity*. New York: Penguin Press.

McQuail, Denis. 1997. *Audience Analysis*. Thousand Oaks, CA: Sage.

Montulli, Lou. 2013. "The Reasoning behind Web Cookies." https://montulli.blog spot.dk/2013/05/the-reasoning-behind-web-cookies.html.

Moody, Glyn. 2001. *Rebel Code: Inside Linux and the Open Source Revolution*. Cambridge, MA: Perseus.

Napoli, Philip. 1998. "The Internet and the Forces of 'Massification.'" *Electronic Journal of Communication* 8 (2). http://www.cios.org/EJCPUBLIC/008/2/00828.HTML.

———. 2003. *Audience Economics: Media Institutions and the Audience Marketplace*. New York: Columbia University Press.

———. 2010. *Audience Evolution: New Technologies and the Transformation of Media Audiences*. New York: Columbia University Press.

Ong, Walter. 1982. *Orality and Literacy: The Technologizing of the Word*. New York: Sage.

Pariser, Eli. 2011. *The Filter Bubble: What the Internet Is Hiding from You*. New York: Penguin Press.

Pope, Daniel. 1983. *The Making of Modern Advertising*. New York: Basic Books.

Roscoe, Timothy. 1999. "The Construction of a World Wide Web Audience." *Media, Culture & Society* 21: 673–684.

Sandvig, Christian. 2013. "The Internet as Infrastructure." In *The Oxford Handbook of Internet Studies*, edited by William H. Dutton, 86–106. Oxford: Oxford University Press.

Servaes, Jan, and Georgette Wang. 1997. "Privatization and Commercialization of the Western-European and South-East Asian Broadcasting Media." *Asian Journal of Communication* 7 (2): 1–11.

Shah, Rajiv, and Jay Kesan. 2007. "The Privatization of the Internet's Backbone Network." *Journal of Broadcasting and Electronic Media* 51 (1): 93–109.

Smulyan, Susan. 1994. *Selling Radio: The Commercialization of American Broadcasting 1920–1934*. Washington, DC: Smithsonian Institution Press.

Smythe, Dallas W. 1977. "Communications: Blindspot of Western Marxism." *Canadian Journal of Political and Social Theory* 1 (3): 1–27.

Turow, Joseph. 2011. *The Daily You: How the New Advertising Industry Is Defining Your Identity and Your Worth*. New Haven, CT: Yale University Press.

Wang, Na, Heng Xu, and Jens Grossklags. 2011. "Third-Party Apps on Facebook: Privacy and the Illusion of Control." Paper presented at CHIMIT '11, 5th ACM Symposium on Computer Human Interaction for Management of Information Technology, Cambridge, MA, December 2011.

Weber, Steven. 2004. *The Success of Open Source*. Cambridge, MA: Harvard University Press.

Williams, Sam. 2002. *Free as in Freedom: Richard Stallman's Crusade for Free Software*. Sebastopol, CA: O'Reilly.

6 Moderating the Public Sphere

Jillian C. York and Ethan Zuckerman

Introduction

More than one billion users worldwide use Facebook on a daily basis to share photos, videos, links, and brief updates about their lives with dozens or hundreds of friends. Many use Facebook not just as a space for personal expression but also as a space for political discussion or organizing. As a result, how platforms like Facebook control speech critically affects the boundaries for freedom of expression. The revenue model in which users produce content for free and platforms monetize that content is a massively profitable one. Facebook earned $15.06 billion in 2015, capturing 16 percent of total online ad revenue in the process (Kint 2016). However, while Facebook's revenue model is a profoundly successful one, the apotheosis of the user-generated content (UGC) businesses has led to the increasing need to address a problem that, in the end, could prove an existential threat to both the platforms and the networked public sphere: content moderation.

Not all users follow a platform's rules when they post to that site. Mixed with quotidian updates about workplace milestones and weekend parties are hate speech and harassment, as well as less serious violations of Facebook's regulations, like nude imagery and misuse of copyrighted material. For UGC businesses to remain viable, they require a steady stream of content posted by users. Nevertheless, for these businesses to maintain their user populations over the long term, they have to control the stream of content so that offensive material does not chase users away from the platform.

As Facebook, Twitter, and other UGC businesses emerge as a key component of the networked public sphere, their decisions about content moderation have increased public importance and come under intense public scrutiny. In the wake of Donald Trump's election to the US presidency in 2016, media commentators accused Facebook of swaying the election toward Trump by enabling the spread of *fake news*, namely, articles, often originating in foreign countries, which made baseless accusations against Hillary Clinton and spread widely on the platform (Silverman and Alexander 2016). Commentators suggested that Facebook had an obligation to identify and warn users of fake news or block the spread of these links.

Others noted that asking Facebook to act as editor for the billions of pieces of content spread on the site daily was both unrealistic and potentially dangerous. Weeks before the controversy about conservative bias, Facebook had experienced a wave of negative publicity not for spreading news but for blocking it. The Norwegian newspaper *Aftenposten* cried foul after Facebook removed *The Terror of War*, a Pulitzer Prize–winning photograph by Nick Ut that portrayed nine-year-old Kim Phúc naked as she ran to escape a napalm attack. It is unclear whether automated algorithms used to detect and block nudity identified the post or whether an overzealous Facebook user or employee flagged the image, but its removal opened a debate about whether it was appropriate for Facebook to act as "the world's most powerful editor" and whether more context was vital to content moderation decisions (Wong 2016).

Facebook's problems with UGC are not limited to decisions about what may be published but include decisions about what content is prioritized. To protect users from being overwhelmed by the posts their friends publish, the Facebook news feed uses an algorithm to decide what posts are most likely to be to a reader's interest. This algorithm generates enormous speculation among publishers who syndicate content to Facebook and wonder how to ensure the widest possible readership for their content and among readers, who worry that Facebook chooses to feature content a reader is likely to ideologically agree with, a problem Eli Pariser (2012) calls "the filter bubble." This algorithmic selection has a clear editorial component, and former Facebook employees have complained that this editorial process was intentionally biased to exclude conservative news sources, preventing such posts from receiving widespread attention on the site and from emerging on Facebook's trending topics list (Nunez 2016). In responding to these complaints, Facebook eliminated its trending topics team and turned over the job of identifying popular news topics to a purportedly more neutral curation algorithm. Almost immediately, Facebook's trending topics began featuring wholly invented news stories, forcing biased humans to intervene on behalf of accurate news (Newitz 2016).

As the brief history above suggests, content moderation is a wicked problem for UGC companies for which there are no easy solutions. Facebook is not alone in its struggles—Reddit, a UGC site organized around volunteer-moderated *subreddits*, which resemble bulletin board systems, has been accused of fomenting hatred, harassment and nurturing a community of far-right-wing trolls accused of chasing others out of political dialogue through the process of *shitposting*, or posting hateful, irrelevant, or other content intended to derail a thread. Since its founding, Twitter has dealt with a number of complex regulation issues, most notably harassment, which saw the company team up with the nongovernmental organization (NGO) Women, Action, & the Media (WAM!) in an attempt to track incidents of harassment and tackle the problem (Lapowsky 2015).

However, content moderation is not just a problem for platform owners. As users of these systems become increasingly dependent on these platforms for news and information, the platforms take on an important civic role. A combination of user choice and algorithmic decision-making tends to lead users toward content that primarily aligns with their ideological preconceptions (Zuckerman 2013). Cass Sunstein's research suggests that communities grow more polarized and less able to compromise with each other as they deliberate among themselves, concluding that isolation within these platforms may be damaging democracy (Sunstein 2006). Beyond concerns about the effects of online dialogue, legitimate concerns exist that a platform like Facebook or Google might influence an election by pointing users to content aligned with one political point of view and suppressing another (Epstein and Robertson 2015). We should expect increasing scrutiny of the decisions made by these platforms, as well as pressure on the companies to increase transparency around their decision-making.

From the perspective of freedom of expression, this pressure needs to increase as platforms have tremendous power over what can and cannot be said online. Strategies favored by platforms that leverage community behavior to identify inappropriate content are gamed by actors in political conflicts, for example, Israelis trying to silence Palestinian speech, and vice versa, by reporting the other side's content as inappropriate. Under current systems, minority voices are in danger of being silenced on UGC platforms, and platforms are ill prepared to protect controversial but legal speech. It is in extreme cases like this that problems of online harassment can escalate to the scale of human rights issues. As these platforms have become important venues for local and international debate, attacks that silence voices by harassing them into nonparticipation or triggering platform policies to remove controversial speech can rise to the level of a freedom-of-expression concern.

In this chapter, we introduce the concepts of *hard control*—a platform's authority over what can be published online—and *soft control*—a platform's authority over what we are likely to see, and what is deprioritized in algorithms that govern a user's view of posts on the network (the feed). Considering these methods of control from the perspective of human rights, we examine the power of the platform within a larger context of threats to freedom of expression, including threats from state actors and threats from individual users acting alone and in consort. We consider these hard and soft controls in terms of not only the power that platforms are able to assert over online speech but what individuals and organized groups can do to influence or silence speech.

Socio-technical problems—like control of UGC—often inspire primarily technical solutions, many of which fail because of their singular focus on a multidimensional problem. At the bleeding edge of Internet development are advocates of decentralized platforms, who believe the only viable counterweights to the power of companies like Facebook and Twitter are alternative platforms that allow individual publishers, not platform owners, to decide what content is appropriate. These novel platforms, just now experiencing the early stage of adoption, replace one set of moderation problems—the massive power of the platform owner—with another problem: the inability to remove offensive or illegal content from the Internet, often without distinguishing between the two. Ultimately, they return the Internet to an earlier model, where users were responsible for choosing what they did and did not see, a solution that may prove entirely unfeasible in the era of mass publics online.

With no easy technical solution in sight, the problems of UGC moderation demand increased transparency and responsiveness from platform owners and vigilance from the human rights community. Ultimately, solutions that protect dialogue in online spaces will require a combination of technical innovation, regulation, transparency, and public pressure from human rights advocates. This chapter explores the challenges all parties—platforms, publishers, users, and advocates—face with the current system and some possible ways forward.

A Brief History of User-Generated Content

The rise of UGC is often referred to with the shorthand "Web 2.0," a piece of marketing slang coined by publisher and tech guru Tim O'Reilly and writer Dale Dougherty (O'Reilly 2005). Web 1.0 was dominated by the idea that businesses could offer products and services online, with the emergence of giants like Amazon and Google. In Web 2.0, the focus was on content, not on products and services, and the key shift was the idea that end users, not professionals, would be responsible for creating online content. While O'Reilly and Dougherty began promoting the term in 2004, UGC long preceded efforts to market it. The preweb Internet, consisting of mailing lists and text-based conversations called *newsgroups*, was entirely user created, as was much of the early web. Outside of the Internet, communities developing around AOL and CompuServe had much the same dynamic, with user content providing much of the value on those early platforms. Until the decommissioning of NSFNET in 1995, much of the Internet was a technically noncommercial space, and UGC was the dominant form of content.

In the late 1990s, commercial publishers flocked to the Internet, now open for business and newly user-friendly with the graphical user interface of the World Wide Web. User-generated content quickly took a back seat as commercial publishers repurposed reams of old content online. Recognizing a shift in the online landscape, companies like GeoCities and Tripod[1] realized that creating web pages was difficult for most inexperienced users, who lacked the technical skills to author HTML documents or set up web servers. The communities of tens of millions of users those sites hosted anticipated the billions hosted on sites like Facebook today, including the use of platforms as a space for controversial political speech and the challenge of moderating these communities. Companies like Tripod had as many staff dedicated to supporting these content creators as they did programmers, and the most challenging customer-facing work involved *abuse* teams, responsible for interpreting the terms of service (ToS) a customer had agreed to and removing material that violated those terms.

User-generated content would likely have failed as a business model if not for a key legal change in 1998. Prior to passage of the Digital Millennium Copyright Act in October 1998, it was unclear whether UGC hosts were liable for copyright infringement committed by their users. On finding copyrighted software or images on a user's web page, content owners would routinely threaten to sue the companies hosting UGC. The Online Copyright Infringement Liability Limitation Act added section 512 to Title 17 of the United States Code, providing *safe harbor* for platform owners as long as they followed a set of procedures designed to protect copyright holders. When being alerted to copyrighted information on their servers, online service providers were required to notify the user who posted it, allow that user to defend his or her ownership of the content, and if the user did not voluntarily remove the content, connect the copyright holder with the alleged infringer.

One aspect of section 512 is worth special notice. If online service providers were aware they were hosting copyright-violating content, they were no longer able to claim safe harbor. Section 512 did not require online service providers to actively monitor their sites for copyrighted content—instead, it discouraged them from doing so, because an active content monitoring strategy might prohibit a later safe harbor defense. For UGC companies hosted in the United States, there is neither incentive nor requirement to uphold the principle of freedom of expression. In addition to section 512, 47 U.S.C. § 230, a provision of the Communications Decency Act often referred to as *section 230* or *CDA 230*, protects UGC platforms—or intermediaries—from legal liability for what they host (with some exceptions, including some related to intellectual property) by treating them as intermediary hosts rather than publishers of content. This intermediary protection has allowed freedom of expression to flourish on UGC platforms.

At the same time, section 230 also provides such platforms with a right to restrict access to a range of materials, regardless of whether such content is constitutionally protected. This provision enables companies to put into place restrictions that—if undertaken by a state—would otherwise raise concerns about censorship. US-based UGC platforms commonly place restrictions on the display of nudity, for example, with some (such as Facebook and its various properties) banning it almost entirely. The combination of fears of lawsuits and the enormous expense of reviewing user-submitted content led toward a paradigm in which the less an online service knew about user content, the better. This paradigm was challenged by the birth of social networks and the increased focus on social interactions.

Early UGC platforms focused on individual expression—they allowed users to post what they wanted but didn't work to connect them with each other. With the rise of Friendster, which connected UGC with the *social graph*, a visualization of people's online relationships, the focus shifted to connecting communities of users through UGC, which became known as *social media*. By the mid-2000s, platforms like YouTube, MySpace, and Flickr and, later, Facebook and Twitter had emerged, offering various options for sharing content, including publicly. Where ToS had previously been sufficient for a world of individual expression, the uptick in public sharing and the ability to create multiple accounts created a need for user-oriented rules, or as they are often called, *community guidelines*.

Online service providers tend to create community guidelines designed to give them maximum flexibility in removing user accounts: almost all ToS include ability to remove content at the company's discretion. These are contracts of adhesion, whereby the individual user has no ability to modify or help shape them. The more user-friendly community guidelines that followed put into clearer terms existing regulations that appeared in ToS, often with further additions. Companies nevertheless set very low barriers to creating new accounts; if users were removed for violating the rules, they were most often able to come back almost immediately under a new identity. While companies sought to remove controversial content, the dynamics of the early web business were centered on growing advertising revenue and, particularly, demonstrating a strong and growing user base. (Most early UGC companies were not profitable—they made money for their founders by being acquired by *old media* content providers who had difficulty finding readers of their content online.) As a result, power often ended up being in users' hands, as UGC businesses had strong disincentives to remove content and users, with the exception of content that led to lawsuits. Other than the nuisance of reposting, users had very few reasons not to share controversial, copyrighted, or otherwise prohibited content.

In today's social web, users who violate such prohibitions face increasingly harsh consequences. Typically, a first post in violation of Facebook's nudity prohibitions will result in removal of the content; a second or third violation will result in increasingly lengthy *bans* from the platform, during which a user cannot post information, send private messages, or administrate pages. Penalties range depending on the severity of the violation; some violations eventually result in full account suspension. Having your Facebook account suspended has become an obstacle to visibility in your social circles, a strong disincentive to post certain types of controversial content. LinkedIn, a social network centered on professional connections, raises the stakes even higher: post content that leads to suspension or elimination of your account, and your professional reputation can suffer. Twitter, perhaps assuming that there's only so much harm a user can do in 280 characters, has remained accepting of anonymous and pseudonymous accounts, authenticating a small number of *verified* accounts with blue check marks, reinforcing the idea that the majority of Twitter accounts are wholly unverified.

While the real-name policy shifts the balance of power from users to platform owners, increasing the costs for bad behavior, it may be accompanied by another effect: a growing reticence on the part of users to produce content. Facebook routinely prompts users to post content, recycling past posts as *memories* ready for reposting, assembling albums commemorating friendships between two users so they have something new to post. Scholar Trebor Scholz points out that platforms like Facebook rely on its users to create content—without user-created content, the sites would have nothing to offer (Scholz 2012). This insight has yet to turn into the workers' rights movement Scholz and others have hoped for. While concerns are sometimes raised that the growth of platforms like Facebook is slowing, UGC sites are the most popular and powerful sites on the Internet.

According to analytics company Alexa, six of the top ten websites in the United States, in terms of traffic, are built on UGC—YouTube, Facebook, Wikipedia, Reddit, eBay, and Twitter—and two others, Google and Yahoo!, are arguably built on indexing UGC. At this point, UGC sites are not the exception to the rule but the dominant model of the social web. The beauty of this model for the platforms is that users do almost all of the work. The platform is responsible only for providing a space where a user can publish, while the user does the work of creating the content. The platform succeeds fiscally if it can make more from advertising on user content than it spends creating and maintaining the space. A major cost in maintaining these spaces is moderating user content, to prevent the site from getting sued or from melting down into a space so abusive and hostile as to chase users away.

The Importance of UGC Platforms to the Human Rights Community

Social media has emerged as a battleground for human rights defenders because of its value in mobilizing resistance movements and in publicizing otherwise invisible points of view. The 2011 uprisings in the Arab world and beyond demonstrated the mobilizing power of UGC platforms, while their aftermath—from the emergence of new democratic norms in some places to war in others—exhibited UGC platforms' value in the documentation of human rights abuses.

In late 2010, a Facebook page emerged in Egypt entitled "We Are All Khaled Said" (in English and in Arabic). Set up to memorialize Khaled Said, a young man killed by police in Alexandria, the page was then used to promote an already-organized set of protests, following in the footsteps of the Tunisian protests that had just effectively deposed the country's autocratic leader of twenty-three years, Zine El Abidine Ben Ali. The page's call to protest went viral among Egyptians, many of whom had previously only used Facebook for ordinary activities and communications, and on January 25, 2011, tens of thousands of people took to the streets in protest. The initial effectiveness of the Egyptian uprising, which deposed long-term autocrat Hosni Mubarak, inspired movements throughout the Arab region and well beyond. Some of those movements, such as that which took hold in Syria in February 2011, sparked violent clashes, leading to civil war. In the case of Syria, social media has been effective both in documenting and sharing human rights abuses, as well as in the dissemination of propaganda. Such content is not immune from the impact of content moderation; Facebook and YouTube have both been accused of contributing to the erasure of evidence from Syria (Ascher-Shapiro 2017).

UGC platforms today are the world's most dominant information carriers. Facebook has more than one billion daily active users, making it more populous than any single entity on earth, save for China and India. It is most certainly the world's largest censorship body, regulating countless unknown pieces of content on a daily basis, both on the basis of its own rules and at the behest of government bodies. The global human rights movement has relied on media attention to support two of its key theories of change. First, naming and shaming human rights abusers requires use of the media to communicate these abuses to a wide audience, and that media is increasingly dependent on social media platforms for distribution.

Second, organizing human rights defenders so that they will lobby legislators and political leaders to defend rights is vastly aided by use of social
media platforms. The importance of social media platforms to the protection of human rights forces us to interrogate their practices of content moderation and to draw attention to cases where such practices might have a
negative impact on freedom of expression.

Platforms and the Public Sphere

From earliest conceptions of democracy in ancient Greek times, through
experiments with representative democracy in the early United States,
democratic theorists have postulated the need for a space where members
of the public can discuss issues of the day and come to a consensus on ways
forward. In Athens, the agora served as a physical space accessible to the
(few, privileged, wealthy) citizens of Athens to meet and have discussions.
In colonial America, town meetings served much the same function for discussion of local issues. However, the sprawling nature of the United States
in the early 1700s led to the need for a mediated public space for discourse.
The combination of newspapers and a massive, heavily subsidized postal
system gave the early republic a textual public space in which literate citizens could share opinions, disagree, and discuss issues with fellow citizens
across the country, despite being separated by time and distance (Gallagher
2016; Starr 2005).

In 1962, German sociologist Jürgen Habermas offered a new conceptual vocabulary for understanding these spaces for democratic discourse.
He examined the ways in which well-to-do merchants in the eighteenth
and nineteenth centuries served as a counterweight to the power of rulers,
even in monarchies (Habermas 1991). Leaders needed to take seriously the
concerns of the bourgeoisie—"public opinion"—lest they find their policies
challenged by commercial interests. The space for the shaping of public
opinion, Habermas explained, was not just the physical spaces of coffee-
houses but a literary space in which writers and thinkers reflected on critical issues through newspapers and journals. Habermas termed this physical
and mediated sphere for discourse "the public sphere" (Habermas 1991).
Numerous critiques of Habermas's public sphere exist, and many center on
the exclusive nature of who could participate in public discussions. Nancy
Fraser's (1990) "Rethinking the Public Sphere" collects many of these

critiques, finding ways in which Habermas excludes women, the poor, and those marginalized by occupation, religion, or race. The public that Habermas celebrates is only a small fraction of the actual public, according to Fraser. Other critiques have examined ways that access to media has restricted access to the public sphere, putting the power of opinion shaping into the hands of those who control broadcast media.

The Habermasian visions of the public sphere have been challenged by developments in media production, from an activist culture of pamphlets and leafleting in the 1960s in resistance to the Vietnam War to the emergence of community access broadcasting in the 1970s, allowing a broader range of citizens to create video content. But the revolutionary shift has been the emergence of digital media technologies (see also Bermejo, this volume).

In *The Wealth of Networks*, Yochai Benkler introduces the idea of the networked public sphere, an updated understanding of this space of discourse for the digital age (Benkler 2006). According to Benkler, the rise of the Internet as the dominant space for discourse leads to two significant changes: it's cheaper for people to participate in discourse, and broadcast media owners no longer have absolute gatekeeping power by sitting at the center of hub-and-spoke networks. Individuals can share perspectives and opinions with each other at very low cost, without the mediation of editors and publishers restricting the flow of opinions. For Benkler, these structural changes solve many of the problems with Habermas's public sphere, opening discourse to a much wider set of actors. Based on comments Habermas made in 2006, Stuart Geiger noted that Habermas did not seem to share Benkler's enthusiasm for the transformations the Internet had made to the public sphere (Geiger 2009). Interrogating the gap between Habermas and Benkler, he offered an important insight on the freedoms offered by the networked public sphere. While powerful individuals and institutions may not have had the ability to shape speech as they had in the age of broadcast media, a new set of actors was sculpting our discourse: the algorithms that determine what ideas were widely shared on sites like YouTube, Reddit, or Digg. Geiger's "algorithmic public sphere" acknowledges the potential openness that Benkler celebrates but recognizes the power that platform owners and algorithm authors have over contemporary discourse.

Our current public sphere is both algorithmically mediated and centrally controlled. Platform owners have enormous power over what speech is possible, and the algorithms they deploy govern which perspectives are seen and which are buried. Moderation, both in terms of blocking content from being published and in terms of promoting or demoting content, is the mechanism through which control is asserted over the networked public sphere. To realize the hopes put forward by Habermas and Benkler, we need a close look at the challenges and paths forward for UGC, the space in which contemporary public discourses unfold.

What's Moderated, and How?

There are two key ways in which UGC platforms enact moderation: they control what users pay attention to, using algorithms that determine what is shown in a given feed (soft control), and they determine what content is acceptable for publication on the platform (hard control). Both types of moderation employ algorithms—often combined with human intervention—through processes that are opaque to users and are therefore difficult to review, analyze, and criticize.

Hard control relies primarily on what Sarah T. Roberts refers to as "commercial content moderation." This control is governed by a company's ToS, a contract of adhesion that gives almost all of the power to the platform, rather than to the user (Roberts 2017). In theory, a user is free to leave a platform and bring his or her content elsewhere, but in practice, a lack of alternatives, the difficulty of migrating the collection of content one has created, and tie-ins to third-party services and apps make leaving difficult. While these platforms are not natural monopolies—you can choose not to participate in social networks, choose Twitter over Facebook, or choose a decentralized alternative like Mastodon over either—the combination of network effects, in which systems grow more valuable as their user base expands, and barriers to interoperability give platforms monopolistic lock-in effects.

In addition to ToS are the aforementioned community guidelines, which aim to educate users about a platform's rules in clear, user-friendly language. These guidelines vary across popular platforms but generally include prohibition of hate speech, sexually explicit content, support for violent extremism, harassment, and copyrighted content. Platforms may have a legal responsibility to remove certain content, depending on the jurisdiction in which they are located, but community guidelines frequently include content that is otherwise legally permitted.

In moderating content, platforms are playing a complex game. They are responsible to their shareholders and advertisers but also seek to keep the cost of content moderation low. They are responsible for responding appropriately to legal requests for content removal. They must mitigate conflict between users to prevent users from abandoning the system because of patterns of abuse. Finally, they are under pressure from users, the media, advocacy organizations, and sometimes their own employees or shareholders to permit certain kinds of speech. Some platforms, such as Twitter, have explicitly oriented themselves toward an ideology of free expression. In order to maintain low overhead, a majority of platforms rely on user reporting, or *flagging* as a means of locating prohibited content for moderation. Flagging is far from a simple behavior—users deploy it not only to identify content that violates ToS but also to attempt to remove content they find politically or socially undesirable or simply do not want to see online. Flagged content is then reviewed by humans, a practice which has had a documented health cost for these workers, who must review graphic violence and other toxic imagery (Roberts 2017). These low-paying jobs are often outsourced to third-party companies, located in countries where the cost of labor is relatively low. Mary Gray and Siddharth Suri (2019) refer to such work as "ghost work," suggesting this invisible human labor is the force that ultimately allows "automated" systems like publishing platforms to operate.

Today, automation appears to be increasingly taking the place of human content moderation. YouTube pioneered the practice with audio fingerprinting of content in 2009. As YouTube increased in popularity and visibility, it became a popular place for users to post copyrighted music, in the form of either music videos recorded from cable television or digital music tracks uploaded as videos. Music publishers began searching for their content and sending reams of takedown notices to YouTube, following the procedures outlined in the Digital Millennium Copyright Act. As the volume of takedown requests became overwhelming, music publishers began arguing that YouTube could not reasonably claim ignorance that it was hosting massive collections of copyright-violating material. In settling these claims, YouTube agreed to implement a process of audio fingerprinting, in which it would accept databases of copyrighted music from publishers and scan videos uploaded to YouTube to identify those that used copyrighted music. Those videos could be blocked from being uploaded or could have their soundtracks altered, or, eventually, publishers could offer limited licenses of their music in exchange for a split of advertising revenues associated with the videos.

Content providers are now using a form of fingerprinting called hashing to identify images they know to be controversial. When they manually remove images of child sexual abuse, images promoting or glorifying terrorism, or images used to harass an individual user, or spam thousands of users with promotional materials, they generate digital signatures—hashes—of each image and store them in a database. As images are uploaded in the future, they are checked against the database of hashes and blocked from being posted if they match an image that was previously removed (Franz 2017). While automation makes aspects of moderation easier for platform owners, it does not eliminate the need for human decision-making. New images and videos are created every day, some of which violate ToS or community guidelines and have to be added to hash databases. Other content requires interpretation to decide whether it is harassing or abusive, decisions that can require local language and subject knowledge to make accurate assessments.

In both the tech and human rights community, innovators are exploring ways to make moderation better and fairer, including empowering users to hold platforms accountable for their content moderation decisions. In the meantime, moderation remains a major cost for platform providers and a frequent place of conflict between platform owners, their users, and the human rights community.

The Human Side of Hard Moderation

A purely algorithmic understanding of hard control misses a key feature of automated systems: these systems are trained using human behaviors, and edge cases are inevitably the responsibility of humans to solve. While human moderation through outsourcing tasks to labor in the developing world raises complex ethical questions, utilizing the free labor of users of the service involves even more complex factors.

Hard content moderation via flagging, as Kate Crawford and Tarleton Gillespie write, may appear simple, but its simplicity "belies a tangle of system designs, multiple actors and intentions, assertions and emotions." Flags use a "narrow vocabulary of complaint" that results in a messy process, "fraught with the vagaries of human interpretation and shaped by competing institutional pressures" (Crawford and Gillespie 2014, 418–419). Further, flagging encourages users to "snitch" on other users—often their friends—effectively creating a culture of reporting.

Indeed, flagging is frequently used by conflicting actors as an attempt to silence opposition. Groups band together to flood a UGC platform with reports of abuse, often reporting users for alleged breaches of guidelines that, when violated, trigger a request to the user to provide ID —policies such as Facebook's *authentic name* requirement or the requirement of US-based sites that users be age thirteen or older. In other cases, reporting abuse focuses on severe violations that trigger an immediate suspension (Brandom 2014).

Governments have enthusiastically adopted the tactic. In Vietnam, activists have documented having their accounts removed en masse, following targeted reporting allegedly by the government. Between June and August of 2014, more than a hundred Facebook accounts belonging to Vietnamese activists were maliciously reported and removed (IFEX 2014). Similarly, WAM! has documented "report trolling" in cases of sexual harassment, "in which people make fake claims about harassment just to gum up the works for reviewers and make it tougher to address legitimate claims" (Lapowsky 2015).

The introduction of automation to flagging and moderation processes may prove to be even more fraught than the status quo. Training artificial intelligence—or humans, for that matter—to distinguish between allowed and prohibited content is a complex task. As Kate Crawford has argued in the *New York Times*, proprietary algorithms are human built and thus contain human biases (Crawford 2016). For example, an image-recognition algorithm learns by being fed images (chosen by humans) and builds a model based on those images; therefore, if such a system is trained on photos of white people, it will have difficulty recognizing nonwhite faces (see also Bechmann's chapter in this volume). A well-known instance of such bias occurred in 2016 when a New Zealand citizen of Asian descent tried to renew his passport and was told his photograph did not meet requirements because "subject eyes are closed" (Titcomb 2016). Content moderation algorithms are likely to unearth similar problems. While replacing human with algorithmic moderation may spare human moderators from having to see horrific images—by having computers scan images before they're posted to a UGC platform—the parameters used to define such images can be inadvertently discriminatory. Unless designed to do so, algorithms do not take into account *who* is posting a given item of content. A news organization sharing a violent image may occur in a different context than an individual doing so.

Context becomes even more essential when algorithmic decisions are applied to text-based content. While Facebook has made strides toward transparency, releasing its content guidelines in late April 2018 in response to scrutiny and criticism following the Cambridge Analytica case, reviewing those standards makes it clear that the devil is in the details. An earlier leak of content moderation guidelines from Facebook's Berlin office, analyzed by the German newspaper *Süddeutsche Zeitung*, reveals that regulation of certain categories of content—such as hate speech—are particularly nuanced, differentiating between examples such as "migrants are scum" (not allowed) and "migrants are so filthy" (allowed). Furthermore, separate rules apply to public figures and nonpublic entities (Krause and Grassegger 2016). Algorithmic moderation is already increasingly being employed by UGC platforms for the purpose of countering violent extremism, a tricky gambit in which context—and expertise—is key. When cultural, political, and legal differences become more pronounced—such as in times of war—decisions on content moderation increase in complexity (Taylor 2014). Lebanese organization Social Media Exchange (SMEX) notes the imperative of UGC platforms "hiring and training teams with cultural and linguistic sensitivity" in order to ensure that any restrictions on freedom of expression are legitimate and limited (Dheere 2016).

Indeed, UGC platforms already struggle with context when dealing with violent content. In the summer of 2015, as police shootings of black men in the United States were making headlines, Facebook removed a live video of the Minneapolis shooting of school cafeteria worker Philando Castile, as filmed by the victim's girlfriend. Facebook called the incident a "technical glitch," which may or may not have involved algorithmic moderation—the company did not comment (Russell 2016). Specific communities are more likely to be impacted by discrimination in content moderation decisions, whether made by humans or computers. Ultimately, content moderation decisions are often highly subjective when made by humans, a problem that algorithms—designed by humans—are unlikely to solve.

Soft Controls

When Michael Brown, an unarmed eighteen-year-old African American man, was killed in Ferguson, Missouri, by police officer Darren Wilson, some corners of the Internet learned the news before television crews arrived in the St. Louis suburb. Twitter, which is disproportionately popular with African American users, lit up with the news of protests erupting in Ferguson and many tweets demanding that mainstream media networks pay attention to the unfolding events. On Facebook, another trend demanded readers' attention: the Ice Bucket Challenge, in which participants dumped a bucket of ice water over their heads to raise awareness of and funds for treatment of amyotrophic lateral sclerosis. Sociologist Zeynep Tufekçi noted this disparity and wondered, "Would Ferguson be buried in algorithmic censorship?" (Tufekçi 2014).

Facebook and Twitter present content to their users through a similar interface, a feed of recent posts from accounts a user has chosen to follow. But those feeds are assembled very differently on the two platforms. Twitter's feed is (largely) uncurated,[2] which means what you see depends on who you follow, how often you check, and which settings you have selected. Facebook's feed is heavily curated, which means you see posts Facebook thinks you most want to see—or, as some have speculated, perhaps what Facebook wants you to see. Tufekçi (2017, 156) have argued that the Ice Bucket Challenge may have been more popular on Facebook than Ferguson posts because Facebook's algorithm favors stories many of your friends engage with, and the Ice Bucket Challenge encouraged friends to pledge their support using Facebook comments. Others, more darkly, wondered if Facebook would weigh the positive stories of charitable giving over the negative stories of racism and protest, hoping to encourage user engagement.[3]

It is not possible to verify or dismiss Tufekçi's concerns. As Christian Sandvig and collaborators have noted, it is virtually impossible to audit the behavior of an algorithm like Facebook's without running afoul of the US Computer Fraud and Anti-Abuse Act, which prescribes severe legal penalties for probing a system with automated queries (Sandvig et al. 2014). Sandvig and others are now suing the US Department of Justice over these provisions, hoping to affirm a right for researchers to audit these systems (Zetter 2016). In the meantime, we face largely unanswerable questions about whether the content Facebook serves users is influenced by commercial motives (favoring a partner's news stories over those from a nonpartner), social engineering (sharing more stories designed to increase engagement over those intended to inform), or political bias (suppressing conservative viewpoints). Soft censorship through algorithmic means has become a major concern in part because it is so difficult to verify whether or not it should be a major concern.

Other forms of soft control are clearly ones we need to worry about. Over the past few years, consensus has emerged among human rights advocates that harassment—in particular, targeted harassment—is, in effect, a form of censorship. One needn't abuse the flagging system to remove someone from a platform—harassment, often by large groups of people, is often just as effective a method. Stories abound of individuals, often women, leaving platforms like Twitter after experiencing weeks of extended harassment. In January 2017, popular writer Lindy West publicly declared her exit from the platform, calling it "unusable for anyone but trolls, robots and dictators" (West 2017). Similarly, Jonathan Weisman—deputy editor of the *New York Times*—quit Twitter in 2016, stating that he would "leave [it] to the racists, the anti-Semites, the Bernie Bros that attacked women reporters yesterday" (Weisman 2016). The hostility evinced on the platform has caused numerous such public departures. Hostile online cultures—be they message boards, subreddits, or Facebook groups—can create a *censorship effect* for users who, when feeling attacked, may choose to self-censor. A 2016 study of US Internet users established that 47 percent of respondents had experienced some form of online harassment or abuse (Lenhart et al. 2016). That same study found that 27 percent of respondents say that they have at some point self-censored online for fear of attracting harassment, and that more than 40 percent of respondents had changed some of their contact information (including, in some cases, a social media user profile) to escape an abuser.

The shift from straightforward hard control to a more complex web of soft and hard controls is a conceptual shift the human rights community needs to understand better. Historically, human rights defenders saw the state as the primary implementer of hard controls. Dozens of countries, ranging from Morocco and Thailand (where key websites were banned for crossing cultural red lines) to Iran, Saudi Arabia, and China (all of which heavily censor UGC platforms and other content) block web pages and/or keywords for users inside each country, barring them from access without a virtual private network or other proxy (Freedom House 2018). The rise of UGC platforms—which have global reach and are difficult to block, as Tunisia learned the hard way in 2010—alleviated some of the pressure being put on states for censorship, as users gravitated away from blocked blogging platforms and news sites and toward Facebook, Twitter, and their competitors.

Nevertheless, as UGC platforms have gained prominence, our perceptions of censorship have shifted. We have begun to face the complex fact that censorship online now often stems from other users, including those in our own networks. Not only are we affected by hard control from platforms and governments and by algorithmic filtering from platforms. We can be silenced and chased off platforms by other users, through harassment or flagging. We have met the enemy, and it is us. Now we must find a way not only to make platforms accountable for hard control but to prevent us from enacting censorship upon each other.

Finding a Way Forward

The reliance on companies to moderate speech is itself problematic. Traditionally, censorship has referred to the restriction of speech or publication rights by the state or religious bodies, but, argue Luca Belli and Jamila Venturini, ToS form a "quasi-legislative function" in defining allowed behaviors on platforms (Belli and Venturini 2016), impacting users' ability to exercise their human rights (see also Land's chapter in this volume). Whereas legislation enacted by a democratic state actor to restrict speech is created transparently and with input from a wide variety of actors, regulations created by UGC platforms are opaquely crafted and may only include input from a handful of individuals. Further, UGC platforms seek to regulate content in the most cost-efficient way, which is not always with the rights of the user in mind. UGC platforms, opaque by design, frequently fail to provide a means by which the user can challenge content moderation decisions: 88 percent of ToS examined in a report by former UN Special Rapporteur Frank LaRue were found to permit platform providers to terminate specific user accounts without notice or a path of redress (United Nations 2011). Even when a path for appeals is offered, such processes can be difficult to use or even locate; in a number of cases tracked by Onlinecensorship.org,[4] users have reported seeking alternative means of redress, such as writing to technical support or advertiser pages (Anderson et al. 2016). Facebook announced in April 2018 that it was implementing an appeals process for content removal, news that is exciting, but also long overdue.

Finally, UGC platforms rarely publish information about the number of ToS-related content removals they make. This lack of transparency makes it difficult for users and human rights groups to advocate for progressive policy changes. Although most popular platforms have for some years published transparency reports that show the percentages of content removed at the request of governments, only Twitter has begun to include some ToS-related takedowns in their reports. These points suggest a combination of transparency, regulation, and careful consumer scrutiny à la Rebecca MacKinnon's Ranking Digital Rights project (Ranking Digital Rights 2018). But transparency is meaningless without real competition in the space—there is a need for competitive platforms that we can use and the right to control our data so we can move to those platforms. The portability provision entailed in Europe's new General Data Protection Regulation is a step in this direction.

One possibility for competition comes from decentralized platforms. Platforms like Diaspora, an open source social network, have promised for years that a user could leave the controlled space of Facebook and move to a server he or she individually controlled or to a server controlled by someone with a consonant approach to content moderation. While Diaspora has failed to develop a critical user base, Mastodon, designed as a decentralized alternative to Twitter, experienced a wave of popularity in 2017 and may emerge as the first prominent decentralized alternative to the megaplatforms. However, while decentralized social networks solve some problems, they generate others. It is near certain that someone will offer a social network with a strong policy designed to protect speech, possibly augmented by storing posts on the InterPlanetary File System, a distributed system of content storage similar to BitTorrent, which will make it virtually impossible for content to be removed from a web server. While this offers strong protections for speech, largely avoiding the problems of both hard and soft control by platforms, it opens the scary notion of content that cannot be removed. Whereas this might sound good to freedom-of-expression absolutists (a stance both authors flirt with), phenomena like revenge porn and other illegal phenomena become deeply problematic in a world where content is technically unremovable.

As we head toward a more complex future, it is necessary that approaches to content control—both soft and hard—recognize that moderation is a major function of successful social media platforms, and that efforts from human beings will be essential, likely in cooperation with algorithms. Both human and algorithmic models of content moderation present challenges but with expert oversight can be improved to limit the effects of bias. *Human-in-the-loop* machine learning is a method by which systems are trained by or with the input of domain experts, in this case, experienced moderators. By incorporating experts—or the broader public—into the training of algorithms employed by UGC platforms, platform owners, and those that regulate them, can work to ensure that such systems take into account diversities and minimize bias. We have witnessed the effects of advocacy toward UGC platforms by NGOs over the past decade. When faced with pressure from the public and media, companies have often changed course on particular policies or content presentation. In the case of the photo *The Terror of War*, removed from the page of a Norwegian news editor, outcry—from NGOs, Facebook users, and the media—led to a shift in content moderation policy (Levin, Wong, and Harding 2016). The hearings in the US Congress in the wake of the Cambridge Analytica scandal in 2018 have led to another move toward transparency by Facebook.

However, perhaps most important is the incorporation of society into the decision-making processes of UGC platforms. As instances of overzealous or erroneous content moderation reach the public, there is the opportunity for a strong citizen movement—that monitors abuse of power by platforms, demands transparency, and fights for freedom of expression—to emerge, building on existing efforts (by NGOs) to hold companies to account.

Notes

1. One of the authors, Ethan Zuckerman, was an early employee at Tripod.com, responsible for setting up much of the company's content moderation infrastructure.

2. In 2015 and 2016, Twitter made a number of tweaks to its interface, adding algorithmically suggested "in case you missed it" and "you might be interested in" tweets. However, users are able to see an unaltered feed by scrolling past these suggestions.

3. See, for example, John McDermott on Digiday UK. https://digiday.com/media/facbeook-twitter-ferguson.

4. One of the authors, Jillian C. York, is the cofounder of Onlinecensorship.org, an advocacy project that tracks user-reported incidents of censorship on UGC platforms.

References

Anderson, Jessica, Kim Carlson, Matthew Stender, Sarah Myers West, and Jillian C. York. 2016. *Censorship in Context: Insights from Crowdsourced Data on Social Media Censorship. Onlinecensorship.org,* November 18. https://s3-us-west-1.amazonaws.com/onlinecensorship/posts/pdfs/000/000/088/original/Censorship_in_Context_November_2016.pdf?2016.

Ascher-Shapiro, Avi. 2017. "YouTube and Facebook Are Removing Evidence of Atrocities, Jeopardizing Cases against War Criminals." *The Intercept.* November 2.

Belli, Luca, and Jamila Venturini. 2016. "Private Ordering and the Rise of Terms of Service as Cyber-Regulation." *Internet Policy Review* 5 (4).

Benkler, Yochai. 2006. *The Wealth of Networks: How Social Production Transforms Markets and Freedom.* New Haven, CT: Yale University Press.

Brandom, Russell. 2014. "Facebook's Report Abuse Button Has Become a Tool of Global Oppression." *The Verge,* September 2. https://www.theverge.com/2014/9/2/6083647/facebook-s-report-abuse-button-has-become-a-tool-of-global-oppression.

Crawford, Kate. 2016. "Artificial Intelligence's White Guy Problem." *New York Times,* June 25. https://www.nytimes.com/2016/06/26/opinion/sunday/artificial-intelligences-white-guy-problem.html.

Crawford, Kate, and Tarleton Gillespie. 2014. "What Is a Flag For? Social Media Reporting Tools and the Vocabulary of Complaint." *New Media & Society* 18 (3): 410–428.

Dheere, Jessica. 2016. "Considering Countering Violent Extremism in Lebanon." *SMEX,* May 1. https://smex.org/considering-countering-violent-extremism-in-lebanon.

Epstein, Robert, and Ronald E. Robertson. 2015. "The Search Engine Manipulation Effect (SEME) and Its Possible Impact on the Outcomes of Elections." *Proceedings of the National Academy of Sciences of the United States of America* 112 (33): E4512–E4521.

Franz, Julia. 2017. "How We Can Use 'Digital Fingerprints' to Keep Terrorist Messaging from Spreading Online." *Public Radio International,* February 12. https://www.pri.org/stories/2017-02-12/how-we-can-use-digital-fingerprints-keep-terrorist-messaging-spreading-online.

Fraser, Nancy. 1990. "Rethinking the Public Sphere: A Contribution to the Critique of Actually Existing Democracy." *Social Text* (25/26): 56–80.

Freedom House. 2018. *Freedom on the Net 2018*, October. https://freedomhouse.org/sites/default/files/FOTN_2018_Final%20Booklet_11_1_2018.pdf.

Gallagher, Winifred. 2016. *How the Post Office Created America: A History*. New York: Penguin Press.

Geiger, Stuart. 2009. "Does Habermas Understand the Internet? The Algorithmic Construction of the Blogo/Public Sphere." *Gnovis. A Journal of Communication, Culture, and Technology* 10 (1): 1–29.

Gray, Mary L., and Siddharth Suri. 2019. Ghost Work: How to Stop Silicon Valley from Building a New Global Underclass. Boston: Houghton Mifflin Harcourt.

Habermas, Jürgen. 1991. *The Structural Transformation of the Public Sphere: An Inquiry into a Category of Bourgeois Society*. 6th ed. Cambridge, MA: MIT Press.

IFEX. 2014. "Hanoi government must stop attacks against Vietnam's Facebook community." *IFEX*, August 13. https://www.ifex.org/vietnam/2014/08/13/attacks_facebook_community.

Kint, Jason. 2016. "Google and Facebook Devour the Ad and Data Pie: Scraps for Everyone Else." *Digital Context Next*, June 16. https://digitalcontentnext.org/blog/2016/06/16/google-and-facebook-devour-the-ad-and-data-pie-scraps-for-everyone-else.

Krause, Till, and Hannes Grassegger. 2016. "Facebook's Secret Rules of Deletion." *Süddeutsche Zeitung*, December 16. https://www.savemysweden.com/facebooks-secret-rules-of-deletion.

Lapowsky, Issie. 2015. "It's Too Easy for Trolls to Game Twitter's Abuse Tools." *Wired*, May 13. https://www.wired.com/2015/05/wam-twitter-harassment.

Lenhart, Amanda, Michele Ybarra, Katherine Zickuhr, and Myeshia Price-Feeney. 2016. "Online Harassment, Digital Abuse, and Cyberstalking in America." *Data and Society Research Institute*, November 21. https://www.datasociety.net/pubs/oh/Online_Harassment_2016.pdf.

Levin, Sam, Julie Carrie Wong, and Luke Harding. 2016. "Facebook backs down from 'napalm girl' censorship and reinstates photo." *The Guardian*, September 9. https://www.theguardian.com/technology/2016/sep/09/facebook-reinstates-napalm-girl-photo.

Newitz, Annalee. 2016. "Facebook Fires Human Editors, Algorithm Immediately Posts Fake News." *Ars Technica*, August 29. https://arstechnica.com/business/2016/08/facebook-fires-human-editors-algorithm-immediately-posts-fake-news.

Nunez, Michael. 2016. "Former Facebook Workers: We Routinely Suppressed Conservative News." *Gizmodo*, May 9. https://gizmodo.com/former-facebook-workers-we-routinely-suppressed-conser-1775461006.

O'Reilly, Tim. 2005. "What Is Web 2.0: Design Patterns and Business Models for the Next Generation of Software." *O'Reilly*, September 30. http://www.oreilly.com/pub/a/web2/archive/what-is-web-20.html.

Pariser, Eli. 2012. *The Filter Bubble: How the New Personalized Web Is Changing What We Read and How We Think.* New York: Penguin Books (reprint edition).

Ranking Digital Rights. 2018. https://rankingdigitalrights.org.

Roberts, Sarah T. 2017. "Social Media's Silent Filter." *The Atlantic*, March 8, 2017. https://www.theatlantic.com/technology/archive/2017/03/commercial-content-moderation/518796.

Russell, Jon. 2016. "Facebook Blames 'Technical Glitch' for Temporary Removal of Falcon Heights Shooting Video." *TechCrunch*, July 7. https://techcrunch.com/2016/07/07/facebook-blames-technical-glitch-for-temporary-removal-of-falcon-heights-shooting-video.

Sandvig, Christian, Kevin Hamilton, Karrie Karahalios, and Cedric Langbort. 2014. "Auditing Algorithms: Research Methods for Detecting Discrimination on Internet Platforms." Paper presented at the annual meeting of the International Communication Association, Seattle, WA, May 2014. http://www-personal.umich.edu/~csandvig/research/Auditing%20Algorithms%20--%20Sandvig%20--%20ICA%202014%20Data%20and%20Discrimination%20Preconference.pdf.

Scholz, Trebor. 2012. *Digital Labor: The Internet as Playground and Factory.* London: Routledge.

Silverman, Craig, and Lawrence Alexander. 2016. "How Teens in the Balkans Are Duping Trump Supporters with Fake News." *Buzzfeed*, November 4, 2016. https://www.buzzfeed.com/craigsilverman/how-macedonia-became-a-global-hub-for-pro-trump-misinfo.

Starr, Paul. 2005. *The Creation of the Media: Political Origins of Modern Communications.* New York: Basic Books.

Sunstein, Cass. 2006. *Infotopia: How Many Minds Produce Knowledge.* Oxford: Oxford University Press.

Taylor, Astra. 2014. *The People's Platform: Taking Back Power and Culture in the Digital Age.* Toronto: Random House Canada.

Titcomb, James. 2016. "Robot Passport Checker Rejects Asian Man's Photo for Having His Eyes Closed." *The Telegraph*, December 7. http://www.telegraph.co.uk/

technology/2016/12/07/robot-passport-checker-rejects-asian-mans-photo
-having-eyes.

Tufekçi, Zeynep. 2014. "What Happens to #Ferguson Affects Ferguson: Net Neutrality, Algorithmic Filtering and Ferguson." *The Message*, August 14. https://medium
.com/message/ferguson-is-also-a-net-neutrality-issue-6d2f3db51eb0.

Tufekçi, Zeynep. 2017. *Twitter and Tear Gas: The Power and Fragility of Networked Protest*. New Haven, CT: Yale University Press

United Nations, General Assembly. 2011. "Report of the Special Rapporteur on the Promotion and Protection of the Right to Freedom of Opinion and Expression, Frank La Rue." A/HRC/17/27. May 16. http://www2.ohchr.org/english/bodies/hrcouncil/docs/17session/A.HRC.17.27_en.pdf.

Weisman, Jonathan. 2016. "Why I Quit Twitter—And Left Behind 35,000 Followers." *New York Times*, June 10. https://www.nytimes.com/2016/06/10/insider/why-i
-quit-twitter-and-left-behind-35000-followers.html.

West, Lindy. 2017. "I've Left Twitter: It Is Unusable for Anyone but Trolls, Robots and Dictators." *The Guardian*, January 3. https://www.theguardian.com/commentisfree/2017/jan/03/ive-left-twitter-unusable-anyone-but-trolls-robots-dictators-lindy-west.

Wong, Julia Carrie. 2016. "Mark Zuckerberg Accused of Abusing Power after Facebook Deletes 'Napalm Girl' Post." *The Guardian,* September 9. https://www.theguardian
.com/technology/2016/sep/08/facebook-mark-zuckerberg-napalm-girl-photo
-vietnam-war.

Zetter, Kim. 2016. "Researchers Sue the Government over Computer Hacking Law." *Wired*, June 29. https://www.wired.com/2016/06/researchers-sue-government
-computer-hacking-law.

Zuckerman, Ethan. 2013. *Rewire: Digital Cosmopolitans in the Age of Connection*. New York: W. W. Norton.

7   Rights Talk: In the Kingdom of Online Giants

Rikke Frank Jørgensen

Introduction

Powerful companies like Facebook and Google have the ability to influence human rights in ways traditionally reserved for governments yet operate outside the direct reach of human rights law. Although their impact on a number of human rights is widely acknowledged, including within the industry itself, the regulation of this impact varies considerably. In the European Union context, for example, the privacy rights of Facebook's and Google's users are regulated via data protection regulation, whereas their potential negative impact on freedom of expression is not. It is fair to say that in most national contexts (including that of the United States), the companies' responsibilities in regard to international human rights law are governed by soft-law frameworks and voluntary measures defined and enforced by the industry itself (for an extensive elaboration of this point, see the chapters by Callamard and Land in this volume).

Whereas some of the subsequent chapters extensively discuss the responsibility of these companies vis-à-vis human rights law, the focus of this chapter is on the internal storytelling around human rights. Using Google and Facebook as empirical case studies, the chapter focus on three corporate narratives related to the companies' commitment to respect human rights. The first narrative concerns the role the companies are depicted to play as safeguards against government overreach. The second narrative relates to their role as cooperators with governments. Finally, the third narrative concerns the way privacy is constructed within company discourse.

With reference to Luhmann's (1993) communicative theory of social systems, the narratives represent specific ways of producing, reproducing, and legitimizing meaning by staff at Facebook and Google. As part of this sense making, the narratives serve to maintain the boundary between a relatively closed system and its environment and to legitimize specific practices within the organizations. The analysis also draws on the notions of *platform* and *infrastructure*, which are used to unpack and critically discuss some of the underlying assumptions in the corporate storytelling.

The chapter will argue that the companies' efforts vis-à-vis human rights tend to focus exclusively on state interference and pays limited attention to the companies' own business practices and the way the data-driven economy informs those practices.

Methodology

The analysis draws in part on empirical data collected as part of a two-year research project on the commercialized public sphere (Jørgensen 2017a, 2017b). The research project relied on a context-oriented qualitative approach, including publicly available statements from the two companies, terms of service, and policies, as well as semistructured interviews with company staff, primarily in Europe and the United States. The interviews focused on the internal discourse and sense making related to human rights; the translation of this normative basis into specific features or products, and the governance mechanisms set up to enforce the norms. The interviewed were staff with responsibility for human rights (e.g., participation in the Global Network Initiative; GNI), public policy, privacy, community operations (Facebook), and removal requests (Google). However, meetings were also conducted with technical staff (Google), as well as more research-oriented staff working on education and user experience (Google). With a few exceptions, the respondents had been with the companies for some years and carried some level of responsibility within the organization. In total, twenty-one interviews were conducted (thirteen Google, eight Facebook), and twenty publicly available talks and testimonies were analyzed in relation to the above themes. The public talks and testimonies were selected on the basis of topic (relevance) and located via YouTube and the Zuckerberg Files, which is a digital archive of all public statements made by Mark Zuckerberg, from 2004 to 2018.[1]

While the three narratives presented in the following are derived from the research project, it is important to note that they are neither exclusive nor exhaustive. Rather, they are chosen for this chapter as telling examples of how the two organizations understand their role and responsibility in relation to human rights.

Analytical Framework

The analysis relies on the concept of frames (Goffman 1974; Johnston 2005; Tannen 1993), as sets of relatively coherent meanings that organize the identity and activities of an individual or organization. As such, frames are used to situate events, fashion a shared understanding of the world, and guide problem-solving (Barnett and Finnemore 2004, 33). In short, concepts such as *freedom of expression* and *privacy* do not have an objective meaning but are framed in particular ways deemed to give meaning in a specific context—in this case, that of Google and Facebook. This implies attention to ways in which individuals and organizations frame and explain particular meanings, as well as how these meanings are translated into practice (Latour and Woolgar 1986).

It also considers organizations as communicative systems, inspired by the German sociologist Niklas Luhmann and his extensive theory on social systems (Luhmann 1993). According to this framework, each system (e.g., an organization) has a distinctive identity that marks the border between system and the environment and is constantly reproduced through communicative processes. These communicative processes (sense making) are governed by "interpretation codes" that guide how information is selected, processed, and understood within the specific organization—for example, true/false (a scientific system), economic gains/losses (a business system), legal/illegal (a justice system) (Luhmann 1992, 253). In relation to human rights such as the right to privacy, this has the function of protecting the boundaries of specific systems—for instance, by preventing sensitive information from one context from proliferating into other ones (Hornung and Schnabel 2009, 85).

In terms of understanding the services that Facebook and Google provide, the analysis is inspired by the literature on platforms and infrastructures as two notions increasingly used to describe the companies, but with different policy implications. The notion of infrastructure is generally used to describe the underlying foundation of a system or organization. Examples include transportation systems such as highway, railway, and airline systems; communication systems such as telephone networks and postal services; and basic public services and facilities such as schools and water systems (Frischmann 2012, 4). Infrastructure often exists as an invisible, taken-for-granted resource, whereas a breakdown in the infrastructure can make its design and effects visible (Bowker et al. 2010, 97–98). The term "platform" is commonly used to characterize the economic model of the social web (Helmond 2015, 5) and connotes openness, functionality, empowerment, and neutrality (Pangrazio 2016, 2–3), whereas in fact the economic model, technical design, and policies of platforms steer user interaction in certain directions. Van Dijck (2013, 29) has importantly noted that "a platform is a mediator rather than an intermediary," because it shapes sociocultural performance rather than merely facilitating it. As such, the owners of the platforms—the companies—hold great power over the wide range of social activities they facilitate, which include small- or large-scale communication, public debate, social interaction, information search, and so forth (van Dijck and Poell 2013). Since online platforms serve varied audiences that include users, shareholders, third parties, and advertisers, part of their governance challenge is to manage expectations between a diverse range of interests in order to serve the company's business interests (Ananny and Gillespie 2016).

Arguably, major online platforms effectively function as social infrastructures—that is, as foundational and largely unseen services that govern public action (Bowker and Star 1999). They are embedded, taken for granted, ruled by unquestioned standards, and visible only when seen to be failing (Star and Ruhleder 1996). While traditional infrastructures undergo *platformization* (Plantin et al. 2016, 298), online platforms experience *infra-structuralization* as companies exploit the power of platforms to "gain footholds as the modern-day equivalents of the railroad, telephone, and electric utility monopolies of the late 19th and the 20th centuries" (Ananny and Gillespie 2016, 14–15). The increasingly infrastructural nature of major platforms makes it difficult for people to leave them (Ananny and Gillespie 2016), just as the platforms benefit from the socio-technical investments users have made over time: "profiles and identities that have been tended to for years; networks and relationships that exist nowhere else and would be nearly impossible to recreate; media and metadata embedded within particular platforms and difficult to extract" (ibid., 1).

The above perspectives on platforms and infrastructures remind us that the notions used to describe the services provided by Google and Facebook carry specific—and often contested—meanings. Moreover, if major platforms are considered to function as societal infrastructures, this prompts consideration of the appropriate regulatory response—a point I return to in the Conclusion.

First Narrative: Google and Facebook Protect Their Users against Government Overreach

In March 2016, US lawyer and commentator Jeffrey Rosen argued that he was happy with the governance of freedom of expression conducted by Facebook, Google, and Twitter. Rosen had previously described these companies as more powerful than any king when it comes to free speech decisions in the online domain (Rosen 2012).

> Especially in light of these new pressures, I really have to express admiration for Monica, and Juniper and their colleagues at Twitter . . . they are trying to tread an incredibly delicate and difficult line where (one has) all of these pressures from Europe and from society to take speech down and to ban speech, and yet this constitutional principle that says it has to stay up unless it is intended to cause harm. . . . I really have concluded that if someone has to do it I would rather that it be these two incredible powerful women than a government, like Europe, or an international body like the illiberal groups that are calling for repression of speech at the network level, led by China and Russia. (Rosen 2016)

The Rosen quotation reflects the first narrative discussed here, namely, how staff at both Google and Facebook frame their human rights responsibility as an obligation to safeguard users against overreach by governments. The interviewees from both companies explicitly acknowledge the importance of protecting and advancing human rights and emphasize their services as enablers of specific rights, most notably freedom of expression. Services such as Google Search and Facebook's social network are seen to counter existing inequalities and contribute to making the world a more just place. "There is asymmetry. Those in power can call a newspaper or television and get access. Ordinary people can't. We want to rectify that asymmetry in communication power" (Facebook interview #2, 2015). "Googlers share a common view of the world; more access to information makes the world a better place" (Google interview #3, 2015). Also, staff at both companies refer to freedom of expression as a crucial element of the corporate identity and as a guiding normative base. "Censorship is against everything Facebook stands for" (Facebook interview #2, 2015). "Freedom of expression runs deep in Google's engineering culture" (Google interview #10, 2015).

When questioned about perceived threats to human rights in relation to their services, all respondents referred to government intervention at either a formal or an informal level. The examples of government intervention included shutting down or blocking access to services, requesting access to user data, or attempting to gain greater control over the platforms. Respondents from both companies stress that they push back fiercely against government attempts to narrow the boundaries for allowed expression, or to withdraw user data, whenever these attempts are not lawful and consistent with international human rights standards. By contrast, none of the respondents highlight the fact that corporate practices may themselves have a negative impact on users' rights, for example, the enforcement of terms of service. "Our purpose is to highlight Government action. That's where the focus should be. That's where the pressure is, and that pressure is increasing. Takedown is not really a user concern" (Facebook interview #6, 2015). "It will impact the scope of expression, but we don't consider ourselves to be deciding on freedom of expression. We take decisions on a specific product. We don't take down political speech; it's hate, pornography, and so on" (Facebook interview #6, 2015). "In relation to human rights, we mostly focus on minimizing harm from governments" (Google interview #7, 2015).

This focus on the company–government relationship is also reflected in the main industry initiative in this field—the GNI, which was established in 2008 as a multistakeholder initiative to help the companies enact policies to anticipate and respond to situations in which local law and practice differ from international standards on the rights to privacy and free expression online (Maclay 2014, 11). The corporate member base is limited and includes Google, Oath, Facebook, Microsoft, and LinkedIn, while seven telecommunication companies have joined the affiliated initiative, the Telecommunications Industry Dialogue. On the basis of international law, the GNI has developed a set of standards that the companies should follow to mitigate violations of privacy and freedom of expression caused by governments. The standards focus entirely on company pushback against illegitimate government requests, while failing to provide similar benchmarks for other types of business practices. It is also unclear how these standards translate into corporate practices. In November 2015, GNI cofounder Rebecca MacKinnon launched the Ranking Digital Rights corporate accountability index in an attempt to increase the transparency of human rights-related business practices.[2] The index measures the human rights commitment of twenty-two major Internet and telecommunication companies at an annual basis, based on the information they disclose on their policy and practices related to freedom of expression and privacy.

In relation to Facebook, the 2017 and 2018 index found evidence that the company's senior leadership exercises oversight of issues related to freedom of expression and privacy, an improvement from the initial 2015 index.[3] Facebook's disclosure regarding its human rights due diligence has also improved, as has as the company's commitment to conduct regular human rights impact assessments. By contrast, there is still a lack of information on remedy and grievance mechanisms for users who allege infringements of their rights. There is also limited information about the volume and nature of content that Facebook restricts or removes in the course of enforcing its terms of service, although this has improved in the 2018 index. Facebook now publishes some data on the volume and nature of content restricted for violating rules against hate speech and inauthentic accounts, yet there should be more transparency on how it identifies and restricts content found to violate its rules. As for privacy, the 2018 index found that while Facebook offers some disclosure about the types of information it collects, it revealed less about what it shares and with whom, for what purpose, and for how long it retains such information. Its disclosure of options users have to control what information the company collects, retains, and uses was especially poor. The company offers some ways to opt out of targeted advertising, suggesting it is on by default. The index found no evidence that Facebook respects the "Do Not Track" standard that allows users to opt out of certain types of web tracking. By contrast, its transparency reporting on government requests for user data is fairly strong.

As for Google, a founding member of the GNI, the 2017 and 2018 index found no evidence of executive oversight of business practices that affect users' freedom of expression and privacy.[4] The index found that although Google is committed to conducting human rights risk assessments when entering new markets, there is no evidence that it conducts assessments of risks related to terms of service enforcement. It also had notably weak remedy and grievance mechanisms. Google discloses more than any other company in the index about how it handles government and private requests to restrict content and accounts, yet the company´s disclosure of private requests could be significantly improved. For example, in 2015, Google reported removing 92 million videos from YouTube for terms of services violations, but there has been no follow-up disclosure since or evidence of similar disclosures for other Google services evaluated. Google does, however, report on requests related to copyright infringement (globally) and the de-indexing of particular search entries following the "right to be forgotten" ruling (for Europe).[5] As for privacy, Google lacks clarity and specificity in its disclosures related to the handling of personal data, in particular the collection of user data from, and the sharing of it with, third parties. The 2018 index noted that Google has improved its disclosure of options users have to control the collection of some user information, including their location, search history and browsing activity. In line with Facebook, there is no evidence that it respects the "Do Not Track" standard that allows users to opt out of certain types of web tracking.

The Ranking Digital Rights assessment highlights the key point of this section, namely, the disproportionate focus on governments as the cause of human rights problems in the online domain. While it must be acknowledged that governments pose significant threats to human rights around the globe, and that standards are needed to ensure that companies respond to government pressure in ways that comply with human rights law, this is only part of the picture. Arguably, Internet giants such as Facebook and Google have a substantial impact on human rights globally through the corporate policies they adopt and enforce for their users. As stressed in the initial quote from Rosen, the companies tread "an incredibly delicate and difficult line" subjected to a complex mix of pressures to take speech down. These pressures are exercised not only by governments but also by users, advertisers, shareholders, specific interest groups, public opinion, and so forth. Effectively, a small minority of removed content is removed because of government requests, whereas the majority of removed content originates from users flagging specific content in violation of the terms of service.[6] With more than a million posts flagged every day at Facebook

(Bickert 2016a) and 400 hours of video uploaded to YouTube every minute (Downs 2016), the exact drawing of this line greatly impacts the scope of allowed expression. "The real hard part is how we can enforce those policies when we receive more than one million reports per day of violations on Facebook" (Bickert 2016a). "We do try to strike a balance to make sure there's plenty of due process and transparency in how we approach this" (Downs 2016).

Likewise, the collection of personal data represents an unprecedented social graph of users' communications, habits, networks, and preferences, with great ramifications for billions of users' ability to enjoy the right to privacy. In this light, focusing entirely on responses to government requests and leaving out, for example, terms of service enforcement and business practices related to data collection and user profiling provides a partial and limited assessment of the potential negative impact on human rights that these companies' business practices may cause.

From a policy perspective, the corporate approach to translating the companies' human rights responsibility is based on a selective understanding of human rights threats, in which governments are depicted as the main violators and the role of the company is to protect users and thus to safeguard the boundaries of the system from unjustified interference. Government requests potentially pose a threat to the autonomy of the companies, which in response have established subsystems to deal with these disturbances in the form of specific organizational units trained to respond to this particular kind of interference. The subsystems dealing with government requests do so through a number of procedures and checks related to due diligence—for example, is the request submitted via a legitimate public authority, does the request have a valid legal basis, is it proportionate, and so on. After having approved a government request, the interference is documented in a transparency report that serves to maintain users' trust in the system and provide evidence that the companies guard the boundaries of their users' rights to freedom of expression and privacy.

In the interviews I conducted, staff from neither Google nor Facebook reflected critically on their potential negative human rights impact, outside the company–government axis. Nor are these human rights impacts addressed in the context of GNI, which is instrumental in developing benchmarks for corporate compliance with human rights law. While both companies are heavily engaged in policy discussions around freedom of expression and privacy in a number of policy venues, not least in Washington and Brussels, these debates have mostly focused on how the companies may support the Internet freedom agenda (Carr 2013; Morozov 2011; Powers and Jablonski 2015) and have rarely involved a critical take on the business practices of these major services vis-à-vis human rights. The companies' potential negative impact on freedom of expression by terms of service enforcement, for instance, has only recently started to emerge as a policy topic, although it has been flagged as a human rights concern for several years, for example, in the Ranking Digital Rights Index. The recent Cambridge Analytica/Facebook case, in which Mark Zuckerberg provided testimony in a joint hearing of the Senate Judiciary Committee and the Senate Committee on Commerce, Science, and Transportation and then to the House Energy and Commerce Committee, marks a significant change in this regard, since it explicitly addresses the democratic implications of Facebook's business practices.[7]

Interestingly, the respondents from both companies describe an organizational culture that is fairly blunt and open to debate with top-level management yet mostly anchored within a technical discourse, for example on specific solutions and developments, rather than a critical sociopolitical discourse. In addition, from a research perspective both companies appeared as closed systems, both in terms of gaining access and in terms of the interview situation itself. Such entry and interview barriers are not unique to these two companies but well described in the literature on elite interviews within corporations (Dexter 2006; Harvey 2011), and in this case included difficulty with obtaining contact details of specific staff members, circular responses referring me continuously to a single point of contact, restrictions on the interview situation itself (no recording of conversations), and difficulty in obtaining more elaborated responses. While both companies have an extensive number of policies available on their website, it was difficult to get staff to elaborate on these policies beyond what is already in the public domain. In relation to obtaining information from policy documents vis-à-vis interviews, the interviews provided limited information beyond the official policies but rather illustrated the high degree of coherence in the way these issues are presented in corporate policies, official statements, and interviews. As for descriptions of internal processes—for example, the escalation procedure for content removal—such information was (not surprisingly) treated as confidential and only provided at a very general level.

Contrary to recent scholarship on platforms that emphasizes the way the economic model, technical design, and platform policies direct social practices in certain directions, the findings indicate that Facebook and Google staff generally depict their services as neutral platforms that facilitate communicative practices among users but have no role in curating this communication. The process of coding is described as detached from political considerations, and algorithms are described as neutral tools for providing the services. "We take all the information that we can find on these crawls and we organize them with algorithms. We try very hard not to have biases" (Schmidt 2013). "The way that Google makes money is by understanding what you want and giving it to you in the moment that you want it. We have the technology, the algorithms that can understand intent" (Green 2015). Specific algorithms (e.g., the PageRank and EdgeRank algorithms) are depicted as important corporate assets, and the respondents generally take great pride in the technical innovations produced by their respective companies. As for policies, these are spoken of as *product guidelines*, not as measures that essentially influence how expression and privacy rights may be exercised. Mark Zuckerberg also emphasized the "neutral platform view" in a response to allegations about the role of Facebook in spreading fake news that influenced the US presidential election. In his response, Zuckerberg stressed that 99 percent of the content users see on Facebook is authentic, that Facebook facilitates access to news of all kinds but does not "identify truth," and that the company has no intention of becoming "arbiters of truth" (Zuckerberg 2016).

In sum, the first narrative refers to Facebook and Google services as neutral products or platforms guided by a commitment to human rights, and free speech in particular. Both companies identify governments as the core threat to their users' rights and freedoms and have established systems and processes to secure their services from governmental interference. From this perspective, the boundaries of their users' right to freedom of expression and privacy is protected by the companies, whereas there is no acknowledgment of the fact that such rights are vulnerable to intrusion by the companies themselves. In short, Facebook and Google treat their users' rights *as part of* the Facebook/Google social system, not as outside systems with independent borders.

Second Narrative: Google and Facebook Assist Law Enforcement by Removing Illegal Content

In May 2016, the European Commission and social media platforms Facebook, Microsoft, YouTube, and Twitter agreed on a Code of Conduct to tackle hate speech online. With the agreement, the companies committed to take the lead on tackling illegal hate speech online. This includes the continued development of internal procedures and staff training to guarantee that they review the majority of valid notifications for removal of illegal hate speech in less than twenty-four hours and remove or disable access to such content if necessary. The companies will also strengthen their partnerships with civil society organizations that will help flag content promoting incitement to violence and hateful conduct. The Code of Conduct on Countering Illegal Hate Speech Online adopted between the European Commission and Facebook, Microsoft, YouTube, and Twitter relates to the second narrative discussed in this chapter—that is, the way that company–government cooperation on law enforcement is framed.

In the fight against unwanted content on the Internet (extremism, terror, hate), governments are increasingly turning to the major online services and enlisting their assistance via more or less formalized cooperation. From a regulatory perspective, this is not surprising, since the private ownership of online communication platforms confronts states with obstacles when they seek to sanction speakers or listeners directly. In consequence, governments enlist private actors as proxy censors to control the online flow of information (Kreimer 2006, 1). Practical measures to control the information flow require either cooperation from these companies, commonly referred to as "gatekeepers" of the online sphere (Laidlaw 2015), or coercion exercised upon them. The policy models that derive from this challenge are addressed extensively in the literature on self- and coregulation as mentioned in the Introduction to this volume. Coregulation refers to a legal model for public authorities based on the voluntary delegation of all or some part of implementation and enforcement of norms to private actors. Self-regulation, by contrast, refers to practices whereby private actors define, implement, and enforce norms without public intervention (Frydman, Hennebel, and Lewkowicz 2008, 133–134). As addressed in the chapters by Land, Callamard, and McGonagle, such policy models carry human rights implications due to the lack of due-process safeguards and the risk of overreach by companies.

While the first narrative concerns the way the companies are seen to safeguard the freedoms of their users from overreach by governments, this narrative relates to their role in assisting law enforcement by removing illegal content. The recently adopted EU Code of Conduct is an example of such cooperation. The code defines illegal hate speech according to EU Framework Decision 2008/913/JHA of November 28, 2008, as "all conduct publicly inciting to violence or hatred directed against a group of persons or a member of such a group defined by reference to race, color, religion, descent or national or ethnic origin" (Code of Conduct on Countering Illegal Hate Speech Online 2016, para. 2). The code is not a legally binding document but establishes a public commitment for the companies, including the requirement to review the majority of valid notifications for removal of illegal hate speech in less than twenty-four hours and to make it easier for law enforcement to notify the companies directly. Currently, there is no uniform definition of what constitutes hate speech around the world, and the Framework Decision has been criticized for lack of compliance with international standards on freedom of expression.[8] When the code was launched in June of 2016, public policy staff at both Google and Facebook stressed that the code is a continuation of work they are already doing in terms of fighting illegal content on their platforms. "We're committed to giving people access to information through our services, but we have always prohibited illegal hate speech on our platforms. . . . We are pleased to work with the Commission to develop co- and self-regulatory approaches to fighting hate speech online" (Junius 2016). "With a global community of 1.6 billion people, we work hard to balance giving people the power to express themselves whilst ensuring we provide a respectful environment. As we make clear in our Community Standards, there's no place for hate speech on Facebook" (Bickert 2016b).

The code is a recent (but not unique) example of the way Internet companies are enlisted to cooperate with law enforcement in the fight against illegal content on their services.[9] It is also an example of the complex mix of legal and nonlegal standards that govern allowed expression and conduct on social media platforms. As stressed in the code, enforcement of criminal law sanctions against perpetrators of hate speech must be complemented by "actions geared at ensuring that illegal hate speech online is expeditiously acted upon by online intermediaries and social media platforms" (Code of Conduct on Countering Illegal Hate Speech Online 2016, para. 6). In other words, law enforcement by public authorities must go hand in hand with privatized enforcement by companies. As stressed in the code, the increased effort to cut down on hate speech online is guided by the companies' *own activities* (Code of Conduct on Countering Illegal Hate Speech Online 2016, para. 7, my emphasis), and the notification of alleged illegal content is assessed against their community standards and "*where necessary* national laws transposing the Framework Decision" (Code of Conduct on Countering Illegal Hate Speech Online 2016, para. 10, my emphasis). In other words, the companies commit to consider expeditiously whether alleged illegal content (i.e., hate speech) is to be removed based on their internally defined community standards, rather than the law on hate speech in the country in question. Effectively, this form of coregulatory arrangement implies that the EU governments sanction a content-removal process based on privately defined standards and enforced by private actors. Hence, companies, rather than courts, decide on the legality of content. As pointed out by several commentators, this raises concerns both from a freedom-of-expression and a due-process perspective.[10] However, from the perspective of Google and Facebook, the process is not controversial, as it basically codifies a practice that is already in place. On the contrary, the code reinforces the narrative of assisting legitimate government requests while maintaining full autonomy over the process. As repeatedly stressed by policy staff at Facebook and Google, their services cover numerous jurisdictions and so the community standards cannot reflect the national law in each country where they operate. Rather, the standards represent a commonly agreed-upon baseline developed over time. This baseline—the corporate constitution for what is allowed—provides the basis for excluding expressions that are potentially unlawful (such as hate speech), as well as those that are lawful but unwanted (such as certain categories of nudity, graphic content, or misleading information). In short, the decision on when to sanction content, remove it, and ultimately close an account is an internal company decision based on the corporate logic that the community standards represent at YouTube and Facebook, respectively. "There's not one single source that provides us with an answer (on hate speech policy). What we have to consider is what is best for the people that are in our community" (Bickert 2016a).

The companies' cooperation with law enforcement on tackling hate speech effectively means that the companies have government approval for removing content according to the corporate version of what constitutes hate speech. From a social system point of view, the partnership constitutes an uneven mix of communicative codes (legal/illegal, profit/ loss). Government practice is driven by a need to target illegal content in a domain that they do not control, whereas company practice is guided by the need to keep users safe in order to maximize the user base and thus profit. Consequently, decisions that should be dealt with by the legal system (ideally a court) are transferred to a commercial system and decided upon on the basis of legally inspired but commercially defined norms. "To expect the kind of heavyweight process you get in the judiciary, or almost expect the police and judiciary to intervene in every dispute that you have in a domestic space or in one of the public spaces like this, is I think unrealistic" (Allan 2013).

In sum, the company narrative on assisting and cooperating with legitimate law enforcement serves several purposes. First, it affirms the role of the companies as law-abiding and socially responsible corporations that commit to assist law enforcement in the countries where they operate. Second, voluntary agreements on public–private cooperation, such as the one on hate speech, reaffirm the autonomy of the companies in deciding exactly how specific categories of unwanted content should be defined and processed within the company. In other words, such an agreement provides the content removal processes with legitimacy and governmental approval, while serving the companies' interest in keeping full control over the processes that determine how content on their platforms is governed.

Third Narrative: Privacy Equals User Control within the Platform

In March 2016, Joe Cannataci, in his position as newly appointed UN Special Rapporteur on the Right to Privacy, called for increasing attention toward companies' collection and use of personal data. Cannataci argued that the data available for the profiling of individuals is now of an unprecedented magnitude and that the extent of the privacy risks associated with this data collection is yet to be understood:

> The first 25 years of the existence of the world-wide web have led to a largely unregulated organic growth of private corporations. . . . One of the hallmarks of this growth has been the collection and use of all forms of personal data: every search, every read, every e-mail or other form of messaging, every product or service purchased leaves hundreds of thousands of electronic tracks about an individual which are capable of being aggregated into forming a very accurate profile of that individual's likes, dislikes, moods, financial capabilities, sexual preferences, medical condition, shopping patterns as well as the intellectual, political, religious and philosophical interests and sometimes even the relevant opinions of the netizen. (Cannataci 2016, para. 9)

The third narrative refers to the way privacy is spoken of within the two companies. This narrative unfolds against the backdrop of an increasingly intense debate on platforms and privacy, raised especially within Europe over the past five years, and brought to the forefront of international attention by high-profile cases such as the class action *Europe v. Facebook* initiated by Austrian privacy advocate Max Schrems.[11] The European focus on privacy is also reflected in the new General Data Protection Regulation, which imposes an updated regime of data protection rules on public authorities as well as private actors that process personal data of European citizens.[12] At the international level, the increased focus on privacy is reflected in the appointment of the first UN Special Rapporteur on the Right to Privacy in 2015.

When interviewing staff at Google and Facebook, it was remarkable how much they emphasized the importance of privacy and acknowledged that the many European cases have made it increasingly important to get privacy right. "It was a very conscious decision to take privacy more seriously. Not only legal compliance, it's much broader than that. The whole idea of privacy is core to what Facebook does. But we often have a different approach compared to what the other companies do. We are very bold as to product development—constantly pushing the use of technology, the limits of what you can do" (Facebook interview #8, 2016). "There are people in every corner of the organization that care deeply about privacy" (Google interview #9, 2015). Arguably, awareness around privacy has developed with dedicated subsystems within both organizations. For example, extensive internal systems of control and governance around compliance with European data protection regulation have been established, including several layers of checks and balances to ensure that no product revision or new product is released without privacy clearance. "So whenever a new product or feature is conceived of, the tech lead for that project has to complete a document that includes a lot of information about how information is going to be collected, processed, shared, used, deleted" (Enright 2015). "Every staff member gets privacy training when joining the company" (Facebook interview #8, 2016). The conversations revealed, however, that the respondents had a very specific understanding of privacy—as user choice *within* the boundaries of the platforms, and as protection against outside interference with these boundaries.

None of the staff I spoke to related privacy to either specific limits or general minimization of data collection by their services.[13] Rather, privacy is described as the ability of the users to foresee and control the sharing of personal information with other users. "Putting people in control is an art. Look at the dashboard in a car" (Facebook interview #8, 2016). "To get privacy right, to provide a solution of choice—is the leadership mantra" (Google interview #8, 2015). As long as users have measures of control, interviewees felt there is not a conflict between the right to privacy and their company's collection and sharing of data. When asked to exemplify how this user control is implemented, the respondents point to Facebook privacy features such as the Facebook Privacy Basics, Privacy Checkup, and Accessing and Downloading Your Information, and within Google, features such as Incognito Mode, Google Takeout, and the Privacy Dashboard, which are repeatedly mentioned as examples of how the idea of user control is implemented into the design of the platforms.

A privacy issue, however, is seen to arise when someone outside the corporate system demands access to user data. In line with the first narrative, governments are depicted as the main cause of privacy problems. "I don't think a democracy functions when your government collects data and doesn't at least fundamentally say what it's doing" (Page 2015). "I hear people say that it's okay to give the government all this data because you're giving it to Facebook anyway, and I'd say that's actually completely different, the power relationship between me and Facebook—however important Facebook is—is just fundamentally different from the power relationship between me and the government" (Allan 2014). In line with the freedom-of-expression safeguards, both companies have subsystems for handling government requests for user data, and there is a corporate sense of protecting user privacy by pushing back against government requests for user data with due diligence standards. "We want to make sure that existing legal processes for legitimate government access to data work appropriately so that we can push governments to use the front door to use legitimate, transparent, accountable legal processes to access information and we will not, have not and have no intention of collaborating with any effort to give governments information through the back door" (Enright 2015).

While many respondents were willing to talk about privacy, both in terms of tools provided to users and due diligence standards in relation to governments, few were willing to discuss the negative privacy impact that may arise from a business model based on harnessing users' personal data. My interviews revealed the absence of a more critical corporate discourse on the companies' potential negative human rights impact as a result of their business model. Relying on the outlined construction of privacy, the respondents saw no conflict between users' privacy and the massive collection of personal data, as raised by Cannataci in the quote given above. The mapping and profiling that inform their business model are seen as an industry default and as uncontroversial as long as users are provides with means of controlling the flow of their information within the services provided. "To a significant degree the privacy discourse is paternalizing; people share what they want to share" (Google interview #8, 2015). "I don't see a conflict between the business model and privacy provided individual users are in control" (Facebook interview #4, 2015).

Whereas Facebook and Google both take great pride in the way their services push the boundaries for technosocial innovation, thereby breaking new ground for connecting people and information, their approach to human rights is conveniently conservative. Despite the explicit commitment to the industry benchmark in the field—the UN Guiding Principles on Business and Human Rights (UNGPs)—their practices do not take into account the practical implications of this soft-law framework. Whereas the UNGPs explicitly call for a human rights impact assessment of *all* business practices that may impact individuals' enjoyment of human rights, the implementation of these principles within the companies only addresses cases in which there is government interference with business practices.

Conclusion

In this final section, I will relate some crosscutting observations on how human rights responsibility is governed by the two companies, as well as the broader implications of these practices.

First, the analysis pointed to an exclusive focus on governments as the cause of human rights violations. While states have a legal obligation to respect human rights law, the UNGPs explicitly state that private companies have a responsibility to assess and mitigate business practices across their entire operations for any negative human impact they may cause. The framing of human rights within the two companies, however, reduces this human rights responsibility to an obligation to safeguard their users against government overreach. Corporate practices that have given rise to human rights concerns among scholars and activists alike, such as the extensive collection of users' personal data, is not framed as a privacy issue within either company. Privacy is constructed in terms of user control and pushback strategies against illegitimate government requests for user data, rather than as data minimization. Nor is the massive content moderation exercised each day, as the platforms govern compliance with their terms of service, spoken of as a human rights issue. These critical debates simply do not resonate with the human rights framing at Facebook and Google.

Second, the way the EU Code of Conduct enlists the companies to effectively carry out privatized law enforcement on their services normalizes a logic whereby decisions on legal/illegal content and behavior are sanctioned by private actors. From the perspective of Google and Facebook, cooperating with governments is part of a narrative of serving legitimate law-enforcement interests as law-abiding and socially responsible companies, while effectively the cooperation (Code of Conduct) legitimizes their internally defined community standards as *the* documents governing what content is allowed or removed within the boundaries of their services.

Third, despite the numerous policies, algorithms, and governance mechanisms that define the boundaries for possible user actions within the Facebook and Google services, these services are depicted as technically neutral products or platforms via which users may communicate, share, search, connect, and so forth. As such, there is limited (public) discourse by company staff on the way specific policies or platform features determine the radius of allowed user action and, in effect, shape users' means of exercising privacy or freedom-of-expression rights. On the contrary, it is emphasized that users may at any time choose not to use the products offered or decide to leave the platform, while taking their data with them. Whereas scholars have called for a repertoire of governance strategies that "sees platforms as something other than simply market actors" or "privately owned public utilities" (Ananny and Gillespie 2016, 16), my analysis pointed to a discourse firmly anchored in free market terminology, emphasizing the right of the companies to set and enforce their own terms in a competitive and deregulated market.

Finally, from a public policy perspective, it is significant how these services are framed. Whereas the notion of infrastructure raises (and legitimizes) expectations of regulation, the notion of platform is anchored in a technology/market perspective with essentially different expectations. Arguably, Google and Facebook serve as a social infrastructure for billions of users, and although they are increasingly referred to as such in the public debate, this has not led to regulatory proposals, despite an increasing debate on these issues. In the United States, the Federal Trade Commission has begun to explore questions of platform governance through algorithmic accountability, but thus far there has not been the political will to address the broader implications that platforms may have for the social and political discourse (Ananny and Gillespie 2016, 2) nor for human rights more generally. Despite the fact that these services have an increasing impact on civic life (Moore 2016), their impact on rights of expression, access to information, public participation, and so forth have remained outside the scope of state regulation. By contrast, their impact on privacy and data protection is subjected to relatively detailed regulation in specific regions, such as the EU. While the companies acknowledge that they influence the rights of billions of users worldwide, they refer to their autonomy as private actors and require the freedom to set and enforce their own rules of engagement. The governance gap with regard to the Internet giants is increasingly giving rise to policy concerns, not only in Europe but also in the United States, and it will be interesting to see whether events such as the Cambridge Analytica/Facebook scandal mark a turning point toward regulation of technology giants such as Google and Facebook.

Notes

1. Available at https://www.zuckerbergfiles.org.

2. See https://rankingdigitalrights.org.

3. https://rankingdigitalrights.org/index2017/companies/facebook.

4. https://rankingdigitalrights.org/index2017/companies/google.

5. See, for example, the European Commission's factcheet on the right to be forgotten ruling (*C-131/12*) https://www.inforights.im/media/1186/cl_eu_commission_factsheet_right_to_be-forgotten.pdf.

6. In June 2018, the UN Special Rapporteur on Freedom of Expression issued a thematic report to the Human Rights Council on the regulation of user-generated online content. The rapporteur recommends among others things that companies apply human rights standards at all stages of their operation. The report is available at https://www.ohchr.org/EN/Issues/FreedomOpinion/Pages/ContentRegulation.aspx.

7. Transcript of Zuckerberg's appearance before the House Energy and Commerce Committee April 11, 2018: https://www.washingtonpost.com/news/the-switch/wp/2018/04/11/transcript-of-zuckerbergs-appearance-before-house-committee.

8. For a critical assessment of the Framework Decision in relation to international standards on freedom of expression, see the brief by Article 19; "EU: European Commission's Code of Conduct for Countering Illegal Hate Speech Online and the Framework Decision", June 2016. https://www.article19.org/resources/eu-european-commissions-code-of-conduct-for-countering-illegal-hate-speech-online-and-the-framework-decision.

9. See, for example, Europol's work with IT companies, covered in EDRi-gram, May 18, 2016: https://edri.org/europol-non-transparent-cooperation-with-it-companies.

10. See, for example, the brief by Article 19; "EU: European Commission's Code of Conduct for Countering Illegal Hate Speech Online and the Framework Decision", June 2016. https://www.article19.org/resources/eu-european-commissions-code-of-conduct-for-countering-illegal-hate-speech-online-and-the-framework-decision.

11. See http://europe-v-facebook.org/EN/en.html.

12. See http://eur-lex.europa.eu/legal-content/EN/TXT/?uri=uriserv:OJ.L_.2016.119.01.0001.01.ENG&toc=OJ:L:2016:119:TOC.

13. These are established data protection principles and part of the EU's General Data Protection Regulation.

References

Allan, Richard. 2013. "Richard Allan, Ulf Buermeyer: Speech at Scale." Keynote conversation at Re:publica 13, May 7. https://www.youtube.com/watch?v=1gSTwa YVERo.

Allan, Richard. 2014. The Campion (President's Invited) Lecture: "The Challenges of Operating at Scale," at RSS International Conference, September 2. https://www .youtube.com/watch?v=BWRjif53qt0.

Ananny, Mike, and Tarleton Gillespie. 2016. "Public Platforms: Beyond the Cycle of Shocks and Exceptions." Paper presented at IPP2016 The Platform Society, Oxford University, Oxford, October.

Barnett, Michael N., and Martha Finnemore. 2004. *Rules for the World: International Organizations in Global Politics*. Ithaca, NY: Cornell University Press.

Bickert, Monica. 2016a. Presentation at SXSW Harassment Summit, March 13. https://www.youtube.com/watch?v=WNgvlCuS6cc.

Bickert, Monica. 2016b. Quoted in Alex Harn, "Facebook, YouTube, Twitter and Microsoft Sign EU Hate Speech Code." *The Guardian*, May 31. https://www.theguardian .com/technology/2016/may/31/facebook-youtube-twitter-microsoft-eu-hate-speech -codequoted.

Bowker, Geoffrey C., Karen Baker, Florence Miller, and David Ribes. 2010. "Towards Information Infrastructure Studies: Ways of Knowing in a Networked Environment." In *The International Handbook of Internet Research*, edited by Jeremy Hunsinger, Lisbeth Klastrup, and Matthew Allen, 97–177. Dordrecht: Springer.

Bowker, Geoffrey C., and Susan Leigh Star. 1999. *Sorting Things Out: Classification and Its Consequences*. Cambridge, MA: MIT Press.

Cannataci, Joseph A. 2016. "Report of the Special Rapporteur on Privacy, Joseph A. Cannataci." Geneva: Human Rights Council.

Carr, Madeline. 2013. "Internet Freedom, Human Rights and Power." *Australian Journal of International Affairs* 67 (5): 621–637.

Code of Conduct on Countering Illegal Speech Online. 2016. European Commission, May 31. http://ec.europa.eu/justice/fundamental-rights/files/hate_speech_code _of_conduct_en.pdf.

Dexter, Lewis Anthony. 2006. *Elite and Specialized Interviewing*. Colchester, UK: European Consortium for Political Research.

Downs, Juniper. 2016. Presentation at SXSW Harassment Summit, March 13. https:// www.youtube.com/watch?v=WNgvlCuS6cc.

Enright, Keith. 2015. "Hot Topics in Privacy: A Conversation with Facebook, Google and Microsoft." Presentation at the RSA Conference, May 5. https://www.youtube.com/watch?v=msc15s52ejc.

Frischmann, Brett M. 2012. *Infrastructure: The Social Value of Shared Resources.* New York: Oxford University Press.

Frydman, Benoit, Ludovic Hennebel, and Gregory Lewkowicz. 2008. "Public Strategies for Internet Co-regulation in the United States, Europe and China." In *Governance, Regulations and Powers on the Internet,* edited by Eric Brousseau, Meryem Marzouki, and Cécile Méadel. Cambridge: Cambridge University Press.

Goffman, Erving. 1974. *Frame Analysis: An Essay on the Organization of Experience.* New York: Harper & Row.

Green, Yasmin. 2015. Panel discussion at the UN Counter-terrorism Centre, June 16. http://webtv.un.org/search/an-exit-for-extermists-digital-solutions-for-online-counter-radicalization-panel-discussion/4302753216001?term=global%20public%20policy%20facebook#full-text.

Harvey, William S. 2011. "Strategies for Conducting Elite Interviews." *Qualitative Research* 11 (4): 431–441.

Helmond, Anne. 2015. "The Platformization of the Web: Making Web Data Platform Ready." *Social Media + Society* 1 (2): 1–11.

Hornung, Gerrit, and Christoph Schnabel. 2009. "Data protection in Germany I: The Population Census Decision and the Right to Informational Self-Determination." *CLSR Computer Law and Security Review: The International Journal of Technology and Practice* 25 (1): 84–88.

Johnston, Hank, and John A. Noakes. 2005. *Frames of Protest: Social Movements and the Framing Perspective.* Lanham, MD: Rowman & Littlefield.

Jørgensen, Rikke Frank. 2017a. "What Platforms Mean When They Talk about Human Rights." *Policy & Internet* 9 (3): 280–296.

———. 2017b. "Framing Human Rights: Exploring Storytelling within Internet Companies." *Information, Communication & Society* 21 (3): 340–355.

Junius, Lie. 2016. Quoted in "Facebook, YouTube, Twitter and Microsoft sign EU hate speech code" by Alex Harn. *The Guardian,* May 31, 2016. https://www.theguardian.com/technology/2016/may/31/facebook-youtube-twitter-microsoft-eu-hate-speech-code.

Kreimer, Seth. F. 2006. "Censorship by Proxy: First Amendment, Internet Intermediaries, and the Problem of the Weakest Link." *University of Pennsylvania Law Review* 155: 11.

Laidlaw, Emily. 2015. *Regulating Speech in Cyberspace*. Cambridge: Cambridge University Press.

Latour, Bruno, and Steve Woolgar. 1986. *Laboratory Life: The Construction of Scientific Facts*. Princeton, NJ: Princeton University Press.

Luhmann, Niklas. 1992. "What Is Communication?" *Communication Theory* 2 (3): 251–259.

———. 1993. *Social Systems*. Copenhagen: Munksgaard.

Maclay, Colin M. 2014. "An Improbable Coalition: How Businesses, Nongovernmental Organizations, Investors and Academics Formed the Global Network Initiative to Promote Privacy and Free Expression Online." PhD diss., The Law and Public Policy Program, Northeastern University, Boston.

Moore, Martin. 2016. *Tech Giants and Civic Power*. London: King's College London.

Morozov, Evgeny. 2011. *The Net Delusion: The Dark Side of Internet Freedom*. New York: PublicAffairs.

Page, Larry. 2015. "One for All." *Zeit Online*, May. Translated by Marc Young. http://www.zeit.de/wirtschaft/unternehmen/2015-05/larry-page-google-inventor/seite-4.

Pangrazio, Luci. 2016. "Technologically Situated—The Tacit Rules of Platform Participation." Paper presented at IPP2016 The Platform Society, Oxford University, Oxford, October.

Plantin, Jean-Chirstophe, Carl Lagoze, Paul N. Edwards, and Christian Sandvig. 2018. "Infrastructure Studies Meet Platform Studies in the Age of Google and Facebook." *New Media & Society* 20 (1): 293–310.

Powers, Shawn M., and Michael Jablonski. 2015. *The Real Cyber War: The Political Economy of Internet Freedom*. Urbana: University of Illinois Press.

Rosen, Jeffrey. 2016. Presentation at the SXSW Harassment Summit Second Panel, March 12, 2016. https://www.youtube.com/watch?v=WNgvlCuS6cc.

Rosen, Jeffrey. 2012. "The Deciders: The Future of Privacy and Free Speech in the Age of Facebook and Google." *Fordham Law Review* 80 (4): 1525–1538.

Schmidt, Eric. 2013. "Eric Schmidt on the New Digital Age." Royal Geographical Society, May 25. https://www.youtube.com/watch?v=etmarYifipE.

Star, Susan Leigh, and Karen Ruhleder. 1996. "Steps toward an Ecology of Infrastructure: Design and Access for Large Information Spaces." *Information Systems Research* 7 (1): 111–134.

Tannen, Deborah. 1993. *Framing in Discourse*. New York: Oxford University Press.

Van Dijck, José. 2013. *The Culture of Connectivity: A Critical History of Social Media.* Oxford: Oxford University Press.

Van Dijck, José, and Thomas Poell. 2013. "Understanding Social Media Logic." *Media and Communication* 1 (1): 2–14.

Zuckerberg, Mark. 2016. Facebook post from November 13, 2016: https://www.facebook.com/zuck/posts/10103253901916271.

III Regulation

The third part of the book looks at the human rights challenges raised by datafication and platforms from a legal perspective. It examines the human rights obligations of non-state actors such as digital platforms and explores options for a stronger framework of protection (Callamard). It considers how a regional human rights institution, Council of Europe, have dealt with Internet intermediaries from a freedom-of-expression and rule-of-law perspective (McGonagle) and explores challenges to protecting online privacy, including the tension between the approaches taken in the United States and Europe (Van Hoboken). Finally, it proposes how content moderation can be addressed under human rights law, and more generally, what a human-rights-based framework could look like for Internet intermediaries (Land).

8 The Human Rights Obligations of Non-State Actors

Agnès Callamard

Introduction

In a world dominated by news of states' violations of human rights, including by encroaching on the digital space to track activists or control political expression, it is easy to forget or downplay the fact that many non-state actors, such as corporations, wield far more power, influence, and reach than a number of governments. This includes the power to do good and bring much needed benefits to populations, as it does the power to cause great harm, alone or in complicity with states, and often enough internationally. "Externally, NSAs [non-state actors] are no longer confined within the territory of a single State but actively operate across national borders. . . . As a result, States now have less control, let alone a monopoly, over developments both within their own territory and at the international level" (International Law Association 2016; see also Drake, Cerf, and Kleinwächter 2016).

The large-scale privatization of state activities and competencies, including law and order, the overall globalization process, which has weakened the factual power of the state, and evidence pointing to the multiplication of actors engaged in a variety of acts, including transborder acts, amounting to violations of human rights—these have all compelled many, particularly within civil society, to call for greater accountability on the part of non-state actors and greater recognition of their human rights obligations, from the 1990s onward. Such calls resulted in a number of initiatives to address the responsibility of these actors, and in so doing mitigate accountability deficits (Ruggie 2013).

Such arguments apply with particular force to the field of the Internet in the twenty-first century, the "geography-defying" sector if ever there was one, challenging the realities and legal constructs of boundaries and sovereignty. As argued elsewhere (Callamard 2017a), the state was largely absent from the early decades of Internet development, with technologists and academics first and Internet companies second largely dominating the field, including in terms of its regulation. While there is no doubt that the state is now a far more central actor, certainly in terms of regulating the digital space and the online actors (de La Chapelle and Fehlinger 2016; Drake, Cerf, and Kleinwächter 2016), it is not, by any stretch, the sole one. Nor is it, necessarily or everywhere, the most powerful one. Internet intermediaries[1] are currently powering this extraordinary technological, social, and economic revolution. The benefits it has brought to humankind are incontestable. So is the vast power some of these companies hold over the global data economy and the production and circulation of news and information, as well as over individuals and commercial entities. Largely mirroring the 1990s process regarding business and human rights, there have been an increasing number of calls for intermediaries to protect human rights online, in the first place freedom of expression but also the right to privacy (Article 19 2017; Kaye 2017; MacKinnon et al. 2014). States too have been particularly vocal, demanding that intermediaries protect the digital space against content inciting terrorism or hate speech or that violates international copyright law. The outcome, so far, has not quite matched the efforts and the rhetoric, and the digital space is slowly transforming into a battlefield, with human rights protection one of its victims.

This chapter focuses on the protection of freedom of expression in the online world and on the role of Internet intermediaries in protecting and abusing human rights online, including freedom of expression. The focus on Internet intermediaries is not meant to suggest that they are the "worst" abusers of free speech online. As argued elsewhere (Callamard 2017a, 2017b), this is far from being the case, with states around the world seeking to control and censor legitimate expressions online. The focus on Internet intermediaries in the violations of freedom of expression online is meant to respond to the legal and normative gaps resulting from the centrality of these non-state actors in the expansion, regulation, and censorship of information and expression. This chapter argues that Internet intermediaries have human rights obligations, different from those of states, which should, ideally, be set in hard international law. Alternatively, failing that, they ought to be established in meaningful and effective self-regulatory mechanisms. The chapter will trace these obligations to international treaty provisions; to the treatment of intermediaries as international human rights law duty bearer; and to their role in influencing, if not shaping, normative development. It will offer an overview of some of the recent broader developments as far as non-state actors' human rights obligations are concerned and assess how these compare to what happened in the Internet field. It will conclude with a set of recommendations.

The Inclusion of Non-State Actors in the Post–World War II International Freedom-of-Expression Protection Regime

The provisions adopted to protect freedom of expression under the Universal Declaration of Human Rights (UDHR) and the International Covenant on Civil and Political Rights (ICCPR) do not explicitly refer to non-state actors, be it the media, private individuals, or others. ICCPR Article 19(3), however, does include a reference to the *"special duties and responsibilities"* of those whose right to freedom of expression must be respected and protected. This is a clause which either has been largely ignored in the years since the ICCPR adoption or has been used rhetorically, politically, and ideologically to insist that "speakers," including the media, have responsibilities, without further elaboration. To offer a possible explanation of the terms, I will have recourse to the UDHR and ICCPR *travaux préparatoires* to determine *who* or *what* the drafters had in mind. In the following sections, I will consider the possible meaning of the clauses in the current context by turning to national and regional jurisprudence regarding Internet intermediaries.

As early as 1946, at its very first session, the UN General Assembly adopted Resolution 59(I), which states "Freedom of information is a fundamental human right and . . . the touchstone of all the freedoms to which the United Nations is consecrated" (UN General Assembly 1946). The resolution goes on to stress that "understanding and co-operation among nations are impossible without an alert and sound world opinion which, in turn, is wholly dependent upon freedom of information." The resolution (which calls for an international conference on freedom of information) conceives of freedom of information as both a fundamental human right and a precondition for global "understanding."

The importance of information to peace (and conflict) immediately after World War II is reflected in the UN's attempts at the time to adopt three related conventions: on freedom of information, on the gathering and international transmission of news, and on an international right of reply. The now long forgotten draft convention on the international transmission of news and the right of correction (UN General Assembly 1949, 22) was seeking to protect the work of foreign correspondents and news agencies while giving states "directly affected by a report which they considered false or distorted" the possibility of securing corrections. The driving force behind the convention was the perception then that inaccurate reporting posed clear dangers to the maintenance of friendly relations among nations. Member states at the time recognized that such a danger could not be addressed "at present" by instituting, at the international level, a procedure for verifying the accuracy of a report. Instead, the drafters go on to suggest that to prevent the publication of such reports or reduce their pernicious effects, "it is above all necessary to promote a wide circulation of news and to heighten the sense of responsibility of those regularly engaged in the production of news" (UN General Assembly 1949, 23). They also suggested a rather complicated process of corrections, involving the UN Secretary General and ultimately a right of reprisal if a member state failed to uphold a correction. The draft convention was reinvented on a couple of occasions but subsequently abandoned, a fate that also beset similar initiatives at the time, including a UK-led Convention on Freedom of Information first adopted by the UN General Assembly in 1949 and abandoned afterward.

These attempts are nevertheless of particular interest because of their focus on private individuals (the journalists) and companies (the media) and the notion that the publication of false and distorted news had "pernicious" effects, which needed to be addressed through a treaty. In the aftermath of World War II, the complex relationship between states, information, and non-state actors certainly was one of the issues dominating the international agenda.

The development of the UDHR and the ICCPR were initiated at the same time. The expectation was that the UDHR and the ICCPR would be proclaimed shortly after one another with the UDHR offering universal and concise principles, elaborated upon by the ICCPR. While this dual track was ultimately respected, twenty years ended up separating the adoption of the two documents.

The drafting of the UDHR article on freedom of expression and that of the ICCPR were initiated together, largely driven by the Sub-Commission on Freedom of Information and of the Press and of the International Conference on Freedom of Information and of the Press, which ended up providing various advice and feedback to the drafting committees tasked with developing and agreeing on the wording of the UDHR and ICCPR.

Article 19 of the UDHR ended up proclaiming that "Everyone has the right to freedom of opinion and expression; this right includes freedom to hold opinions without interference and to seek, receive and impart information and ideas through any media and regardless of frontiers." The individuals involved in drafting UDHR Article 19 (initially, an Article 17) over two years or so debated thoroughly a range of issues (Schabas 2013). These included the role of non-state actors. Drafters discussed the fact that governments alone were not responsible for censorship but that private groups too prevented access to means of communication of ideas, radio stations and time on air. At issue was not whether this was correct (there was no debate on this issue) but whether this should be reflected in the UDHR. Ultimately, member states' representatives agreed that the focus of the declaration was the "moral obligations of governments," not the "question of monopolies." The basis for rejecting the inclusion of non-state actors, particularly media corporations, was thus not substantial but rather procedural: such a focus would involve "going in too much detail" and the focus of the declaration was "a succinct statement of principles." Similar conclusions were reached regarding the discussion on individuals and others' responsibilities, a theme particularly favored by the French delegate, who repeatedly insisted that freedom of expression entailed duties.[2]

The drafters of Article 19 of the ICCPR returned to both themes, which ended up being reflected in the final wording. The twenty-year process cannot be thoroughly described here (see also Land 2013). For the purpose of this chapter, the following debates are highlighted (Bossuyt 1987).

The adopted version of Article 19 of the ICCPR reads as follows:

1. Everyone shall have the right to hold opinions without interference.
2. Everyone shall have the right to freedom of expression; this right shall include freedom to seek, receive and impart information and ideas of all kinds, regardless of frontiers, either orally, in writing or in print, in the form of art, or through any other *media* of his choice.

3. The exercise of the rights provided for in paragraph 2 of this article carries with it *special duties and responsibilities* [italics added]. It may therefore be subject to certain restrictions, but these shall only be such as are provided by law and are necessary:

   a. For respect of the rights or reputations of others;

   b. For the protection of national security or of public order (ordre public), or of public health or morals.

There was discussion on whether to retain the expression "freedom to seek" with some states arguing that "seek had come to imply unrestrained and often shameless probing into the affairs of others, while gather, far from having any passive connotations, merely lacked the aggressive connotations of seek." The amendment (put forward by Ethiopia, Ghana, India, Libya, Nigeria, Saudi Arabia, and the UAE) also suggested replacing "through any other media of his choice" with "any lawfully operated visual or auditory devices of his choice." The proposal was rejected, and the current wording, to this day, offers an inspiring and visionary protection to freedom of expression in the online world, along with a strong normative basis for access to government-held information.

It was suggested that freedom of expression should be protected "against interference by governmental action, save as provided in paragraph 3." This would have been added to the end of paragraph 2 but was rejected because "private financial interests and monopoly control of media and information could be as harmful to the free flow of information as government interference, and that the latter should therefore not be singled out to the exclusion of the former" (Bossuyt 1987, 385). In her in-depth interpretation of Article 19(2), relying on both the travaux préparatoires and the textual analysis of the article, Molly K. Land (2013, 445) argues that the drafting history of Article 19(2) suggests that there is a basis for applying it directly to the conduct of private actors, in other words, that these may be treated like state actors *in some instances* (ibid., 447):

> Private actors do not trigger the application of Article 19(2) unless and until they interfere with a protected right. In most instances, private activity will not rise to this level. For example, if one hosting service declines to display my content, there are plenty of other services for me to choose from. In that instance, the intermediary has "interfered" with my right to seek, receive, and impart ideas and information. When, however, an intermediary assumes such a dominant market position that its decision not to display my content means that I effectively

cannot reach a meaningful audience, that intermediary is "interfering" with my right and must justify its decision according to the three-step test of Article 19(3).

Article 19(3) is introduced with a strong statement about the duties and responsibilities that the exercise of freedom of expression entails: "The exercise of the rights provided for in paragraph 2 of this article carries with it special duties and responsibilities." A number of states opposed the mention of duties and responsibilities because the purpose of the covenant was to "guarantee civil and political rights" rather than impose duties upon individuals (Bossuyt 1987, 386). They also argued that the purpose of the ICCPR was to lay down rights and the corresponding obligations of states, and that there was no other article in the covenant that included such formulation, even though it could be said that each right had also corresponding duties. In contrast, the view that came to prevail maintained that "freedom of expression was a precious heritage as well as a dangerous instrument; that in view of the powerful influence the modern media of expression exerted upon the minds of men and upon national and international affairs, the duties and responsibilities in the exercise of the right to freedom of expression should be especially emphasized" (Bossuyt 1987, 386). Ultimately, the addition of the word "special" before "duties and responsibilities" closed the debate, although how "special" these were was not the object of further clarifications.

A central debate concerned the legitimate restrictions to freedom of expression. There were no debates seemingly as to *whether* restrictions should be imposed, but on how these should be listed and of course *what* these should be. Some states favored an all-encompassing, general wording while others preferred a full catalogue of restrictions. Indeed, one of the drafts submitted included some thirty possible limitations to freedom of expression. The advocates of a general clause argued that a specific list will be far too long and should be included in a separate convention—not in the ICCPR. Those in support of a long list feared that a general clause could be the object of abusive interpretations and that, to be effective at protecting rights, the covenant should set forth in precise and unequivocal terms the permissible limitations to freedom of expression. There were also debates regarding the limitations of freedom of expression when expression amounts to war propaganda, incitement to violence, and so forth. These were rejected for the time being at least on the ground that they could not be well defined. Ultimately, the adopted formulation reflects a balance between those who favored a general clause and those who preferred a list, although clearly the formulation is closer to laying down general principles for limitations.

At the end of this brief overview, the following conclusions may be highlighted. First, throughout the travaux préparatoires, the drafters have discussed the option of including non-state actors (particularly "monopolies") as a duty bearer alongside states. This is well reflected in the discussion relative to Article 19 of the UDHR as well as Article 19(3) of the ICCPR. There is an explicit recognition of the power and monopoly that private actors may exercise over the media, a control which could be as harmful as government interference. However, this explicit recognition did not result in suggesting that private actors bear the same obligations as those of the state. This option was implicitly, if not explicitly, rejected in the course of the discussion regarding Article 19(3).

Second, it is as rights holders that non-state actors have "special duties and responsibilities." It is then incumbent upon the state (the duty bearer under Article 19(2)) to respond to failures by rights holders to uphold their special responsibilities, through regulation, which, to be legitimate, must follow the so-called three-part test.

Third, the travaux préparatoires indicate different types of non-state actors with specific duties and responsibilities: there are private individuals but also private financial interests and monopolies controlling the media. Debates accompanying the development of the three aforementioned conventions indicate that individual journalists and the media in a more general sense were also strong objects of interest and interventions. Land (2013, 407) demonstrates that the reference to the media under Article 19(2) may be said to include new technologies, including the Internet, that have emerged since the adoption of the ICCPR: "The party's intention that the term 'media' evolve over time and be interpreted with reference to current facts is clear from the text itself. The parties chose to use the general term 'media' instead of more specific terms referring to particular technologies." Consequently, "media" might be understood as "any technology that allows individuals to connect with information and expression and with one another." Non-state actors thus include all those who control the technology, from newspaper owners to Internet intermediaries, and corporate actors that may control them, along with individual or private citizens.

A textual analysis of Article 19 and a review of the travaux préparatoires further suggest that duties and responsibilities attached to these non-state actors are not one and the same but "specific." They are distinct from the obligations imposed upon states, and they are distinct from one non-state actor to another.

In subsequent developments, highlighted below, the duties and responsibilities of non-state actors have tended to be played down, if not ignored, by scholars, lawyers, and governments but also regional courts which tended to focus on protecting freedom of expression against state censorship and on guarding Article 19 and human rights more generally against spurious and nonuniversalist interpretations.[3] Before returning to freedom of expression online, the following section will present the legal and theoretical developments regarding the human rights obligations of non-state actors.

Developments: Non-State Actors and Human Rights Obligations

Academic legal debates have gone on for years as to whether human rights obligations should be extended to non-state actors. Many international lawyers and scholars argue that corporations do not have international legal personality and therefore cannot be treated as subjects of international human rights law; they warn against the dilution of international human rights law and point out that non-state actors, including businesses, are already the objects of international human rights law largely through a focus on the role of the state to prevent violations by third parties. In contrast, others have questioned the obsession with the centrality of international legal personality (Alston 2005) or its hegemonic interpretation (Clapham 2006; Higgin 1994; Reinisch 2005), pointing to an outdated vision and an intrinsic lack of imagination and suggesting that whether non-state actors have international duties depends largely on their capacity to bear such obligations (Clapham 2006, 68–69, 2017b). The distinct issue of jurisdiction has also been hotly debated. The result, as summed up in 2016 by a panel of eminent legal experts who reviewed non-state actors under the law, is that "the ascension of NSAs is not yet adequately reflected in international law nor led to another wave of pluralization ratione personae of this law. . . . Thus, though factually interconnected, States and NSAs remain normatively separated at the international level" (International Law Association 2016, 11).

In the remaining part of this section, I will review the legal and doctrinal developments that indicate a path forward in terms of including (some) non-state actors in a human rights framework and holding them to account as duty bearers.

Criminal and Civil Law

It should be first noted that non-state actors, including Internet intermediaries, may be and have been held accountable under legal regimes other than human rights, such as civil and criminal law. In Europe, the national courts of many member states have imposed criminal accountability on companies, although not for their extraterritorial acts. Under certain jurisdictions, a corporation can be held criminally responsible for the conduct of its employees. Criminal responsibility is thus transferred from an agent or employee to the corporation itself, while the agent or employee remains responsible for the crime committed (Heyns 2016).

Regulating corporate behavior, however, may demand legal liability beyond national borders and across corporate groups. There, the developments are ambiguous at best. In Europe, for instance, both corporate criminal laws and civil tort lack extraterritorial reach, making it difficult for companies to be held accountable for extraterritorial abuses (Kirshner 2015, 13–18). Cases alleging extraterritorial liability of corporations or banks are routinely dismissed or settled out of court (United Nations Environmental Programme [UNEP] Finance Initiative and Foley Hoag LLP 2015; Yeginsu and Jones 2016). Under US tort law, it had been possible, albeit difficult, to hold international corporate actors to account for violations committed elsewhere. However, in 2013, in *Kiobel v. Royal Dutch Petroleum Co*, the US Supreme Court reduced the extraterritorial scope of the US Alien Tort Statute by demanding that claims touch and concern the territory of the United States "with sufficient force to displace the presumption against extraterritorial application." According to Kirshner (2015), the withdrawal of the US tort law jurisdiction has produced a governance gap, which the EU or others must or could fill.

Non-State Actors Can Violate Human Rights

Under international human rights law, there seems to be emerging consensus that non-state actors may engage in behaviors amounting to human rights violations or abuses. While particularly true as far as armed groups are concerned, corporations too have been found to be abusing international human rights standards, in the first place those related to workers' rights, the prohibition of forced labor or the forced relocation of communities from their lands (UNEP Finance Initiative and Foley Hoag LLP 2015; Yeginsu and Jones 2016).[4]

The prevailing view, though, is that corporations are not said to have human rights obligations in the legal sense of the word. The state (principally of a company's country of incorporation) does. It is the state that is under the legal human rights obligation to prevent abuses by these corporations. Practically, this means that states are obligated to put in place regulative and legislative frameworks that ensure that private companies, including Internet intermediaries, act in a manner respectful of human rights and are held accountable in instances in which they do not, regardless of whether the contracting party is the state itself (Heyns 2016, 65). Further, under the prevalent interpretation of international human rights responsibilities, states' responsibilities to respect and protect human rights, including freedom of expression, can apply extraterritorially, even though some states dispute this interpretation.[5]

Non-State Actors Should Respect Human Rights

There is also increasing consensus that corporations should *at the very least* respect human rights (Pillay 2009, 63–68). This understanding is particularly reflected in the large development of international or sector-specific soft-law regulations and codes of conduct focusing on strengthening human-rights-based self-regulation and accountability. This includes, for instance, the work of the Special Representative of the Secretary-General on the issue of human rights and transnational corporations and other business enterprises, John Ruggie, culminating in the development of the UN Guiding Principles on Business and Human Rights adopted by the Human Rights Council in 2011 (UN Office of the High Commissioner for Human Rights 2011).

The Guiding Principles' framework rests on three pillars: the state has a duty to protect against human rights abuses by third parties, including business enterprises, through appropriate policies, regulation, and adjudication; business enterprises should act with due diligence to avoid infringing on the rights of others and address adverse impacts with which they are involved; and victims should have greater access to effective remedy, both judicial and nonjudicial (Ruggie 2010, 54–78; UN General Assembly 2008). Corporation acting with due diligence should seek to identify, prevent, and mitigate "human rights risks," defined as the corporations' potential violations of international human rights standards, including with regard to the corporations' customers, workers, or society at large. The corporate responsibility to respect human rights, including freedom of expression, has been further recognized in soft-law instruments such as the Tripartite Declaration of Principles Concerning Multinational Enterprises and Social Policy, the Organisation for Economic Co-operation and Development Guidelines for Multinational Enterprises, and a vast number of initiatives related to corporate social responsibility, which are largely self-regulatory.

Importantly, the Guiding Principles have been cited in a range of state-initiated policies, such as those of the Council of Europe regarding Internet companies. For instance, the Committee of Ministers of the Council of Europe explicitly refers to the Guiding Principles and other self-regulatory schemes to suggest the following:

> The corporate social responsibility of online service providers includes a commitment to combating hate speech and other content that incites violence or discrimination. Online service providers should be attentive to the use of, and editorial responses to, expressions motivated by racist, xenophobic, anti-Semitic, misogynist, sexist (including as regards Lesbian Gay Bisexual and Transgender people) or other bias. (Committee of Ministers of the Council of Europe 2014)

While not legally binding, the Committee of Ministers recommendations are still legal instruments with legal significance.[6] These examples testify as well to the fact that self-regulatory, nonbinding norms of the kind produced by and for corporate actors may have the potential to harden over time. For example, they may inform legal reasoning and jurisprudence by domestic or regional courts, they may be incorporated into legislation, they might become the basis for an international treaty, and they can be included as binding clauses in private party contracts (UNEP Finance Initiative and Foley Hoag LLP 2015, 53–55).

Non-State Actors Should Be Held Accountable for Human Rights Violations

There have been a few judicial developments regarding non-state actors' human rights obligations, which merit attention because of their possible implications for the online world and its corporate actors.

The draft articles adopted by the International Law Commission in 2001 on the responsibility of states for internationally wrongful acts (International Law Commission 2001) identify four instances when the acts of a private entity may be directly attributed to the state. As pointed by Alston (2005, 24), the articles are essentially neutral with regard to the responsibilities of non-state actors in that "they neither discourage nor seek to promote those trends which favor an enhanced role for non-state actors. . . . By the same token, they leave the door open for further developments in the future."

Other developments, though, have moved in the direction of holding non-state actors directly liable for human rights violations. These have tended to concern themselves with core human rights obligations, such as the right to life; the absolute prohibition of torture, cruel, inhuman, and degrading treatment; the recruitment of child soldiers; the prohibition of slavery; and the prohibition of enforced disappearance, as well as freedom of conscience. But other rights have been considered as well.

First, as demonstrated by Heyns (2016), a number of jurisprudence decisions have confirmed that it is the nature of the conduct, and not the entity, that will determine whether or not international human rights law is applicable, thus suggesting that international human rights law does not exclusively govern the conduct of states (Heyns 2016, 108; *Kadic v. Karadzic, Sosa v. Alvarez-Machain*).

Second, there is increasing support for the view that non-state actors, as a group, including armed groups and corporations, have a binding obligation to obey jus cogens and not to engage in conduct amounting to international crimes (UN Independent International Commission of Inquiry 2012, 106–107). The International Criminal Court jurisprudence supports the proposition that non-state actors may be viewed as carrying out crimes against humanity provided they meet the requirements of constituting "an organization" (International Criminal Court 2010; see also Open Society Foundations 2016). The African Union Head of States in 2014 adopted a treaty establishing the African Court of Justice and Human Rights, according to which corporations could be prosecuted for certain international crimes (Clapham, 2018). The protocol applies to fourteen crimes,[7] which, on the surface, may not seem relevant to the operations of companies providing access to the Internet or social media. On the other hand, various developments regarding online "terrorism," cybercrime, and cyberwarfare impact on all the crimes identified by the African Union. Andrew Clapham further suggests that the new protocol comes close to resolving the issues of how to tackle corporate intention, attribution, and corporate knowledge, further suggesting a doctrinal milestone.

Finally, there are also suggestions that armed groups have a range of human rights obligations in the territories they control, including obligations regarding the rule of law (Clapham 2017; the author argues that armed groups have human rights obligations related to fair trial and punishment). Such obligations may also include freedom of expression. For instance, Ben Emmerson, the Special Rapporteur on the Protection of Human Rights while Countering Terrorism, has argued that where the Islamic State of Iraq and the Levant (ISIL) engages in violations that are unrelated to the conflict and not direct consequences of it, the governing legal framework should be international human rights law. In practice, this means that ISIL is legally bound to respect freedom of expression, freedom of assembly, and freedom of movement. These rights should be protected without discrimination on any of the grounds prohibited by international law. The right to a fair trial should also be guaranteed. He further suggested "the more effective control ISIL has over a territory or individuals, the greater is the extent to which human rights law will constitute the appropriate legal framework" (Emmerson 2015, 30–31).

Human Rights Obligations of Non-State Actors in the Online World

Since its adoption, the protection of freedom of expression has been the object of a range of analyses and litigation in domestic, regional, and international courts. Most of these have largely focused, at least until recently, on states' obligation to protect the right to freedom of expression and information, and to respect it, including against actions by non-state actors, such as armed groups or others targeting journalists for killings.

Internet intermediaries had been somewhat shielded from accusations that they too violate human rights, thanks to two forces. The first was cultural and ideological: a number of states and civil society, until the late twentieth century at least, saw intermediaries as the main vehicle for, and allies in, the protection and expansion of freedom of information. This was, and remains to a certain extent, a reasonable conclusion. These actors have been central to the development of the Internet, the first technology ever to potentially realize the vision of the UDHR Article 19 of a borderless freedom. Critiques were few and far between in the first decades of Internet development. Nongovernmental organizations and activists have largely focused their efforts on denouncing censorship by the state and less frequently on the failure of the state to prevent censorship by others. By so doing, the press freedom field has followed conventional interpretations of international law according to which human rights law binds states only: non-state actors are not considered subjects of international law. Toward the end of twentieth century, however, a few voices started raising concerns regarding these actors' business model and the transformation of the global economy and society unleashed by technology (see Callamard 2017a and 2017b for an overview).

The second factor was linked to the various liability regimes devised by states for the purpose of managing the regulation of online content. With notable exceptions discussed below, Internet intermediaries have been largely immune from liability regarding content produced online by others. In the United States, there is a broad immunity regime that has granted them immunity from liability for third-party content, while in some other areas (Europe, Latin America, and India, notably), the so-called safe harbor regime has granted intermediaries immunity, provided they act "expeditiously" to remove or disable access to "illegal" information when they obtain actual knowledge of such content. China and other countries in Asia, on the other hand, are enforcing a strict liability regime, according to which Internet intermediaries are liable for content produced by others—that is, third-party content. In practice, this requires of intermediaries that they monitor all content in order to comply with the law: "if they fail to do so, they face a variety of sanctions, including the withdrawal of their business licence and/or criminal penalties" (Article 19 2013, 7).

In practice, though, the different liability regimes may coexist in a single country. For instance, Europe has devised two, possibly three,[8] different legal regimes that are applicable to Internet intermediaries, depending on the nature of the issue or right (copyright, data protection, right to privacy) and the nature of the intermediaries (passive or mere messengers vs. active or indeed publishers), a diversity which has weakened the presumption of immunity.

Internet Intermediaries Can Violate Human Rights

Increasingly, the tacit understanding that non-state actors are human rights allies has broken down, replaced with increasing skepticism regarding these actors' human rights benevolence, if not outright rejection. In the early twenty-first century, these non-state actors have morphed into some of the largest and most influential monopolies in the world, while their business model demands the collection, analysis, and sale of personal data, not unlike a form of untargeted surveillance on a global scale. These realizations have compelled many within the freedom-of-expression community, along with courts and governments, to question and challenge the human rights behavior of these corporate actors.

Corporations operating in countries with a strict liability regime, such as China, have been accused of complicity in human rights violations. At the time of writing this chapter, for instance, Apple has removed its VPN app from its China App store, creating "one of the biggest setbacks for the free internet in China's history" (Russell 2017). Yahoo! has been the object of a number of accusations and lawsuits for giving information about online activities to Chinese law enforcement, leading to the detention of activists. Under the aforementioned US tort law, Yahoo! has been accused of knowingly and willfully aiding and abetting the commission of torture and other human rights abuses. An earlier case was settled out of court with Yahoo! agreeing to establish a fund "to provide humanitarian and legal aid to dissidents who have been imprisoned for expressing their views online." Subsequently, a Yahoo! shareholder and a Chinese activist have filed a lawsuit alleging misappropriation of the fund's assets by the managers of Yahoo! Human Rights Fund (Business & Human Rights Center 2014).

In places where the notice and takedown regime is in place, Internet intermediaries too have been attacked for their alleged involvement in abuses of freedom of expression. One critique addressed to intermediaries is of willingly or cowardly acting as the state's proxy to regulate and censor content,[9] a process linked to the privatization of censorship (Kreimer 2006, 16–22). Evgeny Morozov, who has written with deep skepticism about the democratic potential of the Internet, wrote, for instance, "Being able to force companies to police the Web according to state-dictated guidelines is a dream come true for any government. The companies must bear all the costs, do all the dirty work, and absorb the users' ire. Companies also are more likely to catch unruly content, as they are more decentralized and know their own online communities better than do the state's censors" (Morozov 2012). An often-heard critique is that intermediaries are over-zealous in their "regulatory role," perceived increasingly as amounting to censorship. The then UN Special Rapporteur on Freedom of Expression well captured this phenomenon in a 2011 report when he wrote that "given that intermediaries may still be held financially or in some cases criminally liable if they do not remove content upon receipt of notification by users regarding unlawful content, they are inclined to err on the side of safety by over censoring potentially illegal content" (La Rue 2011).

On the other hand, intermediaries have also been accused of being too slow in removing problematic content such as hate speech, expression allegedly amounting to bullying or harassment, or more recently "fake news," or failing to remove it at all. Platforms such as Facebook and Twitter in particular have found themselves at the center of multiple controversies linked to their policies on hate speech or "fake news" (see, for instance, Hopkins 2017; ProPublica 2017). States too have been particularly aggressive in pursuing intermediaries and insisting that they remove "terrorist" content or "fake news" in particular (*The Guardian* 2016).

At issue here is the exponential growth of the online space along with the business models of the intermediaries, centered on data production, circulation, and sale, these intermediaries' self-image and normative framework as freedom-of-expression advocates (Jørgensen 2017), and the many contradictory pressures they are confronting. Altogether, these have resulted in potential abuses of both substantive and procedural rights. Substantively, it is often unclear which content is likely to be taken down by intermediaries and on which basis. Procedurally, the process lacks essential guarantees, such as a right of appeal or the involvement of a court backing the takedown demand from a public agency or another user. The result is a move away from the legitimate regulation of "illegitimate" content laid out by the ICCPR and regional conventions toward a censorship regime governed by non-state actors as the censor (by proxy or otherwise), arbitrariness, and lack of due process, as also addressed extensively by Molly K. Land in this volume.

The notion that Internet intermediaries can abuse human rights has also been addressed through formal judicial processes. Internet corporations have been held accountable under criminal or civil law throughout the world, including under charges that are directly related to the exercise of freedom of expression. There are, by now, thousands of cases, which touch on the exercise of online freedom of expression and implicate Internet intermediaries.[10]

One category of cases, rare but worth highlighting, is that of individual users charging Internet companies with censorship. In the United States, such claims are very unlikely to succeed because Internet companies' decisions to remove content, or, in the case of Google, to rank it, are constitutionally protected speech, akin to the decisions of a newspaper editor regarding which content to publish: "The First Amendment protects these decisions, whether they are fair or unfair, or motivated by profit or altruism" (*E-Ventures Worldwide, LLC v. Google, Inc.* 2016). In Europe, such cases are at least more likely to get a full hearing. One such case concerns a French teacher who posted an image of Gustave Courbet's "L'Origine du Monde" on his Facebook page. Facebook suspended Durand-Baissas's account for five years on the grounds that it violated the company's terms and conditions on nudity. Durand-Baissas subsequently sued Facebook France first and then Facebook Incorporated demanding that his account be reactivated. Facebook Incorporated, for its part, argued that the French courts did not have jurisdiction over the matter, and that under its terms of service, only a specific court in California, where Facebook is headquartered, could rule over this lawsuit. The social network also argued that French consumer-rights law does not apply to French Facebook users because its worldwide service is free. In 2016, the Court of Appeal confirmed the lower court findings, dismissing both Facebook arguments[11] (*Facebook Inc. v. Jean Durand* 2016).

The most prevalent cases directly relevant to this chapter concern Internet corporations charged with allowing third-party content which, it is alleged, violates criminal or civil law provisions, such as defamation, privacy rights, hate speech, and incitement to violence, but also consumer rights. The main question asked by courts is whether these companies may be liable for content produced and posted by their users.

In principle, provided Internet companies have removed content deemed to be violating criminal provisions swiftly upon notification, they ought to be held nonliable for such content. For instance, in *Amas M. v. Facebook Ireland*, a German court ruled that Facebook was not the perpetrator or a participant in the alleged defamation of the claimant because under the European Union's electronic commerce rules Facebook, as a "hosting provider," was not obliged to "proactively" search for and remove content unless the content is reported and is clearly unlawful. Facebook had also used geo-blocking to prevent access to the illegal content within Germany and Austria, a measure deemed sufficient for the handling of reported unlawful content (*Amas M. v. Facebook Ireland* 2017). There are, however, an increasing number of exceptions to this rule, particularly in Europe, which tend to indicate inconsistent jurisprudence, and potentially a move away from the nonliability of Internet intermediaries.

Liability is usually found on three bases: (1) the content in question violates criminal or civil law (such as laws related to reputation, privacy, etc.); (2) the platform has been notified that such content should be taken down but failed to do so, or it did not do so expeditiously, or, and more controversially, in the absence of notification, it failed to act *with due diligence*; (3) the court has jurisdiction over the company responsible for the social media platform and/or the company controls and owns the data posted on the platform. Such findings have multiplied with regard to the so-called right to be forgotten or de-indexed. Other recent examples are detailed in the following paragraphs.

In 2017, the Northern Ireland Court of Appeal held Facebook and one of its users liable for "misuse of private information" since the user's posts disclosed a sex offender's photograph, name, address, and previous offences. On the basis of the European Court of Justice decision, the so-called "Right to Be Forgotten" decision, the Irish Court held that Facebook Ireland was a data controller and could therefore be held liable for failing to expeditiously respond to requests to take down the impugned information. However, it found that Facebook was not under an obligation to monitor information it transmits and stores, and it therefore rejected the lower court's assertion that Facebook should have been aware of previous litigation against the plaintiff and proactively removed the private information (*CG v. Facebook Ireland* 2016). The lower court was in effect proposing that a due diligence standard "knew or should have known" should be applied to determine liability.

In Austria, the Court of Appeal ruled that Facebook must delete all hate postings against Austria's Green Party leader, Eva Glawischnig. It reasoned that once Facebook had been notified of at least one infringement, in the past, it should have continued to monitor whether repostings of the original hate posts were occurring and take them down (*Die Grünen v.*

Facebook Ireland Limited 2017). In these circumstances the Court said that Facebook could not rely on the European Community E-Commerce directive, which excludes host-providers from liability for their users' content. The Austria Court is here in essence applying a due diligence standard to Facebook.[12] The Court further dismissed Facebook's argument that it was governed by the laws of California, where it is headquartered, or Ireland, the base of its European operations. It finally ruled that blocking the hate posts in Austria was not enough and they must delete the postings across its global platform.

Most recent developments in countries governed by mixed liability regimes have included enshrining intermediaries' responsibilities in law. In July 2017, the Upper Chamber of the German Parliament approved the Act to Improve Enforcement of the Law in Social Networks, which entered into force on October 1, 2017. The German act demands of Internet platforms such as Facebook, Twitter, and YouTube that they remove hate speech material that is "manifestly unlawful" under German law within twenty-four hours or else face fines that start at five million euros and range up to fifty million euros. If content has been flagged as offensive but is not "manifestly" illegal, it must be examined within seven days. The act further includes a secondary review of unlawful content through self-regulation institutions, which have to be recognized by an administrative body. The act raises a range of concerns regarding the protection of freedom of expression, both substantively and procedurally (Article 19 2017). Its implementation, though, will be the real test: will the act result in increasing instances of removal and blocking of content actually legitimate under German law and international human rights law? Or will it bring some coherence to the existing piecemeal and arbitrary approach? There is little doubt that the implementation will be scrutinized closely by other governments, who may be tempted to follow suit, in Europe and elsewhere.

Internet Intermediaries Should Respect Human Rights
A 2012 recommendation of the European Union Committee of Ministers concluded that social network services may threaten the human rights of users:

> The right to freedom of expression and information, as well as the right to private life and human dignity may also be threatened on social networking services, which can also shelter discriminatory practices. Threats may, in particular,

arise from lack of legal, and procedural, safeguards surrounding processes that can lead to the exclusion of users; inadequate protection of children and young people against harmful content or behaviours; lack of respect for others' rights; lack of privacy-friendly default settings; lack of transparency about the purposes for which personal data are collected and processed. (Committee of Ministers of the Council of Europe 2012)

Two years later, in 2014, Recommendation CM/Rec(2014)6 of the Committee of Ministers on a guide to human rights for Internet users suggests that companies such as social networks may interfere unlawfully with the right to freedom of expression:

It is possible that companies, such as social networks, remove content created and made available by Internet users. These companies may also deactivate users' accounts (e.g. a user's profile or presence in social networks) justifying their action on non-compliance with their terms and conditions of use of the service. Such actions could constitute an interference with the right to freedom of expression and the right to receive and impart information unless the conditions of Article 10, paragraph 2 of the ECHR [European Convention on Human Rights] as interpreted by the Court, are met. (Committee of Ministers of the Council of Europe 2014, 53)

Both recommendations go on to explicitly demand of intermediaries that they "respect human rights and the rule of law" by implementing self- and coregulatory mechanisms, including procedural safeguards and access to effective remedies, as well as by "combating hate speech and other content that incites violence or discrimination. Online service providers should be attentive to the use of, and editorial responses to, expressions motivated by racist, xenophobic, anti-Semitic, misogynist, sexist (including as regards Lesbian Gay Bisexual and Transgender people) or other bias."

Sector-wide regulation has been initiated but remains limited, owing possibly to the fact that the sector is relatively new and evolving constantly. The most important framework is that of the Global Network Initiative (GNI), established in 2008, which includes Internet intermediaries but also participants from civil society and academia. Members commit to implementing GNI core principles on freedom of expression and privacy (thereafter GNI principles).

The GNI principles place a large emphasis on the commitment of the intermediaries in terms of protecting the rights of their users against government interference. On the other hand, little is said of their commitment to respect freedom of expression online, that is, to respect the right of their users vis-à-vis their own activities and decisions. This state focus is also reflected in the transparency reports issued by the intermediaries, which do not include data taken down by the intermediaries as part of the implementation of their terms and conditions. A 2014 United Nations Educational, Scientific, and Cultural Organization study on the role of Internet intermediaries commended the GNI principles but found

> a glaring absence of similar principles, guidelines and standards for companies' self-regulatory practices, including terms of service enforcement. Given the lack of transparency and consistency in how companies enforce their terms of service and other private rules, and given the impact of such enforcement of internet users' freedom of expression, there is a clear need for the development of guidelines and "best practice" standards for intermediaries' own rules on user expression. (MacKinnon et al. 2014, 168)

It is also suggested that while the legal context of the country in which a company is headquartered is particularly important for the respect of user rights, "freedom of expression can be strongly influenced in a positive or negative direction by companies' own rules, processes and mechanisms on matters including terms of service enforcement, user privacy and identity. Companies are much less transparent and accountable with the public on these matters" (MacKinnon et al. 2014, 166).

Since then, a new civil society initiative, Ranking Digital Rights, has been launched, seeking to put more pressure on Internet intermediaries so that they address the "glaring" absence of principles to guide self-regulatory practices. Ranking Digital Rights establishes an index of the most powerful intermediaries' corporate accountability based on their public commitments and disclosed policies affecting users' freedom of expression and privacy (Ranking Digital Rights 2017). Altogether, these critiques point to the privatization of a public space for communication, governed not by the national laws adopted by parliaments but by the rules and regulations drafted by the companies providing Internet services, largely on the basis of commercial interest.

Non-State Actors as Human Rights Norms Developers

Internet intermediaries are also actively involved in formal processes leading to the creation of hard and soft international legal norms. They may do so as part of their active role in the multistakeholder approach, which characterizes Internet governance, such as the Internet Governance Forum or NetMundial. Indeed, according to participants and scholars, the powerful, well-equipped, and well-trained corporate actors are particularly able to influence multistakeholder processes and outcomes, such as NetMundial, for instance.[13] Internet intermediaries may also play a significant role in the development of treaties adopted by states, such as the now defunct Trans-Pacific Partnership Agreement and the Trans-Atlantic Trade and Investment Partnership, which have been regularly denounced by civil society because of their lack of transparency and broad-based consultation. Yet, they may greatly influence the realization of online freedoms, if implemented. It may be argued that through their role and influence, Internet intermediaries are entering into nondisputable commitments over these processes outcomes, including over human rights protection.

Non-State Actors as Human Rights Advocates

Internet intermediaries make explicit commitments to defend freedom of expression, as part of their mission or its implementation, in the context of their interaction and negotiations with states or in court cases as highlighted above. This role is also reflected in the jurisprudence: they challenge states' policies, regulations, or bills which, while targeting intermediaries, are said to impact fundamental human rights. Examples of such cases include Google appealing to the French Conseil d'État against decisions by the French regulator that search results found to be infringing on the right to privacy should be delisted globally. In July 2017, the Conseil d'État ruled to seek European Court of Justice advice on the matter. Google is arguing, among other factors, that a global implementation violates the right to freedom of expression. In the United States, Facebook has challenged search warrants, which it considers to be fishing expeditions by prosecutors against its users, arguing that they are unconstitutionally overbroad, violate the privacy rights of their users, and have serious Fourth Amendment implications. So far, the New York State Court of Appeals affirmed that Internet service providers cannot appeal a judge's decision to issue search warrants in a criminal case, even in situations where the Internet service provider believes the search warrants violate its users' constitutional rights (*In re 381 Search Warrants Directed to Facebook, Inc.* 2017). Recent such cases are mixed in terms of their outcomes. But they are important in terms of human rights commitments and seeking to provide for an access to remedy with a collective dimension.

On the other hand, intermediaries' framing of online freedom of expression embraces largely a state-centered approach consisting in protecting users and private actors against illegitimate interference by governments (Callamard 2017b; Jørgensen 2017). The commitment to freedom of expression is expressed, explicitly or implicitly, as a stand against the state. There is no acknowledgement that private actors, such as intermediaries, may impact negatively on users' freedom of expression, including through enforcing their terms of services: "In sum, there is limited reflection on the power that these internet giants exercise over public participation in the online domain, and the responsibility that follows in terms of systematically assessing all business practices for potential negative impact on their users' rights and freedoms" (Jørgensen 2017, 13).

Conclusion

It is impossible to escape the proposal that Internet intermediaries, by their birth, mission, public expression, and roles, have moral obligations which extend beyond their duties to uphold the interests of their shareholders (Falk 1994). The companies currently powering the Internet have human rights responsibilities. These responsibilities concern not just freedom of expression but also a range of other rights and liberties, which find specific realization in the online world—meaning that their respect and protection take on specific dimensions because of the space within which they are exercised.

It is also difficult to escape the conclusion that these companies have been ill prepared for the range and extent of their human rights responsibilities. Their various attempts at regulating content so far, according to human rights principles, have been at best naive and amateurish and at worst irresponsible (Callamard 2017b). Self-regulation has been weak and hypocritical, including because of the refusal of these intermediaries to consider that the content of their terms of service, and their implementation, may amount to an abusive contractual framework, violating human rights standards.

Andrew Clapham (2017b, 8) suggested that the extent of non-state actors' obligations depends on "what kind of non-state actor they are, the context in which they are operating, and any relevant promises made by them. In other words the scope of their obligations depends on their capacity, context, and commitments." The context as far as the online world is concerned is one characterized by the central role of non-state actors, in the first place Internet intermediaries. Put simply, the online world will not function, and possibly, it will not exist, without the corporate actors that are providing the technologies and services powering this new world. Most importantly, many of these non-state actors are US corporations, operating in situations of quasi-monopoly, whether as Internet service providers, search engines, or platforms. The US monopoly over the technology running the economy of the twenty-first century weighs heavily in the way states, including China or Russia, but also the US traditional allies, such as Europe, approach these non-state actors and seek to regulate them.

It is also a context with great accountability deficits, and a legal vacuum, largely because of the jurisdictional questions over extraterritorial content and nondomestic actors. From a human rights standpoint, the initial claims that the Internet will create a more humane and fairer civilization of the mind (Barlow 1996) are under duress, if not outrightly rejected. Factors include the millions of trolls around the world, threatening and harassing those they disagree with, the multiplication of websites and content preaching hatred, the manipulation and instrumentalization of information directed at an ill-informed and poorly educated public unable to recognize "fake news," to mention a few. Arbitrariness, lack of transparency, political pressures, ad hoc legal developments, and surveillance: all appear to be dominating the working of the online space. Non-state actors at best are playing an ambiguous role and at worst are contributing to the demise of Internet founding claims, through their business models; their normative framework and US-centric culture; and their lack of investment in, and commitment to, effective self-regulation of the kind that other sectors have been forced to embrace.

One of the strongest arguments in support of calling for a reconceptualization of the role of intermediaries in the protection of human rights in the online space comes from their capacities. Internet intermediaries alone have the capacity to ensure respect for human rights online. The sheer quantity of online, transborder content means that it is out of both the technical and jurisdictional range of most states to regulate or protect. Indeed, the current approach, hostage of jurisdictional conflicts results in endless legal uncertainties and accountability vacuums. Many, although not all,[14] potential human rights violations occurring online, including violations of freedom of expression, require the active involvement of Internet intermediaries—to take down content, to lift anonymity, to close accounts, and alternatively, to allow for the circulation of content which may be violating human rights, such as privacy, discrimination, the right to be free of harassment or bullying, and so forth. By the same token, they alone have the technical capacity to ensure rights are protected and fulfilled. To the extent that access to the Internet is a right, this is one right whose realization is heavily dependent upon them. States remain the ultimate duty bearer in terms of *ensuring* that the right is enshrined in law, respected, and protected. But the fulfillment of this right is unlikely to be realized, under the current technological and economic conditions, without the active involvement of these non-state actors.

At the conclusion of this reflection, I see two options for a stronger protection of human rights online. Both require a better understanding and delineation of the specific duties and responsibilities of non-state actors, along with their rights. One option is meaningful self-regulation. Overall, and compared to similarly powerful economic actors, the Internet intermediaries have yet to demonstrate a thorough commitment to meaningful self-regulation or indeed to establish strong sector-wide associations able to regulate their members, individually and collectively. Not only is this situation weakening online freedom, and the rights of users, but it is also weakening the hands of the corporations in their interactions with states. The failure at strong and meaningful self-regulation justifies, if not explains, the multiplication of coregulatory initiatives by states, and their increasing policy and legal pressures on social media platforms to monitor specific content.

One particularly strong example of self-regulation is the 2010 International Code of Conduct for Private Security Service Providers. By adhering to the code, private security companies undertake to respect human rights and comply with international humanitarian law when providing security services in regions where the rule of law has been undermined. They undertake to respect all applicable laws, including local, regional, and/or national laws. In September 2013, multistakeholder negotiations established an independent governance and oversight mechanism in the form of an association under Swiss law: the International Code of Conduct for Private Security Providers' Association (ICoCA), based in Geneva. The ICoCA Board of Directors is made up of representatives from government, industry, and civil society. The ICoCA has developed procedures for certification, monitoring, reporting, assessing performance, and addressing complaints. Governments are also considering integrating membership to the self-regulatory body when recruiting private security providers.

Meaningful self-regulation demands not only agreed-upon standards of behavior but also a system of accountability that can be trusted by users and other actors, including governments. This requires complaints mechanisms, effective and independent investigation of alleged violations of agreed standards, and measures to address the violations. As presented above, existing self-regulation within the online world still has a long way to go to meet minimum requirements for effective self-regulation. On the other hand, there appears to be increasing awareness that the current approach is failing to deliver human rights protection in the online world, while strengthening the hands of those intent on controlling and censoring. There are a number of multistakeholder processes, such as the Internet Governance Forum, which offer avenues and opportunities to put together meaningful self-regulation. But time is running out.

The second option, more difficult to realize, is through international law. As suggested by Bethlehem (2014, 23),

> [I]ncreasingly aged treaties and other crystallized rules of international law are left to carry the burden of addressing conduct, and of shaping an international system, that may bear little relation to the conduct and system for which the rules were originally crafted. This is ultimately unsatisfactory. . . . In the era of Globalization 3.0, in which the principal agents of change are individuals and corporations, international law needs to develop a more sophisticated appreciation of international legal personality and of subject-hood of international law, and more inclusive, responsive, and efficient mechanisms to address the interests and voices of these subjects.[15]

The development of an appropriate and relevant international legal framework for the online space, including through the adoption of a treaty, ought to be on the agenda of actors concerned with the protection of human rights online. At this point in time, a number of factors militate against considering practically the emergence of a new body of international public law. To name a few such factors, human rights indicators are on the decline, particularly those related to freedom of expression and association; the birth of a new global governance system, to replace US hegemony and the bipolar system of the cold war, is proving to be particularly painful and bloody, characterized by the multiplication of proxy wars and conflicts; around the world, electorates have brought to power populist leaders who embrace nationalism and reject the globalization project and human rights protection; and so forth. Any international treaty-based regulation, if it were to occur, will thus be likely to result in a shrinking of human rights protection, online and offline.

Still, it is worth reflecting on what an international legal framework for the online space, protecting human rights, and incorporating Internet intermediaries as duty bearers, would require. At a theoretical and conceptual level, this may require rethinking the notion of territory, with the view of defining and incorporating the concepts of digital territory and digital boundaries, and of identifying the international legal implications and content of these concepts.[16] Such a process, no doubt, demands rethinking the sources of law, to include industry-driven and coregulatory standards, and to give legal meaning and weight to the principles that would have been the objects of "raw consensus" through multistakeholder discussions and gatherings such as the Internet Governance Forum. It will, also, and most importantly, require a better appreciation of the working of the world and global society of the twenty-first century, understanding Internet corporations and other non-state actors as subjects of international law, with specific rights and duties.

Notes

1. As mentioned in the Introduction to this volume, "internet intermediaries" refers to "third-party platforms that mediate between digital content and the humans who contribute and access this content" (DeNardis 2014, 154).

2. The French delegate proposed that the clause "Every one shall have the right to freedom of thought and expression" should be followed by "provided that he shall be answerable, in cases defined by the law, for abuses of that freedom."

3. These include the "Asian values" interpretation of freedom of expression, for instance.

4. See, for instance, the many reports by international human rights organizations, including Amnesty International and Human Rights Watch, on corporate accountability.

5. As far back as 1995, the United States has argued that obligations under the ICCPR, including those related to freedom of expression or the right to privacy, only apply to individuals who are both within the territories of a state party and

subject to that state party's sovereign authority. This position ran contrary to the jurisprudence of the Human Rights Committee, according to which a state party must respect and ensure the rights laid down in the covenant to anyone within the power or effective control of that state party, even if not situated within the territory of the state party (UN Human Rights Committee 2004). In a subsequent 2014 development related to the protection of the right to privacy (UN Office of the High Commissioner for Human Rights 2014), the OHCHR has endorsed this position and further stated that "where the State exercises regulatory jurisdiction over a third party that physically controls the data, that State also would have obligations under the Covenant. If a country seeks to assert jurisdiction over the data of private companies as a result of the incorporation of those companies in that country, then human rights protections must be extended to those whose privacy is being interfered with, whether in the country of incorporation or beyond."

6. Among other things, they are cited by European Convention on Human Rights decisions and listed under the "Relevant International Instruments Section."

7. (1) Genocide, (2) Crimes Against Humanity, (3) War Crimes, (4) the Crime of Unconstitutional Change of Government, (5) Piracy, (6) Terrorism, (7) Mercenarism, (8) Corruption, (9) Money Laundering, (10) Trafficking in Persons, (11) Trafficking in Drugs, (12) Trafficking in Hazardous Wastes, (13) Illicit Exploitation of Natural Resources, and (14) the Crime of Aggression.

8. The E-commerce directive, the data protection directive, and the European Court are establishing three different liability regimes (Van der Sloot 2015).

9. Content censored upon demands from the states has been reported (on a metadata basis) biannually by a number of intermediaries since 2010.

10. The cases discussed below are taken from the Columbia Global Freedom of Expression database of free speech jurisprudence from around the world. It includes a large number of cases implicating Internet companies, including social media platforms and search engines.

11. The ruling points to the many revenues extracted by and through the Facebook platform. It also argues that under French consumer law, a noncommercial/nonprofessional party to a contract can sue the other party of the contract in either his or her country or that of the other party. It finds that the teacher in this particular case acted for noncommercial purposes. It further points to the "abusive clause" provision under French consumer law according to which some contractual engagements may be found to be "abusive" because they result in a significant imbalance (déséquilibre) between the parties to the contract.

12. However, the Court also said that while Facebook could easily delete verbatim repetitions of the hate posts by automated process, it would be unreasonable to require it to monitor and control all content on its platform for postings similar to

the ones in the original posting because of the vast number of its users. Accordingly, the Court reversed the lower court's decision in this regard.

13. Critiques over their influence included the following: Just Net Coalition "The Caravan Has Set Out for a Neo-liberal Capture of Global Governance," "They have forcefully declared that the Internet is special and that its governance is to be left to vaguely defined "stakeholders" among whom of course would be the dominant Internet corporations, thus for example allowing Amazon to share in decision-making concerning global taxation of its Internet e-commerce activities and Facebook to be a partner in deciding what should be the power of citizens in controlling their own information" (Just Net Coalition 2014); the Internet Governance Civil Society Coordination Group, "Civil Society Coordination Group and NETmundial Initiative Information," "Among the underlying concerns of many are that the involvement of the World Economic Forum in the initiative signals an attempt by economic and political elites to secure a central role in Internet governance; that the Initiative has been organised in a top-down manner that privileges its three promoters above other stakeholders" (NETmundial Initiative 2014).

14. The clear exception is Internet shut-down.

15. Bethlehem also suggests reconceiving notions of jurisdiction, for instance by seeking to develop a consensual approach around the notion of "deemed jurisdiction," "a notion that, for certain given forms of conduct, jurisdiction will be deemed to rest with x or y or z, or with some configuration of all of them. An approach along these lines might be particularly appropriate, for example, in respect of cyber activity, given the challenges of saying with any clarity where, in geographic space as opposed to virtual space, such conduct occurs. . . . A deemed jurisdiction approach could craft a flexible conception of jurisdiction that may be more appropriate to the virtual geography of the medium."

16. The 2017 Microsoft-led proposal for a Digital Geneva Convention to prevent warfare in cyberspace seeks to adapt a treaty-like approach to the multistakeholder nature of Internet governance. It somehow radically suggests a set of legal obligations imposed on states, along with the adoption of self-regulatory principles for tech companies and the establishment of an independent multistakeholder oversight mechanism responsible for investigating cyberattacks (Smith 2017). Yet, the proposal fails to acknowledge the active role of the tech corporate actors in violating human rights and contributing to cyber insecurity (Microsoft 2017).

References

Alston, Philip, ed. 2005. *Non-State Actors and Human Rights*. Oxford: Oxford University Press.

Amas M. v. Facebook Ireland. 2017. 11 O 2338/16 UVR (Würzburg Court of Justice, March 7).

Article 19. 2013. "Internet Intermediaries: Dilemma of Liability." August 29. https://www.article19.org/resources.php/resource/37242/en/internet-intermediaries:-dilemma-of-liability.

Article 19. 2017. "Getting Connected: New Policy on Freedom of Expression, Telcos and ISPs." Policy Brief. June 14. https://www.article19.org/resources.php/resource/38792/en/getting-connected:-new-policy-on-freedom-of-expression,-telcos-and-isps.

Barlow, John Perry. 1996. "A Declaration of the Independence of Cyberspace." https://www.eff.org/cyberspace-independence.

Bethlehem, Daniel. 2014. "The End of Geography: The Changing Nature of the International System and the Challenge to International Law." *The European Journal of International Law* 25 (1), 9–24.

Bossuyt, Marc J. 1987. *Guide to the "Travaux Préparatoires" of the International Covenant on Civil and Political Rights.* Dordrecht: Martinus Nijhoff.

Business & Human Rights Resource Centre. 2014. "Yahoo! Lawsuit (Re China)." February 18. https://business-humanrights.org/en/yahoo-lawsuit-re-china-0.

Callamard, Agnès. 2017a. "Are Courts Re-inventing Internet Governance?" *International Review of Law, Computers and Technology.* March 23. 1–17.

———. 2017b. "The Control of 'Invasive' Ideas in a Digital Age." *Social Research: An International Quarterly* 84 (1): 119–145.

CG v. Facebook Ireland. 2016. [2016] NICA 54 (Court of Appeal in Northern Ireland, December 21).

Clapham, Andrew. 2006. *Human Rights Obligations of Non-State Actors.* Oxford: Oxford University Press.

———. 2017. "Detention by Armed Groups under International Law." *International Law Studies* 93. Stockton Center for the Study of International Law.

———. 2018. "Human Rights Obligations for Non-State-Actors: Where Are We Now?" In *Doing Peace the Rights Way: Essays in International Law and Relations in Honour of Louise Arbour*, edited by Fannie Lafontaine and François Larocque. Cambridge, UK: Intersentia.

Committee of Ministers of the Council of Europe. 2012. "Recommendation on the Protection of Human Rights with Regard to Social Networking Services." Recommendation CM/Rec(2012)4. Strasbourg, France: Council of Europe

———. 2014. "Recommendation on a Guide to Human Rights for Internet Users." Recommendation CM/Rec(2014)6. Strasbourg, France: Council of Europe.

de La Chapelle, Bertrand, and Paul Fehlinger. 2016. "Jurisdiction on the Internet: From Legal Arms Race to Transnational Cooperation." Global Commission on Internet Governance Paper Series. April 1. https://www.cigionline.org/publications/jurisdiction-internet-legal-arms-race-transnational-cooperation.

DeNardis, Laura. 2014. *The Global War for Internet Governance*. New Haven, CT: Yale University Press.

Die Grünen v. Facebook Ireland Limited. 2017. 5 R 5/17t (Austrian Court of Appeal, May 5).

Drake, William J., Vinton G. Cerf, and Wolfgang Kleinwächter. 2016. "Internet Fragmentation: An Overview." Future of the Internet Initiative White Paper. Cologny-Geneva: World Economic Forum.

Emmerson, Ben. June 16, 2015. "Report of the Special Rapporteur on the Promotion and Protection of Human Rights and Fundamental Freedoms while Countering Terrorism." A/HRC/29/51. Geneva: Human Rights Council.

E-Ventures Worldwide, LLC v. Google, Inc. 2016. 2:14-cv-646-FtM-29CM (US District Court for the Middle District of Florida, May 12).

Facebook Inc. v. Jean Durand. 2016. 2016–58 (Cour D'Appel de Paris, February 12).

Falk, Richard. 1994. "Democratizing, Internationalizing and Globalizing." In *Global Transformation: Challenges in the State System*, edited by Yoshikazu Sakamoto. Tokyo, Japan: United Nations University Press.

Global Network Initiative. n.d. "GNI Principles on Freedom of Expression and Privacy." https://globalnetworkinitiative.org/gni-principles/

Guardian, The. 2016. "Facebook Won't Block Fake News Posts because It Has No Incentive, Experts Say." November 15. https://www.theguardian.com/technology/2016/nov/15/facebook-fake-news-us-election-trump-clinton.

Heyns, Christof. 2016. "Report on the Right to Life and the Use of Force by Private Security Providers in Law Enforcement Contexts." A/HRC/32/39. UN May 6. Geneva: Human Rights Council. https://documents-dds-ny.un.org/doc/UNDOC/GEN/G16/092/21/PDF/G1609221.pdf?OpenElement.

Higgin, Rosalyn. 1994. *Problems and Processes: International Law and How We Use It*. Oxford: Clarendon Press.

Hopkins, Nick. 2017. "Revealed: Facebook's Internal Rules on Sex, Terrorism and Violence." *The Guardian*. May 21. https://www.theguardian.com/news/2017/may/21/revealed-facebook-internal-rulebook-sex-terrorism-violence?CMP=twt_gu.

In re 381 Search Warrants Directed to Facebook, Inc. 2017. 2017 NY Slip Op 02586 Docket Number 16 (New York State Court of Appeals, April 4).

International Criminal Court. 2010. *Decision Pursuant to Article 15 of the Rome Statute on the Authorization of an Investigation into the Situation in the Republic of Kenya.* ICC-01/09 (International Criminal Court, March 31). https://www.refworld.org/cases.ICC.4bc2fe372.html.

International Law Commission. 2001. "Report of the International Law Commission on the Work of Its Fifty-third Session." A/56/10. http://legal.un.org/docs/?symbol=A/CN.4/L.602/Rev.1

International Law Association. 2016. Report of the Seventy Seventh Conference, Johannesburg Conference. Johannesburg. http://www.ila-hq.org/index.php/orderssdb.

Jørgensen, Rikke Frank. 2017. "Framing Human Rights: Exploring Storytelling within Internet Companies." *Information, Communication & Society* 21 (3).

Just Net Coalition. 2014. "The Caravan Has Set Out for a Neo-liberal Capture of Global Governance." The Just Net Coalition. November 17. https://justnetcoalition.org/NMI-neoliberal-caravan.

Kadic v. Karadzic, 70 F.3d 232 [2nd Cir. Circuit, 1995], cert. denied [1996] 518 US 1005 [1996].

Kaye, David. 2017. "Report on the Roles Played by Private Actors Engaged in the Provision of Internet and Telecommunications Access." A/HRC/35/22. Geneva: Human Rights Council.

Kiobel v. Royal Dutch Petroleum Co., 133 Supreme Court. 1659 [2013].

Kirshner, Jodie A. 2015. "A Call for the EU to Assume Jurisdiction over Extraterritorial Corporate Human Rights Abuses." *Northwestern University Journal of Human Rights* 13 (1): 1–26.

Kreimer, Seth F. 2006. "Censorship by Proxy: The First Amendment, Internet Intermediaries, and the Problem of the Weakest Link." *University of Pennsylvania Law Review* 155 (1): 11–101.

Land, Molly. 2013. "Towards an International Law of the Internet." *Harvard International Law Journal* 54 (2): 393–458.

La Rue, Frank. 2011. "Report on Key Trends and Challenges to the Right of All Individuals to Seek, Receive and Impart Information and Ideas of All Kinds through the Internet." A/HRC/17/27. May 6. Geneva: Human Rights Council.

MacKinnon, Rebecca, Elonnai Hickok, Allon Bar, and Hae-in Lim. 2014. *Fostering Freedom Online: The Role of Internet Intermediaries.* Paris: United Nations Educational, Scientific, and Cultural Organization.

Microsoft. 2017. "A Tech Accord to Protect People in Cyber Space." Microsoft Policy Paper. https://dig.watch/sites/default/files/Policy-Paper-Industry-Accord.pdf.

Morozov, Evgeny. 2012. "Whither Internet Control?" In *Liberation Technology: Social Media and the Struggle for Democracy*, edited by Larry Diamond and Marc F. Plattner. Baltimore: Johns Hopkins University Press.

NETmundial Initiative. 2014. "Civil Society Coordination Group and NETmundial Initiative Information." *Diplo Internet Governance Community*. November 26. http://www.diplointernetgovernance.org/profiles/blogs/civil-society-coordination-group-and-netmundial-initiative-inform.

Open Society Foundations. 2016. "Undeniable Atrocities: Confronting Crimes against Humanity in Mexico." New York, USA: Open Society Foundation.

Pillay, Navanethem. 2009. "The Corporate Responsibility to Respect: A Human Rights Milestone." *International Labour and Social Policy Review*. Geneva, Switzerland: International Organisation of Employers.

ProPublica. 2017. *Facebook's Secret Censorship Rules Protect White Men from Hate Speech but Not Black Children*. June 28. https://www.propublica.org/article/facebook-hate-speech-censorship-internal-documents-algorithms.

Ranking Digital Rights. 2017. *2017 Ranking Digital Rights Corporate Accountability Index*. https://rankingdigitalrights.org/index2017.

Reinisch, August. 2005. "The Changing International Legal Framework of Dealing with Non-State Actors." In *Non-State Actors and Human Rights*, edited by Philip Alston, 37–90. Oxford: Oxford University Press.

Ruggie, John. 2010. "Business and Human Rights: Further Steps toward the Operationalization of the 'Protect, Respect and Remedy' Framework." A/HRC/14/27. Geneva: Human Rights Council.

Ruggie, John. 2013. *Just Business: Multinational Corporations and Human Rights*. New York: W. W. Norton.

Russell, Jon. 2017. "Apple Removes VPN Apps from the App Store in China." *Tech Crunch*. July 29. https://techcrunch.com/2017/07/29/apple-removes-vpn-apps-from-the-app-store-in-china.

Schabas, William A. 2013. *The Universal Declaration of Human Rights: The Travaux Préparatoires*, vol. 1. Cambridge: Cambridge University Press.

Smith, Brad. 2017. "The Need for a Digital Geneva Convention." February 14. https://blogs.microsoft.com/on-the-issues/2017/02/14/need-digital-geneva-convention.

Sosa v. Alvarez-Machain, 542 US 692, 725 [2004].

United Nations Environmental Programme Finance Initiative and Foley Hoag LLP. 2015. *Banks and Human Rights: A Legal Analysis.* December. http://www.unepfi.org/publications/banking-publications/banks-and-human-rights-a-legal-analysis-2.

UN General Assembly. 1946. "Resolution 59(I)."

UN General Assembly. 1949. "Draft Convention on the International Transmission of News and the Rights of Correction." Official records of the 3rd session of the General Assembly, part 2, April 5–May 18, 1949—A/900.—.—pp. 22–30.

UN General Assembly. 2008. "Protect, Respect and Remedy: A Framework for Business and Human Rights." A/HRC/8/5. April 7. https://www.ohchr.org/en/issues/transnationalcorporations/pages/reports.aspx.

UN Human Rights Committee. 2004. "General Comment No. 31." CCPR/C/21/Rev.1/Add. 1326. May 26. https://www.refworld.org/docid/478b26ae2.html.

UN Independent International Commission of Inquiry. 2012. "Report of the Independent International Commission of Inquiry on the Syrian Arab Republic." February 22. A/HRC/19/69.

UN Office of the High Commissioner for Human Rights. 2011. "Guiding Principles on Business and Human Rights: Implementing the United Nations 'Protect, Respect and Remedy' Framework." March 21. A/HRC/17/31.

UN Office of the High Commissioner for Human Rights. 2014. "The right to privacy in the digital age." June 30. A/HRC/27/37.

Van der Sloot, Bart. 2015. "Welcome to the Jungle: The Liability of Internet Intermediaries for Privacy Violations in Europe." *Journal of Intellectual Property, Information Technology and Electronic Commerce Law* 6: 211–228.

Yeginsu, Can, and Jones, Anthony. 2016. "The Emerging Human Rights Liability of Banks?" *Butterworths Journal of International Banking and Financial Law* 6 (June): 353–355.

9   The Council of Europe and Internet Intermediaries: A Case Study of Tentative Posturing[1]

Tarlach McGonagle

Internet intermediaries wield enormous power in the evolving digital ecosystem. The extent of their power, as detailed insightfully throughout this book, has prompted increased scrutiny of their activities and the impact they have on the human rights of Internet users. This chapter offers a critical analysis of the suitability of the Council of Europe's system for the protection of freedom of expression as a framework for regulating the activities of Internet intermediaries. The title of the chapter refers to the Council of Europe's "tentative posturing" in respect of the roles and regulation of Internet intermediaries. The institutional posturing can be described as "tentative" for a number of reasons, not least of which is the difficulty of (re-)calibrating regulation for a relatively new and complex medium. Another reason is the difficulty of bringing powerful private actors under the scope of an international system of human rights protection that is built around the relationship between states and individuals.

The chapter opens with a brief overview of the Council of Europe's system for the protection of freedom of expression, the centerpiece of which is Article 10 of the European Convention on Human Rights (ECHR) (Council of Europe 1950). It will then explore the efforts of the European Court of Human Rights (ECtHR) to keep apace of technological developments and to retain and revamp its general freedom-of-expression principles in an information and communications environment that is increasingly dominated by the Internet and the intermediaries which strongly influence its operation. This exploration will focus in particular on the growth spurts and growing pains of the ECtHR's case law. Besides the court, other bodies within the Council of Europe contribute to and strengthen the system of protection for freedom of expression, in particular the Committee of Ministers with its political standard-setting activities. The chapter will also focus on the legal complications involved in bringing Internet intermediaries into the fold of a traditional, international, and treaty-centric system of human rights protection. It will conclude with a reflection on the rights, duties, and responsibilities of Internet intermediaries that flow from the existing system. "Hate speech" will be used to illustrate how frictional the relationship between intermediaries' rights, duties, and responsibilities—and those of their users—can be in practice.

A System for the Protection of Freedom of Expression

The Council of Europe has developed an elaborate system for the protection of freedom of expression, which is a source of guidance for the organization's forty-seven member states in respect of their national media laws and policies. The system comprises principles and rights, as enshrined in treaty law and developed in case law; political and policy-making standards; and state reporting/monitoring mechanisms. Each of the instruments and mechanisms has its own objectives and emphases and/or mandates and working methods. To understand these instruments and mechanisms as a systemic whole is to "take into account the actual forces at work and make possible the realistic achievement of the objectives sought" (Emerson 1970, 4). Each has its place in the system due to the overall "unity of purpose and operation" (ibid.).

The interplay between each of the system's components determines how the right to freedom of expression is exercised in practice. The system strives to operationalize abstract theories of freedom of expression and turn them into a right to freedom of expression that is meaningful and effective in practice. It seeks to create an enabling environment for freedom of expression, including as exercised by journalists, the media, and others who contribute to public debate. Internet intermediaries are important actors within this enabling environment, insofar as they can facilitate or obstruct access to the online forums in which public debate is increasingly conducted. The operators of social network services, for instance, "possess the technical means to remove information and suspend accounts," which makes them "uniquely positioned to delimit the topics and set the tone of public debate" (Leerssen 2015, 99–100; see also Jørgensen's Introduction to this volume and Land's chapter in this volume). Search engines, for their part, have the aim and the ability to make information more accessible and prominent, which gives them influence over how people find information and ideas and what kinds of information and ideas they find (see, generally, van Hoboken 2012). Both of these types of Internet intermediary therefore have clear "discursive significance" in society (Laidlaw 2015, 204).

The ECHR is the most important instrument in this system. Article 10 protects the right to freedom of expression (see further below), but that protection is integrated into the ECHR's broader, more general scheme of protection for human rights. The rights safeguarded by the ECHR, as interpreted by the ECtHR in its jurisprudence, are the drivers of the whole. This must remain the case when exploring new dimensions to freedom of expression, such as Internet intermediary regulation, and when overcoming persistent and emerging threats and challenges to the exercise of the right to freedom of expression.

Over the years, various other treaties have been adopted by the Council of Europe, which reflect the general principles of the ECHR in their own theme-specific focuses. A systemic approach to freedom of expression helps to ensure that relevant treaties remain largely consistent and complementary in their focuses.

There is an important measure of interplay between the Council of Europe's treaties, which are legally binding on contracting states, and political standard-setting texts, which typically take the form of declarations and recommendations and are not legally binding. Political and policy-making texts (hereinafter, "standard-setting texts") ought to be grounded in the ECHR and the case law of the ECtHR, but they can also influence the development of that case law.

As standard-setting texts tend to focus on particular (human rights) issues or (emerging) situations with democratic or human rights implications, they can serve to supplement existing treaty provisions and case law. They can do so by providing a level of detail lacking in treaty provisions or by anticipating new issues not yet dealt with in treaty provisions or case law. It is noteworthy that judgments of the ECtHR refer to the Committee of Ministers' standard-setting texts in an increasingly systematic and structured way. It has referred to Recommendation CM/Rec(2011)7 of the Committee of Ministers to member states on a new notion of media (Committee of Ministers of the Council of Europe 2011a), in its *Yildirim* and *Delfi* judgments (ECtHR 2012a and 2015a, respectively).[2] These standard-setting texts can also facilitate the interpretation of existing treaties by applying general principles to concrete situations or interpreting principles in a way that is in tune with the times.

The Basics and Centrality of Article 10 of the ECHR

Article 10(1) sets out the right to freedom of expression as a compound right comprising the freedom to hold opinions and to receive and impart information and ideas. As such, there are three distinct components to the right, corresponding to different aspects of the communicative process, that is, holding views, receiving content, and sending content. A distinct right to seek information and ideas is conspicuous by its absence. In this respect, Article 10 of the ECHR contrasts with equivalent provisions in other international human rights treaties, such as Article 19 of the International Covenant on Civil and Political Rights (ICCPR). It should be noted, though, that the evolution of the court's case law has served to compensate for and, to an extent, close the gap between the texts of Article 10, ECHR, and Article 19, ICCPR, on this point (ECtHR 2016a).

Article 10(1), ECHR, countenances the possibility for states to regulate the audiovisual media by means of licensing schemes. This provision was inserted as a reaction to the abuse of radio, television, and cinema for Nazi propaganda during the Second World War. Article 10(2) then proceeds to delineate the core right set out in the preceding paragraph. It does so by enumerating a number of grounds, based on which the right *may* legitimately be restricted, *provided that* the restrictions are *prescribed by law* and are *necessary in a democratic society*. It justifies this approach by linking the permissibility of restrictions on the right to the existence of *duties* and *responsibilities* which govern its exercise. Whereas the right to freedom of expression is regarded as being subject to general duties and responsibilities, the ECtHR sometimes refers to the specific duties or responsibilities pertaining to specific professions, for example, journalism, education, military service, and so forth. The court has held that those duties or responsibilities may vary, depending on the technology being used. In light of the case-by-case nature of the court's jurisprudence on duties and responsibilities and in light of its ongoing efforts to apply its free expression principles to the Internet (see further, below), it is only a matter of time before it begins to proffer indications of the nature of Internet actors' duties and responsibilities in respect of freedom of expression.

Notwithstanding the potential offered by Article 10(2) to restrict the right to freedom of expression on certain grounds (although legitimate restrictions must be narrowly drawn and interpreted restrictively), as the ECtHR famously stated in its *Handyside* judgment, information and ideas which "offend, shock or disturb the State or any sector of the population" must be allowed to circulate in order to safeguard the "pluralism, tolerance and broadmindedness without which there is no 'democratic society'" (ECtHR 1976). The question of how far the *Handyside* principle actually reaches in practice is very pertinent as regards online content because of the widely perceived permissiveness of the Internet as a medium. It is of particular relevance for the reflection, below, on what duty of care can be expected of Internet intermediaries to combat hate speech.

Aside from the permissible grounds for restrictions set out in Article 10(2), ECHR, the right to freedom of expression may also be limited, or rather denied, on the basis of Article 17, ECHR ("Prohibition of abuse of rights"). It reads, "Nothing in this Convention may be interpreted as implying for any State, group or person any right to engage in any activity or perform any act aimed at the destruction of any of the rights and freedoms set forth herein or at their limitation to a greater extent than is provided for in the Convention." In the past, the court has applied Article 17 to ensure that Article 10 protection is not extended to racist, xenophobic, or anti-Semitic speech; statements denying, disputing, minimizing or condoning the Holocaust; or (neo-)Nazi ideas (McGonagle 2013b). This means that in practice, sanctions for racist speech do not violate the right to freedom of expression of those uttering the racist speech. In other words, national criminal and/or civil law can legitimately punish racist speech. The straightforward application of Article 17 can lead to a finding that a claim was manifestly ill founded and a declaration of inadmissibility. Such a finding means that the court will usually not examine the substance of the claim because it blatantly goes against the values of the ECHR. That is why Article 17 is sometimes referred to as a "guillotine" provision (Tulkens 2012, 284). However, the criteria used by the court for resorting to Article 17 (as opposed to Article 10(2)) are unclear, leading to divergent jurisprudence (Cannie and Voorhoof 2011; Keane 2007).

The scope of the right to freedom of expression is not only determined by the permissible restrictions set out in Articles 10(2) and 17, ECHR. It is also determined by the interplay between the right and other ECHR rights, including the right to privacy, freedom of assembly and association, and freedom of religion.

The ECtHR has developed a standard test to determine whether Article 10, ECHR, has been violated. Put simply, whenever it has been established that there has been an interference with the right to freedom of expression, that interference must first of all be prescribed by law. In other words, it must be adequately accessible and reasonably foreseeable in its consequences. Second, it must pursue a legitimate aim (i.e., correspond to one of the aims set out in Article 10(2)). Third, it must be necessary in a democratic society, that is, it must correspond to a "pressing social need," and it must be proportionate to the legitimate aim(s) pursued.

The particular importance of the media for democratic society has been stressed repeatedly by the court. The media can make important contributions to public debate by (widely) disseminating information and ideas and thereby contributing to opinion-forming processes within society. As the court consistently acknowledges, this is particularly true of the audiovisual media because of their reach and impact. The court has traditionally regarded the audiovisual media as more pervasive than the print media. It has yet to set out a clear and coherent vision of online media, but it has ventured to say, in 2013, that "the choices inherent in the use of the Internet and social media mean that the information emerging therefrom does not have the same synchronicity or impact as broadcasted information" (ECtHR 2013a, para. 119). It continued by stating that notwithstanding "the significant development of the Internet and social media in recent years, there is no evidence of a sufficiently serious shift in the respective influences of the new and of the broadcast media in the [United Kingdom] to undermine the need for special measures for the latter" (ibid.). Commentators have been left guessing as to what *would* amount to a "sufficiently serious shift" in the eyes of the court (Plaizier 2018). The media can also make important contributions to public debate by serving as forums for discussion and debate. This is especially true of new media technologies which have considerable potential for high levels of individual and group participation (see further: ECtHR 2012a).

Furthermore, the role of "public watchdog" is very often ascribed to the media in a democratic society. In other words, the media, acting as the Fourth Estate, should monitor the activities of governmental authorities vigilantly and publicize any wrongdoing on their part. In respect of information about governmental activities, but also more broadly in respect of matters of public interest generally, the court has held time and again that "[n]ot only do the media have the task of imparting such information and ideas: the public also has a right to receive them" (ECtHR 1979, para. 65). The extent to which Internet intermediaries also fulfill or facilitate the public watchdog role depends on their actual functions (see further, below).

To date, the ECtHR has engaged meaningfully with the Internet generally (ECtHR Research Division 2015; Murphy and Ó Cuinn 2010, 636), and the specific features of the online communications environment in particular, in a surprisingly limited number of cases (ECtHR Press Unit 2017; McGonagle 2013a). It has focused on the duty of care of Internet service providers (ECtHR 2008a, para. 49), the added value of online newspaper archives for news purposes (ECtHR 2009a, 2013b), and the challenges of sifting through the informational abundance offered by the Internet (ECtHR 2011a). How the court dealt with the final point is of interest:

> It is true that the Internet is an information and communication tool particularly distinct from the printed media, in particular as regards the capacity to store and transmit information. The electronic network serving billions of users worldwide is not and potentially cannot be subject to the same regulations and control. The risk of harm posed by content and communications on the Internet to the exercise and enjoyment of human rights and freedoms, particularly the right to respect for private life, is certainly higher than that posed by the press. Therefore, the policies governing reproduction of material from the printed media and the Internet may differ. The latter undeniably have to be adjusted according to the technology's specific features in order to secure the protection and promotion of the rights and freedoms concerned. (ibid., para. 63)

The court made these observations in a case involving a newspaper that, owing to a lack of funds, "often reprinted articles and other material obtained from various public sources, including the Internet" (ibid., para. 5). In short, the court is calling for a rethink of familiar principles of media freedom and regulation in the expansive, global context of the Internet.

Again, these findings by the court focus on journalists and professional media, but in light of the expanding understandings of the roles such professions play, they are also of relevance for other actors. This reading is confirmed by the reference to the importance of the Internet "for the exercise of the right to freedom of expression generally" (ECtHR 2009a, para. 27). The court has repeatedly recognized that besides professional journalists and media, an expanding range of actors—such as individuals, civil society organizations, whistle-blowers, academics, and bloggers—can all make valuable contributions to public debate, thereby playing a role similar or equivalent to that traditionally played by the institutionalized media (ECtHR 2016a; McGonagle 2015, 19 et seq.).

From the passage cited above, it is clear that the court places the onus on states' authorities to develop a legal framework clarifying issues such as responsibility and liability. It is unclear, however, to what extent an equivalent self-regulatory framework would suffice. The court has held in other case law that self- and coregulatory mechanisms can suffice, provided they include effective guarantees of rights and effective remedies for violations of rights (Hans-Bredow-Institut 2006, 147–152, especially paras. 108 and 109). In any case, it is clear that "the State cannot absolve itself from responsibility by delegating its obligations to private bodies or individuals" (ECtHR 1993c, para. 27, and 1983, paras. 29–30). As will be explained below, state responsibility can, in certain circumstances, be triggered indirectly by the acts or omissions of private bodies.

In its *Ahmet Yildirim v. Turkey* judgment of December 18, 2012, the court recognized in a very forthright way the importance of the Internet in the contemporary communications landscape. It stated that the Internet "has become one of the principal means for individuals to exercise their right to freedom of expression today: it offers essential tools for participation in activities and debates relating to questions of politics or public interest" (ECtHR 2012a, para. 54).

This recognition clearly places great store by the participatory dimension of free expression. The court found that a measure resulting in the wholesale blocking of Google Sites in Turkey "by rendering large quantities of information inaccessible, substantially restricted the rights of Internet users and had a significant collateral effect" (ibid., para. 66; ECtHR 2015b, para. 64). The interference "did not satisfy the foreseeability requirement under the Convention and did not afford the applicant the degree of protection to which he was entitled by the rule of law in a democratic society" (ibid., para. 67). In addition, it produced arbitrary effects (ibid., para. 68).

Furthermore, the court found that "the judicial-review procedures concerning the blocking of Internet sites are insufficient to meet the criteria for
avoiding abuse, as domestic law does not provide for any safeguards to
ensure that a blocking order in respect of a specific site is not used as a
means of blocking access in general" (ibid.). This reasoning suggests that
the court would also disapprove of other intrusive or overly broad blocking
techniques.

In the case of *Delfi AS v. Estonia*, the Estonian courts held a large online
news portal liable for the unlawful third-party comments posted on its site
in response to one of its own articles, despite having an automated filtering
system and a notice-and-takedown procedure in place (ECtHR 2015a). The
Grand Chamber of the ECtHR found that this did not amount to a violation
of Article 10, ECHR. The judgment has proved very controversial, particularly among free speech advocates, who fear that such liability would create
proactive monitoring obligations for Internet intermediaries, leading to private censorship and a chilling effect on freedom of expression.

The contentious nature of the judgment stems from a number of the
court's key lines of reasoning therein. First, the court took the view that
"the majority of the impugned comments amounted to hate speech or
incitements to violence and as such did not enjoy the protection of Article 10" (ibid., para. 136). By classifying the comments as such extreme
forms of speech, the court purports to legitimize the stringent measures
that it sets out for online news portals to take against such manifestly
unlawful content. The dissenting judges objected to this approach, pointing out that "[t]hroughout the whole judgment the description or charac-
terisation of the comments varies and remains non-specific" and "murky"
(ibid., Joint Dissenting Opinion of Judges Sajó and Tsotsoria, paras. 12 and
13, respectively).

Second, the court endorses the view of the Estonian Supreme Court that
Delfi could have avoided liability if it had removed the impugned comments "without delay" (ibid., para. 153). This requirement is problematic
because, as pointed out by the dissenting judges, it is not linked to notice
or actual knowledge (ibid., Joint Dissenting Opinion, para. 8) and paves the
way for systematic, proactive monitoring of third-party content.

Third, the court underscored that Delfi was "a professionally managed
internet news portal run on a commercial basis which sought to attract a
large number of comments on news articles published by it" (ibid., para.

144). The dissenting judges aptly argued that the economic activity of the news portal does not cancel out the potential of comment sections for facilitating individual contributions to public debate in a way that "does not depend on centralised media decisions" (ibid., Joint Dissenting Opinion, paras. 39 and 28).

Fourth, the court failed to appreciate or articulate the broader ramifications of far-reaching Internet intermediary liability for online freedom of expression generally. It was at pains to stress that "the case does not concern other fora on the Internet where third-party comments can be disseminated, for example an Internet discussion forum or a bulletin board where users can freely set out their ideas on any topics without the discussion being channelled by any input from the forum's manager; or a social media platform where the platform provider does not offer any content and where the content provider may be a private person running the website or a blog as a hobby" (ibid., para. 116). The dissenting judges again took great exception to this line of reasoning, describing it as an exercise in "damage control" (ibid., Joint Dissenting Opinion, para. 9).

The court subsequently revisited the issues of the responsibility and liability of Internet service providers for comments posted on their sites by users of their services in *MTE & Index.hu v. Hungary* (ECtHR 2016b). Unlike in *Delfi* and perhaps smarting from the critical fallout to *Delfi*, the court seemed keen in *MTE & Index.hu* to talk up the importance of Internet intermediaries in fostering public debate online. It referred to them as "protagonists of the free electronic media" (ibid., para. 88; see also para. 69). This is an important realization of the broader implications of intermediary liability for robust public debate. Similarly and more recently, in *Tamiz v. the United Kingdom*, the court referred to "the important role that ISSPs [Information Society Service Providers] such as Google Inc. perform in facilitating access to information and debate on a wide range of political, social and cultural topics" (ECtHR 2017a, para. 90).

The court emphatically distinguished the *Delfi* and *MTE & Index.hu* cases on the basis of the nature of the comments. Whereas it had deemed that some of the comments in *Delfi* amounted to hate speech, it described the comments at issue in *MTE & Index.hu* as "offensive and vulgar," but found that they "did not constitute clearly unlawful speech" and "certainly did not amount to hate speech or incitement to violence" (ECtHR 2016b para. 64). The court has followed this line in a more recent inadmissibility decision in

Pihl v. Sweden, a case involving a defamatory blog post and an anonymous online comment (ECtHR 2017b). This distinction shows how important it is to be clear-sighted about what "hate speech" entails in legal terms.

Political Standard Setting by the Council of Europe

While the above developments remain quite tentative in the case law of the ECtHR, they are more advanced in other Council of Europe standard-setting activities (see, generally, Benedek and Kettemann 2013). Although such standard-setting work, notably by the organization's Committee of Ministers and Parliamentary Assembly (see Nikoltchev and McGonagle 2011a and 2011b, respectively), is not legally binding, it is politically persuasive and offers a number of advantages over treaty-based approaches. It can, for example, engage with issues in a more detailed way than is possible either in treaty provisions or case law or monitoring pursuant to treaty provisions. It can also address issues that have not arisen in case law but are nevertheless relevant. In the same vein, it can identify and address emergent or anticipated developments, thereby ensuring a dynamic/modern approach to relevant issues.

Standard setting by the Committee of Ministers includes a number of focuses that are relevant for Internet intermediaries (as also noted by Jørgensen in her Introduction to this volume), for example, self-regulation concerning cybercontent; human rights and the rule of law in the information society; freedom of expression and information in the new information and communications environment; the public service value of the Internet; respect for freedom of expression and information with regard to Internet filters; network neutrality; freedom of expression, association, and assembly with regard to privately operated Internet platforms and online service providers; human rights and search engines; human rights and social networking services; risks to fundamental rights stemming from digital tracking and other surveillance technologies; human rights for Internet users; the free, transboundary flow of information on the Internet; and Internet freedom. These normative texts generally explore their subject matter in an expansive way, while grounding the exploration in relevant principles that have already been established by the ECtHR. As such, the texts tease out the likely application of key legal principles to new developments, thereby also giving an indication of the likely content of specific state obligations in respect of those principles. Their role and influence, while not legally binding, can nevertheless be seen as instructive.

Thus, the Committee of Ministers has highlighted the gravity of violations of Articles 10 and 11, ECHR ("Freedom of assembly and association"), "which might result from politically motivated pressure exerted on privately operated Internet platforms and online service providers" (Committee of Ministers of the Council of Europe 2011b, para. 7). It has insisted that the use of filters be strictly in accordance with Articles 10 and 6, ECHR ("Right to a fair trial"), and specifically be targeted, transparent, and subject to independent and impartial review procedures. It encourages member states and the private sector to "strengthen the information and guidance to users who are subject to filters in private networks, including information about the existence of, and reasons for, the use of a filter and the criteria upon which the filter operates" (Committee of Ministers of the Council of Europe 2008, Guidelines, section 3). It has also called on member states to "promote transparent self- and coregulatory mechanisms for search engines, in particular with regard to the accessibility of content declared illegal by a court or competent authority, as well as of harmful content, bearing in mind the Council of Europe's standards on freedom of expression and due process rights" (Committee of Ministers of the Council of Europe 2012a, para. 8). Finally, in the present string of examples, the Committee of Ministers has stated that social networking services should refrain from "the general blocking and filtering of offensive or harmful content in a way that would hamper its access by users" (Committee of Ministers of the Council of Europe 2012b, para. 11); develop and communicate editorial policies about "inappropriate content," in line with Article 10, ECHR (ibid., para. 10, and see also para. 3), and "ensure that users are aware of the threats to their human rights and able to seek redress when their rights have been adversely affected" (ibid., para. 15). It has called on member states to "encourage the establishment of transparent co-operation mechanisms for law-enforcement authorities and social networking services," which "should include respect for the procedural safeguards required under Article 8 ["Right to respect for private and family life"], Article 10 and Article 11," ECHR (ibid., para. 11).

Another prong to the Committee of Ministers' standard setting that is important for Internet intermediaries, without addressing their role explicitly, is its Recommendation CM/Rec(2016)3 to member states on human rights and business. A central aim of this recommendation is to ensure that states "effectively implement the UN Guiding Principles on Business and Human Rights as the current globally agreed baseline in the field of business and human rights" (CM 2016, Appendix, para. 1). The recommendation includes focuses on the state's obligation to protect human rights as well as on the kinds of state action that can enable corporate responsibility to respect human rights. Such action includes the application by states of "such measures as may be necessary to encourage or, where appropriate, require that" businesses based within their jurisdiction apply "human rights due diligence throughout their operations" and businesses "conducting substantial activities" within their jurisdiction "carry out human rights due diligence in respect of such activities" (ibid., para. 20). States should also ensure that access to judicial mechanisms, namely, courts and remedies, is available for everyone in respect of (allegations of) business-related human rights abuses (ibid., para. 31).

Many of the above principles and recommendations are played out in detail in the Committee of Ministers' Recommendation CM/Rec(2018)2 to member States on the roles and responsibilities of Internet intermediaries (Committee of Ministers of the Council of Europe 2018). In the Preamble to the recommendation, the Committee of Ministers observes, "A wide, diverse and rapidly evolving range of players, commonly referred to as 'Internet intermediaries,' facilitate interactions on the internet between natural and legal persons by offering and performing a variety of functions and services" (ibid., Preamble, para. 4). It goes on to acknowledge that individual intermediaries are capable of performing different functions and services simultaneously (ibid., para. 5). Referencing the UN Guiding Principles on Business and Human Rights, it further states, "Owing to the multiple roles intermediaries play, their corresponding duties and responsibilities and their protection under law should be determined with respect to the specific services and functions that are performed" (ibid., para. 11). Taken together, these observations and recommendations plead for a targeted and differentiated regulatory approach—not a "one-size-fits-all" model.

In its Appendix, the recommendation sets out detailed and extensive Guidelines for states on actions to be taken vis-à-vis Internet intermediaries with due regard to their roles and responsibilities. The Guidelines have a dual focus: obligations of states and responsibilities of Internet intermediaries. The identified obligations of states include ensuring the legality of measures adopted; legal certainty and transparency; safeguards for freedom of expression, privacy, and data protection; and access to an effective remedy. The responsibilities of Internet intermediaries include respect for human rights and fundamental freedoms, transparency and accountability, responsibilities in respect of content moderation, the use of personal data, and the ensuring of access to an effective remedy.

Positive Obligations

General Observations

The international legal system for the protection of human rights pivots on the linear relationship between individuals (rights holders) and states (duty bearers). The recognition that different types of non-state/private actors should also be (explicitly) positioned within the system has come about in a gradual and frictional manner. And even that reluctant recognition has only been achieved through the dynamic interpretation of existing legal norms and the interplay between those norms and policy-making documents. As noted by Land in her chapter in this volume, this presents a real conceptual and regulatory "dilemma" (for extensive and insightful analysis, see the chapters by Land and Callamard and the Introduction by Jørgensen in this volume).

All international human rights treaties share the primary objective of ensuring that the rights enshrined therein are rendered effective for everyone. There is also a predominant tendency in international treaty law to guarantee effective remedies to individuals when their human rights have been violated. In order to achieve these dual objectives, it is not always enough for the state to simply honor their negative obligation to refrain from interfering with individuals' human rights: positive or affirmative action will often be required as well. This may, on occasion, require the state to intervene in relations between third parties. It is therefore important to acknowledge the concomitance of negative and positive state obligations to safeguard human rights. While this acknowledgement typically informs treaty interpretation, relevant formulas and approaches tend to vary per treaty.

In the context of Internet intermediary self-regulation as well, in addition to the traditional *negative obligations* that bind public authorities, the *positive obligations* of the state to safeguard human rights can mean that public authorities may be obligated to prevent private parties from engaging in different types of behavior that endanger the fundamental rights of third parties. This can result in restrictions by public authorities on the use of self-regulation as a regulatory paradigm for the online environment.

The positive obligations doctrine has developed in piecemeal fashion, and its precise scope and finer details continue to evolve (for extensive analysis, see McGonagle 2015). As correctly noted by Land (see chapter 11 of this volume), the doctrine is germane to European human rights law. Besides the doctrinal evolution in the case law of the ECtHR, it is also instructive to consider the potential guidance offered by relevant standard-setting work by the Council of Europe's Committee of Ministers. For analytical purposes, it is useful to group positive state obligations relating to the rights to freedom of expression, privacy, and data protection as well as media freedom (hereinafter, for convenience, "communication rights") online into three categories: preventive, promotional, and remedial. These categories are not, however, mutually exclusive. As will be shown, preventive and promotional obligations, for example, overlap to an extent.

Preventive Obligations

States are required to put in place regulatory frameworks (including legislative frameworks) to ensure the effective exercise of communication rights in the online environment. These frameworks should include legislative frameworks (ECtHR 2011a) and, more specifically, criminal-law frameworks, as appropriate—for instance, for combating child pornography (ECtHR 2008a). In respect of medical data, which constitutes "highly intimate and sensitive" data, states must ensure that the law affords "practical and effective protection to exclude any possibility of unauthorised access" to such data (ECtHR 2008b, paras. 38, 39, and 47, and 1997, paras. 95–96). States must ensure that laws not only meet the *Sunday Times* criteria concerning the quality of law (foreseeability and accessibility (ECtHR 1979); see also Council of Europe Commissioner for Human Rights 2014, Recommendation 16, p. 24) but in particular for surveillance of communications, for example, additional criteria apply in the interests of transparency/avoiding chilling effect and to ensure safeguards against various possible abuses (see, in particular, ECtHR 2006a, para. 95, and, generally, ECtHR 1984, 1990, and 1993b, and Eskens, van Daalen, and van Eijk 2015).

The obligations described in the previous paragraph exist regardless of the existence of self-regulatory mechanisms. While states may enjoy discretion as to the means they use to fulfill their fundamental rights obligations, they may not delegate those obligations to private parties (ECtHR 2006b, 2012b; see also ECtHR 1985, 2000, 2003; see also Land's chapter in this volume). Relatedly, these obligations also exist regardless of states' obligations under other international treaties, especially when the source of those obligations is an international organization with "equivalent" levels of human rights protection (ECtHR 2005, 2011b). Thus, EU law, for example, may neither displace nor dilute positive state obligations identified and developed by the ECtHR pursuant to the ECHR.

Promotional Obligations

States also have positive obligations to actively promote different values, such as pluralistic tolerance in society and media pluralism. Whereas the role of the state as "ultimate guarantor" of media pluralism has traditionally concerned the audiovisual media sector (ECtHR 1993a, 2001, 2009b), it is likely—in light of the living instrument and practical and effective doctrines—that this principle will have to be developed and applied mutatis mutandis to the online environment. Similarly, states' positive obligation to ensure an environment that is favorable to freedom of expression (ECtHR 2010, para. 137) necessitates adaptation for optimal realization in the online environment. Étienne Montero and Quentin Van Enis (2011, 24) have posited that states' positive obligations, when "[t]ransposed to the digital universe," include the adoption of "a genuinely reassuring framework for intermediaries in order to avoid the private censorship they are liable to effect through fear of liability action."

Remedial Obligations

Review and redress are also important elements of states' positive obligations to uphold communication rights in an online environment. In accordance with Article 13, ECHR ("Right to an effective remedy"), states must, first and foremost, ensure that effective remedies are available for violations of communication rights. Remedies should have corrective, compensatory, investigative, and punitive functions and effects. These obligations mean that states must ensure that alleged violations of communication rights by private parties are subject to independent and impartial judicial review (see also Council of Europe Commissioner for Human Rights 2014, Recommendation 16, p. 24). Such review would necessarily consider the extent to which policies and practices of private actors, for example, for blocking and filtering content, show due regard for process values such as transparency and accountability, as well as respect for rule of law (ECtHR 2003).

General Guidance

Primary guidance for ongoing attempts to clarify the scope and content of states' positive obligations to guarantee the effective exercise of communication rights in an online environment is provided by the ECHR, as interpreted by the ECtHR. In that context, the ECtHR has stated that the legitimate aims of restrictions on, for example, the rights to privacy and freedom of expression (as set out in Articles 8(2) and 10(2)) may be relevant for assessing whether states have failed to honor relevant positive obligations (ECtHR 1986, 2012c). The ECtHR has also found that the margin of appreciation is, in principle, the same for Articles 8 and 10, ECHR (2012c, para. 106). In all cases involving competing rights guaranteed by the ECHR, a fair balance has to be struck between the rights involved, as relevant for the particular circumstances of the case. However, when restrictions are imposed on a right or freedom guaranteed by the ECHR, in order to protect "rights and freedoms" which are not guaranteed by the ECHR, the ECtHR has insisted that "only indisputable imperatives can justify interference with enjoyment of a Convention right" (ECtHR 1999, para. 113).

Internet Intermediaries and "Hate Speech"

Intermediaries have a complex relationship with freedom of expression and "hate speech." Under the "safe harbour" regime created by the EU's E-commerce Directive, a neutral or passive stance would ordinarily entitle intermediaries serving as hosting providers to exemption for liability for the hosted content (European Parliament and the Council 2000). Service providers hosting third-party content may avail themselves of this exemption on the condition that they do not have "actual knowledge of illegal activity or information and, as regards claims for damages, is not aware of facts or circumstances from which the illegal activity or information is apparent" and that "upon obtaining such knowledge or awareness, acts expeditiously to remove or to disable access to the information" (ibid., Article 14). The directive also stipulates that states shall not impose a general obligation on (hosting service) providers to "to monitor the information which they transmit or store, nor a general obligation actively to seek facts or circumstances indicating illegal activity" (ibid., Article 15). Although the E-Commerce Directive is extraneous to the Council of Europe's regulatory system, it is an essential reference point for the twenty-eight EU member states which are also members of the Council of Europe. EU Directives require EU member states to achieve certain results but give them some flexibility as to the measures used to achieve those results.

Yet, the binary distinction between active and passive intermediaries that held sway at the time of the adoption of the directive in 2000 no longer adequately reflects the varied relationships that many intermediaries have with third-party content today. Some activities carried out by Internet intermediaries go beyond passive hosting toward editorial, presentational, recommendation, and ranking functions.

The optic through which the Council of Europe examines the question of Internet intermediary liability is rather that of rights, duties, and responsibilities. Intermediaries contribute to public debate by facilitating (or impeding) access to the arenas—and thereby also the content of—public debate. Their ensuing duties and responsibilities are shaped by the nature of their gatekeeping functions and the techniques they employ to carry out those functions. The Committee of Ministers of the Council of Europe (2011a, para. 7) has called for a "new, broad notion of media" encompassing all relevant actors. It advocates "a graduated and differentiated response for actors [. . .], having regard to their specific functions in the media process and their potential impact and significance in ensuring or enhancing good governance in democratic society" (ibid.). Furthermore, evolving international norms and expectations of corporate social responsibility and human rights due diligence can provide useful guidance (Committee of Ministers of the Council of Europe 2016; see also Land, this volume). The size and dominance of the intermediary and whether there are viable alternative opportunities for individuals to exercise their right to freedom of expression in a practical and effective manner are all contextual variables that are taken into account in this calculus. The commercial or noncommercial character of the intermediary is another and somewhat controversial contextual variable (see the discussion of the *Delfi* case above). The nature of the expression at issue in a given case is also a central consideration.

When the expression at issue is "hate speech," it is important to recall that the term does not appear in the ECHR and the court, having first used the term in 1999, does not have a hard-and-fast definition of the term (see, generally, McGonagle 2013b). Its understanding of the term is subject to continuous development on a case-by-case basis in which the interplay between Articles 10 and 17, ECHR, is crucial. From the court's case law to date, it is possible to distill an approximation of a definition. Hate speech is any type of expression via any medium that intentionally targets someone on the basis of certain fundamental characteristics shared with other members of a specific group, which is hateful in essence and/or incites to hatred, discrimination, or violence or amounts to a grave assault on human dignity and therefore is devoid of redeeming social value and constitutes an abuse of the rights and freedoms safeguarded by international and European human rights law. However, as already noted, the *Delfi* judgment has added to the murkiness of this understanding by omitting a reference to the group dimension usually present in relevant cases.

The upshot of this is that in the absence of a legally binding definition of hate speech, as well as inconsistencies in the court's application of the term, the precise scope of the term remains uncertain and problematic from the perspective of legal certainty and foreseeability. If the Grand Chamber of the ECtHR is prone to depart—without explanation or motivation—from previously held understandings of what hate speech involves, intermediaries cannot be expected to be able to accurately identify types of expression which, from a legal perspective, amount to hate speech. The sophisticated legal knowledge and diagnostic skills required to determine what is hate speech and whether it should be removed are therefore far beyond the competences of what could reasonably be expected of ordinary content moderators employed by intermediaries. Moreover, as submitted by some of the intervening parties in *Delfi*, many intermediaries are small enterprises, compared to the leading global players, and would often lack the resources to proactively make the necessary legal assessment and then, if warranted, block or remove hate speech and other illegal content (ECtHR 2015a, para. 108).

Nevertheless, the problem remains that if hate speech is not removed expeditiously, the harm it causes to victims is aggravated by its perpetuation and/or further dissemination. If multiple postings, cross-posting, or extensive hyperlinking has taken place, the removal of particular material from a particular online source cannot guarantee the unavailability of the same material elsewhere, thus strengthening its "incessant and compounding" aspects (Delgado and Stefancic 2009, 367–368). This pleads strongly for the need for Internet intermediaries to raise their game when it comes to countering hate speech, a call that is resonating in legal and political circles across Europe at the moment.

Conversely, if the urgency for action leads to intermediaries erring on the side of caution (including to avoid liability) and blocking or removing content that may be offensive while not being illegal, the consequences for freedom of expression can be severe. The practice of private actors making and acting on their own determinations about the (il)legality of content is sometimes described as *privatized law enforcement* or *privatized censorship*, terms which—out of concern for rule of law—question the legitimacy of private actors to determine whether particular content is illegal.

Tentative Conclusions about Tentative Posturing

The analysis in this chapter offers some modest, initial guidance on the seemingly intractable problem of how to calibrate and operationalize the duties and responsibilities of Internet intermediaries regarding hate speech that is disseminated via their platforms or networks without jeopardizing users' right to freedom of expression. First, states may not delegate their obligation to counter hate speech in an effective manner by passing the buck to Internet intermediaries and requiring them to take sole responsibility for eradicating hate speech within their services/networks. States' positive obligation to uphold individuals' human rights may be triggered when the action or inaction of an intermediary amounts to a human rights violation (see, further, Callamard's chapter in this volume). If such a scenario could and should have been prevented by proactive measures by the state, then the state could well have failed to honor its relevant positive obligations.

Not all interferences with individual human rights involving Internet intermediaries will trigger states' positive obligations, however (ECtHR 2017a, paras. 82–84). If an interference does not attain a certain level of seriousness and the person(s) whose right to freedom of expression has been interfered with can still exercise their right effectively in alternative ways, such as in other forums or through other networks, a state will ordinarily not have a positive obligation to take a particular course of action. It is also important to recall that states' (positive) obligations are not solely grounded in the ECHR but (at least for EU member states) can also arise from the Charter of Fundamental Rights of the European Union (European

Union 2010; Angelopoulos et al. 2016; Kuczerawy 2017, 2018). Moreover, EU member states are also subject to the E-Commerce Directive—another detailed regulatory frame of reference. The intertwined character of relevant regulatory frameworks points to a second piece of guidance: regulators need to have very keen positional awareness, in order to be able to properly gauge the requirements, implications, and interaction of different regulatory instruments.

Third, even though states may not delegate their obligation to counter online hate speech to Internet intermediaries, the latter are coming under increasing political and public pressure to raise their own game in this regard. But this is by no means a straightforward task. "Hate speech" has not been pinned down by an authoritative, legally binding definition, and its precise scope remains somewhat unclear. This makes it very difficult for private actors such as Internet intermediaries to make accurate assessments of borderline cases; it often leaves them trying to hit a moving target. These definitional difficulties, coupled with a desire to avoid legal liability for illegal third-party content, will inevitably lead to instances of intermediaries blocking or removing contested content as a precautionary measure. Such scenarios violate—or at least jeopardize—the right to freedom of expression of their users. Conversely, though, persons targeted by illegal types of expression have the right to be protected against such expression. This is a very difficult circle to square. Emerging principles of corporate social responsibility and human rights due diligence, if developed and operationalized further, may be able to help Internet intermediaries to safeguard their users' rights to freedom of expression, equality, and nondiscrimination and their right to an effective remedy.

The Committee of Ministers' Recommendation CM/Rec(2018)2 on the roles and responsibilities of Internet intermediaries would have been an obvious place to provide further, detailed guidance on these issues. However, while it provides much valuable guidance on the roles and responsibilities of Internet intermediaries in various contexts, the recommendation does not contain any explicit references to "hate speech" and only a couple of passing references to "hatred" (Committee of Ministers of the Council of Europe 2018). It therefore remains to be seen how the Council of Europe will concretely engage with these issues in the future. Growing awareness and use of the Committee of Ministers' standard-setting work and a number of pending cases before the ECtHR focusing on Internet intermediaries and freedom of expression are sure to keep, and sharpen, the focus on these relevant issues.

This chapter has focused primarily on the approach of the Council of Europe, with intermittent references to the EU's approach. Although the approaches taken by the Council of Europe and the EU are broadly congruent and sometimes overlap and influence each other, they remain distinct legal and political systems, each with its own particular objectives and emphases. All of this can create consistency in European states' national law and policy, but it can also give rise to confusion and uncertainty in situations where the approaches (appear to) diverge. Recent standard-setting work at the Council of Europe has sought to clarify the human rights framework governing the roles and responsibilities of Internet intermediaries, paying particular attention to freedom of expression, privacy, and data protection and effective remedies. The EU's current approach, as typified by the 2016 Code of Conduct on Countering Illegal Hate Speech Online, adopted by leading tech companies and driven by the European Commission (for an overview and analysis, see Jørgensen's chapter in this volume), focuses on the responsibility of intermediaries to remove illegal hate speech very expeditiously. The code pays scant attention to the importance of, and the need for, freedom-of-expression safeguards. This is a significant difference between both approaches and one that will have to be addressed "expeditiously": #WatchThisSpace.

Notes

1. This is an abridged, updated, and adapted version of the present author's contribution to Christina Angelopoulos, Annabel Brody, Wouter Hins, Bernt Hugenholtz, Patrick Leerssen, Thomas Margoni, Tarlach McGonagle, Ot van Daalen, and Joris van Hoboken, "Study of Fundamental Rights Limitations for Online Enforcement through Self-regulation," commissioned by the Open Society Foundations, Institute for Information Law (IViR), 2016.

2. For further discussion of the added value of standard-setting texts for the court's decision-making, especially on Internet-related issues, see Spano (2016).

References

Angelopoulos, Christina, Annabel Brody, Wouter Hins, P. Bernt Hugenholtz, Patrick Leerssen, Thomas Margoni, Tarlach McGonagle, et al. 2016. "Study of Fundamental

Rights Limitations for Online Enforcement through Self-regulation." Commissioned by Open Society Foundations. Amsterdam: Institute for Information Law (IViR).

Benedek, Wolfgang, and Matthias C. Kettemann. 2013. *Freedom of Expression and the Internet.* Strasbourg: Council of Europe.

Cannie, Hannes, and Dirk Voorhoof. 2011. "The Abuse Clause and Freedom of Expression in the European Human Rights Convention: An Added Value for Democracy and Human Rights Protection?" *Netherlands Quarterly of Human Rights* 29 (1): 54–83.

Committee of Ministers of the Council of Europe. 2008. "Recommendation CM/Rec(2008)6 to Member States on Measures to Promote the Respect for Freedom of Expression and Information with Regard to Internet Filters." Strasbourg: Council of Europe.

———. 2011a. "Recommendation CM/Rec(2011)7 of the Committee of Ministers to Member States on a New Notion of Media." Strasbourg: Council of Europe.

———. 2011b. "Declaration on the Protection of Freedom of Expression and Freedom of Assembly and Association with Regard to Privately Operated Internet Platforms and Online Service Providers." Strasbourg: Council of Europe.

———. 2012a. "Recommendation CM/Rec(2012)3 to Member States on the Protection of Human Rights with Regard to Search Engines." Strasbourg: Council of Europe.

———. 2012b. "Recommendation CM/Rec(2012)4 to Member States on the Protection of Human Rights with Regard to Social Networking Services." Strasbourg: Council of Europe.

———. 2016. Recommendation CM/Rec(2016)3 to Member States on Human Rights and Business." Strasbourg: Council of Europe.

———. 2018. "Recommendation CM/Rec(2018)2 to Member States on the Roles and Responsibilities of Internet Intermediaries." Strasbourg: Council of Europe.

Council of Europe. 1950. "Convention on the Protection of Human Rights and Fundamental Freedoms (ECHR)," ETS no. 5, November 4, 1950 (entry into force: September 3, 1953).

Council of Europe Commissioner for Human Rights. 2014. "The Rule of Law on the Internet and in the Wider Digital World" (author: D. Korff). Issue paper published by the Commissioner for Human Rights. Strasbourg: Council of Europe.

Delgado, Richard, and Jean Stefancic. 2009. "Four Observations about Hate Speech." *Wake Forest Law Review* 44: 353–370.

Emerson, Thomas I. 1970. *The System of Freedom of Expression*. New York: Random House.

Eskens, Sarah, Ot van Daalen, and Nico van Eijk. 2015. "Ten Standards for Oversight and Transparency of National Intelligence Services." Amsterdam: Institute for Information Law (IViR).

European Court of Human Rights. 1976. *Handyside v. the United Kingdom*, December 7, 1976, Series A, no. 24.

———. 1979. *The Sunday Times v. the United Kingdom* (no. 1), April 26, 1979, Series A no. 30.

———. 1983. *Van der Mussele v. Belgium*, November 23, 1983, Series A no. 70.

———. 1984. *Malone v. the United Kingdom*, August 2, 1984, Series A no. 82.

———. 1985. *Barthold v. Germany*, March 25, 1985, Series A no. 90.

———. 1986. *Rees v. the United Kingdom*, October 17, 1986, Series A no. 106.

———. 1990. *Kruslin v. France*, April 24, 1990, Series A no. 176-A.

———. 1993a. *Informationsverein Lentia and Others v. Austria*, November 24, 1993, Series A no. 276.

———. 1993b. *Klaas v. Germany*, September 22, 1993, Series A no. 269.

———. 1993c. *Costello-Roberts v. the United Kingdom*, March 25, 1993, Series A no. 247-C.

———. 1997. *Z. v. Finland*, judgment of February 25, 1997, Reports of Judgments and Decisions 1997-I.

———. 1999. *Chassagnou and Others v. France* [GC], nos. 25088/94, 28331/95 and 28443/95, ECHR 1999-III.

———. 2000. *Fuentes Bobo v. Spain*, no. 39293/98, February 29, 2000.

———. 2001. *VgT Verein gegen Tierfabriken v. Switzerland*, no. 24699/94, ECHR 2001-VI.

———. 2003. *Peck v. the United Kingdom*, no. 44647/98, ECHR 2003-I.

———. 2005. *Bosphorus Hava Yolları Turizm ve Ticaret Anonim Şirketi v. Ireland* [GC], no. 45036/98, ECHR 2005-VI.

———. 2006a. *Weber and Saravia v. Germany* (dec.), no. 54934/00, ECHR 2006-XI.

———. 2006b. *Woś v. Poland*, no. 22860/02, ECHR 2006-VII.

———. 2008a. *K.U. v. Finland*, no. 2872/02, ECHR 2008.

————. 2008b. *I. v. Finland*, no. 20511/03, July 17, 2008.

————. 2009a. *Times Newspapers Ltd. (nos. 1 & 2) v. the United Kingdom*, nos. 3002/03 and 23676/03, ECHR 2009.

————. 2009b. *Manole and Others v. Moldova*, no. 13936/02, ECHR 2009.

————. 2010. *Dink v. Turkey*, nos. 2668/07 and 4 others, September 14, 2010.

————. 2011a. *Editorial Board of Pravoye Delo and Shtekel v. Ukraine*, no. 33014/05, ECHR 2011.

————. 2011b. *M.S.S. v. Belgium and Greece* [GC], no. 30696/09, ECHR 2011.

————. 2012a. *Ahmet Yıldırım v. Turkey*, no. 3111/10, ECHR 2012.

————. 2012b. *Michaud v. France*, no. 12323/11, ECHR 2012.

————. 2012c. *Von Hannover v. Germany (no. 2)* [GC], nos. 40660/08 and 60641/08, ECHR 2012.

————. 2013a. *Animal Defenders International v. the United Kingdom* [GC], no. 48876/08, April 22, 2013.

————. 2013b. *Węgrzynowski and Smolczewski v. Poland*, no. 33846/07, July 16, 2013.

————. 2015a. *Delfi AS v. Estonia* [GC], no. 64569/09, June 16, 2015.

————. 2015b. *Cengiz and Others v. Turkey*, nos. 48226/10 and 14027/11, ECHR 2015.

————. 2016a. *Magyar Helsinki Bizottság v. Hungary* [GC], no. 18030/11, ECHR 2016.

————. 2016b. *Magyar Tartalomszolgáltatók Egyesülete and Index.hu Zrt v. Hungary*, no. 22947/13, February 2, 2016.

————. 2017a. *Tamiz v. the United Kingdom* (dec.), no. 3877/14, October 12, 2017.

————. 2017b. *Pihl v. Sweden* (dec.), no. 74742/14, February 7, 2017.

European Court of Human Rights (Press Unit). 2017. "Fact Sheet—New Technologies." Strasbourg: Council of Europe.

European Court of Human Rights (Research Division). 2015. "Internet: Case-law of the European Court of Human Rights." Strasbourg: Council of Europe.

European Parliament and the Council. 2000. "Directive 2000/31/EC of the European Parliament and of the Council of 8 June 2000 on Certain Legal Aspects of Information Society Services, in Particular Electronic Commerce, in the Internal Market." [2000] OJ L 178/1 (Directive on Electronic Commerce).

European Union. 2010. "Charter of Fundamental Rights of the European Union." [2010] OJ C 83/389.

Hans-Bredow-Institut for Media Research, University of Hamburg. 2006. "Study on Co-regulation Measures in the Media Sector," Final Report, Study for the European Commission, Directorate Information Society and Media.

Keane, David. 2007. "Attacking Hate Speech under Article 17 of the European Convention on Human Rights." *Netherlands Quarterly of Human Rights* 25 (4): 641–663.

Kuczerawy, Aleksandra. 2017. "The Power of Positive Thinking: Intermediary Liability and the Effective Enjoyment of the Right to Freedom of Expression." CiTiP Working Paper 30/2017. Leuven, Belgium: KU Leuven Centre for IT & IP Law.

———. 2018. "Private Enforcement of Public Policy: Freedom of Expression in the Era of Online Gatekeeping." PhD diss., KU Leuven Faculty of Law.

Laidlaw, Emily B. 2015. *Regulating Speech in Cyberspace: Gatekeepers, Human Rights and Corporate Responsbility*. Cambridge: Cambridge University Press.

Leerssen, Patrick. 2015. "Cut Out by The Middle Man: The Free Speech Implications of Social Network Blocking and Banning in the EU." *JIPITEC* 6: 99–119.

McGonagle, Tarlach. 2013a. "User-Generated Content and Audiovisual News: The Ups and Downs of an Uncertain Relationship." In *Open Journalism, IRIS plus* 2013-2, edited by Susanne Nikoltchev, 7–25. Strasbourg: European Audiovisual Observatory.

———. 2013b. "The Council of Europe against Online Hate Speech: Conundrums and Challenges," Expert paper, Doc. No. MCM 2013(005), the Council of Europe Conference of Ministers Responsible for Media and Information Society, Freedom of Expression and Democracy in the Digital Age: Opportunities, Rights, Responsibilities, Belgrade, November.

———. 2015. "Positive Obligations Concerning Freedom of Expression: Mere Potential or Real Power?" In *Journalism at Risk: Threats, Challenges and Perspectives*, edited by Onur Andreotti, 9–35. Strasbourg: Council of Europe.

Montero, Étienne, and Quentin Van Enis. 2011. "Enabling Freedom of Expression in Light of Filtering Measures Imposed on Internet Intermediaries: Squaring the Circle." *Computer Law & Security Review* 27: 21–35.

Murphy, Thérèse, and Gearóid Ó Cuinn. 2010. "Works in Progress: New Technologies and the European Court of Human Rights." *Human Rights Law Review* 10 (4): 601–638.

Nikoltchev, Susanne, and Tarlach McGonagle, eds. 2011a. *Freedom of Expression and the Media: Standard-Setting by the Council of Europe, (I) Committee of Ministers—IRIS Themes*. Strasbourg: European Audiovisual Observatory.

———. 2011b. *Freedom of Expression and the Media: Standard-Setting by the Council of Europe, (II) Parliamentary Assembly—IRIS Themes*. Strasbourg: European Audiovisual Observatory.

Plaizier, Cees. 2018. "Micro-targeting Consent: A Human Rights Perspective on Paid Political Advertising on Social Media." Unpublished LL.M. thesis, Informatierecht LL.M. Programme, Faculty of Law, University of Amsterdam (on file with author).

Spano, Robert. 2016. Presentation at "Internet Freedom: A Constant Factor of Democratic Security in Europe", Conference, Council of Europe, Strasbourg, September 9. http://www.coe.int/en/web/freedom-expression/internetfreedom2016.

Tulkens, Françoise. 2012. "When to Say Is to Do: Freedom of Expression and Hate Speech in the Case-Law of the European Court of Human Rights." In *Freedom of Expression: Essays in Honour of Nicolas Bratza*, edited by Josep Casadevall, Egbert Myjer, Michael O'Boyle, and Anna Austin, 279–295. Oisterwijk, The Netherlands: Wolf Legal Publishers.

Van Hoboken, Joris. 2012. *Search Engine Freedom: On the Implications of the Right to Freedom of Expression for the Legal Governance of Web Search Engines*. Alphen aan den Rijn, The Netherlands: Kluwer Law International.

10 The Privacy Disconnect

Joris van Hoboken[1]

Introduction

In the last decade, a flurry of regulatory, legislative and judicial activity has taken place responding to concerns over commercial and government interferences with data privacy.[2] Europe stands out in this regard. In May 2018, the highly anticipated new General Data Protection Regulation (GDPR) came into force.[3] The European legislature is debating revision to the regulatory framework for electronic communications privacy (European Commission Proposal for ePrivacy Regulation 2017a).[4] New frameworks for cross-border access to digital evidence are being discussed.[5] Privacy regulators are stepping up enforcement in relation to Internet companies and adopting a growing stream of regulatory guidance.[6] National courts as well as the Court of Justice of the European Union (CJEU) and the European Court of Human Rights have been asked to rule, as a consequence of citizen and privacy activist initiatives, on the legality of government surveillance measures and the legality of international data flows in view of the fundamental right to privacy and the protection of personal data.[7] The CJEU has been particularly impactful, by invalidating the Data Retention Directive (CJEU 2014a), imposing a right to be forgotten on search engines (CJEU 2014b), and invalidating the Safe Harbour agreement for data flows between the EU and the United States in a sweeping ruling on the need to guarantee data privacy in the context of personal data flowing outside of the EU. The UN General Assembly adopted several resolutions on the right to privacy in the digital age and has also appointed a UN Special Rapporteur on the Right to Privacy.

From these developments alone, one would be tempted to draw the conclusion that, at least in Europe, we are living in a golden age of privacy. Finally, the conditions are being set for the right to privacy and the protection of personal data to be valued and enforced. Research and practice appear to be following suit. Privacy has become an increasingly active field of study in law, economics, social science, computer science, and engineering.[8] Nongovernmental privacy organizations are understaffed but growing; professional organizations of privacy practitioners such as the International Association of Privacy Professionals (IAPP) have seen membership soar and conferences and educational programs fill up with professionals seeking to make a new living.[9]

This contribution's starting point is that the amount of energy, resources, and good intentions going into privacy alone is a bad measure for evaluating whether fundamental challenges to data privacy are being addressed in practice. Clearly, when the European Commission proposes new rules for electronic communications privacy with the headline that they "will increase the protection of people's private life and open up new opportunities for business" (European Commission 2017a), close scrutiny of whether the specifics of the proposals back up this claim is warranted.[10] However, the problem with the protection of data privacy may run deeper than can be uncovered by a close reading of specific legislative acts and their particular legal consequences. Ultimately, the question is whether the current legal and policy frameworks for data privacy provide robust underpinnings for the legitimacy of pervasive processing of personal data in our societies. It is through this divide between the demands for such legitimacy and what current privacy governance offers in practice, a divide I will call "the Privacy Disconnect," that developments in the realm of privacy may be running into a wall.

With the aim to sketch some of the contours of a Privacy Disconnect, this chapter will review some of the major challenges related to the establishment of legitimacy for the pervasive processing of personal data. First, I will discuss the consolidation in the Internet service industry and its transformation into a data-driven environment, where the continuous capture and analysis of data in individualized networked relationships between services, third parties, and users has become an inseparable ingredient for the production of digital functionality and the accumulation of data-driven power (Gürses and Van Hoboken 2018). This transformation challenges established core principles of data privacy, such as transparency and purpose limitation, in ways that are not easily addressed without radical reform. The way in which the environment is currently shaped along the principle of modularity also challenges the attribution of responsibility for observing data privacy laws and principles, without which the project of protecting and enforcing privacy is perhaps most fundamentally challenged.

Second, the discussion turns to the continuing erosion of restrictions on data collection and the recent debates about a refocus on regulating use instead. Historically, a debate has existed in privacy scholarship on whether privacy law, policy, and engineering should concern itself centrally with limiting the collection and flow of personal information (data minimization) or whether it is enough to put entities processing personal data under an obligation to act fairly, transparently, and lawfully, observing the right of individuals to exercise relative control over the collection and use of their personal data (De Hert and Gutwirth 2006; Gürses and Diaz 2013; Warren and Brandeis 1890; Westin 1967). More recently, a somewhat more radical position has emerged, arguing that regulation should turn away from regulating collection altogether and regulate the use of personal data instead.[11] This proposition may be understandable in the face of ever more pervasive data collection practices, the value that can be extracted from data through advances in data analytics and machine learning, and the limited success of data minimization standards. However, relevant legal frameworks, in Europe, but also in the United States, would require a rather unfeasible overhaul to facilitate this shift in practice. At a theoretical level, the argument for use regulation, as an alternative to the current broader focus of data privacy, is weak.[12] In addition, considering the repeated news about large-scale data breaches, most recently Equifax, Uber, and the use of Facebook by Cambridge Analytica,[13] the argument that people should no longer be concerned about the mere collection of their data rings hollow.

Third, the chapter will discuss the continued reliance on the concept of informed consent for providing legitimacy to data privacy interferences and the related emphasis on giving individuals control over their personal data. This is striking considering the theoretical issues with consent as central to privacy as well as the mountain of evidence that in current-day settings, meaningful consent and control are not practically possible in the first place. The European Union's legislature doubled down on the importance of consent and individual control over personal data in the GDPR.

Consent is the one legitimate ground for the processing of personal data, out of six, that is enshrined in the fundamental right to the protection of personal data in the Charter of Fundamental Rights.[14] Data subject rights to gain access to and erasure of personal data are strengthened, and a new right to data portability has been added to the legal mix.[15] It is possible that allowing people to reap some of the benefits of the economic value in personal data with a right to data portability could strengthen the legitimacy of pervasive personal data processing in certain regards.[16] However, there are reasons to doubt this will work in practice and whether this will further privacy or other values entirely, potentially with significant unintended distributive effects across industries and populations.

Finally, we will turn to the international level, specifically the tension between the different regulatory approaches to data privacy in the United States and Europe and the role of the human rights framework at the international level. In the commercial sphere, the comprehensive and rights-based approach to data privacy regulation in Europe stands in clear contrast to the sectoral and market-oriented approach to privacy law in the United States.[17] In addition, the fact that the dominant firms of the data-driven economy are US-based companies has turned the enforcement of European privacy law into a trans-Atlantic battle of the regions, in which a lot more than privacy is at stake. The latter is also true in the area of lawful access by government agencies. The frameworks for lawful access have been under pressure because of the Snowden revelations and generally need a rigorous internationally coordinated update in view of globally operating cloud service providers that see themselves confronted with growing pressure to provide access to data at home and abroad. While a series of efforts to bridge some of the divides between Europe and the United States on privacy remains ongoing and some strengthening of data privacy in the human rights context can be observed, the political realities seem to have become more challenging over the last years.

The chapter will conclude with some observations of the way in which the multiplicity of concerns and values that has informed privacy frameworks, debates, and practices can lead to a situation in which significant resources are spent on protecting certain aspects of data privacy while other aspects remain unaddressed. In my conclusion I call for data privacy regulation and discourse to move beyond a concern with the organizational handling of people's "personal data" and become more centrally concerned with the value of the fair accumulation and exercise of data-driven power and the material and political conditions for this value to thrive.

Consolidation in a Networked Internet Service Industry

Over the last decade, we have witnessed a remarkable concentration of power in the hands of a handful of dominant technology companies, which are together providing the services and platforms that are giving shape to the digital environment. Personal information, including data from and about individualized interactions between users and Internet-based services, has become a key ingredient in the production of digital functionality in this environment in ways that challenge existing approaches to data privacy rights.

While some of the underlying developments in the Internet services industry are discussed in more detail and more eloquently elsewhere in this book, it is worth taking note of some of the basics. Of the top ten global companies in terms of market capitalization, the first seven are technology companies, that is, Apple, Alphabet, Amazon, Alibaba, Facebook, Microsoft, and Tencent.[18] The valuations of these companies are so staggering that they raise macroeconomic concerns beyond the specifics of the digital economy itself (Wolf 2017). The monetary assets controlled by these major companies amount to more than four trillion USD, and a general sense has emerged that there is a widespread problem of monopoly and supernormal profits (ibid.).

One of the most important ways in which these companies have become as dominant as they are is through acquisitions, including of potential future competitors. Facebook, for instance has bought Instagram, WhatsApp, and more than fifty other companies since 2005; Google has bought YouTube, Nest Labs, and Motorola and more than 200 other companies since 1999; and Microsoft recently bought Skype, Nokia, and LinkedIn.[19] The role of user data assets in these acquisitions raises important issues at the interface of data privacy and competition law.[20] It is undeniable that in many regards, the dominant tech companies are in competition with one another. Facebook and Alphabet, for instance, are in competition over digital advertising revenues in a market that is now seen as an effective duopoly, earning more than half of all digital advertising revenues worldwide.[21] In the cloud computing market, Amazon is firmly in the lead but has competition from

Alphabet, Microsoft, IBM, and a variety of strong niche players.[22] Without exception, however, leading technology companies have moved toward and built a technology and services environment in which service offerings and innovation have become dependent on the continuous capture of data about users, their behavior, and their interactions (Gürses and Van Hoboken 2018; Zuboff 2015).

Considering the reliance of the tech industry on the processing of data in individualized relationships with users, data privacy concerns abound. At a high level, a question that has to be tackled is how macrolevel concerns about the accumulation and exercise of data-driven power can be better incorporated into discussions of data privacy, which have a tendency to focus on microlevel, decontextualized, and individualized relations with users. Still, existing data privacy laws do offer ample opportunities for regulatory scrutiny. In Europe, in particular, consumer-facing major tech companies are facing regular enforcement actions with respect to their data-related practices.[23] Besides the enforcement of the so-called right to be forgotten since the *Google Spain* ruling,[24] Google has faced considerable pushback related to the consolidation of its privacy policies across its wide portfolio of different consumer-facing services.[25] Such combination of data from different sources easily breaks with the principle of purpose limitation enshrined in European data protection law, raising the question of lawfulness and often requiring a renegotiation of consent. Facebook, too, has been hit with a variety of enforcement actions, including litigation by privacy activist Max Schrems in relation to data flows to the United States and lawful access for intelligence purposes, as well as enforcement with respect to the pervasive tracking of Internet users, the breaking of its promises with respect to the use of WhatsApp user data, and the lack of proper oversight over the collection of data from the platform by Facebook apps.[26] Microsoft is being investigated over its privacy policy with respect to the Windows 10 operating system,[27] which signals a clear and final break with the age of shrink-wrapped software.

Gone are the days in which users bought software and technology products after which they would enjoy these in their relative private sphere, removed from direct interaction with software and technology producers. In the age of the cloud and the emerging Internet of Things, access to technology and software amounts to entering into continuous data-driven relationships that require significant individualized data flows to function properly (Gürses and Van Hoboken 2018).

There is one aspect of the Internet services environment that is worth highlighting here, considering the resulting complications for the attribution of responsibility for privacy rights and values. This is the deployment of the concept of modularity in the cloud environment (ibid.). The term "modularity" is used to describe the degree to which a given (complex) system can be broken apart into subunits (modules), which can be coupled in various ways. As a design or architectural principle, modularity refers to the "building of a complex product or process from smaller subsystems that can be designed independently yet function together as a whole" (Baldwin and Clark 2003). Modularity can operate within the boundaries of tech companies, leading to the internal decomposition of software into so-called microservices. These components talk to each other through service interfaces and can get loosely coupled in integrated service offerings to users. Separate service components can grow into successful industry-wide offerings, as in the case of the cloud, which was developed internally by Amazon and Google before being offered as a service to others.

The principle of modularity can be seen in action outside the boundaries of technology companies, too. The integration of services into other services and organizational offerings is most simply illustrated by the so-called mash-up, which was pioneered by services such as HousingMaps.[28] It is also well illustrated by the start-up mantra of doing one thing really well. The range of basic service components that is available for integration into the offering of companies and organizations has grown significantly over the last decade.[29] All of these services tend to have direct privacy implications for users. Typical service components for publishers, retailers, and other organizations include[30] user analytics,[31] advertisement,[32] authentication,[33] captcha,[34] performance and (cyber)security,[35] maps and location,[36] search,[37] sales and customer relation management,[38] data as a service,[39] payment,[40] event organizing and ticketing,[41] stockage,[42] shipping,[43] reviews,[44] sharing and social functionality,[45] commenting,[46] and embedded media.[47] Notably, the amount of attention that has been paid to the privacy-invasive practices of online advertising may have distracted privacy researchers and regulators from looking at the integration of a variety of other service components (Englehardt 2017).

The strength and attraction of these third-party services is strongly linked to the fact that they can be built in such a way that they can be offered across organizational offerings and domains, at so-called "internet scale." The unbundling of service components leads to a situation in which users, when interacting with one organization, let us say a newspaper app or website or the IT infrastructure of one's employer, are pulled into a whole set of additional service relationships (Gürses and Van Hoboken 2018). Each of those relationships has its own (dynamic) privacy implications for users. The resulting network of relationships between different services and users raises the question of who the proper addressee is for privacy norms in such an environment. Privacy law and practice are struggling to provide an answer. Should the organization that decides to integrate a particular third-party service simply be held responsible for that service's compliance with data privacy laws? The CJEU is set to rule on these issues, which boil down to the interpretation of the concept of "controller" and the possibility of contributory liability of platforms for data privacy violations in the coming years.[48] Without answering this question precisely and effectively, data privacy law and policy can hardly be hoped to be achieving their more substantive aims.

Furthermore, even though the Internet industry may have become organized according to this principle of modularity, this does not appear to be the case in the way that users are offered a chance to negotiate and give shape to the value of data privacy that is affected by different service components. When using available software and services online, users are defaulted into bundles of relationships with first- and third-party service providers, which are collecting their information in ways that leave little room for real choice or escape.[49]

Erosion of Restrictions on Personal Data Collection

As mentioned in the introduction, one of the key debates has been whether data privacy centrally involves a restriction on the collection of personal data (data minimization) or whether data privacy should merely guarantee that the collection and use of personal data take place in ways that observe the fairness, transparency, and lawfulness of personal data-processing operations. In the first view, privacy involves the respect of a private sphere, the possibility of keeping information about oneself confidential and the respect of the so-called right to be let alone. In the second view, data privacy can still be possible once data has been collected by others for further use if it is put under appropriate conditions that guarantee the respect for data protection principles.

It will come as no surprise that many have concluded that data minimization principles have failed entirely.[50] The growing commercial and government appetite for personal data has created a situation in which it is hard to imagine any social, economic, or administrative relationship that does not involve the collection of one's personal data. The data-driven nature of service offerings discussed in the previous section plays a role in this regard as well. In addition to developments in the commercial realm, governments have increasingly pushed for legal frameworks that ensure the general availability of personal data for administrative and law-enforcement purposes—for instance, through interagency data-sharing arrangements, data-retention obligations on telecommunications companies, license-plate-scanning programs, and fraud detection.

Where does this state of affairs lead us in terms of the connection between privacy regulations and the collection of personal data?[51] Answering this question, some have put forward the argument that privacy regulation should turn its focus toward the use of data instead of its mere collection.[52] The main argument for this shift tends to be pragmatic, namely, that the collection of personal data has become the normal state of affairs. As a result, focusing the regulation of personal data-driven processes by limiting the collection of data (data minimization) is considered to be no longer feasible and desirable. It is not feasible since the current environment can only function properly when data collection is left relatively unrestrained. It is not desirable considering the societal value involved in big data, which would be unduly restrained by the regulation of data collection practices. Thus, the argument goes, privacy regulation should focus (more) on issues arising from the actual use of personal data.

The arguments for "use regulation" tend to involve two specific elements. First, the existing mechanisms for establishing the *legitimacy* of personal data collection and further use need to move away from a negotiation from the moment of the collection, in terms of specified, legitimate purposes, toward a focus on data use and management practices. Second, a use-based approach would provide the *flexible reuse of data across contexts*, which is argued to be required to extract the optimal value from data analytics. Cate et al. (2014) argue as follows:

The evolution of data collection and data use necessitates an evolving system of information privacy protection. A revised approach should shift responsibility away from individuals and toward data collectors and data users, who should be held accountable for how they manage data rather than whether they obtain individual consent. In addition, a revised approach should focus more on data use than on data collection because the context in which personal information will be used and the value it will hold are often unclear at the time of collection.[53]

Variations of the argument can be found in the technical literature on privacy engineering, too. Weitzner et al. (2008), for instance, argue for a refocusing of privacy engineering practices away from the implementation of data minimization strategies, which have been developed in the community working on privacy-enhancing technologies, toward information accountability architectures.

The resulting debate about regulatory flexibility for big data analytics may be one of the core data privacy debates of our time. Privacy scholar Helen Nissenbaum, known for her work on providing a theory of privacy in terms of contextual norms, has characterized the argument as "big data exceptionalism" (Nissenbaum 2017). For the purposes of this chapter, the problem with the argument for use regulation is that it proposes to redefine the legal and political question as regards the legitimacy of pervasive personal data processing in a way that is instable, both from a legal point of view and from a broader societal perspective (Van Hoboken 2016).

From a legal and fundamental rights point of view, the establishment of the legitimacy of processing of personal information is still very much connected to the situation that comes into being once personal data is collected. This is the case in Europe, where the fundamental rights guarantee for the protection of personal data in Article 8 of the EU Charter kicks in as soon as personal data is collected. Once personal data is collected, the legal framework requires that this happens transparently and in view of specified lawful and legitimate purposes, in observance of data subject rights and the guarantee of independent oversight.[54] In the United States, there is some more flexibility, considering the lack of a comprehensive regulatory framework for data privacy. Still, consent requirements in sectoral legislation tend to connect to the question of whether data is collected. In addition, the constitutionally grounded third-party doctrine in the United States, while ever under scrutiny, generally implies that once data has been collected by a third party, one loses one's expectation of privacy in relation to government surveillance (Kerr 2009, 561).

There may be a variety of reasons for hoping that people can be stopped from caring about privacy in terms of the mere access of organizations to information about their identity, behavior, and preferences in their personal, professional, and social lives. However, the empirical support that can help ground this wish is lacking. In fact, the growing impact that collected information has on the conditions for living one's life, through the potential use as well as misuse of such data, only makes such concerns about the mere collection of information more pertinent to address.

In conclusion, even if one were to support the attempt to answer the question about the legitimacy of pervasive personal data processing in terms of data use, instead of in terms of data collection, the legal and societal conditions for this attempt to succeed simply do not exist. If the use regulation argument is in essence a project of deregulation, as Chris Hoofnagle (2014) has argued, a shift to use regulation would increase the Privacy Disconnect even further. As long as the law provides legal standing to individuals, individually or in a more organized fashion, to investigate and contest personal data-processing practices from the moment of data collection, a shift to use regulation in practice would hardly respond to deeply entrenched legal data privacy dynamics. Perhaps even more importantly, a shift in privacy governance toward use regulation is not informed by empirical evidence that people will stop worrying about pervasive data processing from the moment data is being collected. In fact, the more data is collected about oneself for more purposes, ever more flexibly defined, the more reason there seems to be to simply worry about the accumulation of data-derived power in the first place. This does not mean this is a productive stance toward current pervasive data-processing operations but simply that a negotiation around use involves even more complexity than a realistic, be it abstract, concern about the existence of data-derived power. In sum, the argument for use regulation may be more informed by our current inability to find robust mechanisms for establishing the legitimacy of pervasive personal data processing than anything else.

Legitimacy and Informed Consent

The mechanisms for establishing the legitimacy of personal data processing lie at the core of any privacy theory and data privacy framework. The core mechanism for establishing this legitimacy in the commercial sphere has been the mechanism of informed consent.[55] In the sphere of public administration, informed consent plays a diminished or differently constructed role. There, the legitimacy requirement is anchored in democratic legitimacy of legislation underlying personal data-processing operations by public administrations, including the observance of the principles of necessity and proportionality of the related interference in view of relevant constitutional and fundamental rights safeguards.

If we restrict ourselves for a moment to the commercial sphere, we are confronted with a paradoxical situation. Even though the conditions for realizing meaningful informed consent to work in practice seem weaker than ever,[56] current privacy regulations, such as the GDPR, place more focus than ever on informed consent and the control over personal data as the primary standard for legitimacy.[57] In the following, I will discuss some of the core challenges for informed consent to work and what lessons have been and could be drawn from that.

At the practical level, informed consent has been demonstrated to be difficult to realize. Even if privacy policies and related service architectures would provide the levels of transparency that would allow people to inform themselves about privacy-relevant practices, people would lack the time, let alone stamina, to inform themselves properly before making informed decisions (McDonald and Cranor 2008). The data-driven nature of the production of digital functionality and the increasingly dynamic nature of all the features that are offered make things significantly harder (Gürses and Van Hoboken 2018). If meaningful consent with respect to a certain data-processing operation has been established, when and how should and can consent be renegotiated? Once we add the integration of third-party services, as discussed previously, to the mix, the situation becomes even more challenging.

Take the situation of the smartphone ecosystems as an example. Smartphones are an ideal site for the offering of individualized data-driven services. They tend to be personal and contain and provide access to a host of sensors and personal data, such as photos, messages, contacts, rich behavioral patterns, and location (de Montjoye et al. 2013). Enforcement initiatives and research in academia and civil society continue to show a lack of respect for basic data privacy guarantees that would be necessary for the establishment of informed consent in this context.[58] For instance, many apps do not even have a privacy policy, the most basic means through which transparency is offered to users.[59] While the relevant operating systems have implemented increased controls (and policies) for accessing personal data such as location, the permission architectures do not provide the granularity that would be needed to address integration of a growing number of third-party trackers.[60] Considering the high levels of standardization that are possible through the policies and designs of dominant smartphone ecosystem providers (Android and Google Play, Apple Store and iOS), smartphones would be one of the best places to hope for data privacy to work in practice.

In addition to the practical problems with respect to the establishment of informed consent, there are fundamental theoretical objections with informed consent as the primary mechanism for establishing legitimacy. And in fact, in the European context, informed consent is just one of the possible grounds for establishing the lawfulness for the processing of personal data.[61] There are two main other grounds available in the commercial realm. The first one requires that the processing of personal data is necessary for the delivery of a service, or more specifically "the processing is necessary for the performance of a contract to which the data subject is party or in order to take steps at the request of the data subject prior to entering into a contract" (Article 6(1)(b), GDPR). The second is that the processing "is necessary for the purposes of the legitimate interests pursued by the controller or by a third party, except where such interests are overridden by the interests or fundamental rights and freedoms of the data subject which require protection of personal data, in particular where the data subject is a child" (Article 6(1)(f), GDPR). Notably, these two standards are objective and subjective elements meant to play a role in individual cases only.[62] But the most striking aspect of the role of informed consent in the European legal framework is that regardless of consent being required or not, entities processing personal data always need to do so fairly, transparently, for specific, legitimate purposes, in observance of data subject rights, and subject to independent oversight by privacy regulators.[63]

There are further objections to data privacy frameworks relying on informed consent. First, the requirement of informed consent and the underlying conception of privacy as the control over one's personal data, as most famously articulated by Westin (1967), may get the value of privacy wrong. This argument has been made most eloquently and convincingly by Nissenbaum (2009) in her theory of privacy as contextual integrity. It may be so that in a certain context, respect for privacy implies the respect for a norm regarding the flow of personal data that involves the negotiation of consent, but such a context-specific norm does not generalize to a theory of privacy (ibid.). Respect for privacy, Nissenbaum argues, involves the respect for contextual norms with respect to the flow of personal information. This more objective contextual definition of privacy places the respect for privacy firmly outside of the realm of individualized negotiations around the processing of "one's personal data."

In addition, the fact that informed consent aims to protect privacy by giving individuals (a certain amount of) control over the collection and use of *their* personal information runs into deeper trouble every year (see also Mai's chapter in this volume). First of all, the practical boundaries of what has to be negotiated are unclear as the boundaries of the concept of personal information (personal data under the European data protection framework) are contested and legally uncertain. In the United States, consumer privacy protections tend to focus on providing control mechanisms related to the personal information of individuals that is collected in the interaction of a particular service with that specific individual.[64] This implies that the collection and use of personally identifiable information gathered through other means, or the information related to others collected through those individuals, simply falls through the cracks.[65] If one follows the guidance of the European Union's Article 29 Working Party on the concept of personal data, one could wonder what would still escape this broad definition in the context of data flows in digitally mediated contexts.[66] In practice, many entities processing information falling under the definition of personal data do not easily acknowledge this (Christl and Spiekermann 2016). The removal of identifiers and the application of similar privacy engineering practices, however, do not easily lead to the legal conclusion that such information is no longer personal data. A similar problem with respect to the legal definition of personal data exists for the designated special categories of sensitive data, such as information revealing someone's ethnicity, race, sexual orientation, or medical data. The boundaries of this concept are legally consequential as EU law imposes some significant roadblocks for the processing of these data.[67]

Finally, the structures of relevant sets of personal data reflect the social and interconnected contexts in which data is collected and processed. It is difficult to meaningfully separate someone's personal data from the personal data of others. As a result, the individualized negotiations around privacy in terms of informed consent are simply too narrow, while functional mechanisms for negotiating the pervasive collection of the personal information of nonusers are lacking.[68] But perhaps more fundamentally, because of predictive analytics and machine learning, the personal data "of others" may be as significant, from the perspective of privacy and related concerns about the data-driven exercise of power, as one's own data (Barocas and Nissenbaum 2014). In sum, it seems unwise to continue to frame data privacy issues in terms of a subjective concern over the relative control over one's "own" personal data, that is, the subset of information that relates to you.

International Data Flows and the US–EU Divide in Data Privacy Governance

Some of the differences between the US and EU approaches to data privacy have already been discussed in passing. These differences are many and exist at the level of legal culture, regulatory design, constitutional safeguards, and enforcement mechanisms.[69] While a deeper understanding of the differences is of theoretical as well as practical value, this is not the place to discuss these differences in depth. It seems entirely unsurprising that different approaches to data privacy exist in the world and would continue to exist in the future.

In fact, the diversity of approaches to data privacy in the European context is often overlooked. In Scandinavian countries, mandatory transparency requirements with respect to taxation data exist that would be unthinkable elsewhere in Europe. The right to be forgotten ruling came out of a minority position of the Spanish Data Protection Authority with respect to the application of data protection obligations on search engines.[70] It is quite unthinkable that a similar case would have emerged in the Netherlands, and a number of right to be forgotten rulings in the Netherlands have demonstrated the relative unease with the conclusions of the CJEU at the EU level.[71]

The European approach to privacy is the result of a combination of the concern for the protection of personal data, already codified into national data protection laws since the 1970s, with the project of European integration (Fuster 2014; Gutwirth 2002; Lynskey 2015; Schwartz 2013). The latter project necessarily continues to involve harmonization efforts to allow for the free flow of personal data in the European context. To allow for such free flow of personal data, the Data Protection Directive established a European Union–wide framework for respect for privacy in the context of the processing of personal data.[72] To address legal fragmentation as a result of different implementation and enforcement practices of the directive, the new framework established by the GDPR provides for further harmonization in view of digital single-market aims.

The real complexity and trouble emerge, in the relationship with Europe, in the context of increasingly pervasive international data flows and the relative lack of legal and political integration outside the boundaries of the European integration project. The Organisation for Economic Co-operation and Development (OECD) principles and the increased interest in data privacy in the human rights context provide some legal baseline.[73] Furthermore, a variety of more specific intergovernmental and international regulatory initiatives have been undertaken. In addition, more pragmatic efforts exist, including through corporate privacy governance frameworks, as well as standardization and engineering practices. These can all serve to increase interoperability in view of differences in data privacy protections and the economic and political interests connected to international data flows. Even so, the divide between Europe and the United States on privacy has lately looked as wide and challenging as it ever may have been, and the stakes have grown considerably.

It is only since relatively recently that the EU has had its own binding fundamental rights instrument, including the newly established fundamental right to the protection of personal data. Until well into the 1990s the status of fundamental rights in the EU context was weak and heavily debated.[74] The European institutions, except perhaps for the Council of the European Union, have enthusiastically received the new charter right to the protection of personal data with far-reaching regulatory efforts and judgments. Such European harmonization in the area of personal data protection sometimes overlooks the lack of enforcement of relevant norms in the European Union and the member states itself, in favor of establishing a common ground. Also, often overlooked is the reality that national security and foreign intelligence surveillance practices, an area in which data privacy violations tend to be most severe, are not harmonized at the EU level in the first place. Clearly, Article 8 of the European Convention of Human Rights and related Council of Europe instruments, including Convention 108, provide a fundamental baseline of protection. Still, it is sometimes hard to escape the impression that the increased attachment to the protection of fundamental rights at the EU level, which were predominantly informed by the European integration project, is causing international tensions about international flows of personal data partly for the sake of Europe's self-image.

Looking at the United States, the main challenges for data privacy in the international context exist at two levels. The first level is the relative inability and unwillingness of the US political system to adopt meaningful legislative reforms in the area of data privacy, including in relation to offering meaningful protection of the privacy-related rights and freedoms of non-US persons. Recent efforts to adopt a commercial privacy bill of rights have stalled, and internationally controversial United States surveillance laws remain in place without fundamental reforms, in the view of many observers. It seems entirely possible that such lack of reforms and the apparent lack of support of the current US administration to rigorously implement the recently adopted Privacy Shield will lead to another trans-Atlantic privacy breakdown now that the CJEU has been asked to look at it again.[75]

Second, the international dominance of US-based technology firms complicates dynamics in relation to the protection of privacy in commercial settings as well as in relation to the issue of government surveillance.[76] In a purely national setting the interaction between commercial data collection practices and lawful access regimes is already a complicated matter. Respect for privacy and the legitimacy of pervasive personal data processing involves consideration of the standards under which data held in private hands can become accessible to government agencies. This ideally requires the calibration of privacy standards for commercial and government surveillance at the national level. When lawful access is not meaningfully restrained, domestically or abroad, people are right to worry about entrusting their data to internationally operating private entities. Internationally operating cloud companies and the resulting transnational relationships between service providers and users in multiple jurisdictions across the world take place under the shadow of a multiplicity of lawful access regimes. The legal complexity is staggering, goes well beyond the EU–US relationship, and is likely to keep privacy researchers and practitioners busy for decades.

All of these transnational data privacy tension points put significant pressure on the existing international framework for data privacy at the international level, and the human rights framework in particular. The extent to which the right to privacy as enshrined in human rights treaties will be able to trickle down and play a constructive role in addressing some of the challenges discussed in this chapter remains to be seen. There are positive signs in the establishment of a UN Special Rapporteur on the Right to Privacy and the increased attention to data privacy in the human rights area more generally, including in relation to the practices of online service providers. However, these are minor steps in comparison to what may be needed in terms of institutional and legal reform at the international level to ensure respect for data privacy in a globalized world in the long run.

Conclusion

This chapter has created a bleak picture in sketching some of the current challenges to data privacy. Specifically, I have argued that current privacy laws and policies fall short in providing for the legitimacy of current-day pervasive personal data-processing practices. This falling short, which I have summarized as the Privacy Disconnect, exists at the socio-technical, the regulatory, and the political levels. The Privacy Disconnect may not be new, but I find it safe to argue that the intensity of some of the challenges for the establishment of legitimacy has increased. The complexity of the socio-technical environment has increased, existing legal mechanisms and institutional arrangements are wearing out, and solutions are hard to come by.

When one takes a step back and looks at all the efforts that go into the protection of privacy, should not one conclude that the glass is at least half full? Undoubtedly so. Still, the reality is also that privacy laws, policies, and engineering practices respond to a multiplicity of concerns and values. This can easily lead to a situation in which significant resources are spent on protecting certain aspects of data privacy while other aspects remain unaddressed. Moving forward, it seems particularly important that privacy law and policy discussions become more firmly connected to the underlying power dynamics they aim to resolve. Although this is certainly ambitious, we should aim to ensure that data privacy law and policy respond more directly to the social, economic, and political needs of people confronted with a world in which power is increasingly mediated through data-driven practices.

Notes

1. I would like to thank the editor, Rikke Frank Jørgensen, the anonymous reviewers, and the participants in the Author Workshop for their valuable comments and suggestions with respect to this chapter.

2. Data privacy as a conceptual term referring to the subset of privacy issues that stem from the collection and use of (personal) information, including data protection.

3. Regulation 2016/679 of April 27, 2016, on the protection of natural persons with regard to the processing of personal data and on the free movement of such data, and repealing Directive 95/46/EC (General Data Protection Regulation).

4. The European Commission also published a new proposal for a Regulation on the processing of personal data by EU institutions, a Communication on International Data Protection and a Regulation on the free flow of nonpersonal data.

5. In early 2018, the US Congress passed the Clarifying Lawful Overseas Use of Data Act (as a last-minute addition to a trillion-dollar spending bill), and the European Commission has put forward proposals in the area of law enforcement on electronic evidence gathering through Internet-based services. Internationally, the United Kingdom and the United States appear closest to reaching an agreement on cross-border access in the law-enforcement area.

6. In the last two years, the Article 29 Working Party has issued new guidelines on data portability, data protection officers, the lead supervisory authority, the data protection impact assessment, transparency, the rules on profiling and automated decision-making, and the setting of administrative fines.

7. See, for example, the proceedings of the European Court of Human Rights in the Big Brother Watch application relating to government surveillance, https://t.co/PyAhfgq5cc. See also CJEU (2014a, 2015). See *Europe v. Facebook* for more background on litigation of privacy advocate Max Schrems, mostly in relation to Facebook. Available at http://europe-v-facebook.org/EN/en.html. Schrems recently launched a new data privacy enforcement nongovernmental organization, called noyb ("none of your business").

8. Several (increasingly interdisciplinary) conferences have successfully established themselves in the area, including Institute of Electrical and Electronics Engineers Symposium on Security and Privacy, the Computers, Privacy and Data Protection conference, the Privacy Law Scholars Conference, the Amsterdam Privacy Conference, and the Privacy Enhancing Technologies Symposium.

9. IAPP recently reported it now has 40,000 members worldwide; see Ashford (2018).

10. For a discussion of the proposals, see Zuiderveen Borgesius et al. (2017).

11. For a discussion, see Van Hoboken (2016). See also Nissenbaum (2017).

12. For a discussion, see Nissenbaum (2017).

13. See Brian Fung (2017), Todd Shields and Eric Newcomer (2018), and Carole Cadwalladr and Emma Graham-Harrison (2018).

14. Article 8, Charter of Fundamental Rights of the European Union. The charter was solemnly proclaimed at the Nice European Council in 2000 and became binding with the entry into force of the Lisbon Treaty on December 1, 2009.

15. See Paul De Hert et al. (2017).

16. For a discussion, see, for example, Graef, Husovec, and Purtova (2017).

17. See recently, for example, Paul M. Schwartz and Karl-Nikolaus Peifer (2017).

18. See, for example, Nicole Bullock (2017). The most highly valued tech company in Europe is SAP, which is the world's sixtieth most valued company.

19. Basic information about these acquisitions can be found on Wikipedia.

20. For a discussion, see, for example, European Data Protection Supervisor Opinion, March 2014.

21. For a discussion, including of the potential rise of Amazon in ad sales, see Sorrell (2018).

22. See Miller (2017).

23. See, for example, Esteve (2017).

24. Note that the case of the right to be forgotten is different in character, as it does not relate to the processing of user data, but to the public accessibility of personal data through search engines.

25. See, for example, Dutch Data Protection Authority reports for 2014.

26. *Supra* note 7. See also Van Alsenoy et al. (2015), Samuel Gibbs (2018), European Commission (2017b), and Federal Trade Commission (2018).

27. See Bodoni (2017).

28. See http://www.housingmaps.com.

29. Consider the wide range of companies and organizations that are offering (information) goods and services, connecting to users through digital channels, including retailers, publishers, political parties, educational institutions, health services, government agencies, nongovernmental organizations, and so forth.

30. This is a nonexhaustive list meant to illustrate the argument. The question of what the current array of service components in different online service sectors

looks like is the kind of future research that we think needs to happen and is likely to provide further insights into how privacy governance may be organized.

31. Statcounter (https://statcounter.com) or market leader Google Analytics (https://analytics.google.com/analytics/web/provision).

32. RevenueHits (http://www.revenuehits.com) or market leader Google AdSense (https://www.google.com/adsense).

33. See, for example, SwiftID by CapitalOne (two-factor authentication; https://developer.capitalone.com/products/swiftid/homepage), OpenID (http://openid.net), or Facebook Login (https://developers.facebook.com/docs/facebook-login).

34. See, for example market leader Google reCaptcha (https://www.google.com/recaptcha/intro/index.html).

35. See, for example, Cloudflare (https://www.cloudflare.com); Symantec's Web Security Service, (https://www.symantec.com/products/web-security-services); or the free and open https as a service, Let's Encrypt (https://letsencrypt.org).

36. OpenStreetMap (https://www.openstreetmap.org) or market leader Google (https://developers.google.com/maps).

37. See, for example, Google Custom Search (https://cse.google.com/cse).

38. See one of the earliest movers to the cloud, Salesforce (http://www.salesforce.com).

39. See, for example, Oracle Data Cloud (https://www.oracle.com/applications/customer-experience/data-cloud/index.html) or Acxiom's LiveRamp Connect (https://liveramp.com/blog/customer-data-liveramp-connect).

40. See, for example, PayPal's Braintree v.zero SDK (https://developer.paypal.com).

41. See Eventbrite (https://developer.eventbrite.com) or Ticketmaster (http://developer.ticketmaster.com).

42. See, for example, Fulfillment by Amazon (https://services.amazon.com/fulfillment-by-amazon/benefits.htm).

43. See, for example, Amazon's Delivery Service Partner program (for delivery suppliers; https://logistics.amazon.com) and UPS Shipping API (for delivery demand) (https://www.ups.com/us/en/services/technology-integration/online-tools-shipping.page).

44. See, for example, Feefo (https://www.feefo.com/web/en/us).

45. See, for example, AddThis (http://www.addthis.com) and Facebook Sharing (https://developers.facebook.com/docs/plugins).

46. See, for example, Facebook Comments (https://developers.facebook.com/docs/plugins/comments) or Disqus (https://disqus.com).

47. See, for example, Google's YouTube (https://www.youtube.com/yt/dev/api-resources.html) and SoundCloud (https://developers.soundcloud.com/docs/api/sdks).

48. See CJEU (2017a). See also CJEU (2017b).

49. A discussion of whether cookie walls are permissible in Europe is ongoing. See, for example, Zuiderveen Borgesius et al. (2018).

50. See, for example, Koops (2014).

51. For an in-depth discussion, see Van Hoboken (2016).

52. See, for example, Mundie (2014), United States President's Council of Advisors on Science and Technology (2014), Cate et al. (2014), and Weitzner et al. (2008).

53. See Cate et al. (2014) for the application of this argument to the revision of international data privacy guidelines.

54. See Article 8 of the Charter of Fundamental Rights of the European Union.

55. In the United States, informed consent tends to be phrased as the requirement of "notice and choice."

56. For a discussion of core issues with consent, see Solove (2013), Reidenberg et al. (2015), Koops (2014), and Nissenbaum (2009).

57. See, for example, European Commission (2012, 2018).

58. Federal Trade Commission Protecting America's Consumers (2013); European Commission, Article 29 Working Party (2013); European Union Agency for Network and Information Security (2017); and Future of Privacy Forum (2016).

59. App distribution platforms (Google Play for Android and the Apple Store for iOS) require apps that process personal information to have a privacy policy and have started to enforce this requirement more strictly in the last year.

60. See, for example, European Union Agency for Network and Information Security (2017).

61. See Article 6 of the GDPR and Article 7 of the Data Protection Directive. See also Article 8 of the Charter of Fundamental Rights of the European Union.

62. See, for example, European Commission, Article 29 Working Party (2014) Opinion on the notion of legitimate interests of the data controller.

63. This stands in contrast to the market-oriented approach to data privacy in the United States.

64. See, for example, the California Online Privacy Act, which defines "personally identifiable information" as "individually identifiable information about an individual consumer collected online by the operator from that individual and maintained by the operator in an accessible form."

65. For a discussion of the definition of the US concept of personally identifiable information, see Schwartz and Solove (2011).

66. European Commission, Article 29 Working Party, Opinion on the Concept of Personal Data (2007). See also Purtova (2018). Specifically, the definition of personal data includes information relating to an identified or identifiable individual. This, in the view of the Article 29 Working Party, encompasses information that is about an individual, information that has the purpose to be used in relation to an individual, or information that is likely to have an impact on a particular individual.

67. The CJEU is expected to rule on this definition in an upcoming ruling on the obligations of search engines with respect to sensitive personal data in their index.

68. Think of the implications to others of providing access to one's messages, e-mails, pictures, and contacts in the smartphone context.

69. See, for example, Bennett and Raab (2006) and Bygrave (2014).

70. The Spanish Data Protection Authority Agencia Española de Protección de Datos took a different position from the Article 29 Working Party in 2009, by arguing that a right to request delisting from search engines followed from the data protection directive. The Article 29 Working Party itself took a more careful approach in its Opinion 1/2008 on data protection issues related to search engines.

71. For a discussion of Dutch right to be forgotten cases, see Kulk and Zuiderveen Borgesius (2018).

72. Directive 95/46/EC of the European Parliament and of the Council of 24 October 1995 on the protection of individuals with regard to the processing of personal data and on the free movement of such data (European Parliament and the Council 1995).

73. See OECD (2013). In the human rights context, see, for example, United Nations (2014).

74. On the relation of the EU to fundamental rights, see Alston and Weiler (1999), Leben (1999), Williams (2004), and Coppell and O'Neill (1992).

75. The Irish High Court has recently referred questions to the CJEU, in a new case of Schrems, involving standard contractual clauses and the privacy shield. See the Irish High Court (2016).

76. For a US perspective, see, for example, Clarke et al. (2013). See also Van Hoboken and Rubinstein (2013).

References

Alston, Philip, and Joseph H. H. Weiler. 1999. "An Ever Closer Union in Need of a Human Rights Policy: The European Union and Human Rights." In *The EU and Human Rights*, edited by Philip Alston, 3–69. Oxford: Oxford University Press.

Article 29 Working Party. 2007. Opinion 4/2007 on the concept of personal data. June. https://www.clinicalstudydatarequest.com/Documents/Privacy-European-guidance .pdf.

———. 2013. Opinion 02/2013 on apps on smart devices. February 27. https://www. datatilsynet.no/globalassets/global/regelverk-skjema/artikkel29gruppen/opinion _on_mobile_apps_wp_202_en_.pdf.

———. 2014. Opinion 06/2014 on the notion of legitimate interests of the data controller under Article 7 of Directive 95/46/EC. April 9. http://www.dataprotection.ro/ servlet/ViewDocument?id=1086.

Ashford, Warwick. 2018. "Data Protection Is a Business Issue, Says IAPP." *Computer Weekly.com*, April 20. https://www.computerweekly.com/news/252439642/Data -protection-is-a-business-issue-says-IAPP.

Baldwin, Carliss Y., and Kim B. Clark. 2003. "Managing in an Age of Modularity." In *Managing in the Modular Age: Architectures, Networks, and Organizations*, edited by Raghu Garud, Arun Kumaraswamy, and Richard N. Langlois, 84–93. Oxford: Blackwell.

Barocas, Solon, and Helen Nissenbaum. 2014. "Big Data's End Run around Procedural Privacy Protections." *Communications of the ACM* 57 (11): 31–33.

Bennett, Colin, and Charles Raab. 2006. *The Governance of Privacy: Policy Instruments in Global Perspective*. Cambridge, MA: MIT Press.

Bodoni, Stephanie. 2017. "Microsoft Faces European Privacy Probes over Windows 10." *Bloomberg*, February 21. https://www.bloomberg.com/news/articles/2017-02-21/ microsoft-faces-european-privacy-probes-over-windows-10.

Bullock Nicole. 2017. "Tech Surge Boosts Year's Momentum Trade." *Financial Times*, November 23. https://www.ft.com/content/4c34a416-cfd4-11e7-b781-794ce08b24dc.

Bygrave, Lee A. 2014. *Data Privacy Law: An International Perspective*. Oxford: Oxford University Press.

Cadwalladr, Carole, and Emma Graham-Harrison. 2018. "50 Million Facebook Profiles Harvested for Cambridge Analytica in Major Data Breach." *The Guardian*, March 17. https://www.theguardian.com/news/2018/mar/17/cambridge-analytica-facebook -influence-us-election.

Cate, Fred H., Peter Cullen, and Viktor Mayer-Schonberger. 2014. "Data Protection Principles for the 21st Century: Revising the 1980 OECD Guidelines." https://www.oii.ox.ac.uk/archive/downloads/publications/Data_Protection_Principles_for_the_21st_Century.pdf.

Clarke, Richard A., Michael J. Morell, Geoffrey R. Stone, Cass R. Sunstein, and Peter Swire. 2013. "Liberty and Security in a Changing World." Report and Recommendations of the President's Review Group on Intelligence and Communications Technologies. https://obamawhitehouse.archives.gov/sites/default/files/docs/2013-12-12_rg_final_report.pdf.

Coppell, Jason, and Aidan O'Neill. 1992. "The European Court of Justice: Taking Rights Seriously?" *Common Market Law Review* 29: 669–692.

Court of Justice of the European Union. 2014a. *Digital Rights Ireland Ltd v Minister for Communications, Marine and Natural Resources and Others and Kärntner Landesregierung and Others.* Joined Cases C-293/12 and C-594/12, April 8, 2014.

———. 2014b. *Google Spain SL and Google Inc. v Agencia Española de Protección de Datos (AEPD) and Mario Costeja González.* Case C-131/12, May 13, 2014.

———. 2015. *Maximillian Schrems v Data Protection Commissioner.* Case C-362/14, October 6, 2015.

———. 2017a. Opinion of Advocate General. *Unabhängiges Landeszentrum für Datenschutz Schleswig-Holstein v Wirtschaftsakademie Schleswig-Holstein GmbH, in the Presence of Facebook Ireland Ltd, Vertreter des Bundesinteresses beim Bundesverwaltungsgericht.* Case C-210/16, October 24, 2017.

———. 2017b. *Fashion ID GmbH & Co.KG v Verbraucherzentrale NRW eV.* Case C-40/17, January 26, 2017.

Christl, Wolfie, and Sarah Spiekermann. 2016. *Networks of Control: A Report on Corporate Surveillance, Digital Tracking, Big Data & Privacy.* Vienna: Facultas.

De Hert, Paul, and Serge Gutwirth. 2006. "Privacy, Data Protection and Law Enforcement: Opacity of the Individual and Transparency of Power." In *Privacy and the Criminal Law,* edited by Erik Claes, Antony Duff, and Serge Gutwirth, 61–104. Cambridge: Intersentia.

De Hert, Paul, Vagelis Papakonstantinou, Gianclaudio Malgieri, Laurent Beslay, and Ignacio Sanchez. 2017. "The Right to Data Portability in the GDPR: Towards User-centric Interoperability of Digital Services." *Computer Law & Security Review* 32 (2): 193–203.

de Montjoye, Yves-Alexandre, Cesar A. Hidalgo, Michel Verleysen, and Vincent Blondel. 2013. "Unique in the Crowd: The Privacy Bounds of Human Mobility." *Scientific Reports* 3 (1376).

Dutch Data Protection Authority. 2013. "Investigation into the Combining of Personal Data by Google: Report of Definitive Findings." https://autoriteitpersoon sgegevens.nl/sites/default/files/downloads/mijn_privacy/en_rap_2013-google -privacypolicy.pdf.

Englehardt, Steven. 2017. "No Boundaries: Exfiltration of Personal Data by Session-Replay Scripts." *Freedom to Tinker*. November 15. https://freedom-to-tinker.com/ 2017/11/15/no-boundaries-exfiltration-of-personal-data-by-session-replay-scripts.

Esteve, Asunción. 2017. "The Business of Personal Data: Google, Facebook, and Privacy Issues in the EU and the USA." *International Data Privacy Law* 7 (1): 36–47.

European Commission. 2012. "Commission Proposes a Comprehensive Reform of Data Protection Rules to Increase Users' Control of Their Data and to Cut Costs for Businesses." January 25. http://europa.eu/rapid/press-release_IP-12-46_en.htm.

————. 2017a. "Commission Proposes High Level of Privacy Rules for All Electronic Communications and Updates Data Protection Rules for EU Institutions." January 10. https://ec.europa.eu/digital-single-market/en/news/commission-proposes-high -level-privacy-rules-all-electronic-communications-and-updates-data.

————. 2017b. "Mergers: Commission Fines Facebook €110 million for Providing Misleading Information about WhatsApp Takeover." May 18. https://europa.eu/ newsroom/content/mergers-commission-fines-facebook-%E2%82%AC110-million -providing-misleading-information-about_en.

————. 2017c. "Proposal for a Regulation on Privacy and Electronic Communications." January 10. https://ec.europa.eu/digital-single-market/en/news/proposal -regulation-privacy-and-electronic-communications.

————. 2018. *It's Your Data—Take Control.* May 4. https://publications.europa.eu/da/ publication-detail/-/publication/fe2cb115-4cea-11e8-be1d-01aa75ed71a1.

European Data Protection Supervisor Opinion. 2014. Preliminary Opinion Privacy and Competitiveness in the Age of Big Data: The Interplay between Data Protection, Competition Law and Consumer Protection in the Digital Economy. March. https://edps .europa.eu/sites/edp/files/publication/14-03-26_competitition_law_big_data_en.pdf.

European Parliament and the Council. 1995. Directive 95/46/EC of the European Parliament and of the Council of 24 October Official Journal L 281, November 23, 1995, 31–50.

European Union Agency for Network and Information Security. 2017. "Privacy and Data Protection in Mobile Applications: A Study on the App Development Ecosystem and the Technical Implementation of GDPR." November. https://www.enis .europa.eu/publications/privacy-and-data-protection-in-mobile-applications/ at_download/fullReport.

Federal Trade Commission Protecting America's Consumers. 2013. "Mobile Privacy Disclosures: Building Trust through Transparency." https://www.ftc.gov/sites/default/files/documents/reports/mobile-privacy-disclosures-building-trust-through-transparency-federal-trade-commission-staff-report/130201mobileprivacyreport.pdf.

————. 2018. "Statement by the Acting Director of FTC's Bureau of Consumer Protection Regarding Reported Concerns about Facebook Privacy Practices." March 26. https://www.ftc.gov/news-events/press-releases/2018/03/statement-acting-director-ftcs-bureau-consumer-protection.

Fung, Brian. 2017. "Equifax's Massive 2017 Data Breach Keeps Getting Worse." *The Washington Post*, March 1. https://www.washingtonpost.com/news/the-switch/wp/2018/03/01/equifax-keeps-finding-millions-more-people-who-were-affected-by-its-massive-data-breach.

Fuster, Gloria González. 2014. *The Emergence of Personal Data Protection as a Fundamental Right of the EU*. Berlin: Springer Science & Business.

Future of Privacy Forum. 2016. "FPF Mobile Apps Study." https://fpf.org/wp-content/uploads/2016/08/2016-FPF-Mobile-Apps-Study_final.pdf.

Gibbs, Samuel. 2018. "Facebook Ordered to Stop Collecting User Data by Belgian Court." *The Guardian*, February 16. https://www.theguardian.com/technology/2018/feb/16/facebook-ordered-stop-collecting-user-data-fines-belgian-court.

Graef, Inge, Martin Husovec, and Nadezhda Purtova. 2017. "Data Portability and Data Control: Lessons for an Emerging Concept in EU Law." TILEC Discussion Paper. https://papers.ssrn.com/sol3/papers.cfm?abstract_id=3071875.

Gürses, Seda, and Claudia Diaz. 2013. "Two Tales of Privacy in Online Social Networks." *IEEE Security and Privacy* 11 (3): 29–37.

Gürses, Seda, and Joris van Hoboken. 2018. "Privacy after the Agile Turn." In *Cambridge Handbook of Consumer Privacy*, edited by Evan Selinger, Jules Polonetsky, and Omer Tene. Cambridge: Cambridge University Press.

Gutwirth, Serge. 2002. *Privacy and the Information Age*. Oxford: Rowman & Littlefield.

Hoofnagle, Chris J. 2014. "The Potemkinism of Privacy Pragmatism." *Slate*, September 2. http://www.slate.com/articles/technology/future_tense/2014/09/data_use_regulation_the_libertarian_push_behind_a_new_take_on_privacy.html?via=gdpr-consent.

Irish High Court. 2016. "Request for Preliminary Ruling." http://www.europe-v-facebook.org/sh2/ref.pdf.

Kerr, Orin S. 2009. "The Case for the Third-Party Doctrine." *Michigan Law Review* 107 (2): 561–602.

Koops, Bert-Jaap. 2014. "The Trouble with European Data Protection Law." Tilburg Law School Research Paper. https://papers.ssrn.com/sol3/papers.cfm?abstract_id=2505692.

Kulk, Stefan, and Frederik Zuiderveen Borgesius. 2018. "Privacy, Freedom of Expression, and the Right to Be Forgotten in Europe." In *Cambridge Handbook of Consumer Privacy*, edited by Evan Selinger, Jules Polonetsky, and Omer Tene, 301–320. Cambridge: Cambridge University Press.

Leben, Charles. 1999. "Is There a European Approach to Human Rights?" In *The EU and Human Rights*, edited by Philip Alston, 69–99. Oxford: Oxford University Press.

Lynskey, Orla. 2015. *The Foundations of EU Data Protection Law*. Oxford: Oxford University Press.

McDonald, Aleecia M., and Lorrie Faith Cranor. 2008. "The Cost of Reading Privacy Policies." *I/S: A Journal of Law and Policy for the Information Society* 4: 543–568.

Miller, Ron. 2017. "AWS Won't Be Ceding Its Massive Market Share Lead Anytime Soon." *TechCrunch*, July 28. https://techcrunch.com/2017/07/28/aws-wont-be-ceding-its-massive-market-share-lead-anytime-soon.

Mundie, Craig. 2014. "Privacy Pragmatism: Focus on Data Use, Not Data Collection." *Foreign Affairs*, March/April. https://www.foreignaffairs.com/articles/2014-02-12/privacy-pragmatism.

Nissenbaum, Helen. 2009. *Privacy in Context: Technology, Policy, and the Integrity of Social Life*. Stanford, CA: Stanford University Press.

———. 2017. "Deregulating Collection: Must Privacy Give Way to Use Regulation?" SSRN Scholarly Paper ID 3092282. Rochester, NY: Social Science Research Network. https://ssrn.com/abstract=3092282.

Organisation for Economic Co-operation and Development. 2013. "Protection of Privacy and Transborder Flows of Personal Data." http://www.oecd.org/sti/ieconomy/oecdguidelinesontheprotectionofprivacyandtransborderflowsofpersonaldata.htm.

Purtova, Nadezhda. 2018. "The Law of Everything: Broad Concept of Personal Data and Future of EU Data Protection Law." *Law, Innovation and Technology* 10 (1): 40–81.

Reidenberg, Joel R., Cameron N. Russel, Alexander J. Callen, Sophia Qasir, and Thomas B. Norton. 2015. "Privacy Harms and the Effectiveness of the Notice and Choice Framework." *I/S: A Journal of Law and Policy for the Information Society* 11 (2): 485–524.

Schwartz, Paul. M. 2013. "The EU-US Privacy Collision: A Turn to Institutions and Procedures." *Harvard Law Review* 126 (7): 1966–2009.

Schwartz, Paul M., and Karl-Nikolaus Peifer. 2017. "Transatlantic Data Privacy." 106 *Georgetown Law Journal* 115 (November). https://papers.ssrn.com/sol3/papers.cfm ?abstract_id=3066971##.

Schwartz, Paul M., and Daniel J. Solove. 2011. "The PII Problem: Privacy and a New Concept of Personally Identifiable Information." *N.Y.U. Law Review* 86: 1814–1893.

Shields, Todd, and Eric Newcomer. 2018. "Uber's 2016 Breach Affected More Than 20 Million U.S. Users." Bloomberg. April 12. https://www.bloomberg.com/news/ articles/2018-04-12/uber-breach-exposed-names-emails-of-more-than-20-million -users.

Solove, Daniel. 2013. "Introduction: Privacy Self-Management and the Consent Dilemma." *Harvard Law Review* 126 (7): 1880–1903.

Sorrell, Martin. 2018. "How Amazon Will Crash Google and Facebook's Advertising Duopoly." *Wired*, January 2. http://www.wired.co.uk/article/amazon-advertising -threaten-google-facebook.

United Nations. 2014. "The Right to Privacy in the Digital Age." Report of the Office of the United Nations High Commissioner for Human Rights. June 30. A/HRC/ 27/37. Geneva: Human Rights Council.

United States President's Council of Advisors on Science and Technology. 2014. Report to the President. "Big Data and Privacy: A Technological Perspective." https:// bigdatawg.nist.gov/pdf/pcast_big_data_and_privacy_-_may_2014.pdf.

Van Alsenoy, Brendan, Valerie Verdoodt, Rob Heyman, Ellen Wauters, Jef Ausloos, and Gunes Acar. 2015. *From Social Media Service to Advertising Network: A Critical Analysis of Facebook's Revised Policies and Terms.* SPION and EMSOC. Draft August 25. https://www.researchgate.net/publication/291147719_From_social_media_service _to_advertising_network_-_A_critical_analysis_of_Facebook's_Revised_Policies_and _Terms.

Van Hoboken, Joris. 2016. "From Collection to Use in Privacy Regulation? A Forward Looking Comparison of European and U.S. Frameworks for Personal Data Processing." In *Exploring the Boundaries of Big Data*, edited by Bart Van der Sloot, Dennis Broeders, and Erik Schrijvers, 231–259. The Hague: The Netherlands Scientific Council for Government Policy.

Van Hoboken, Joris, and Ira Rubinstein. 2013. "Privacy and Security in the Cloud: Some Realism about Technical Solutions to Transnational Surveillance in the Post-Snowden Era." *Maine Law Review* 66: 488–533.

Warren, Samuel D., and Louis D. Brandeis. 1890. "The Right to Privacy." *Harvard Law Review* 193–220.

Weitzner, Daniel J., Harold Abelson, Tim Berners-Lee, Joan Feigenbaum, and Gerald J. Sussman. 2008. "Information Accountability." *Communications of the ACM* 51 (6): 82–87.

Westin, A. 1967. *Privacy and Freedom*. New York: Atheneum.

Williams, Andrew. 2004. *EU Human Rights Policies: A Study of Irony*. Oxford: Oxford University Press.

Wolf, Martin. 2017. "Taming the Masters of the Tech Universe." *Financial Times*, November 14. https://www.ft.com/content/45092c5c-c872-11e7-aa33-c63fdc9b8c6c.

Zuboff, Shoshana. 2015. "Big Other: Surveillance Capitalism and the Prospects of an Information Civilization." *Journal of Information Technology* 30 (1): 75–89.

Zuiderveen Borgesius, Fredrik. J., Joris van Hoboken, Kristina Irion, and Max Rozendaal. 2017. "An Assessment of the Commission's Proposal on Privacy and Electronic Communications." European Parliament's Committee on Civil Liberties, Justice and Home Affairs research paper. https://www.ivir.nl/publicaties/download/IPOL_STU2017583152_EN.pdf.

Zuiderveen Borgesius, Frederik J. J., Sanne Kruikemeier, Sophie C. Boerman, and Helberger Boerman. 2018. "Tracking Walls, Take-It-Or-Leave-It Choices, the GDPR, and the ePrivacy Regulation." *European Data Protection Law Review* 3 (3): 353–368.

11   Regulating Private Harms Online: Content Regulation under Human Rights Law

Molly K. Land[1]

Introduction

Online expression today is largely governed by private companies exercising authority outside the purview of public control. Companies such as Google, Facebook, and Twitter moderate our conversations, deliver our news, and keep us connected with acquaintances, friends, and family. Business entities now manage our communication and social relationships in ways that can affect everything from our emotions to our dignity, our livelihoods, and even our elections.

In the context of human rights law, however, private regulation—however pervasive—presents a dilemma. Both state and private actors can cause human rights harms, but international human rights law traditionally has only regulated the former. Human rights law requires governments to protect individuals from violations of their rights by non-state actors but generally stops short of imposing legal obligations on private actors themselves. Non-state actors typically have only a moral responsibility, not a legal obligation, to respect rights and remedy their violation.

Although nonbinding, the responsibility of companies to respect rights has gradually evolved into a framework of "corporate social responsibility" (CSR) that is now being applied across a range of industries, including in the context of Internet content moderation. The UN Special Rapporteur on Freedom of Opinion and Expression, for example, has called on Internet companies to follow the UN Guiding Principles on Business and Human Rights (Kaye 2018, para. 11). Yet the application of the UN Guiding Principles to Internet intermediaries[2] raises a host of questions for human rights law and institutions. Do content "intermediaries" such as Facebook and

Google truly not have any obligations under international human rights law when they determine what content we see in our news feed or search results? If they do, what are these obligations and where do they come from? And how should these companies resolve disagreements about what content is indexed or displayed?

This chapter responds to these questions by developing a human rights–based approach to understanding the legal obligations of Internet intermediaries that engage in content moderation activities. The chapter makes two contributions to the literature on Internet governance and human rights. First, it develops a definition of state action online that takes account of the myriad ways in which states are currently pressuring Internet content providers to implement state policies. Much of what is currently characterized as "private" action should instead be seen as action by the state, since in many cases the state has expressly or implicitly imposed an obligation on these private companies to regulate speech on its behalf. In order to understand the scope of state responsibility for the actions of private intermediaries, the chapter develops a new typology for describing the activities of states seeking to influence, control, or appropriate these private entities: *control, command, delegation, notice and takedown, co-optation,* and *informal pressure.* The chapter applies this framework to delineate between action that can and should be governed directly by human rights law as state action and "private" action that requires a modified approach to account for its non-state character.

Second, this chapter provides such a modified approach for understanding the "private" actions of non-state content intermediaries. It argues that Article 19 of the International Covenant on Civil and Political Rights (ICCPR) imposes some duties directly on online intermediaries. These duties do not mirror those of the state, but they do require intermediaries to respect basic principles of due process and remedy. Direct obligations may be strongest for Internet companies that are Internet gatekeepers—a position defined by an intermediary's dominance, the nature of the intermediary's service, and the availability of market alternatives. These intermediaries in particular must be transparent about their terms of service and provide grievance mechanisms for users wishing to contest their decisions about content.

Harms that are neither "state action" nor a violation of a direct obligation on an Internet company can be addressed through the exercise of positive state obligations. States have positive obligations to create an enabling environment in which the right to freedom of expression is not threatened by terms of service enforcement. In meeting this obligation, states should not only regulate to enforce the direct obligations of due process and remedy but should also take steps to ensure competition in the Internet ecosystem and to consider the rights of speakers in addition to the companies' business objectives and the desires of users when they make decisions about content moderation and curation.

The chapter begins by briefly describing ways in which Internet intermediaries can affect freedom of expression online. It then discusses current CSR responses to these harms as well as the gaps and limitations of these approaches: the conflation of private and public action, the difficulty of identifying a "violation" of expressive rights, and the challenge of reconciling the interests of speakers with business objectives and user preferences. The final section identifies concrete recommendations that can be adopted by human rights institutions, such as the United Nations bodies that monitor state compliance with human rights treaties, in responding to the human rights impact of such intermediaries.

Internet Intermediaries under Human Rights Law

For human rights law and institutions, harms caused by private actors can present a challenge. Both states and non-state entities can cause human rights harms, but international human rights law generally only regulates the former. This section first discusses the way in which current approaches to protecting rights online have tended to neglect the harms of private regulation. It then provides a roadmap of the kinds of harms associated with private regulation of online speech and identifies several conceptual challenges in fitting these harms within a traditional human rights framework.

Current Approaches to Business and Human Rights Online

Human rights law typically responds to the impact of business on human rights through a combination of national regulation and nonbinding frameworks. States are obligated to regulate non-state actors to protect human rights, and many do so in a variety of ways. This duty to protect is a central pillar of human rights law and was recently reaffirmed in the reports of John Ruggie, who served as the UN Secretary-General's Special Representative for Business and Human Rights from 2005 to 2011. The approach that

Ruggie advocated, which was eventually affirmed by the UN Human Rights Council in the UN Guiding Principles on Business and Human Rights, puts primary emphasis on the state's obligation to regulate business to protect rights (Jørgensen 2018; Ruggie 2011).

Efforts to promote greater respect for human rights by business enterprises have been largely voluntary, relying on aspirational statements and self-regulation to push forward the CSR agenda (De La Vega 2017, 446).[3] Ruggie's framework, which provides the foundation for the Guiding Principles, reflects an attempt to give CSR more teeth by introducing the idea of a business "responsibility"—a moral (but not a legal) obligation to respect rights and to remedy their violation. The moral responsibilities of business under the Guiding Principles include the duty to "[a]void causing or contributing to adverse human rights impacts through their activities" and to "[s]eek to prevent or mitigate adverse human rights impacts that are directly linked to their operations" (Ruggie 2011, 14).

Efforts to apply this framework to Internet companies have tended to focus on two kinds of problems. First, significant efforts have been made—including by the companies themselves in many cases—to develop a way to respond to state requests to censor content online (Jørgensen 2018, 263). Second, activists have also emphasized transparency and process, including the need for more disclosure about the nature of company activities regulating online content and the importance of creating procedures for receiving and responding to complaints (Laidlaw 2015, 112).

The first issue—how companies respond to state requests to censor online content—came to prominence in the mid-2000s with revelations about the complicity of Yahoo! and other companies in human rights violations in China. These revelations led to Congressional hearings at which representatives of the major Internet companies had to respond to questions about their role in state human rights abuses. These events prompted the formation in 2008 of a multistakeholder organization, the Global Network Initiative (GNI),[4] composed of company, investor, academic, and nongovernmental organization representatives (Maclay 2010). GNI helps companies navigate "pressure by governments to act in ways that may impact the fundamental human rights of privacy and freedom of expression" by providing a framework of human rights standards, a process for holding companies accountable to these standards, as well as opportunities for policy engagement and learning (GNI 2017).

Advocates and experts have also identified Internet companies' lack of transparency about their policies and procedures as an issue of human rights concern. As Sullivan notes, "the lack of transparency and accountability for how those policies [the terms of service of Internet providers] are enforced can lead to human rights risks" (Sullivan 2016, 16). The issue of transparency about companies' policies and how they are enforced has also been raised by the UN Special Rapporteur on Freedom of Opinion and Expression (Kaye 2016, para. 65). Ranking Digital Rights, a nonprofit advocacy group, assesses Internet companies' compliance with human rights principles, including by reference to whether the company communicates about changes in their terms of service and is transparent about enforcement (Ranking Digital Rights 2018).

Human Rights Impacts of Content Regulation

Clearly, the question of how companies can and should respond to state requests plays a central role in promoting respect for human rights on the Internet. Yet the decisions that these companies make about their *own* policies and procedures can also have significant consequences for rights. Although UN experts have identified private harms as an important human rights issue (Kaye 2016, 2018), companies themselves have been "reluctant to view content moderation undertaken to enforce their terms of service (TOS) as a human rights issue" (Sullivan 2016). Jørgensen's chapter in this volume, for example, explores how this focus on state overreach is reflected in the narratives of company employees and executives. Nonetheless, the thousands of decisions each day that these "new speech governors" (Klonick 2018) make about the content on their platforms have significant effects on our ability to generate and share information and expression.

This section will discuss three primary ways in which private terms of service can affect freedom of expression online: content moderation, content curation, and account suspension or termination (Bradley and Wingfield 2018, 12).

Content Moderation. Internet platforms can affect expression and participation online by moderating (removing, de-indexing, or deprioritizing) particular user content. As the chapter in this volume by Jillian York and Ethan Zuckerman makes clear, content moderation policies and practices routinely go beyond what is required by either domestic or international law. Terms of service enforcement often removes content that platforms believe might be unpleasant or harmful to users—including content that is violent, explicit, or abusive or which models harmful behaviors (such as pro-anorexia content). Content that might violate a platform's terms of service is often first identified by other users or through the use of algorithms (Cook 2016). After potentially harmful content is identified, it is reviewed by paid moderators and potentially escalated for further review within the company (Hopkins 2017).

Content Curation. Private companies are also increasingly taking on the role of curating the information world in which we live. Internet platforms and services do not just show us information randomly—they organize, curate, and manage information for us. Often, these processes of curation are algorithmic. Platforms use proprietary formulas to decide what content to provide to users: what search results to display, what content to show, and what related content to offer (Pasquale 2015, 59–100). Because these formulas are proprietary and central to their business models, platforms do not share many details about how they make these decisions; some do, however, offer users the ability to provide input into the choices that are made about the content they experience.

In some instances, platforms may also intentionally display particular content to users. Examples include not only the infamous Facebook feed incident (Goel 2014) but also recent reports that YouTube redirects users who search for extremist content to antiterrorism videos (Brogan 2017). Facebook has partnered with Homeland Security and an analytics firm to support campaigns aimed at creating counterspeech against hate and extremism, although it has denied using its algorithm to direct people to such material (Solon 2017).

Account Suspension and Termination. Platforms also affect freedom of expression online when they suspend or terminate user accounts for repeated terms of service violations. Users whose accounts have been terminated often have relatively few options for contesting those decisions (Angwin and Grassegger 2017).

Two Conceptual Challenges

There are several different types of human rights problems raised by the processes of content moderation, curation, and account suspension/termination. Nonetheless, the extent to which human rights law governs these activities is unclear. This section discusses the human rights impact of these activities in light of the two central challenges to applying human rights law to content moderation policies.

Challenge 1: Identifying the Violation   The first challenge in applying human rights law to these activities has to do with identifying when, if ever, content moderation by Internet companies constitutes a violation of international human rights. When does a company's decision to remove content or terminate a user account trigger a human rights obligation? As David Kaye, the current UN Special Rapporteur on Freedom of Opinion and Expression, noted in his 2016 report to the Human Rights Council, Internet companies can affect rights when they engage in "overzealous censorship of a wide range of legitimate but (perhaps to some audiences) 'uncomfortable' expressions" (Kaye 2016, para. 52).[5] Clearly, restricting access to information via moderation or curation limits the rights of both speakers and listeners under Article 19 of the ICCPR, which includes the "freedom to seek, receive and impart information and ideas of all kinds, regardless of frontiers." But does that transform every content decision by an intermediary—not only large social media companies but also individual website operators and online newspapers with comments sections—into an action that must be justified pursuant to Article 19?

From the perspective of users, the fact that expression is silenced by a private rather than a public actor may not matter. Apple's decision to remove from the iTunes App Store an application that distributed publicly available data about drone strikes (Biddle 2015) or Facebook's deletion of a Syrian artist's photos of refugees who had drowned off the coast of Libya (Mirzeoff 2015)—look and feel like censorship. For individuals affected by such decisions, it may be of little comfort that their content was blocked or removed by a private rather than a public actor.

Human rights institutions, to the extent they have addressed this gap, have simply tended to equate public and private censorship and have condemned both as inconsistent with freedom of expression. A joint declaration by UN and regional freedom of expression experts, for example, contends, "Content filtering systems which are imposed by a government or commercial service provider and which are not end-user controlled are a form of prior censorship and are not justifiable as a restriction on freedom of expression" (Joint Declaration on Freedom of Expression and the Internet 2011, para. 3(b)). Nonprofits as well have advocated that companies adopt the standards of Article 19 in their content moderation policies (Bradley and Wingfield 2018, 15–18). And David Kaye's 2018 report recommends that companies "recognize that the authoritative global standard for ensuring freedom of expression on their platforms is human rights law, not the varying laws of States or their own private interests, and they should re-evaluate their content standards accordingly" (Kaye 2018, para. 70).

Yet it cannot be the case that every content moderation decision made by every digital platform should be subject to human rights scrutiny. And if not, how and where do we draw the line in terms of when freedom of expression (or any other human right) is implicated? Is the decisive factor the platform's size and impact, the presence of alternative avenues for expression, the type of content—or a combination of all of the above? Although any interference with free expression, if done by a state actor, would trigger human rights scrutiny, it is not clear under which circumstances *private* content moderation or curation interferes with a protected right.

Challenge 2: Human Rights Norms on Commercial Platforms The second challenge is understanding *how* human rights norms might apply to content moderation and curation activities. Typically, when free expression norms are applied to states, the state is not in the business of moderating or curating content; indeed, it would be highly suspect for a government to take on the role of making content-based decisions about speech in order to curate the information space. Companies, in contrast, are not only engaged in curating content as a central element of their business model but users seek these platforms precisely because of the choices the companies make about the information they deliver.

The explicit role that information management plays in the business of Internet content providers complicates the human rights analysis. When a company chooses to prioritize some content over other, what values should guide its decision? Imagine, for example, the off-line equivalent—that Facebook were put in charge of determining who should speak at a public rally in order to curate an information experience for listeners, who then paid it for this service. If we truly believe that the Internet is the new public forum, what criteria should Facebook use to determine who is heard in that forum? And is it legitimate for those criteria to be driven by business incentives designed to make our speech a desirable commodity for other users—for Facebook, a commodity that generated over $40 billion in revenue in 2017 (Roettgers 2018)?

At its core, the conflation of public and private raises questions about values. These platforms generally purport to be showing us information that we *want to see* based on a complex formula that takes into account our past information consumption habits combined with the habits and preferences of others. But is "what we want" the right metric for making those decisions? Shouldn't they also consider what information we "need" to have? Are they obligated to show us what we do not want to see, and if so, under what circumstances? Curation algorithms that display content based on past user behavior, for example, will bias content in favor of material for which the user has already expressed a preference and thus limit the extent to which the user encounters content with which he or she disagrees (Bakshy, Messing, and Adamic 2015; Tufekci 2015).

Some have advocated a principle of neutrality in content moderation, arguing that neutrality should be the governing principle not only for online transmission of data (i.e., "net neutrality") but also for the "over the top" content delivery services. Such services, in this view, should act in a "neutral way" with respect to the content they deliver (Observacom 2017, 11). It is not clear, however, what "neutrality" means, since even a principle of "most recent" reflects value choices. Further, given the amount of content on the largest platforms, some moderation is inevitable.

The question of public speech on private platforms also raises the question of how "freedom of expression concerns raised by design and engineering choices should be reconciled with the freedom of private entities to design and customize their platforms as they choose" (Kaye 2016, para. 55). Content moderation is deeply intertwined with companies' business models as well as being part and parcel of the products that they offer to consumers (Jørgensen 2018, 251). Internet platforms make decisions about content because of their brand or image and what they think consumers want from their product or service. Shocking or unpleasant material, even if it constitutes core political speech, could still be "bad for business" (Benedek and Kettemann 2014, 105). How should the values of "free speech" be reconciled with business values, individual choice, and consumer rights? How should claims for transparency be reconciled with the need of companies to protect proprietary information about their algorithms?

Internet intermediaries view content moderation and filtering as essential to the nature of the services they provide and thus the value they offer to consumers. Moreover, these pressures cause companies to be highly risk averse. In navigating the demands of consumers, business models, and governments, "[t]oo often, companies err on the side of caution and forbid much more speech than states would have to prohibit because of their human rights obligations" (Benedek and Kettemann 2014, 104).

A Proposed Human Rights Framework for Protecting Rights Online

This section proposes a framework for resolving these challenges. First, it argues that much of what might seem to be "private" speech is actually undertaken pursuant to state authority and thus should be treated as government action under human rights law. Second, it argues that platforms are subject to some limited but direct responsibilities under human rights law. With respect to private conduct of intermediaries that is not governed by human rights law, the section then argues that states have a positive obligation to create a rights-enabling environment to protect against and remedy harms to freedom of expression.

Identifying State Action

At the outset, human rights institutions and experts must first recognize that a good deal of "private" censorship is being done pursuant to state authority. From China to the European Union, private companies are being asked to "voluntarily" regulate speech on their platforms under the threat of regulation and liability (Bradley and Wingfield 2018; Xu and Albert 2017). Governments have strong interests in controlling the communications sector, and they are using a variety of sophisticated techniques to leverage the power of intermediaries in order to achieve their objectives. Jørgensen and Pedersen acknowledge this problem, asking "at what stage may freedom of expression limitations be attributed to the state, when caused by 'voluntary' measures taken by intermediaries following state encouragement to do so?" (Jørgensen and Pedersen 2017, 187). This section argues that the extent of *government interference* should determine whether a particular action—removal of content, for example—should be viewed as the action of a private entity or a state (ibid., 183).

Under international human rights law, there are two ways in which a state can incur responsibility for the act of a private entity. First, the private action may be attributable to the state under principles of state responsibility. The International Law Commission's Articles on State Responsibility, which the UN General Assembly commended to the attention of states in 2001, provides a framework for understanding the conditions under which action by an entity other than the state is attributable to the state for purposes of state responsibility. Second, states have special obligations under human rights law to ensure and protect rights, which includes the obligation to protect individuals from violations of their rights by non-state actors. This means that private harms can give rise to state responsibility if the state fails to respond adequately to these harms (Velásquez Rodríguez 1988, para. 182). This second form of liability is not derivative liability for the acts of a private actor but rather a new and independent wrongful act by the state—namely, the systematic failure to prevent, prosecute, and punish harms to rights perpetrated by non-state actors (Hessbruegge 2004, 269; Bodansky and Crook 2002, 783).

This section addresses the first type of state responsibility—direct or vicarious responsibility. (State responsibility derived from the failure to protect and punish violations will be considered later in the chapter.) Broadly, there are three provisions of the Articles on State Responsibility relevant to understanding when the actions of an Internet intermediary are the acts of a state governed by human rights law:

- **Article 4 (State Organ):** Under Article 4 of the Articles on State Responsibility, "[t]he conduct of any State organ shall be considered an act of that State under international law, whether the organ exercises legislative, executive, judicial or any other functions, whatever position it holds in the organization of the State, and whatever its character as an organ of the central Government or of a territorial unit of the State."

- **Article 8 (Instruction, Direction, or Control):** States are responsible for wrongful private acts done pursuant to their instruction, direction, or control. Article 8 of the Articles on State Responsibility provides, "The conduct of a person or group of persons shall be considered an act of a State under international law if the person or group of persons is in fact acting on the instructions of, or under the direction or control of, that State in carrying out the conduct." The three terms in Article 8 are disjunctive, and thus any one of the elements—"instructions," "direction," or "control"—will satisfy the test (Commentary, 47). The ILC Commentary notes that Article 8 largely encompasses two situations: "The first involves private persons acting on the instructions of the State in carrying out the wrongful conduct. The second deals with a more general situation where private persons act under the State's direction or control" (ibid.).

Instruction: State responsibility for acts carried out pursuant to state instruction is clearly established by international law. When the state instructs a private party to carry out a wrongful act, the act will be attributable to the state (ibid.). Key to establishing attribution under this provision is a specific charge. A broad rallying cry by the state, or statements that seek to instigate or encourage action, even in the context of a shared goal with private actors, will not constitute instruction (Mačák 2016, 415-416).

Direction or Control: The second situation, involving direction and control, is more complicated. Much of the law in this area has involved direction and control by a state over military operations, so the extent to which this law may be extrapolated to other contexts is unclear. Nonetheless, the Commentary emphasizes that private conduct can be attributed to the state only if the state "[1] directed or controlled *the specific operation* and [2] the conduct complained of was an *integral part of* that operation. The principle does not extend to conduct which was only incidentally or peripherally associated with an operation and which escaped from the State's direction or control" (ibid.). Discussing the drafting history of this article, Mačák notes that the ILC's Special Rapporteur, Professor Crawford, intended this second situation to provide for attribution in the absence of a "specific charge" since "the existence of an express instruction will be very difficult to demonstrate" (Mačák 2016, 413).

- **Article 5 (Empowered by Law):** Article 5 provides that states also incur responsibility for the wrongful acts of entities, which, although not officially organs of the state, are "empowered by the law of that State to exercise elements of governmental authority." Article 5 includes entities that exercise state authority on behalf of state agencies as well as "former State corporations [that] have been privatized but retain certain public or regulatory functions" (Commentary, 42). What is key is that the entity "is empowered by the law of the State to exercise functions of a public character normally reserved by State organs" (ibid., 43). This might include a private airline delegated authority over immigration issues or a private company running a prison and exercising the governmental power of detention. (Ibid.)

To understand the application of these principles to government control of intermediaries, this section develops a typology of state activities seeking to control, influence, or appropriate the regulatory power of Internet intermediaries. To date, there has been no systematic attempt to identify and describe the increasingly sophisticated ways in which states are bringing their power to bear on intermediaries.[6] This typology is urgently needed to ensure that states do not evade responsibility for their wrongful acts by cloaking them in the garb of private power. Jørgensen and Pedersen (2017, 180), for example, note concern "that the intermediaries are being used to implement public policy with limited oversight and accountability with severe implications on human rights." Among other things, this could allow states to "de facto neglect their human rights obligations and escape the strict requirements, which would have been otherwise incumbent upon them had they applied the restrictions themselves" (ibid.; Jørgensen 2013, 98–100).

Broadly, there are five different ways in which governments use Internet companies to control speech online: *control, command, delegation, notice and takedown, co-optation,* and *informal pressure.* These are ideal types, however, and any given government action may exhibit characteristics of more than one of these categories. Nonetheless, categorizing government action in this way provides a foundation for understanding how principles of state responsibility might apply to the various ways in which states interact with Internet intermediaries engaged in content regulation.

Control. A state might be responsible for the acts of an intermediary if it either controls the *intermediary itself* or controls the *activities* of the intermediary (Hathaway et al. 2017, 547).[7] This might occur if the intermediary is an organ of the state under Article 4 of the Articles on State Responsibility. State ownership is most common with telecommunications companies and mobile operators, and the actions of those state-owned companies with respect to access and content are attributable to the state. State organs may also be directly involved in managing online content. A recent paper by King, Pan, and Roberts (2017), for example, describes the way in which the Chinese government engages in reverse censorship by hiring individuals to post social media comments. Analyzing documents from the Internet

Propaganda Office of Zhanggong in Jiangxi Province, King and his colleagues find that these posts are not aimed at countering but rather distracting readers from antigovernment speech. Individuals hired by a state to influence the information space are acting on behalf of a state organ and their activities are attributable to the government.

States might also be responsible for the acts of intermediaries under Article 8 if the intermediary is acting under the state's direction or control. Mačák (2016) notes that although "direction" and "control" are often addressed as one element (411–412), the explicit change from "and" to "or" indicates that the ILC intended these to operate separately (414). Thus, "direction" could encompass situations in which a state has an ongoing relationship with a private actor, such that a suggestion or innuendo by the state would be understood as a command (418). The control test, in contrast, has been interpreted fairly narrowly (Hathaway et al. 2017, 552), and would likely require either "effective" or at least "overall" control (Wittich 2002, 894). Mačák (2016) argues however that international law may be moving toward a more permissive interpretation of "control," either in general or on a case by case basis (423–425).

In some instances, the requisite level of state direction or control over a private platform might be demonstrated. Certainly, there are several situations in which states have relationships with private actors that would lead the private actor to view the state's "suggestion" as a command. For example, although the precise contours of China's relationships with its three largest Internet intermediaries—Baidu, Alibaba, and Tencent—is unclear, it seems that these relationships would meet the definition of direction or even control, including under some of the more restrictive interpretations of the control test. The Chinese government has discussed taking a direct stake in these companies (Borak 2017), for example, and reports note these intermediaries are "careful to demonstrate loyalty to the party" and that they have significant power because "the government trusts them to heed [its] call to do whatever the regulatory bodies want" (Feng 2017). To the extent that the government directs and controls the content moderation activities of Internet companies, these decisions should be governed by the requirements of human rights law.

Command. Under Article 8 of the Articles on State Responsibility, states may also be responsible for the actions of intermediaries that, while not state organs, are acting under the instructions of a state. Thus, a legal command directing an intermediary to take a particular action with respect to content on its platform should be considered state action. This might include, for example, court injunctions to block illegal file sharing sites (Laidlaw 2015, 170), or orders from the government directing platforms to remove particular apps (Manjoo 2017). Commands might also include enforcement actions seeking to apply existing laws to the Internet. Pakistan, for example, has used blasphemy laws to restrict access to Facebook, while in Lebanon, authorities used defamation law to justify the arrest of three Facebook users who had posted criticism of the Lebanese president (Deibert and Rohozinski 2012, 25–26). When the government directs the intermediary's actions with respect to content removal or account termination, the resulting conduct should be considered state action subject to human rights principles.

Delegation occurs when a state places legal responsibility on the intermediary to regulate content, thereby thrusting the intermediary into the role of state censor. Article 5 of the Articles on State Responsibility provides that states incur responsibility for the wrongful acts of entities that, although not officially organs of the state, are "empowered by the law of that State to exercise elements of governmental authority." The Commentary to the Articles on State Responsibility notes that what is essential to this category is that the private entity is "empowered by the law of the State to exercise functions of a public character normally reserved by State organs" (Commentary, 43). In the examples provided in the Commentary—including private airlines exercising immigration authority or private prisons exercising detention authority—the private actors are carrying out essential government functions and are therefore deemed to be state actors.

When governments create liability regimes that require Internet companies to censor the speech of their users, they risk delegating essential governmental authority to the intermediaries and the resulting actions of the intermediaries could be considered state action subject to the requirements of human rights law. For example, in many jurisdictions Internet intermediaries are strictly liable for the speech on their platforms and thus must proactively police speech. The Chinese Cybersecurity Law of 2016 prohibits dissemination of "false" information as well as information that disrupts national unity or national security and "requires companies to monitor their networks and report violations to the authorities," and failure to comply with the law can lead to heavy fines (Kaye 2018, para. 15). Thailand's

Computer Crimes Act also imposes strict liability on intermediaries for content prohibited by the government (Bradley and Wingfield 2018, 31). Kenyan law requires companies to "'pull down accounts used in disseminating undesirable political contents on their platforms' within 24 hours" (Kaye 2018, para. 16).

The essential government function delegated to intermediaries in this context is the authority to regulate the rights and remedies of others. This "delegated censorship" (Deibert and Rohozinski 2012, 26; DeNardis 2014, 158) is problematic because it calls for a private company to make decisions about the meaning, applicability, and enforcement of law. The making and enforcement of law is an essential government function and should not be delegated to a private entity without any framework of accountability.

Notice and Takedown. Governments also seek to influence the conduct of intermediaries through conditional liability. In these frameworks, intermediaries are liable for offending content only if they fail to remove that content after being notified of its presence on their systems. For example, the new German network enforcement law (NetzDG) requires social media companies to remove unlawful content after being notified of its presence on their networks or risk up to fifty million euros in fines (Kaye 2018, para. 16; McGoogan 2017). The European Union is pushing for similar legislation to make companies responsible for hate speech online (Fioretti 2017). In the United States, intermediaries are protected from liability for copyright violations only if they fail to remove offending content after being provided with notice (17 U.S.C. § 512(c)(1)(C)). Like direct delegation, notice and takedown or other forms of conditional liability have the potential to delegate essential governmental authority to intermediaries to make decisions about whether the content of users on their networks is unlawful, and therefore could be considered state action if the delegated authority is not properly circumscribed.

There are two other types of state influence of Internet intermediaries that would not appear to rise to the level of state action.

Co-optation. States increasingly co-opt the enforcement systems developed by Internet intermediaries to achieve their own ends. The Counter-Terrorism Internet Referral Unit in the United Kingdom, for example, uses providers' terms of service to initiate removal of content the government wishes to suppress. This Counter-Terrorism Internet Referral Unit employs state agents to review content online and upon finding "extremist" content, notifies the platform on which it was found and suggests that this content should be removed as a terms of service violation (Kaye 2018, para. 19; Llanso and Cant n.d.). More informally, governments also "refer" matters to Internet companies for their review. In the wake of controversy following the publication of the video "The Innocence of Muslims," for example, the US government asked Google to consider whether the video violated its Community Guidelines (DeNardis 2014, 158). David Kaye notes that "[i]n South-East Asia, parties allied with Governments reportedly attempt to use terms of service requests to restrict political criticism" (Kaye 2018, para. 19).

Although state co-optation of private enforcement systems is troubling, it does not seem to rise to the level of state action. Under principles of state responsibility, the fact that a government has referred a matter to an intermediary for evaluation under the intermediary's terms of service does not make a subsequent takedown an act of the state. Absent facts that would indicate a close relationship between the intermediary and the state (which would imbue the "referral" with greater authority), there has been no exercise of governmental authority by the intermediary, nor is the intermediary acting "on the instructions of, or under the direction or control of" the state. Nonetheless, while the activity of the private company is not state action, the referral or request is the activity of a state and thus can be judged on its own merits (Commentary, 47). Thus, the work of the UK Referral Unit, which co-opts providers' terms of service to achieve its ends, should be judged in light of the UK's human rights obligations—but the action of the intermediary itself remains a private, not a state, action.

Informal Pressure. Governments also regularly exert informal pressure on Internet intermediaries to take actions entirely outside of public law mechanisms.[8] Governments pressure companies in a variety of ways, including through public condemnation and telephone calls. Following the WikiLeaks revelations, for example, the US government exerted pressure on PayPal, Amazon, and others to cease doing business with WikiLeaks (Balkin 2014, 2328; DeNardis 2014, 162). As David Kaye notes in his most recent report to the Human Rights Council, governments "also place pressure on companies to accelerate content removals through nonbinding efforts, most of which have limited transparency. A three-year ban on YouTube in Pakistan compelled Google to establish a local version susceptible to government demands for removals of 'offensive' content" (Kaye 2018, para. 20).

Informal pressure alone, absent other facts that could give this pressure greater coercive force, would not seem to meet the definition of state action—it is neither delegated governmental authority nor action taken under the instruction, direction, or control of the state. That said, there are instances in which informal pressure appears to border on delegation or instruction. For example, some instances of what appears nominally to be self-regulation are actually a form of delegation achieved through the *threat* of regulation. The 2016 European Union Code of Conduct addressing hate speech online, for example, is an "agreement" between the European Union and Facebook, Microsoft, Twitter, and YouTube that the companies will, among other things, review notifications and remove unlawful hate speech within 24 hours of notice (Aswad 2016, 3-4; Kaye 2018, para. 21). The European Union has also made demands that illegal content be removed within two hours, invoking the threat of legislation if platforms did not "voluntarily" comply with this demand (Bradley and Wingfield 2018, 10).

Under principles of state responsibility, the first four categories of state influence—control, command, delegation, and notice and takedown—transform the resulting private activity into state action that should be evaluated pursuant to human rights norms. While this conclusion is likely unproblematic with respect to the first two categories, it may be somewhat more controversial to view actions taken pursuant to delegation and notice and takedown as state action. That said, this conclusion is supported not only by law but also policy. The risks of overcensorship are extremely high in cases of delegated government authority.

Delegation is a problem for human rights law because it makes private actors responsible for governing the conduct of others. Clearly, a state can impose liability on private actors. Doing so is an important way for governments to force individuals and corporations to internalize the costs of their behavior and thereby to enforce the law. What is unique about delegated authority to remove harmful speech is that it is responsibility to govern the speech of others—what Jack Balkin (2014, 2298) calls "collateral censorship." There is an important difference between holding a newspaper responsible for the defamatory material it publishes and holding a platform responsible for defamatory material that third parties publish on its site.[9]

It is appropriate to view this as a delegation of essential government authority because private entities do not have the proper incentives to regulate the content of others. Internet companies do have an interest in protecting freedom of expression on their platforms as a general matter, since the content that users generate is an essential component of the product that they are providing. However, while they may have an interest in protecting freedom of expression generally, they do not have a strong interest in protecting any particular individual instance of speech. When faced with a choice of taking down a post that might be problematic and fighting to keep it up in the face of potential liability, the incentives weigh in favor of removal. Delegation thus leads inevitably to overbroad limits on speech (Balkin 2014, 2309–2310). As a result of these concerns, both the current and former UN Special Rapporteurs have expressed significant concerns with the impact of intermediary liability on expressive rights (Kaye 2016, para. 40–44; La Rue 2011, para. 38–48). The Office of the Special Rapporteur for Freedom of Expression of the Inter-American Commission on Human Rights has similarly argued that strict liability and notice and takedown are both inconsistent with the American Convention on Human Rights (Special Rapporteur for the Inter-American Commission 2013, para. 98, 105).

The primary consequence of viewing content moderation undertaken pursuant to delegated authority or notice and takedown as state action is that the resulting moderation should be evaluated under human rights norms. This means that content removals, for example, must pursue a legitimate purpose, follow lawful procedure, and be proportional to the ends to be achieved (La Rue 2011, para. 24). This ensures that states cannot delegate public authority to private entities and thereby evade lawful human rights, constitutional, and rule-of-law checks. In delegating responsibility to Internet platforms, states must take care to ensure that the regulation occurs in ways that comport with its human rights obligations.

Limited but Direct Obligations

Under human rights law, the activities of non-state actors are generally not governed by international law, except in limited instances (Knox 2008; Land 2013; Weissbrodt and Kruger 2005). I argue that with respect to the regulation of speech, international law imposes a limited set of obligations directly on intermediaries in some circumstances.

The text and negotiating history of Article 19 of the ICCPR, which protects freedom of expression and opinion, indicates that it applies, at least in part, to private actors. As I have written elsewhere and Agnes Callamard addresses in this volume, the drafters of Article 19 recognized that private actors can have significant effects on freedom of expression and therefore settled on a text that protected not only against governmental interference but also interference from private actors (Land 2013, 445). This is reinforced by the term "media" in Article 19(2), which protects the channel of communication, as well as the term "duty" in Article 19(3), which makes clear that "opinion makers" are obligated "not to abuse their power at the expense of others" (Nowak 1993, 351).

If they do have direct obligations under human rights law, however, these obligations would only be triggered when there has been an "interference" with a protected right. But under what circumstances would an Internet company's decision to remove my comment from its site be a violation of my freedom of expression? Because users often have a variety of options for expression online, an interference is likely to occur primarily when an Internet intermediary has assumed such a dominant position in the market that the user is not able to easily find another venue for his or her expression. This understanding of an "interference" with freedom of expression draws on the work of scholars who have written about dominant intermediaries as the "gatekeepers" of expression. Reliance on gatekeeper theory is particularly appropriate given that the rationale behind including private actors within the scope of Article 19 was the drafters' concern with media concentration and monopolies in the communications arena.

Gatekeeper theory argues that some intermediaries may have special responsibilities by virtue of their dominance, status, or influence on democracy. Emily Laidlaw (2015), for example, argues that companies with greater impacts on democracy should have greater obligations to ensure that discourse can take place. According to Laidlaw, the human rights responsibilities of these entities "increase or decrease based on the extent that its activities facilitate or hinder democratic culture" (Laidlaw 2015, 48). Jørgensen similarly asks whether Google should merely be treated as a private company or whether the importance of its services mean it has "an extra obligation to respect human rights standards" (Jørgensen 2013, 95).

Gatekeepers may be defined both by reference to market dominance as well as the extent to which there are reasonably adequate alternatives. As danah boyd argues, Facebook is structured in a way that does not reasonably enable exit. Even if one disagrees with Facebook's policies, it is difficult to leave the platform, which has become such a central nexus not only for social connection but also for professional advancement (boyd 2010). This is complicated by network effects. A user might reasonably choose to use a different blog hosting service, but it is more difficult to recreate a social network that includes one's friends or followers (York 2010). Impact might also be measured by the extent to which a platform is used for political speech, which generally enjoys higher protections (Laidlaw 2015, 50). Platforms that host high levels of political speech, such as Twitter, may need to be more attentive to human rights concerns than those that are aimed solely at social connection.

Thus, intermediaries will have differential duties based on the extent to which their activities affect freedom of expression. All intermediaries would be subject to a limited set of duties, including obligations of process, transparency, and remedy—the obligation to provide grievance processes for individuals who alleged they have been harmed by the company's decision; the obligation to provide information about the company's policies, practices, and impacts; and the obligation to remedy harms to expression with which they are linked (see Kaye 2018, para. 58–59, 71–72, recommending conformity with the Guiding Principles in these respects; see also Aswad 2018). Because their market dominance means they are able to interfere with freedom of expression, gatekeeper intermediaries should also be required to evaluate their content moderation policies under the legality, necessity, and legitimacy requirements of Article 19(3) of the ICCPR.

At the same time, it is not clear that even dominant intermediaries should be treated like states for all purposes. State and private action can have different impacts on communication, and private entities cannot be held responsible for the full range of obligations that states have with respect to freedom of expression. Internet companies are private entities, and even the most dominant of them should be able, at least to some extent, to take into account their own business needs and the preferences of the users of their platforms, including in eliminating offensive content. Internet intermediaries may also have their own expressive rights under domestic law to consider (cf. Hein 2014, 326). Nonetheless, these differential interests can be addressed within the framework provided by Article 19(3), as legitimate goals of content moderation. Article 19(3) allows limitations on speech that are necessary "[f]or respect of the rights or reputations of others." This includes not only the expressive and association rights of others but also the domestic property rights and commercial rights of the company, since the terms of Article 19(3) are not limited to "fundamental rights or Covenant rights" (Nowak 1993, 463).

There may be a second type of situation in which direct duties are triggered—namely, situations in which the challenged action has a significant impact on a protected right. For example, interrupting access to the Internet can affect the ability of users not only to express themselves and associate with others but also to fulfill a range of basic needs, including applications for employment or social support. Thus, the decision of an intermediary to suspend or terminate the account of a user would be more likely to trigger human rights duties than decisions about content moderation, regardless of the dominance of the platform. Similarly, violations of the right to be free from discrimination, or to give meaningful consent prior to being involved in an experiment, should be judged directly under human rights law. Thus, an intermediary of any size that suspends or terminates an account, or engages in discriminatory content moderation, could be bound by human rights law on the same terms as a state.

Positive Obligation to Regulate Private Harms

Much of the activity of Internet intermediaries that affects freedom of expression can be addressed either as state action or by virtue of direct obligations on intermediaries to guard against interferences or particularly serious violations of rights. There will, however, be some amount of private regulation of content beyond these measures of accountability. With respect to this private activity, companies can and should follow the UN Guiding Principles (Kaye 2018; see also Aswad 2018). In addition, however, it also falls to the state to create an enabling regulatory environment to ensure that the right to freedom of expression is protected.

States have positive obligations to create a regulatory environment in which all users' rights can be respected, online as off-line (Del Campo 2017, 5–6). Human rights institutions and advocates have largely neglected the positive obligations of the state to regulate intermediaries to protect rights online by focusing on harmful regulation by states or the harms of content itself. Nonetheless, it is a fundamental principle of human rights law that states are required to protect individuals from human rights harms and to provide remedies when rights have been violated (Ruggie 2011, 3). Failure to do so can give rise to state responsibility. As the Inter-American Court of Human Rights noted in the case of *Velásquez Rodríguez v. Honduras*: "An illegal act which violates human rights and which is initially not directly imputable to a State (for example, because it is the act of a private person or because the person responsible has not been identified) can lead to international responsibility of the State, not because of the act itself, but because of the lack of due diligence to prevent the violation or to respond to it as required by the Convention" (para. 172). The Court has explained further in *Ximenes-Lopes* that these positive duties are particularly urgent when the state has outsourced the exercise of essential governmental authority:

> Rendering public services implies the protection of public interests, which is one of the objectives of the State. Though the States may delegate the rendering of such services, through the so-called outsourcing, they continue being responsible for providing such public services and for protecting the public interest concerned. Delegating the performance of such services to private institutions requires as an essential element the responsibility of the States to supervise their performance in order to guarantee the effective protection of the human rights of the individuals under the jurisdiction thereof and the rendering of such services to the population on the basis of non-discrimination and as effectively as possible. (*Ximenes-Lopes* 2006, para. 96).

There are several components to a rights-respecting information ecosystem. States must enable access to the Internet (La Rue 2011, para. 61), and they must regulate to ensure the Internet is free and open (Kaye 2016, para. 30). States must take positive steps to protect individuals from harmful speech posted by others online, while avoiding the imposition of intermediary liability that can negatively affect freedom of expression (Arun 2015, 9–10). States must also take positive steps to protect users from harms that might result from terms of service enforcement—content removal, content curation, or account suspension or termination—undertaken by the platform itself. In addition to being more transparent about their *own* requests of intermediaries, states should require transparency, process, and remedies of these content regulators. They might also impose fiduciary duties on Internet companies to ensure they fully consider the rights of users.

One way in which public regulation could provide greater protection for users is to obligate intermediaries to be transparent about the decisions they make regarding content regulation and account suspension or termination and to provide for grievance procedures if individuals are harmed in the process. Transparency about platform terms of service and their enforcement is needed both to ensure that individuals know what content is allowed and what is prohibited and to enable them to hold the platform accountable for violations. This might be complemented by regulations requiring a remedy or grievance procedure for responding to alleged harms. Robust remedies designed to respond to harms of online content might in many cases be preferable to prior restraints that seek to avoid the harm; this approach could minimize both limits on content as well as regulatory burdens on intermediaries.

States can also take steps to promote competition and reduce market concentration—for example, through competition law. Media consolidation can have a significant impact on diversity and pluralism (Jørgensen 2013, 94). States might use antitrust law to ensure there are enough avenues for expression and that markets do not become unduly concentrated, thus limiting choices available to users of these platforms (Kaye 2018, para. 6). Competition would be promoted by protecting user rights, such as rights to data ownership and portability (Thierer 2013, 283–284). Tim Wu (2011, 304) argues in favor of a separations principle, or "the idea of maintaining a salutary distance between differing functions in the information economy." Comparing it to the governmental separation-of-powers principle, Wu argues that this principle could both protect young industries from incumbents as well as prevent against the consolidation of too much power in any one industry player (ibid.).

In some cases, states might also consider regulating intermediaries as public utilities to ensure basic minimum quality and access requirements (boyd 2010; Thompson 2010). Regulation of this sort is not without cost, of course, including costs to innovation and competition (Heins 2014, 326–327; Lao 2013, 314–317; Thierer 2013, 270–278). Nonetheless, thinking about a public utility framework offers "a way to diagnose problematic concentrations of power" and "suggest[s] a concrete way forward for today's reformers seeking to secure access to basic necessities and impose checks and balances on providers" (Rahman 2018).

States might also impose substantive obligations in some instances. For example, a state could prevent particularly dominant intermediaries or intermediaries that hold themselves out as public forums from discriminating based on the content on their platforms. Twitter, for example, as a forum that is aimed at generating public speech, might reasonably be subject to greater regulation than Facebook, which positions itself as promoting private speech. Although the public forum doctrine has not been applied to the Internet under US law (Gey 1998; Nunziato 2005), positive substantive obligations may be more consistent with European law (Laidlaw 2015, 157).

Conclusion

The purpose of this chapter has been to outline two central challenges that arise in applying human rights law online and providing starting points for human rights institutions and experts seeking accountability for private harms online. Clearly, much more work needs to be done to identify the normative commitments that should drive answers to these questions—to address what Gillespie calls the "basic paradox" of social media platforms: that "these are private companies policing public speech, and are often intervening according to a culturally specific or financially conservative morality" (Gillespie 2015). Nonetheless, the growing impact that Internet intermediaries have on freedom of expression compels the task.

Many of the challenges in this process stem from the fact that Internet intermediaries often do not fit traditional roles. They are generally not speakers themselves; in general they do not solicit and curate content like a newspaper; nor are they in most cases mere conduits, such as a telephone company. Increasingly, albeit to varying degrees depending on the business at issue, these companies are the guardians and curators of speech of others. Failing to recognize this new and unique role has obscured the importance of an enabling regulatory environment in addressing harms associated with these activities.

Understanding better the responsibilities of non-state actors with respect to their private activity in defining the boundaries for public debate is particularly important given the poor track records most governments have in protecting rights online. The usual human rights response, which is to rely on states to regulate non-state actors to protect rights, may be ineffective given the incentives that states also have to exert their control over the communication space. Articulating independent responsibilities for private actors—and being clear about the limits of those responsibilities—will have beneficial effects for human rights in this sector because they can supplement state responsibilities when the latter fall short.

Finally, addressing these challenges will also be important for efforts to promote business and human rights more generally. Understanding the complicated relationship between business responsibility and protecting freedom of expression in this area could prove crucial for eventual efforts in obtaining a treaty on the human rights obligations of private companies. Further study is warranted, particularly with respect to how any treaty obligations would apply across various sectors, before moving forward, and understanding the obligations of Internet intermediaries would be a step forward in that process.

Notes

1. The author is grateful to Evelyn Aswad, Bethany Berger, Larry Helfer, Rachel Lopez, Federica Nieri, and Richard Wilson, as well as the faculty at Drexel Law School and the participants in the Business and Human Rights Scholars Association 4th Annual Conference, for their helpful feedback and comments, and to Zeynep Aydogan and Camden Weber for excellent research assistance.

2. "Internet intermediaries are third-party platforms that mediate between digital content and the humans who contribute and access this content" (DeNardis 2014, 154).

3. The exception was the Draft Norms on the Responsibility of Transnational Corporations and Other Business Enterprises with Regard to Human Rights, which was not adopted by the UN General Assembly (De La Vega 2017, 443–446). Although efforts to develop a new treaty on business and human rights are ongoing at the United Nations, the future of these efforts is uncertain given uneven state support and the opposition of many within the business community (ibid., 433; Response of International Business Community 2017).

4. The author participates in GNI's academic constituency and is an alternate on its board on behalf of the Human Rights Institute at the University of Connecticut, which became a member of GNI in 2015. All views expressed here are the author's own.

5. To the extent that curation results in content not being seen, it can be analyzed like moderation. There is generally little difference to the end user whether content is removed or simply made invisible.

6. Deibert and Rohozinski (2012) come the closest in their discussion of next-generation controls employed by government to control content online. Their framework, however, focuses broadly on all controls—legal and technical, public and private—while this typology seeks to understand and categorize the various forms of influence that governments can exert on intermediaries to control content.

7. Hathaway et al. (2017, 547) explain: "Under Article 4, the question is the level of control the state exercises over the *actor* that undertakes the act, whereas under

Article 8, it is the level of control the state exercises over the *operation* during which the act occurs."

8. Deibert and Rohozinski (2012, 26) call this category "informal requests" but include in this category slowdowns by state-owned Internet service providers and pressure from government officials to remove requests.

9. This does not mean that all forms of secondary liability or even privatization of services transform private action into state action. It is the particular way in which incentives align in this instance to incentivize overcensorship that make delegated censorship especially pernicious.

References

Angwin, Julia, and Hannes Grassegger. 2017. "Facebook's Secret Censorship Rules Protect White Men from Hate Speech but Not Black Children." *ProPublica*, June 28. https://www.propublica.org/article/facebook-hate-speech-censorship-internal -documents-algorithms.

Arun, Chinmayi. 2015. "Gatekeeper Liability and Article 19(1)(a) of the Constitution of India." Working Paper Series, Centre for Communication Governance at National Law University Delhi, May 20. https://papers.ssrn.com/sol3/papers.cfm ?abstract_id=2643278.

Aswad, Evelyn. 2016. "The Role of U.S. Technology Companies as Enforcers of Europe's New Internet Hate Speech Ban." *Columbia Human Rights Law Review Online* 1(1): 1–14.

Aswad, Evelyn. 2018. "The Future of Freedom of Expression Online." *Duke Law and Technology Review* 17: 26–70.

Bakshy, Eytan, Solomon Messing, and Lada A. Adamic. 2015. "Exposure to Ideologically Diverse News and Opinion on Facebook." *Science* 348 (6239): 1130–1132.

Balkin, Jack. 2014. "Old-School/New-School Speech Regulation." *Harvard Law Review* 127 (8): 2296–2342.

Benedek, Wolfgang, and Matthias C. Kettemann. 2014. *Freedom of Expression and the Internet.* Strasbourg: Council of Europe.

Biddle, Sam. 2015. "Apple: Drone Strikes Are Offensive, Farts and Poop Are Cool." *Gawker*, September 28. http://gawker.com/apple-kills-drone-strike-news-app-for-being -too-crude-1733402994.

Bodansky, Daniel, and John R. Crook. 2002. "Symposium: The ILCs State Responsibility Articles." *American Journal of International Law* 96: 773–791.

Borak, Masha. 2017. "WSJ: Chinese Government Wants to Enter Boards of Chinese Tech Giants." *Technode*, October 13. https://technode.com/2017/10/13/wsj-chinese -government-wants-to-enter-boards-of-chinese-tech-giants.

boyd, danah. 2010. "Facebook Is a Utility; Utilities Get Regulated." *Apophenia* (blog), May 5. http://www.zephoria.org/thoughts/archives/2010/05/15/facebook-is-a-utility -utilities-get-regulated.html.

Bradley, Charles, and Richard Wingfield. 2018. *A Rights-Respecting Model of Online Content Regulation by Platforms*. London: Global Partners Digital.

Brogan, Jacob. 2017. "YouTube Starts Redirecting People Who Search for Certain Key- words to Anti-Terrorism Videos." *Slate*, July 21. http://www.slate.com/blogs/future _tense/2017/07/21/youtube_redirects_those_who_search_for_terrorist_keywords _to_anti_terrorist.html.

Cook, Kristina. 2016. "Facebook Developing Artificial Intelligence to Flag Offen- sive Live Videos." *Reuters*, December 1. http://www.reuters.com/article/us-facebook -ai-video-idUSKBN13Q52M.

Deibert, Ronald, and Rafal Rohozinski. 2012. "Liberation vs. Control: The Future of Cyberspace." In *Liberation Technology: Social Media and the Struggle for Democracy*, edited by Larry Diamond and Marc F. Plattner, 18–32. Baltimore: Johns Hopkins University Press.

De La Vega, Connie. 2017. "International Standards on Business and Human Rights: Is a Drafting New Treaty Worth It?" *University of San Francisco Law Review* 51: 431–468.

Del Campo, Agustina. 2017. *Content Moderation and Private Censorship: Standards Drawn from the Jurisprudence of the Inter-American Human Rights System*. Buenos Aires: Universidad de Palermo.

DeNardis, Laura. 2014. *The Global War for Internet Governance*. New Haven, CT: Yale University Press.

Draft Articles on Responsibility of States for Internationally Wrongful Acts, with Commentaries. 2001. *Yearbook of the International Law Commission*, vol. 2, part 2 ("Commentary"). New York: United Nations.

Feng, Emily. 2017. "Chinese Tech Giants Like Baidu and Sina Set Up Communist Party Committees." *Financial Review*, October 11. https://www.afr.com/news/world/ asia/chinese-tech-giants-like-baidu-and-sina-set-up-communist-party-committees -20171011-gyyh5u.

Fioretti, Julia. 2017. "EU States Approve Plans to Make Social Media Firms Tackle Hate Speech." *Reuters*, May 23. http://www.reuters.com/article/us-eu-hatespeech-social media-idUSKBN18J25C.

Gey, Steven G. 1998. "Reopening the Public Forum—From Sidewalks to Cyberspace." *Ohio State Law Journal* 58:1535–1634.

Gillespie, Tarleton. 2015. "Facebook's Improved 'Community Standards' Still Cannot Resolve the Central Paradox." *Culture Digitally*, March 18. http://culturedigitally.org/2015/03/facebooks-improved-community-standards-still-cant-resolve-the-central-paradox.

Global Network Initiative. 2017. "About Us." http://globalnetworkinitiative.org/about/index.php.

Goel, Vindu. 2014. "Facebook Tinkers with Users' Emotions in News Feed Experiment, Stirring Outcry." *New York Times*, June 29. https://www.nytimes.com/2014/06/30/technology/facebook-tinkers-with-users-emotions-in-news-feed-experiment-stirring-outcry.html?_r=0.

Hathaway, Oona A., Emily Chertoff, Lara Domínguez, Zachary Manfredi, and Peter Tzeng. 2017. "Ensuring Responsibility: Common Article 1 and State Responsibility for Non-State Actors." *Texas Law Review* 95: 539–590.

Heins, Marjorie. 2014. "The Brave New World of Social Media Censorship." *Harvard Law Review Forum* 127 (June): 325–330.

Hessbruegge, Jan Arno. 2004. "The Historical Development of the Doctrines of Attribution and Due Diligence in International Law." *New York University Journal of International Law and Politics* 36; 265–306.

Hopkins, Nick. 2017. "Facebook Moderators: A Quick Guide to Their Job and Its Challenges." *The Guardian*, May 21. https://www.theguardian.com/news/2017/may/21/facebook-moderators-quick-guide-job-challenges.

Jørgensen, Rikke Frank. 2013. *Framing the Net—The Internet and Human Rights*. Cheltenham, UK: Edward Elgar.

———. 2018. "Human Rights and Private Actors in the Online Domain." In *New Technologies for Human Rights Law and Practice*, edited by Molly K. Land and Jay D. Aronson, 243–269. Cambridge: Cambridge University Press.

Jørgensen, Rikke Frank, and Anja Møller Pedersen. 2017. "Online Service Providers as Human Rights Arbiters." In *The Responsibilities of Online Service Providers*, edited by Mariarosaria Taddeo and Luciano Floridi, 179–199. Cham, Switzerland: Springer Press.

Joint Declaration on Freedom of Expression and the Internet. June 1, 2011. http://www.oas.org/en/iachr/expression/showarticle.asp?artID=848.

Kaye, David. 2016. "Report of the Special Rapporteur on the Promotion and Protection of the Right to Freedom of Opinion and Expression." May 11. A/HRC/32/38. Geneva: United Nations.

———. 2018. "Report of the Special Rapporteur on the Promotion and Protection of the Right to Freedom of Opinion and Expression." April 6. A/HRC/38/35. Geneva: United Nations.

King, Gary, Jennifer Pan, and Margaret E. Roberts. 2017. "How the Chinese Government Fabricates Social Media Posts for Strategic Distraction, Not Engaged Argument." *American Political Science Review* 111: 484–501.

Klonick, Kate. 2018. "The New Governors: The People, Rules, and Processes Governing Online Speech." *Harvard Law Review* 131: 1598–1670.

Knox, John H. 2008. "Horizontal Human Rights Law." *American Journal of International Law* 102 (1): 1–47.

Laidlaw, Emily B. 2015. *Regulating Speech in Cyberspace: Gatekeepers, Human Rights and Corporate Responsibility.* Cambridge: Cambridge University Press.

Land, Molly. 2013. "Toward an International Law of the Internet." *Harvard Journal of International Law* 54 (2): 393–458.

Lao, Marina. 2013. "Search, Essential Facilities, and the Antitrust Duty to Deal." *Northwestern Journal of Technology & Intellectual Property* 11: 275–319.

La Rue, Frank. 2011. "Report of the Special Rapporteur on the Promotion and Protection of the Right to Freedom of Opinion and Expression." May 16. A/HRC/17/27. Geneva: Human Rights Council.

Llanso, Emma, and Rita Cant. n.d. "'Internet Referral Unit' Co-Option of Private Content Moderation Systems for Extralegal Government Censorship." Draft on file with author.

Mačák, Kubo. 2016. "Decoding Article 8 of the International Law Commission's Articles on State Responsibility: Attribution of Cyber Operations by Non-State Actors." *Journal of Conflict and Security Law* 21(3): 405–428.

Maclay, Colin M. 2010. "Protecting Privacy and Expression Online: Can the Global Network Initiative Embrace the Character of the Net?" In *Access Controlled: The Shaping of Power, Rights and Rule in Cyberspace*, edited by Ronald Deibert, John Palfrey, Rafal Rohozinski, and Jonathan Zittrain, 87–108. Cambridge, MA: MIT Press.

Manjoo, Farhad. 2017. "Clearing Out the App Stores: Government Censorship Made Easier." *New York Times*, January 18. https://www.nytimes.com/2017/01/18/technology/clearing-out-the-app-stores-government-censorship-made-easier.html.

McGoogan, Cara. 2017. "Germany to Fine Facebook and YouTube €50m if They Fail to Delete Hate Speech." *The Telegraph*, June 30. http://www.telegraph.co.uk/technology/2017/06/30/germany-fine-facebook-youtube-50m-fail-delete-hate-speech.

Mirzoeff, Nicholas D. 2015. "Facebook Censors Refugee Photographs." *How to See the World*, September 1. https://wp.nyu.edu/howtoseetheworld/2015/09/01/auto -draft-78.

Nowak, Manfred. 1993. *U.N. Covenant on Civil and Political Rights: CCPR Commentary*. Kehl, Germany: N. P. Engel.

Nunziato, Dawn. 2005. "The Death of the Public Forum in Cyberspace." *Berkeley Technology Law Journal* 20: 1115–1171.

Observacom. 2017. "Key Points for the Democratic Regulation of "Over-the-Top" Services so as to Ensure a Free and Open Internet." *Ifex*, September 19. https://www .ifex.org/international/2017/09/19/regulacion-servicios-internet.

Office of the Special Rapporteur for Freedom of Expression of the Inter-American Commission on Human Rights. 2013. *Freedom of Expression and the Internet*. December 31. OEA/Ser.L/V/II, CIDH/RELE/INF.11/13 ("Special Rapporteur for the Inter-American Commission").

Pasquale, Frank. 2015. *The Black Box Society: The Secret Algorithms That Control Money and Information*. Cambridge, MA: Harvard University Press.

Rahman, K. Sabeel. 2018. "Constructing Citizenship: Exclusion and Inclusion Through the Governance of Basic Necessities." *Columbia Law Review* 118.

Ranking Digital Rights. 2018. *2018 Corporate Accountability Index*. April. https:// rankingdigitalrights.org/index2018/assets/static/download/RDRindex2018report .pdf.

"Response of the international business community to the 'elements' for a draft legally binding instrument on transnational corporations and other business enterprises with respect to human rights." October 20, 2017. https://cdn.iccwbo.org/ content/uploads/sites/3/2017/10/business-response-to-igwg-draft-binding-treaty -on-human-rights.pdf.

"Responsibilities of States for Internationally Wrongful Acts," G.A. Res. 56/83, Annex, A/RES/56/83 (December 12, 2001) ("Articles on State Responsibility"). Geneva: United Nations.

Roettgers, Janko. 2018. "Facebook Says It's Cutting Down on Viral Videos as 2017 Revenue Tops $40 Billion." *Variety*, January 31. http://variety.com/2018/digital/news/ facebook-q4-2017-earnings-1202683184.

Ruggie, John. 2011. "Guiding Principles on Business and Human Rights: Implementing the United Nations 'Protect, Respect and Remedy' Framework." March 21. A/HRC/ 17/31 (Annex). Geneva: United Nations.

Solon, Olivia. 2017. "Facebook Policy Chief: Social Media Must Step Up Fight against Extremism." *The Guardian*, March 12. https://www.theguardian.com/culture/2017/mar/12/facebook-policy-chief-social-media-must-step-up-fight-against-extremism.

Sullivan, David. 2016. "Business and Digital Rights: Taking Stock of the UN Guiding Principles for Business and Human Rights in the ICT Sector." *Association for Progressive Communications*. https://www.apc.org/sites/default/files/BusinessAndDigital Rights_full_report.pdf.

Thierer, Adam. 2013. "The Perils of Classifying Social Media Platforms as Public Utilities." *CommLaw Conspectus* 21: 249–297.

Thompson, Ambrose. 2010. "Social Media as Public Expectation: The New Public Utility." *New York Public Library Blog*.

Tufekci, Zeynep. 2015. "How Facebook's Algorithm Suppresses Content Diversity (Modestly) and How the Newsfeed Rules Your Clicks." *Medium*, May 7. https://medium.com/message/how-facebook-s-algorithm-suppresses-content-diversity -modestly-how-the-newsfeed-rules-the-clicks-b5f8a4bb7bab.

Velásquez Rodríguez, Inter-Am. Ct. H.R. (Ser. C) No. 4 (1988).

Weissbrodt, David, and Muria Kruger. 2005. "Human Rights Responsibilities of Business as Non-State Actors." In *Non-State Actors and Human Rights*, edited by Philip Alston, 315–350. Oxford: Oxford University Press.

Wittich, Stephan. 2002. "The International Law Commission's Articles on the Responsibility of States for Internationally Wrongful Acts Adopted on Second Reading." *Leiden Journal of International Law* 15: 891–919.

Wu, Tim. 2011. *The Master Switch: The Rise and Fall of Information Empires*. New York: Vintage Books.

Ximenes-Lopes v. Brazil, Inter-Am. Ct. H.R. (Ser. C) No. 149 (2006).

Xu, Beina, and Eleanor Albert. 2017. "Media Censorship in China." *Council on Foreign Relations*, February 17. https://www.cfr.org/backgrounder/media-censorship-china.

York, Jillian C. 2010. "Policing Content in the Quasi-Public Sphere." *OpenNet Initiative Bulletin*. https://opennet.net/policing-content-quasi-public-sphere.

Contributors

Anja Bechmann is Professor of Media Studies and director of Datalab—Center for Digital Social Research at Aarhus University. She is guest professor at Political Science, Antwerp University, and Thinker in Residence at Royal Flemish Academy for Science and the Arts. She conducts research at the intersection between algorithms and digital sociology, disentangling how algorithms create meaning from digital human communication and behavioral data, and on the challenges—regulatory, ethical, and in relation to sociology and information design—in doing so. She has served as an appointed member of the EU Commission high-level expert group on Disinformation (2017–2019). Her work on user data, machine learning, and privacy has been published in, for example, *Big Data & Society*, *New Media & Society*, *Information Communication & Society*, *Digital Journalism*, and *The Information Society*, and she is among others the coeditor of *The Ubiquitous Internet* (Routledge, 2014).

Fernando Bermejo is a Faculty Associate at the Berkman Klein Center and the research and program director of Media Cloud at MIT. He is also Profesor Asociado at IE University in Madrid. His research focuses on the different forms of measuring the Internet—content, infrastructure, people, activity—and he is the founder of Net Data Directory. He is also interested in the evolution of the different forms of online advertising and the process of commercialization of interactivity. He is the author of *The Internet Audience: Constitution and Measurement* (Peter Lang, 2007) and the editor of *On Communicating: Otherness, Meaning, and Information* (Routledge, 2009).

Agnès Callamard is the Director of Columbia University Global Freedom of Expression, an initiative seeking to advance understanding on freedom-of-expression global norms. On August 1, 2016, she was appointed the UN Special Rapporteur on Extra-Judicial Summary or Arbitrary Executions. Agnès spent nine years as the Executive Director of ARTICLE 19, the international human rights organization promoting and defending freedom of expression and access to information globally. Prior to this, she was Chef de Cabinet for the Secretary General of Amnesty Internationa (AI) and AI's Research-Policy Coordinator, leading AI's policy work and research on women's human rights. She has advised senior levels of multilateral organizations and governments around the world and has led human rights investigations in more than thirty countries.

Mikkel Flyverbom is Professor (mso) of Communication and Digital Transformations at Copenhagen Business School. His research interests concern how digital technologies shape communication and governance processes in organizational settings. His research addresses how the Internet has emerged as a key concern in global politics (see *The Power of Networks*, Edward Elgar, 2011), how big data relates to knowledge production and the politics of transparency, how transparency ideals shape the Internet domain, and how power and transparency intersect (see *The Digital Prism: Transparency and Managed Visibilities in a Datafied World*, Cambridge University Press, 2019). Most recently, he has been a member of the European Commission's expert group TrustForesight and has been appointed to the Danish governments' Data Ethics Council. Mikkel also serves on the Editorial Boards of the international journals *Communication Theory, Organization Theory,* and *Big Data & Society*.

Rikke Frank Jørgensen is a Senior Researcher at the Danish Institute for Human Rights focusing on the interface between technology and human rights. Her experience includes technology policy making within the Danish government, Internet rights advocacy within European Digital Rights, as well as participation in the UN World Summit on the Information Society as human rights expert in the Danish delegation and co-coordinator of civil society's Human Rights Caucus (see *Human Rights in the Global Information Society*, MIT Press, 2006). She has served as an international expert in the Council of Europe's working group on Rights of Internet Users (2013–2014) and is on the advisory board of DataEthics and Ranking Digital Rights, among others. Her book, *Framing the Net—The Internet and Human Rights* (Edward Elgar, 2013), deconstructs four commonly applied Internet metaphors and examines how each of them shapes human rights debates.

Molly K. Land is Professor of Law and Human Rights at the University of Connecticut School of Law and Associate Director of the Human Rights Institute. Drawing on her human rights expertise and background as an intellectual property litigator, her scholarship focuses on the effect of new technologies on human rights fact-finding, advocacy, and enforcement, as well as the role of human rights norms and framing strategies in organizing around human rights issues. Her current work explores the opportunities and challenges for using new technologies to achieve human rights objectives (see *New Technologies for Human Rights Law and Practice*, Cambridge University Press, 2018). Her work has been published in the Yale, Harvard, and Michigan journals of international law, among other places.

Tarlach McGonagle is a Senior Researcher/Lecturer at the Institute for Information Law (IViR), Faculty of Law, University of Amsterdam. He is a senior researcher at the Netherlands Network for Human Rights Research and is co-chair of its Working Group on human rights in the digital age. He specializes in a broad range of topics relating to international and European human rights law, especially the rights to freedom of expression and religion, minority rights, participatory rights, and cultural and linguistic rights. His other main area of expertise is international, European, and comparative media law and policy. He was Rapporteur of the Council of Europe's Committee of Experts on protection of journalism and safety of journalists (2014–2015) and of its Committee of Experts on media pluralism and transparency of media ownership (2016–2017). He is currently a member of its Committee of Experts on quality journalism in the digital age. He is also a member of the Euromedia Research Group.

Jens-Erik Mai is Professor and Head of Department of Information Studies at the University of Copenhagen. His work concerns basic questions about the nature of information phenomena in contemporary society—he is concerned with the state of privacy and surveillance given new digital media, with classification given the pluralistic nature of meaning and society, and with information and its quality given its pragmatic nature. His publications on the nature of classification have been recognized by Emerald's "Outstanding Paper Award" for the paper "The Modernity of Classification," published in *Journal of Documentation*—and by the International Society for Knowledge Organization's (ISKO) "Best Paper in KO Award" for the paper "Ethics, Values and Morality in Contemporary Library Classifications," which was published in *Knowledge Organization*.

Joris van Hoboken is Professor of Law at the Vrije Universiteit Brussels, appointed to the Fundamental Rights and Digital Transformation Chair. The Chair is established at the interdisciplinary Research Group on Law, Science, Technology & Society, with the support of Microsoft. He is also a Senior Researcher at the Institute for Information Law (IViR), Faculty of Law, University of Amsterdam. Joris works on the intersection of fundamental rights protection and the governance of platforms and Internet-based services. His research interests include data privacy, smartphone ecosystems, data-driven discrimination, intermediary liability, algorithms, and platforms. Joris obtained his PhD from the University of Amsterdam on the topic of search engines and freedom of expression (see *Search Engine Freedom*, Kluwer Law International, 2012) and has graduate degrees in law and theoretical mathematics.

Glen Whelan is Course Lecturer at McGill University and Visiting Scholar at York University, Toronto. His research focuses on how high-tech corporations impact society. From 2014–2016 he completed a project, "Internet Privacy," as a Marie Curie Research Fellow at Copenhagen Business School. From 2017 to 2021, he is collaborating on a Canadian Social Sciences and Humanities Research Council Insight Grant on "Artificial Intelligence, Corporate Accountability and Public Understanding." He regularly publishes with leading university presses and has published in such journals as *Business & Society, Business Ethics Quarterly, Ephemera, Journal of Business Ethics,* and *Journal of Management Inquiry*. He is the current social media editor for *Journal of*

Business Ethics and is in the process of coediting a special issue on the sharing economy for the same journal. He is also currently coediting a special issue for *Organization* on "Exploring the Dark Side of Digitalization."

Jillian C. York is Electronic Frontier Foundation's (EFF's) Director for International Freedom of Expression; a fellow at the Centre for Internet & Human Rights in Berlin, and a founding member of the Deep Lab collective. Her work encompasses a broad range of topics, from digital security to the privatization of censorship. Jillian's writing has been featured in *Al Jazeera, The Guardian, Foreign Policy, The Atlantic,* and the *New York Times,* among others. She is also a regular speaker at global events. Prior to joining EFF, Jillian worked at the Berkman Klein Center for Internet & Society at Harvard University, where she researched Internet censorship. She currently serves on the Board of Directors of Global Voices, the IFEX Council, and the advisory boards of Social Media Exchange (SMEX) and R-Shief.

Shoshana Zuboff is an author and scholar whose new work, *The Age of Surveillance Capitalism: The Fight for a Human Future at the New Frontier of Power* (Public Affairs/ Hachette, 2019), integrates her lifelong themes: the rise of the digital and its meaning for knowledge and power, the evolution of capitalism, the historical emergence of psychological individuality, and the conditions for human development. Zuboff is also the author of *In the Age of Smart Machine: The Future of Work and Power* and *The Support Economy: Why Corporations Are Failing Individuals and the Next Episode of Capitalism* (with James Maxmin), along with many scholarly and popular articles. Her 2015 paper, "Big Other: Surveillance Capitalism and the Prospects of an Information Civilization" was the recipient of the Best Paper Award from the International Conference of Information Systems Senior Scholars. Zuboff joined the Harvard Business School in 1981 where she became the Charles Edward Wilson Professor of Business. In 2014 and 2015 she was a Faculty Associate at the Berkman Klein Center for Internet & Society at Harvard University. Zuboff has been a frequent contributor to the *Frankfurter Allgemeine Zeitung* writing at the intersection of capitalism and the digital, as well as a featured columnist for both *Fast Company* and BusinessWeek Online.

Ethan Zuckerman is director of the Center for Civic Media at MIT and associate professor of the practice in the Program in Media Arts and Sciences at the MIT Media Lab. His research focuses on the distribution of attention in mainstream and new media, the use of technology for international development, and the use of new media technologies by activists. He is the author of *Rewire: Digital Cosmopolitans in the Age of Connection* (W. W. Norton, 2013). In 2005, Zuckerman cofounded the international blogging community Global Voices together with Rebecca MacKinnon. Global Voices showcases news and opinions from citizen media in over 150 nations and thirty languages, publishing editions in twenty languages. Through Global Voices and the Berkman Klein Center for Internet and Society at Harvard University, where he served as a researcher and fellow for eight years, Zuckerman is active in efforts to promote freedom of expression and fight censorship in online spaces.

Index

Information Policy Series

Edited by Sandra Braman

The Information Policy Series publishes research on and analysis of significant problems in the field of information policy, including decisions and practices that enable or constrain information, communication, and culture irrespective of the legal silos in which they have traditionally been located as well as state–law–society interactions. Defining information policy as all laws, regulations, and decision-making principles that affect any form of information creation, processing, flows, and use, the series includes attention to the formal decisions, decision-making processes, and entities of government; the formal and informal decisions, decision-making processes, and entities of private and public sector agents capable of constitutive effects on the nature of society; and the cultural habits and predispositions of governmentality that support and sustain government and governance. The parametric functions of information policy at the boundaries of social, informational, and technological systems are of global importance because they provide the context for all communications, interactions, and social processes.